Development-Induced Displacement

Development-Induced Displacement

Case of Kerala

Jose Murickan
M.K. George
K.A. Emmanuel
Jose Boban
Prakash Pillai R.

A Joint Study by

Indian Social Institute, Bangalore
and
Loyola College of Social Sciences, Thiruvananthapuram

RAWAT PUBLICATIONS
Jaipur and New Delhi

ISBN 81-7033-813-1

Published by
Prem Rawat for ***Rawat Publications***
Satyam Apts., Sector 3, Jawahar Nagar, Jaipur 302 004 (India)
Phone: 0141 265 1748 / 7006 Fax: 0141 265 1748
E-mail : info@rawatbooks.com
Website: www.rawatbooks.com

Delhi Office
4858/24, Ansari Road, Daryaganj, New Delhi 110 002
Phone: 011-23263290

Typeset by Rawat Computers, Jaipur
Printed at Chaman Enterprises, New Delhi

Contents

Foreword

Persons involved in struggles against development, particularly dams, have been frequently pitted against the state and the judiciary in recent times. The Supreme Court judgment on Sardar Sarovar is its best example during 2000. A few months later came the Report of the World Commission on Dams and the government even refused to discuss it. Some put the tag of anti-developmental on those wanting to have a dialogue around it. In the meantime, displacement is continuing. Many more people will be deprived in future of their livelihood in the name of liberalisation, than in the last five decades.

Amid these unequivocal stands, the struggles against displacement are bringing new issues to the fore. The present study is an integral part of a national effort to deal with these issues. An issue being debated at present is the number of people the large dams have displaced since 1951. The country does not have an official database on the numbers deprived of their livelihood in the name of national development. So, some like Arundhuti Roy speak of 56 millions displaced by large dams while others give a ridiculously low figure. Based on the average worked out by Indian Institute of Public Administration (IIPA), some like Surjit Bhalla (*Seminar*, January 2001) have arrived at an average of 1,300 per large dam. The main reason for this difference is that IIPA and others like Arundhuti Roy take all the "large dams" above 15 metres together. As the Kerala and other studies show, one has to divide them into major, medium and minor according to their irrigation potential (IP). Displacement is linked to land and IP is based on the land they submerge.

Fewer than 300 of India's 4,200 large dams are major and the rest medium. Major dams affect 25,000 to 2,50,000 and medium dams 400 to 6,000 persons each. At least fifteen major dams have displaced more than a lakh each. For every ten persons they displace, dams deprive six more of their livelihood without relocating them. Their situation is often worse, because they receive only meagre compensation for *patta* land. Those living on common revenue land or in forests do not even get that. Based on these and other studies, we tend to put the number of water resource DPs/PAPs at 30 to 40 million till today: some 25 million of them displaced and 15 million deprived of livelihood.

On the other side, the tribals, the main victims of national development, and other rural poor are resisting dams, industries and mines like Utkal Alumina in Orissa. A few of them were killed in police firing in Orissa in December 2000. But, instead of redressing their grievances, the Centre is planning to amend the draconian Land Acquisition Act, 1894 to make acquisition easier. It is also planning to change the fifth schedule in order to remove obstacles to transfering tribal land to private companies.

The present study is an effort to face these issues. In an earlier estimate, we had arrived at a figure of 213 lakh affected by all the development projects during 1951-1990. By now, we have completed data-based studies of all displacements during 1951-1995 in Andhra Pradesh (AP), Goa, Jharkhand and Orissa and have preliminary data from three more states. The present study on Kerala adds to our knowledge. We hope to do these studies in the remaining states if funds are available. Based on these studies, we realise that 213 lakh is an underestimate and that the IIPA method of putting all large dams together is not acceptable. Our estimate for dams was 164 lakh. But our studies show that AP, Orissa, West Bengal and Jharkhand have together deprived nearly 100 lakh, about 61 per cent of them by dams, during 1951-1995. That is nearly 50 per cent of the above estimate of 213 lakh and that does not include other high displacement states like Chhatisgarh and the western zone.

Thus, one can see that our underestimate is not limited to dams, but to all types of projects. We had come to a figure of 12.5 lakh deprived by industry. Our studies show that only AP and Orissa account for half that figure. We had put the numbers deprived by wildlife sanctuaries at 6,00,000. Jharkhand, Orissa and AP together exceed this figure. We had calculated those affected by schemes like transport and communications at 5,00,000. AP and Orissa together account for that number. AP, Orissa and Jharkhand account for more than 10 lakh victims of mines, while our all-India figure was 23.5 lakh. So, one should not be surprised if the total of the DPs/PAPs from 1951 exceeded 50 million.

Equally important is the poor record of rehabilitation. Orissa has resettled about 32 per cent of those it displaced during 1951-1995, AP around 27 per cent and Goa 42 per cent. Though Kerala, claims to be progressive and high on human development, it has resettled the DPs of only a handful of projects. Compensation, though relatively high in Kerala, cannot be a substitute for rehabilitation because the law limits it to *patta* land. The victims of big projects even in Kerala are tribals and Dalits. At the national level, around 40 per cent of the victims are tribals, some 20 per cent Dalits and a similar number of other rural poor like fish workers and stone cutters. The fact that around 80 per cent belong to the powerless classes may explain why after depriving millions of their livelihood, India does not have a rehabilitation policy even fifty years after it has been declared a Republic.

Misery is usually the consequence of this neglected field as experience and studies have shown. But the right of the displaced to a life with dignity is not a concern of the law or of the project staff. As a result, people are resettled only when they agitate against displacement or when the World Bank orders India to do so. The Bank is interested in getting land for the multinationals and demands rehabilitation to satisfy human rights activists in the rich countries. But, even five decades after independence, the Bank has to tell those who swear by *swadeshi* to rehabilitate persons displaced in the name of national development. And those who agitate on their side are called anti-national!

Besides, the "public purpose" under which land is acquired has not been defined till today. Therefore, more land than needed is acquired and later misused. For example, the ICRISAT campus near Secunderabad has come up on excess land acquired for BHEL. Two-thirds of the land acquired for the HAL-MIG plant at Sunabeda, Koraput district, Orissa in 1966 is lying vacant. But, the 3,000 tribal families it displaced have not been resettled. The land is reportedly being sold at high profit. Much land was acquired on both sides of the Roro irrigation canals in Jharkhand for a "public purpose" and given to relatives of the officials for housing co-operatives.

It is in this context that one has to look at the proposal to amend the Land Acquisition Act 1894 and the fifth schedule and the failure to finalise a rehabilitation policy. A national rehabilitation policy was mooted in 1985, but was drafted only in 1993 and revised in 1994. The drafts were not made public but obtained through other means and circulated to thousands of NGOs and displaced persons who found them unsatisfactory. The drafts took displacement for granted and did not define the "public purpose" for which people are displaced. So, abuses are inevitable. There are indications that they were drafted under pressure from the World Bank, not out of conviction. The 1994 draft began by stating that more land than in the past has to be acquired to encourage private investment.

Most states take this part of the policy seriously, but not the sections on rehabilitation. Our studies show that in most states an average of 6 per cent of the landmass has been acquired during 1951-1995. That comes to more than 15 million hectares all over the country, a quarter of it forest land and about 20 per cent other common property resources (CPRs). The CPRs are the livelihood of the tribals and other rural poor. But, they are paid no compensation. So, these communities that have preserved forests for centuries have no choice, but to destroy the little left, for sale as firewood since that is the only income they can earn. Because of it, those who have deprived them of their livelihood call them enemies of forests.

Our studies also show that the tempo of acquisitions has increased with liberalisation. For example, Orissa had acquired 40,000 hectares for industries during 1951-1995. The present trend is to acquire 1,00,000 hectares in a decade. AP has already acquired in five years half as much land for industry as it did in 45 years. The acquisitions for mining are higher than that, mainly for foreign companies that are eyeing this sector. About 12 per cent (actually, 11.5%) of the landmass of Goa has been on perpetual mining leases to private companies since 1948 and 38 per cent is under forests. Another 3.2 per cent of the landmass was acquired for other projects from 1965 to 1995. If the plans go through, another 7.2 per cent of its landmass will be acquired during the next five years.

The rationale for many new projects is questionable. For example, the Indian Navy that controls the Goa Airport as well as People's Committee that studied the proposed new private airport, are of the view that the present one can be expanded to accommodate future needs for some decades. But, the proponents of the new airport are not impressed. Questions are asked about the need for a second airport in Bangalore. Ritu Dewan's economic analysis shows that any new airport in Maharashtra or Gujarat can survive only by stealing traffic from the three existing major ports in these states. But, plans are afoot to build a private port in Gujarat. Repression follows when these actions are opposed. For example, a retired senior defence officer who was leading the agitation against the proposed port in Gujarat, died in police custody in May 2000.

Moreover, the private sector goes where the infrastructure is. Mostly fertile rice growing land near roads and railway lines is acquired, when alternatives are available. For example, the agitation around the Konkan Railway in Goa was not to stop it as some allege but to save the *khazan* lands that are a pre-Portuguese irrigation system whose technology and flora and fauna have not been studied. Thousands of fishing families depended on them. Studies on similar systems in Kuttanadu in Kerala show that bisecting them without proper drainage results in a rise in the mosquito menace and malaria. And, Goa is known for Japanese encephalitis. Studies show that about 10,000 hectares of abandoned mining land were available for industry if the line was diverted. It would have also saved the *khazan* lands. But, the line was built right on the coast. Today, fertile land is being acquired on both sides of it for new industries. In West Bengal, the land to the north of the Midnapore railway station is rocky and undulating, while that closer to Kharagpur was fertile. But being close to the highway, 200 acres of the latter were acquired for Tata Metalliks in 1992 and later 96 acres more for a proposed Birla firm that has not even taken off. Hundreds of Lodha tribal families have thus been sacrificed to private profit.

These are some of the reasons why the displaced and persons active with them are dissatisfied with the draft policy and oppose the plan to amend the Land Acquisition Act, 1894. In fact, they have prepared alternatives both to the rehabilitation policy and the Act, and presented them to the Secretary, Ministry of Rural Development, in October 1995. That is where they remained till the next policy draft was prepared in 1997. They found it an improvement over the previous drafts. It recognised that displacement causes "state-induced impoverishment" (2.1a) and the "no developmental project can be justified if a section of society is pauperised by it" (3.1.2). It said that displacement should be minimised and that the displaced should be resettled. But, it did not accept people's right not to be displaced without their consent based on proper information on the project.

Despite these and other shortcomings, they were ready to dialogue with the Ministry on this draft. That is when they heard of the plans to amend the Land Acquisition Act, 1894 to support the effort to acquire more land. The amendments went contrary to most clauses of the draft policy. Social activists protested when news leaked out in October 1998 that the Union Cabinet had accepted this Bill but had rejected the draft policy apparently because the private sector was not ready to invest on rehabilitation. In response, at a meeting convened in January 1999, the Minister for Rural Development gave an impression of being ready to discuss a policy before enacting a law. Today, we find the Union Government non-committal on the policy, but seems to be determined to go ahead with the amendments.

The present study is an effort to support this search for people-oriented alternatives. The main question it asks is whether it is necessary to impoverish and marginalise the already powerless in the name of national development and liberalisation. Is it possible to have another type of people-oriented development? This search is the main reason why the researchers have tried to involve social activists in this study. They are aware that the proposed amendments to the Land Acquisition Act, 1894 will legalise such plunder in the name liberalisation. They would like to join all people of good will in search for people-oriented alternatives. It is to them that this study is presented.

Walter Fernandes

Preface

In the post-independence period, India has been grappling with the problem of fast economic development through the implementation of numerous projects like dams, industries, mines, airports, railways and roads. For this purpose large areas of land have been acquired, displacing millions of people without proper concern for their resettlement and rehabilitation. Most of the victims belong to the very poor sections like the Dalits, the tribals and the backward classes. Unfortunately, no systematic effort has been made at the national level to collect reliable data on the immensity of this problem nor has the government succeeded to formulate a national policy on rehabilitation.

It is in this context, the Indian Social Institute, Delhi initiated a nationwide study under the direction of Dr. Walter Fernandes, on development-induced displacement, resettlement and rehabilitation. It is a comprehensive project covering all the major issues around this problem from 1951 to 1995. The study aims at creating a national database, which can provide the policy makers with abundant evidence regarding the urgency to formulate a more humane policy on displacement and rehabilitation.

The study has been carried out by Dr. Fernandes himself in several states of India in collaboration with local partners. The Indian Social Institute, Bangalore took up the task of implementing the project in the four southern states of India. The Kerala study was carried out in partnership with Loyola College of Social Sciences, Thiruvananthapuram.

Acknowledgements

In carrying out the present study the research team has sought help from many institutions and individuals. We are grateful to the Ministry of Rural Areas and Employment, Government of India and to MISEREOR for providing financial assistance to implement this research project. We are also thankful to the officials of Kerala government who granted sanction to initiate the study. Our thanks are due to the librarians of the Public Library, Secretariat General Library, Legislature Library, University Library and the CDS Library who co-operated in the first phase of Gazette search. We also thank the librarians of Centre for Earth Sciences Studies, State Planning Board, Thiruvananthapuram and Kerala Forest Research Institute, Peechi.

We acknowledge the help offered by various officials in different government offices, especially those in the Collectorates, Land Acquisition Offices, Irrigation Department, and Electricity Board, Public Office, Vikas Bhavan, Secretariat, Irrigation Research Development Bureau and Forest Office as well as the several project offices concerned. We thank the social activists from all over the state and staff of various NGOs who helped us in identifying the displaced and affected people, as well as in the data collection. We acknowledge the encouragement and inspiration from many scholars.

We gratefully remember the respondents (displaced and affected people) who wholeheartedly co-operated with our investigators by sharing the traumatic experiences of displacement.

We are thankful to Mr. C Ramesh Kumar of Public Relations Department who supported and helped us, with all possible effort, throughout the study.

We thank Mr. Suresh, Mr. Sreeju and other staff members of Volks Computers, Thiruvananthapuram and Ms. Beena for their help in data processing and analysis. We acknowledge the services of Fr. Antony and his team in Yuvadeepthi Press, Thiruvananthapuram. We are grateful to the Rector, Principal, faculty, students and staff members of Loyola College for their help.

A whole lot of our friends, colleagues, even strangers have put in their energy to gather information for this report. We wish to place on record our sincere appreciation of their sustained support.

Research Team

Indian Social Institute, Bangalore and

Loyola College of Social Sciences, Thiruvananthapuram

Research Team

Walter Fernandes, the Project Consultant, is currently the Director, North Eastern Social Science Research Centre, Guwahati and formerly Director, Indian Social Institute, New Delhi.

Jose Murickan, Director of the present study, has been the Programme Co-ordinator at Indian Social Institute, Bangalore and formerly Principal of Loyola College of Social Sciences, Thiruvananthapuram.

M.K. George is the Vice-Principal and Faculty in the Post Graduate Department of Sociology, Loyola College of Social Sciences, Thiruvananthapuram.

K.A. Emmanuel is the Senior Faculty, Loyola Extension Services, Loyola College of Social Sciences, Thiruvananthapuram.

Jose Boban is the Faculty in the Post Graduate Department of Sociology, Loyola College of Social Sciences, Thiruvananthapuram.

Prakash Pillai R. is the Faculty in the B.C.M. College, Kottayam and a research scholar of the University of Kerala.

Abbreviations

CADA	Command Area Development Authority
CCA	Cultivable Command Area
CDS	Centre for Development Studies
CEPZ	Cochin Export Promotion Zone
CESS	Centre for Earth Sciences Studies
CPCRI	Central Plantations Crops Research Institute
CPRs	Common Property Resources
CTCRI	Centre Tuber Crops Research Institute
CWC	Central Water Commission
CWRDM	Centre for Water Resource Development and Management
DPs	Displaced Persons
GCA	Gross Command Area
GN	General Category (Forward Castes)
Ha.	Hectare
IDA	Industrial Development Area
IDP	Industrial Development Plots
IRDB	Irrigation Research and Development Bureau
ITI	Industrial Training Institute
KFRI	Kerala Forest Research Institute
KTDC	Kerala Tourism Development Corporation
LES	Loyola Extension Services
MES	Muslim Education Society
MT	Metric Tonne

NP	National Park
OBCs	Other Backward Castes
PAPs	Project Affected Persons
R&R	Resettlement and Rehabilitation
SCs	Scheduled Castes
SDP	State Domestic Product
SIKL	Steel Industries Kerala Ltd.
SNDP	Sree Narayana Dharma Paripalana Sangham
STs	Scheduled Tribes
TBGRI	Tropical Botanical Research Institute
TTC	Teacher Training Course
WRD	Water Resource Department

List of Tables

1

Displacement in India: Issues and Methodology

The content of this book is the outcome of a two year long study conducted by a research team regarding the nature, extent and consequences of displacement brought about by the implementation of development projects in Kerala during the period 1951-1995. This study is an integral part of an All India effort to examine the state of displacement in the country as a whole since Independence.

In the ongoing discourse on development and the search for a model of sustainable development, displacement has become a crucial concern. Though a vast amount of literature is available on the concept of development and its benefits, there is a striking paucity of data on the problems created by it especially displacement, resettlement and rehabilitation. There is also a conspicuous lack of any national policy regarding these issues. In the context of growing human rights consciousness, this problem acquires serious dimensions challenging the administrators, academicians and activists to respond to this issue pro-actively. The ultimate purpose of this research is to raise national consciousness on the enormity of human suffering created by development projects through displacement, often without resettlement, of large masses of the Indian population, particularly the weaker sections, and to support the victims through policy changes in their favour.

The Focus of the Study

The study dealt only with planned and often forced displacement created in the name of national development. Though a great amount of dislocation of life had taken place in the pre-Independence era, and even during the Ancient and Medieval period by the construction of dams and other projects, the actual dislocation they caused was minimal in the context of the abundance of land and the small population of those times. Displacement became a significant problem during the colonial period and got intensified after Independence (Mankodi, 1989). With the onset of globalisation, it has assumed larger proportions and it is today a serious concern of national significance.

The concept of displacement we use in this study is exclusively confined to the dislocation of people brought about by development projects. It excludes refugees fleeing from natural disasters like floods, droughts, earthquakes and cyclones. It also excludes process induced displacement such as that caused by the introduction of new technologies like trawlers for fishing and those resulting from other changes in the nature of the economy. It further excludes voluntary or involuntary migration caused by wars and other human made upheavals in society, as well as displacement of Tribals through land alienation and eviction of non-Tribal encroachers in the reserve forests. The characteristic of displacement brought about by such tragedies is their unpredictability and inevitable helplessness.

The type of displacement investigated by this study is caused by pre-planned projects like dams, mines, thermal power plants, industries, roads, railways, ports, national parks, tourist resorts and the like. They have necessitated the acquisition of private and community lands (Common Property Resources - CPRs) mostly in the rural areas. CPRs affect the very life sustenance of the Tribals and other forest and mountain dwellers. Displaced Persons (DPs) are persons forced to move out of their home when their homestead is acquired by the project. Project Affected Persons (PAPs) are deprived of their livelihood fully or partially without being physically displaced. In some cases, their individual land may be acquired, but not their homestead. PAPs also include those people who are affected by environmental degradation due to development projects. In other cases, the CPRs that are the livelihood of some traditional communities like the Tribals are taken over by the project without evicting them from their homestead.

The UN organised World Conference on Human Rights, held at Vienna in June 1993, clearly identified 'forced eviction' as 'gross violation of human rights'. In order to conceal the trauma it causes to the affected people, policy makers and international financial institutions use the pretentious phrase, '*involuntary relocation*', though in reality, it is nothing but 'forced eviction'. The policy makers even claim that the displaced persons are beneficiaries of the compensation and rehabilitation package. It is ironical that the ones who suffer the most from the project itself are called beneficiaries. Another argument, the policy makers use to justify displacement is that "some people have to suffer if the nation has to prosper." Studies show that it is invariably the weaker sections like the Tribals and Dalits who are sacrificed again and again at the "altar of development". As Fernandes and Paranjpye (1997: 3) point out,

> though involuntary displacement occurs at a point of time, it sets in motion a series of inevitable events, which often constitute several years of psychological trauma due to the disruption in the established pattern of life of the people displaced. Production systems are dismantled, close knit kinship groups get scattered, long established relationships are disrupted, traditional sources of employment are lost, market links broken and customs related to child care, food security, intra-community credit transfers etc., get dissolved. The obvious result of such sudden changes is impoverishment, both economic and social. The psychological trauma is profound, because people find themselves landless, jobless, without food and access to community resources.

Moreover, when environmentalists and social activists demand that displacement be minimised and rehabilitation be taken seriously, they are often accused of being 'anti-developmental'.

These groups are by no means against development per se, but oppose that type of lopsided development which causes environmental destruction, human rights violation and social injustice. The exclusive emphasis of most development projects on productivity leads to the neglect of the justice issue. On the other hand, some activists lay excessive emphasis on the negative side of development without sufficiently recognising the positive benefits. This misunderstanding can be cleared if both issues are juxtaposed and seen in the total perspective of human and economic development.

The main reason for this controversy is the lack of awareness on the part of policy makers, and the urban middle and upper class who invariably stand to benefit from these projects. The poor availability of data, inaccessibility of official records and absence of reliable documentation on the question of displacement and rehabilitation add to the accentuation of this conflict. This study is undertaken precisely to gather such badly needed data and sensitise the elite as well as the policy makers, project authorities, the public and the government to the deeper issue of the wanton human sufferings caused by the implementation of these projects. The lack of sensitivity on the part of the ruling class is evidenced by the fact that during the past 50 years after Independence, the government has not felt the need to promulgate a National Policy on Resettlement and Rehabilitation for serving its own people. It was only when the World Bank brought this to their attention that our policy makers woke up to this grim reality.

Displacement in India

Displacement is not a recent phenomenon. There is evidence of development-induced displacement already from the era of the Guptas from the 3rd to the 6th century A.D. It seems to have continued to some extent in the Mughal Age and picked up momentum under the British. The post-independence measures have resulted in much more displacement than in the colonial times with the difference that now it is in the name of national development. That was the reason for fixing 1951, the year of the

First Five-year Plan, as the starting point for the study. The study covered the period upto 1995, which was originally meant to be the last year of the Eighth Plan. Besides, it comes four years after the promulgation of the New Economic Policy in 1991. This also enables us to understand its impact by looking at future trends.

The Pre-Independence Scenario

Much of 19th century displacement is process induced rather than project induced. The economy and the legal system of the Indian Empire (the present day Bhutan, India, Nepal, Pakistan and Bangladesh) were changed to suit the needs of the British economy. That also caused displacement. From the first coal mines in the 1820s in Raniganj, to the coffee plantations in Karnataka, tea plantations in Assam, the construction of the Grand Trunk Road in the 1830s, and the Railways in the 1860s, creation of the Public Works Department in the 1840s and other projects later, the colonialists needed more and more land in order to change the Indian economy to suit the needs of the British Industrial Revolution (Mankodi, 1989: 140-143).

This effort culminated in the *Land Acquisition Act 1894.* Other laws and policies followed around land and forests, and all of them resulted in direct or indirect displacement of people. It has intensified after independence, thanks to the industrial policy enunciated in 1947 and the Five-Year Plans launched in 1951. These were an integral part of the process of changing the economy of the sub-continent to such colonial needs. Basic to it was the de-industrialisation of the colony in order to turn it into a supplier of capital and raw materials for the British Industrial Revolution and captive market for its finished products. The second step was to change land laws to make its acquisition easy for British plantations and raw material producers. The landless agricultural labourers, most of them Dalits and service groups from other "low" castes, felt its negative effects more than the others did (Sen, 1979: 8-12).

The best known change is *The Land Acquisition Act, 1894* (LAQ). It was preceded by other changes, beginning with the

Permanent Settlement 1793. A new land law was enacted in Calcutta in 1824, to make land available for salt pans and other purposes. Three other major laws followed till finally the LAQ was enacted in 1894 (Upadhyay and Raman, 1998). Simultaneously in 1864, the forest laws were changed to suit British revenue needs and to provide timber for railway sleepers and to build ships for colonial wars. "By one stroke of the executive pen, (it) attempted to obliterate centuries of customary use by rural populations all over India" (Gadgil and Guha, 1992: 134). The exact number affected by these legal and economic changes is not known. According to one estimate, it deprived 35 million persons of their livelihood (Naoroji, 1988). It remains an estimate. But, one knows that these changes resulted in the impoverishment and disruption of life of the poor, mainly the Tribals and Dalits. They also led to many struggles (Savyasaachi, 1998: 15-16).

The distinguishing feature of these laws is the establishment of State monopoly over land and other community assets and natural resources. In Australia, the principle on which this legal system is based is called *terra nullius* (nobody's land). White colonisation of indigenous land in Australia, in the Americas and Southern Africa was based on the principle that land without an individual title belongs to nobody as such can be occupied by anyone. In 1993, the Australian judiciary declared it unconstitutional (Brennan, 1995: 4-5). But, it continues to be the basis of land legislation in India, under its American expression of 'eminent domain'. Its first facet is that land not having an individual *patta* is State property. The second is that the State alone has the right to decide what is a "public purpose". But, the public purpose has not been defined till today (Ramanathan, 1999).

Displacement in Post-Independence India

There were several cases of struggles against these changes already in the colonial times, the best known among them being the one of Mulshi-Peta near Pune in the 1920s (Bhuskute, 1997: 170-172). The struggle was appropriated by the freedom fighters. But, though they opposed the colonial Government on this particular issue, the nationalist leaders had themselves internalised much of the colonial value system including that of the eminent domain. So, the thinking behind development in India remains more or less unchanged even half a century after independence. When they became the decision-makers of independent India, the freedom fighters who had earlier supported the Mulshi-Peta struggle, continued to use the same colonial legislation to displace people in the name of national development.

As a result, there has been much greater displacement and many more struggles after independence, because investment strategies for economic progress envisaged by India's five-year plans entail changes in the use of land, water, forests and other resources. They also result in often irreversible changes in the lives of millions who are displaced or otherwise deprived of access to the resources that are their livelihood. Studies indicate that it has resulted in the further impoverishment of the already poor. As such, the issue of displacement has become one of the rights of the poor, much more so after liberalisation.

Thus, the first feature of the post-independence scenario is an enormous increase in the number of DPs and other PAPs. The present state of development induced displacement and rehabilitation has to be studied within this context. Its outstanding feature is that despite an enormous increase in their numbers, no official database exists on the total number and the type of DPs/PAPs. The official figures are not reliable. Besides, most DPs and PAPs belong to the powerless classes. The country does not have a rehabilitation policy or law though millions have been deprived of their livelihood. Briefly, post-independence displacement scenario is characterised by the following:

Absence of a Database

The country lacks an official database on the number of DPs/PAPs, the state of their rehabilitation etc. The few estimates available put their number at a minimum of 21.3 million between 1951 and 1990 (Fernandes, 1998a: 251). By now, they must have crossed 30 to 35 millions. A researcher puts the dam DPs,

1951-1985 at 21.6 million (Reddy, 1989: 419) and another even at 50 million (Roy, 1999). All of them are based on estimates and extrapolation of secondary data.

A database is a basic, not the only, tool to help the DPs/PAPs to demand their rights and work for a rehabilitation policy and law that respond to their aspirations, because today we have only scanty official statistics and a few case studies. In an effort to build a reliable database, studies were made by extrapolating official and unofficial data. One of the studies (Fernandes, 1998a: 251) indicates that by and large dams lower than 15 meters from the foundation built on streams in the plains, displace very few or none. Those in the hills displace around 1,000 each. Medium dams (say 15-30m.) displace 2,000 to 10,000 each. Some major dams like Tawa and Nagarjunasagar have displaced around 25,000 each and many others more than 100,000 and some above 100,000. Some like Upper Krishna have caused 2.5 lakh DPs each (Guggenheim, 1990: 14).

Official and research data were available also for several mines and industries. For example, by official count, the major coal companies displaced 32,751 families in 1981-85. The four steel plants displaced 1.25 lakhs in the 1950s and 60s (Govt. of India, 1985: 18; Commissioner of SC & ST, 1961: 115). Singrauli displaced 50,000 (Guggenheim, 1990). Korba in Madhya Pradesh and other industries like HEC and thermal plants in the Damodar Valley gave similar figures (Dani, 1991). Figures for industries and mines show that displacement by coal-mines has increased. It is because till 1960s the focus was on underground mines that cause PAPs, but relatively few DPs. With the rise in the demand for low-grade coal for thermal plants and need to raise its production rapidly, focus since 1970 has been on opencast mines that displace many (Krishna and Sachdeva, 1990: 106).

Data on parks and sanctuaries are difficult to obtain, because of a veil of secrecy surrounding matters environmental, particularly forests. Studies (e.g. Kothari, 1999) indicate that protected areas displace very few, but 4 to 5 millions live inside their core area. The present law allows them to live inside the sanctuaries, but not parks. But, they are denied access to the non-wood forest produce that were their livelihood. Besides, a large number of persons in their periphery depend on this resource, but are denied access to it. Though physically living in the protected area, they are considered intruders. So, in reality, protected areas have PAPs running into millions, and relatively few DPs. But, in the absence of accurate data, the researchers extrapolated the available data and arrived at an approximate number of 6 lakh DPs, most of them PAPs.

Table 1.1

A Conservative Estimate of Persons Displaced by Various Categories of Projects (1951-1990)

	Type of Project	*No. Displaced*	*No. Rehabilitated*	*Per cent of all DPs*	*Backlog*	*Per cent of DPs*
1	Mines	25,50,000	6,30,000	24.71	19,20,000	75.29
2	Dams	1,64,00,000	41,00,000	25.00	1,23,00,000	75.00
3	Industries	12,50,000	3,75,000	31.25	8,75,000	69.75
4	Sanctuaries	6,00,000	1,25,500	20.83	4,75,000	79.17
5	Others	5,00,000	1,50,000	30.00	3,50,000	70.00
	Total	2,13,00,000	53,80,000	25.26	1,59,20,000	74.74

Source: Fernandes 1998: 251

Besides, there has been an enormous increase in "miscellaneous schemes" like roads, railways, universities and government offices (Mankodi, 1989). Fernandes and Raj (1992) based on their estimates added five lakhs on this count. They could not make an estimate for urban DPs. So, Table 1.1 gives figures mainly for rural DPs. The number would be higher if urban DPs were added to it.

The situation can be expected to deteriorate with liberalisation, because efforts are being made to acquire more land than in the past. As the 1994 draft policy says:

> With the advent of the New Economic Policy, it is expected that there will be large-scale investments, both on account of internal generation of capital and increased inflow of foreign investments, thereby creating an enhanced demand for land to be provided within a shorter time span in an increasingly competitive market ruled economic structure (MRD, 1994: 1.1).

Differences Between Sources

Added to this is the confusion in the few sources that are available. Table 1.2 in which we contrast official data with researchers and

Table 1.2

Difference in the Number of DPs/PAPs in Some Projects

No.	*Project*	*Official*	*Researchers*	*Others*
1.	Hirakud	110,000 to 160,000 (GOO)	180,000 (PDM)	NA
2.	Koel-Karo	50,000 (D&S)	66,000 (D&S)	NA
3.	Singrauli	40,000 (HB)	80,000 (MG)	50,000 (SG)
4.	Pochampad	200,000 (GOAP)	200,000 (R&R) 150,000 (COL)	240,000 (SG)
5.	Nedumbassery Airport	1937 families[#]	NA	820 families[+]
6.	Pong	NA	80,000 (MG) 150,000 (ET)	NA
7.	Sardar Sarovar	45,000 (Verma) 52,000 (NCA) 90,000 (Babbar)	120,000 (MG) 70,000 (D&D) 108,000 (NIUA)	199,500 (MB) 125,000 (SG) 114,000 (RAI)
8.	Srisailam	NA	100,000 (MG)	125,000 (SG)
9.	Rihand	NA	150,000 (EGT) 200,000 (HB)	NA
10.	Tehri	NA	70,000 (MG) 85,000 (PAR)	NA
11.	U. In'vati	15,500 (GOO)	18,500 (LKM)	20,500 (SCST)
12.	U. Kolab	51 Villages (GOO)	50,771 (F&R)	44 Vil (SCST)
13.	Farakka	None	NA	53,500 (WB)
14.	Singrauli I & II		None	49,000 (WB)
15.	MP Medium Irrigation		8,800	19,000 (WB)
16.	AP Irrigation II		63,000	1,50,000 (WB)

N.B.: Most figures of MG are official.

N D: Not Dated

Sources: Areeparampil, 1987 (MA); Babbar, 1992; Colchester, 1986: 246 (COL); Das and Singh, 1985 (D & S); Datta and De Roy, 1986: 14 (D & D); Fernandes and Raj, 1992: 32 (F & R); Govt. of Andhra Pradesh, 1989: 8 (GOAP); Govt. of Orissa, 1968 (GOO): 13; Guggenheim, 1990: 14 (SG); Heuze Brigant, 1991 (HB); Laskshmi, (n.d.) (G L); Mahapatra, 1994: 50-57 (LKM); Monkodi and Gangopadhyay, 1983: 5 (MG); Morse and Berger, 1992 (MB); NCA, 1984; NIUA, (n.d.); ORG, 1992: 17; Paranjpye, 1988: 23; (PAR) Pattanaik, Das and Mishra, 1987 (PDM); Rai, 1994; Reddy and Reddy, 1987 (R & R); Ganguly Thukral, 1989: 44 (EGT); Verma, 1985: 3; World Bank, 1994 (WB). Vishtapit Mukthi Vahini, 1996: 1 (VMV). # Land Acquisition-1 Office, Ankamaly; + Dhanam Bimonthly, Feb 15-28, 1999.

other unofficial sources, shows the confusion about the numbers involved. It also shows that official sources by and large underestimate the number of DPs and PAPs. For example by official count, the Hirakud dam displaced one lakh persons. But according to researchers, the DPs were more than 1.8 lakhs and out of Rs. 9.66 crores allotted for compensation, only Rs 3.43 crores (35.5%) have been paid. Official figures for Sardar Sarovar DPs range from 70,000 to 1,08,000 persons. Officially, the Farakka Super-thermal Plant was to cause no DPs/PAPs. But, World Bank estimates put the number of PAPs at 53,500.

The Type of DPs/PAPs

The next feature of displacement is the proportion of DPs/PAPs from the weaker sections, particularly Tribals and Dalits. It has been high in the past and is increasing today. Most DPs/PAPs are assetless rural poor like landless labourers and small and marginal farmers. The Tribals who constitute 8.08 per cent of the country's population, are estimated to be more than 40 per cent of the DPs/PAPs of dams and mines, and 90 per cent of wildlife sanctuaries (Fernandes, 1998a: 265). Another 20 per cent are Dalits (Mahapatra, 1990). An unknown, but big proportion of the rest are other rural poor. That may be the main reason why the country does not have a rehabilitation policy and law till today. These voiceless communities can be displaced without their consent and conveniently ignored. Most of them are not even resettled. The compensation they receive is low and they are unable to start a new life with it. The benefits reach another class.

A reason for the high proportion of Tribals among the DPs is that the number of projects in their areas has been growing since the 1970s. For example, of the 117 dams above 50m completed or under construction in 1990, 47 (40.17%) were built between 1971 and 1989, and 38 (32.48%) were under construction. Forty of them (53.33%) are in the Tribal areas, so also 73 (43.45%) of those with height between 30.1 and 50m (CWC, 1990). Simultaneously, the thrust during the last quarter of a century is towards major dams that displace a large number. For example, Upper Krishna, in

Karnataka, will displace 2,40,000, Somasila (AP) 1,00,000, Koel-Karo (Jharkhand) 70,000, Sardar Sarovar (Gujarat) more than 1,00,000. Some of them have a big proportion of Tribals and others have Dalits. For example, 90 per cent of those to be displaced by Koel-Karo are Tribals and 75 per cent of the Somasila dam are Dalits.

Besides, the Tribal regions witness what Gadgil (1989: 367-368) calls sequential exhaustion while analysing deforestation. The industrialist begins with spatial exhaustion, i.e. by cutting the forest near the village since it is accessible at least by a bullock cart. Then, he goes to the next village, next district or State, and then to distant regions, thus, depriving more persons of their livelihood. Thus, the paper mills in South India are today getting raw material from as far away as the northeast. The third is the sequence of species. After exhausting species like bamboo, industry changes over to hardwood like fruit trees that are essential for people's survival. The people, thus, deprived of their livelihood, go against their tradition of conservation and destroy the resources for their very survival. They cut for sale as fuel-wood, trees that are close to the village, then go further away, thus intensifying the vicious circle initiated by the industrialist.

Spatial sequence is visible today also in the location of developmental schemes, particularly dams, the biggest displacing agents. A comparison between the number of Tribals and the location of dams can give one an idea of the extent of Tribal displacement. Initially, relatively few dams were in the Tribal regions. Out of the 206 dams of less than 30m from the lowest foundation constructed before 1950, 44 (21.36%) were in these areas, so also 4 (19.05%) of those between 30.1 and 50m and 4 out of 16 (25.00%) above 50m.

The rest were mostly in the hilly tracts close to the rice growing regions of Tamil Nadu, Andhra Pradesh, Maharashtra, Gujarat, UP and Western MP. The non-rice growing, relatively powerless non-Tribals were displaced to provide irrigation to the rice growers. Once the accessible areas were exhausted, focus shifted to the Tribal regions. Only 9 out of 32 dams above 50m completed till 1970 (22.13%) were in the Tribal areas, so also 22 out of 58 between 30.1 and 50m (44.83%). After 1970, Maharashtra, Western MP and Gujarat concentrated on medium dams. They accounted for 1860 of the 2,162 built between 1971 and 1990, 1,165 of them on local streams. But, most major dams in these and other states came up in the Tribal areas (Fernandes and Asif, 1997).

Table 1.3

Large Dams in India in 1994

Year	*Height (meters) from the lowest foundation*						
Completed	*0.1-15m*	*15.1-20m*	*20.1-30m*	*30.1-40m*	*40.1-50m*	*>50.1m*	*NA*
Before 1950	147 (51.8)	64 (22.6)	45 (15.8)	10 (3.6)	8 (2.8)	7 (2.4)	3 (1.0)
	(7.5)	(5.6)	(6.0)	(4.9)	(8.7)	(5.1)	(13.0)
1951-60	86 (32.7)	63 (23.9)	73 (27.8)	13 (4.9)	12 (4.5)	11 (4.2)	5 (1.9)
	(4.4)	(5.5)	(9.9)	(6.4)	(13.1)	(8.1)	(22.0)
1961-70	191 (44.2)	126 (29.2)	61 (14.1)	23 (5.3)	8 (1.8)	21 (4.9)	2 (0.4)
	(9.8)	(11.0)	(8.2)	(11.3)	(8 7)	(15.4)	(0.9)
1971-80	564 (46.2)	365 (29.9)	179 (14.6)	63 (5.2)	20 (1.6)	28 (2.3)	2 (0.2)
	(28.9)	(31.9)	(24.0)	(30.9)	(21.7)	(20.6)	(0.9)
1981-90	505 (46.7)	311 (28.7)	200 (18.5)	30 (2.8)	12 (1.1)	20 (1.6)	4 (0.3)
	(25.9)	(27.3)	(26.8)	(14.7)	(13.0)	(14.7)	(1.8)
1991-93	60 (59.4)	17 (16.8)	13 (12.9)	1 (0.9)	6 (5.9)	4 (4.0)	0 (0.0)
	(3.1)	(1.5)	(1.7)	(0.5)	(6.5)	(2.9)	(0.0)
N. A	162 (76.1)	30 (14.1)	15 (7.0)	2 (0.9)	1 (0.4)	3 (1.4)	0 (0.)
	(8.3)	(2.6)	(2.0)	(0.9)	(1.1)	(2.2)	(0.)
Under Construction	234 (33.7)	166 (23.9)	160 (23.1)	62 (8.9)	25 (3.6)	42 (6.0)	6 (0.8)
	(12.1)	(14.5)	(21.4)	(30.4)	(27.2)	(30.9)	(27.0)
Total	1949	1142	746	204	92	136	22

N.B.: The Central Water Commission (CWC) and the Water Resources Department (WRD) have two different classifications of dams. Even some of what WRD calls minor irrigation schemes are classified by CWC as large dams. In Table 1.4, we have given the projects according to their year of completion. In Chapter 2, we shall give the number according to what WRD considers major and minor.

Source: CWC 1994.

Multiple Displacement

Lack of long term planning results in multiple displacement. For example, many Rihand dam oustees in MP of the early 1960s were displaced again in the 1970s for coal mines, a third time for industrial units and a fourth time for the Singrauli Super-Thermal Plant (Ganguly Thukral, 1989: 47-48). The Soliga Tribals in Karnataka displaced by the Kabini dam in the 1970s are threatened with displacement a second time by the Rajiv Gandhi National Park (Cheria, 1996). Many fishing families displaced by the Mangalore Port in the 1960s and resettled as agriculturists were displaced again by the Konkan Railway in the 1980s, after they had adapted themselves to farming (Fernandes, 1991). Many more such cases are found all over the country.

Absence of Rehabilitation

A sign of ignoring the social component is the absence of a rehabilitation law or policy. Fewer than *a third of the DPs have been resettled even partially* (Fernandes, 1998a: 251). Three states have laws and two have policies for the rehabilitation of irrigation project DPs. One more state is drafting its policy. Two public sector companies have promulgated their policies in the 1990s. The Central Government drafted a policy in 1993 and it was revised in 1994. This process culminated in the Ministry of Rural Area and Employment preparing in 1998, a draft National Rehabilitation Policy (NCPRR, 1998). But, the Union Cabinet is reported to have rejected this policy in October 1998, but approved the Land Acquisition (Amendment) Bill, 1998 that attempted to further reduce the few rights the DPs/PAPs have under the existing legislation. However, under pressure from social activists, DPs/PAPs and researchers working with them, the then Minister for Rural Development seems to have agreed to formulate a new rehabilitation policy and then draft a law based on it. The process and dialogue were continuing at the time of the study. A detailed discussion on the efforts made by the government in policy formulation is presented in the concluding chapter.

The main reason for the apathy towards rehabilitation is that in most cases it is not an integral part of the scheme. It is either neglected or is left to be worked out later. Even when planned, by and large it is viewed as one time resettlement. Besides, the displacing agency itself is put in charge of rehabilitation. The work of its personnel is judged according to the speed and the cost-effectiveness of project implementation. So, rehabilitation becomes a casualty. Moreover, rehabilitation schemes are only for the DPs. Parks, sanctuaries and several mines displace relatively few, but destabilise the life support system of many communities. The PAPs they create lose their employment, market, kin groups and access to the outside world, but are not rehabilitated.

Besides, groups depending on CPRs or on the village as a community do not get compensation since it is guided exclusively by the Land Acquisition Act 1894. It deals with individual patta holders (Vaswani, 1992: 156-160) and has the market value of quantifiable commodities as the basis for compensation though around 80 per cent of the DPs belong to the informal economy and very few have pattas. The loss of CPRs, the psychological trauma of forced displacement, the break up of community institutions and support structures are ignored in its calculation (Fernandes and Chatterji, 1995: 6-7). Moreover, most displacement is in regions that have been administratively neglected, as such considered backward. The market price of the little land the DPs own is inadequate for them to begin a new life. Land records do not exist at times. When they do, they are inaccurate or outdated (Fernandes and Raj, 1992: 91-93).

Moreover, displacement results in a conflict between the informal society to which most DPs belong and the formal one into which they are inserted. These societies are based on contradictory frameworks and value systems (Sharma, 1978: 6-10). For example, land-based resettlement can be viable if the social, psychological and cultural aspects are attended to. Many DPs belong to the second and at times, the first generation of a monetised economy. Monetary compensation is by and large ineffective in societies based on a barter economy. As a result, the compensation they receive is, more often than not, appropriated by middlemen coming from outside (Viegas, 1992: 40-45).

Studies also show that these communities find it difficult to adapt themselves to the new production pattern into which they are inserted without any psychological or socio-cultural preparation. As a result, they often turn out to be 'undisciplined' workers and take to alcohol and even to crime as a way out of their trauma. Many of them lose their job, because of these problems (Baboo, 1991: 298-299). Moreover, the social pollution aspect, for example, the introduction of new diseases, because of the change of the environment and the introduction of exotic species is ignored (Mahapatra, 1990: 97).

Besides, the implementation of most rehabilitation schemes is weak. For example, a 'land for land' scheme has existed in Maharashtra and Gujarat for about two decades and in Orissa since 1994; but, it is limited to irrigation schemes. In Maharashtra, only 27.74 per cent of the 94,387 families got its benefits under the scheme by a decade since 1976. The percentage was 15.18 for the 10,147 Tribal families and 31.4 for the others. In Gujarat, out of 19,619 families displaced by World Bank financed medium irrigation projects by a decade since 1979, only 15,560 landowners were entitled to its benefits. Six thousand (38.61%) of those entitled were given a total of 6,632 ha. of land against 22,171 ha. acquired from them. For the land acquired, they were paid an average of Rs. 8,780 per ha. when its market rate was Rs.16,000 to 20,000 (Fernandes, 1990: 35-36).

The T.N. Singh Formula 1967 stipulated that one job be given per family of DPs. But, the illiterate did not possess the skills required by the project. So, they were given mainly low-paid unskilled jobs, often temporary in nature. The job was limited to the "head of the family", usually men. Despite these shortcomings, it was a step in the right direction. But, with the reduction in unskilled jobs, because of mechanisation, the Bureau of Public Enterprises abandoned the scheme in 1986 (MRD, 1993: 4.3) instead of finding alternatives to help the DPs/PAPs. This trend can be expected to intensify since mechanisation is intrinsic to liberalisation.

It is obvious then that displacement and rehabilitation are not a one-time event pertaining to physical transfer to the new place, but a series of happenings, many of them of a qualitative nature, affecting the lives of the DPs in a myriad ways. Total rehabilitation should, therefore include, apart from physical resettlement, replacement of CPRs and socio-cultural systems, psychological preparation and technical training to deal with the new society and economy (Nayak, 1996).

Focus on Economic Growth

The consequence of all these factors is impoverishment and marginalisation of most DPs/PAPs. By impoverishment, we refer to their status as individuals and communities after loss of livelihood, not to economic poverty that may have been their state prior to it. The consequences of deprival of livelihood are felt differentially. Some PAPs from the better off sections of the high castes living in the "advanced" districts may improve their livelihood by getting a somewhat high price for their not very fertile land. But, most Tribals and Dalits experience deterioration in their financial, social and cultural status (Fernandes and Raj, 1992: 142-143). In every category, particularly among the disadvantaged sections, women are the worst hit and pay the highest price of development (Ganguly Thukral and Singh, 1995).

A conclusion one can draw from the above is that the project authorities plan the financial and technical aspects meticulously, but make little effort to get a clear idea of the people to be affected by it or to plan their resettlement. In the few cases where rehabilitation is planned, the specificity of the problems faced by the disadvantaged groups is rarely attended to. In reality, the poor are displaced and left to fend for themselves. But, no compromise is made on the engineering and economic aspects of the project. In other words, economic growth gets priority over the people affected by it.

Another feature of modern development is monopolistic acquisition of the resource. Land, forests and other resources are alienated from the communities directly dependent on them to the benefit of the class to which they are not its livelihood, but a source of profit or a raw material for producing other goods. This can be seen, inter-alia, in the resource utilisation pattern by mines, industries, parks and sanctuaries. Most minerals like coal, bauxite and chromite are in the Tribal areas. In 1983, 440 of the 498 coal-mines (87.23%) were in the states with a large Tribal population. In 1994, the number of coal-mines in these states had gone up to 490 out of 548 (89.42%) (Ministry of Mines, 1994).

Some Issues Around Deprival

It is clear then that the issue of displacement without rehabilitation should be tackled and a solution found to the process that impoverishes, and further marginalises the already powerless. To ensure change in the condition of the DPs/PAPs, one has first to arrive at a consensus on some basic issues beginning with the very meaning of displacement-induced impoverishment. Deprival of livelihood results both in the economic deprival of the DPs/PAPs and in their marginalisation. So, in defining impoverishment, one has to go beyond the economic factor, particularly the formal economy, which those inclined to justify displacement (e.g. Kar, 1991) use as the sole criterion. Calculating losses and gains on the basis of monetary income alone, they conclude that in many cases, the financial status of the DPs improves after displacement, because often their monetary income rises.

In this assessment, they ignore the fact that before displacement most DPs/PAPs belong to the non-monetised or semi-monetised informal economy. Many of their communities sustain themselves on the CPRs or by rendering services to the village as a community (Dhagamwar, 1989). Neither source of their livelihood is recognised, compensated or replaced. Those who limit their analysis to monetary income and marketable commodities, exclude from their calculation what the DPs/PAPs used to get from the informal economy. They ignore the fact that even when monetary income rises after displacement, they are often impoverished also in economic terms, because the CPRs and other sources of their non-monetised livelihood are not replaced.

Another issue is their total marginalisation by which is meant deterioration in their social status and psychological attitudes. These changes deprive them of the very motivation required for improvement of their status. The DPs and other marginalised categories internalise a sense of helplessness and powerlessness, because of their encounter with the powerful external world they are pushed into without adequate preparation. They also internalise the value system of the formal society that does not recognise their economy and culture, and begin to consider their own society and culture of little value. Such internalisation makes it impossible for them to rebuild their lives, leave alone improve their lifestyle (Fernandes, 1996). As a result, their standard of living deteriorates, so do their social status and self-esteem, though most policy makers (e.g. Sinha, 1996: 1455) insist that improvement of lifestyle is the primary objective of rehabilitation.

In other words, studies point to two facts of displacement-induced impoverishment: (a) economic deterioration; (b) loss of the social and psychological infrastructure. So, most persons who are active among the DPs/PAPs have long discarded an exclusively economic measurement of impoverishment and have gone beyond it to factors like the social, psychological, cultural and health parameters. For example, among the eight areas of impoverishment risks identified by Cernea (1995: 11-12) includes factors like the CPRs that belong to the informal economy and non-economic ones like social disintegration.

Lack of Awareness

Despite the enormity of the problem, awareness about displacement is very low in the country. The number of DPs/PAPs is double the 15 million persons transferred between India and Pakistan at the Partition in 1947 (Mankodi, 1989: 150). The sub-continent is yet to recover from its trauma. But, millions of people deprived of their livelihood in the name of national development have not entered India's national consciousness.

Its main reason is the lopsided developmental planning which has excluded people's participation from below and concentrated all decision-making in the hands of politicians, bureaucrats and professional experts. The focus has been on GNP growth and economic development without a social component.

Objectives, Hypotheses and Methodology

With this understanding of the situation in the country as a whole, we present the objectives, hypotheses and methodology used to carry out this study in Kerala.

Objectives of the Study

Our study was designed with the following objectives:

1. To create a quantitative and qualitative database on the nature and extent of displacement projects in Kerala from 1951-1995.
2. To examine the socio-economic, cultural and psychological consequences of development induced displacement on the oustees.
3. To understand the process involved in planning rehabilitation, the nature and extent of its implementation, and to search for alternatives in the process with a view to creating an integrated perspective on development, displacement and rehabilitation.
4. To generate awareness among decision-makers regarding the magnitude of the problem and to contribute to the formulation of a more humane and rational rehabilitation policy for the country.
5. To assess the environmental impact of development projects in Kerala-though the technical aspects of environment may be beyond our ken, we shall, nevertheless, look into the environmental impact on the displaced people.
6. To indicate future trends regarding the magnitude of displacement and its impact on the weaker sections.
7. To mobilise public opinion regarding the extent and magnitude of human suffering involved in the displacement process and initiate remedial measures through people's organisations.

The Hypotheses

Kerala has high levels of human development, but one of the lowest per capita incomes in the country: Rs.6,983 per annum as against Rs.8,399 for the whole of India in 1994-95. It comes to Rs.582 per month for Kerala as against the all India figure of Rs.670. This is in sharp contrast to the figures of the State of Punjab, Rs.14,188 and Rs.1,182 respectively (CMIE, March 1997). Kerala's performance in productive sectors has been abysmal with the industrial sector being the poorest. Because of the high levels of awareness and political organisation, demands for higher compensation, resorting to legal action etc., are common.

In spite of this, there has been sizeable investment in development projects and a considerable amount of displacement in Kerala. Official response has always been that the projects provide handsome compensation and hence, rehabilitation is not their concern. Data on these, especially official data are hard to come by. The image of a Model State and official apathy are likely to be serious blocks in getting an objective picture and applying suitable remedies to such a crucial human problem. Therefore, we believe that the complexity of this issue is serious enough to mandate a scientific inquiry. In the context of these contradictory claims, we proposed the following hypotheses:

1. In spite of low levels of industrialisation, displacement is quite high in Kerala.
2. A proportionately large number of project DPs are Scheduled Castes (SCs), Other Backward Communities (OBCs), Tribals and other economically weaker sections. Their socio-economic situation deteriorates further as a result of displacement.
3. The impact of displacement is higher on women than on men.

Methodological Issues

It is important that the methodology one chooses for research should correspond to the nature and requirements of the objectives of the study. Our study pursues three main thrusts:

(1) collection, anlaysis and systematisation of quantitative and qualitative data regarding all the major aspects of displacement with a view to preparing a comprehensive database;
(2) sensitising and mobilising the affected people and the activists working with them to demand their right to just compensation and humane resettlement and rehabilitation;
(3) influencing the government and the decision-makers to formulate a just rehabilitation policy, minimising displacement and providing all the facilities required for the betterment of the lives of those who have made enormous sacrifices for the development of the nation.

Corresponding to these three approaches, there are three methodologies, namely conventional research methodology, action research and participatory research. For the first part of our study with quantitative data, we followed the conventional methodology to collect quantitative data from secondary sources like Kerala Gazette, Government Records, and the existing research publications. For the second part, namely the empirical study done through the examination of selected projects, we attempted a combination of action research and participatory method. A word of comment on these approaches might explain the rationale of our evolving a unique type of methodology, which alone would suit a complex study of this kind, which calls for a creative approach to modern research. We have drawn inspiration for this methodological innovativeness from the studies carried out by other scholars. In so doing, we have gone beyond the conventional method of research developed by social sciences, particularly in sociology and anthropology which consists of collecting data and quantifying, classifying and analysing the information for systematic generalisation.

Questioning the Past

The classical methodology was developed in the context of the colonial need to know the subordinate peoples in order to better control and administer them. So, the questioning of this traditional system had begun already in the 1960s. Some questioned it from the perspective of methodology and others from that of the development paradigm. To begin with the first, to be accepted in one's own country, a Third World scholar had to be trained abroad. Their professional recognition depended less on their peers than on getting their papers published in foreign journals (Desai, 1981). So, a few began to search for methodologies that could free scholarship from its dependence on the West. They thought that the scholar had to understand the aspirations of the newly independent countries and gear research to their developmental and cultural needs (Hursh-Cesar and Roy, 1971). During the 1970s, some funding agencies such as the World Bank were feeling the need to get feedback on their inputs. Action Research was a tool they chose to respond to this need.

On the other side, a section of the youth was getting disillusioned with the pattern of development. Unemployment was rising as the products of mass education were getting out of school. The 1960s were also the years of drought particularly in Bihar. Food shortages were being felt and dependence on imports grew. The Green Revolution, presented as the panacea for all ills, made a section of middle and big farmers prosperous, but impoverished most small and marginal farmers and landless agricultural labourers (Kulkarni, 1993). This resulted in a section of university students questioning the pattern of development. Some of them abandoned the system and went to the rural areas to organise the rural poor to resist their marginalisation (Kothari, 1984: 50-51).

These were also the years of questioning among a section of researchers. Many of them felt that methodologies developed by Third World scholars and by funding agencies, could at best deal with the symptoms, but not the causes of the alienation of the poor (Roy, 1983: 61-62). Many of those who took this stand, questioned the very basis of traditional research. They viewed it as capitalist in nature in the sense that the researcher, whether following a western or Third World methodology, was appropriating to him/herself the knowledge of the people just as the factory owner appropriated the product of his workers. In their thinking, the basic issue was not the methodology, but the ownership of the process and product of research. Besides, these scholars could not accept the assumption that the researcher can study the people objectively without getting involved in issues concerning them. It amounted to objectifying human communities, as such, against their very humanity. They thought that the researcher could not study the people without getting involved in their struggles. Thus, research had to be turned into a tool of mobilisation.

To achieve it, the external researcher has to recognise that knowledge belongs to the people. Outsiders can give it a new form, but not appropriate it for themselves. They have to develop a partnership with the communities that share their knowledge with them. In this partnership, researchers have to be the interface between these communities and the macro world. Their task, among others, is to translate the demands and aspirations of the people into a language the decision-makers and other outsiders understand. Besides, social activists require tools meant to evaluate themselves constantly and be more effective both ideologically and in their action. Tools had to be developed for it. Some of those who took this stand viewed participatory research as a possible alternative (Fernandes, 1989: 7-9).

As far as our theme is concerned, while field experience showed us that displacement went against the people, we lacked a professionally acceptable database in support of or against this contention. To arrive at such a database, we had to move away from individual village studies and take a macro-approach in order to understand the impact of displacement on the social, economic and cultural life of the affected people. For this, we had to establish a rapport with them and grasp their emotional link with the livelihood which they had lost as a result of displacement. With this end in view, we had to work in tandem with the social activists and also win the people's confidence. The ultimate objective of this search is to find ways of supporting the struggles of the people who were trying to defend their livelihood. Besides, since the government is in the process of formulating a new policy regarding displacement and rehabilitation, our study could make a meaningful and substantial contribution to it.

With these goals in mind, we had to work on new methodologies that could function as tools of mobilisation, while at the same time ensuring that a professional report was prepared that could influence policy formulation. The former required a flexible timeframe without being totally undisciplined. The latter had to be done within definite deadlines. It also meant that various methodologies had to be combined. While participatory research required a mobilisation approach together with adequate data collection and analysis, a report acceptable to the policy makers had to be based on the traditional individual interviews and an academic methodology. In this study, therefore, we have tried to combine the two. In this attempt, we are aware that the traditional researchers and decision-makers who disagree with our analysis would not question our conclusions since it would not be politically correct. Instead, they would question our methodology. So, we had to be very faithful to the traditional data collection and analysis methods. We have ensured this in the study.

The Study was planned in three phases, the first of them being studying the notifications. In Kerala, the process of land take-over is as follows:

The First Phase

The first notification is published in the Gazettes for the information of the people concerned as per section 4 (1) of the Land Acquisition Act, 1894. The second notification (known as declaration) is published in Gazettes and/or newspapers. The third notification is the award. Award registers are kept in the district collectorates and the land acquisition offices concerned. The area of land acquired and the amount of compensation paid for each holding are entered in the award register.

In the first phase, all gazette notifications of the Government of Kerala regarding land acquisition during the period 1951-1995 were thoroughly scanned by using a detailed pro forma. For projects which acquired less than five hectares, data like date of notification, notification number, district, taluk, village, panchayat and extent of area were collected. For projects which acquired 5 Hectares or more, apart from identification details the following details were sought:

(i) Notification Law
(ii) Dates of Notification
(iii) Area acquired and type of land
(iv) Names of villages
(v) Compensation
(vi) Number of people displaced and caste-wise

The first notification does not necessarily lead to land acquisition. Many a time, it is followed by cancellation and correction. Hence, our investigators went through all the corrections and cancellations in the Gazettes during the period (1951-1995) in order to make our assessment of the extent of land take-over more accurate. This work was massive involving seven researchers for a period of six months. The number of gazette notifications during the period 1951-95 totalled 34233. Out of these, only 1,105 notifications were of above 5 hectares each. Thus, a majority of the notifications were for acquiring small plots of land like a few cents to one acre, two acres or three acres etc.

The Second Phase

In the second phase, secondary data regarding the acquisition of land and related matters connected with the implementation of different projects in the various districts were collected from government departments, collectorates, universities, research centres etc. Specifically the following aspects were looked into:

— extent of area acquired for the projects
— the type of projects for which land was acquired
— the number of persons displaced
— specific communities affected
— amount of monetary compensation paid to displaced families
— number of persons and families resettled and the manner of their rehabilitation

— problems of those who were not rehabilitated and possible solutions.

This phase was the most disappointing part of the study from the point of view of data collection. The investigators had to approach the officials of government departments and collectorates several times as their response was not encouraging. In spite of their repeated efforts, they could collect only incomplete information on several areas. The records and files were not even available in several departments. Despite these constraints, we managed to collect data on major projects from collectorates and a set of representative projects.

The following reasons were identified for this poor state of affairs:

1. Inadequate record keeping and filing in the various departments.
2. Government/official refusal to divulge the data on the pretext of official secrecy e.g. Naval Base.
3. Government policy of destroying files after 15 years.
4. Closure of offices for each project or merging of different offices.
5. Ignorance of the present staff of the details regarding projects of the 1950s, 60s and even early 70s.
6. Lack of time and interest on the part of certain officers.
7. A certain amount of complacency on the part of higher officials that they have fulfilled the government's responsibility by paying compensation to the affected people.
8. The belief of some officials that the magnitude of the problem of displacement is not significant in Kerala.
9. Lack of provision on the part of the Government to follow up on the rehabilitation of the displaced persons.
10. Lack of previous studies on the problem of displacement even in research centres.

These constraints were, to an extent, compensated by the data the research team collected from different collateral sources.

Since displacement is directly proportionate to the area acquired, we took into consideration the possible magnitude of displacement besides the area acquired. Out of the 1,105 notifications in above 5 ha., 153 projects were identified as having a significant magnitude of displacement. They were selected according to the following criteria:

(a) Nature and type of project according to the 14 categories identified in Kerala.

(b) Location: district, taluk and village with focus on district and its stage of development; 3 categories were identified: advanced, medium and backward districts.

(c) Period of implementation or age of the Projects.
(1) More than 25 years, (2) 11-25 years, (3) 1-10 years, (4) Ongoing (5) Future.

The Third Phase

The third phase was primary data collection. It is to be noted that displacement and rehabilitation are viewed as a process and not a one time event. In order to understand the process, during the third phase, out of the 153 projects, 15 were specifically selected for detailed study based on the following criteria:

1. Nature of the project (two each from mines, defence, power, irrigation, 3 from industries and one each from harbour, wildlife, tourism and airport).
2. Year of the project-projects started in all decades from 1951-1995 (see Table 1.4).
3. Type of people affected-based on caste, class and nature of affected people (DPs & PAPs).
4. Type of project-major, medium and small according to the size of the project. In the case of irrigation, the size of the project refers to major, medium and minor as per the standard classification. A major project is one with a Cultural Command Area (CCA) of more than 10,000 hectares. A medium project is one with a CCA of 2000-10000 ha. (Planning Commission, 1987). Similarly, for industries, the classification is small scale, medium scale and large scale.

5. Type of district-forward, medium and backward according to the stage of economic and social development.

This phase was preceded by a series of meetings with social activists in three regions of Kerala in order to ensure their involvement in the study in the areas of collection of data, sensitisation and mobilisation of the affected people, and influencing the process of policy formulation. A total of 45 social activists were included in these consultations. At each of these meetings, the research team presented the objectives and relevance of the study along with the background work already done. It was followed by a sharing by the participants of their knowledge of the projects and the experience of displaced persons. This led to a joint planning by the research team and the activists of the procedure to be followed in selecting and training the field investigators, identifying the respondents and conducting the interviews.

Later on, a thorough training was given to the joint team of field investigators. Primary data collection was done thoroughly, thanks to the co-operation we received from the affected people and NGO activists in each locality.

Based on these criteria we selected the projects shown in Table 1.4.

Selection of Respondents

For the selection of respondents for primary data collection, two methods were employed:

(1) *Focus Group Discussion* with affected people in each project area: Its purpose was to get a general idea of the socio-economic and other characteristics of the village or colony where DPs/PAPs were living. For some projects, this could not be done, because the DPs were scattered in different places, even districts. That was the case with Steel Industries Kerala Ltd. (SIKL), Karappuzha, Idukki and Muvatupuzha Valley Irrigation Project.

(2) *Individual Interviews:* The criteria for selecting respondents were caste, tribe, sex, age group, land ownership of the DPs/PAPs and DPs resettled by the project or by themselves.

Table 1.4

Projects Selected for Primary Data Collection

Sl. No.	Name of the Project	Code	Category	Year	District	Location	Number of respondents DPs/ PAPs		Total
1	Indian Rare Earths	IRE	Mine	1965	Kollam	Chavara	42	1	43
2	Kerala Minerals and Metals	KML	Mine & Industry	1972	Kollam	Chavara	17	0	17
3	Idukki Hydro Electric Project	IHP	Hydel	1967	Idukki	Kulamavu	70	0	70
4	Karappuzha Irrigation	KIP	Irrigation	1970	Wayanad	Ambala vayal	33	29	62
5	Industrial Development Area	IDA	Industry	1983	Palakkad	Kanjikode	45	0	45
6	Steel Industries Kerala Ltd.	SIKL	Industry	1978	Alappuzha	Cherthala	30	0	30
7	National Thermal Power Corpn.	NTP	Power	1994	Alappuzha	Kayamku lam	14	57	71
8	Vikram Sarabai Space Centre	VSC	Defence	1961	Thiruvananthapuram	Pallithura	60	0	60
9	Mavoor Gwalior Rayons	MGR	Industry	1958	Kozhikode	Mavoor	31	10	41
10	Vizhinjam Harbour	VZM	Harbour	1967	Thiruvananthapuram	Vizhinjam	40	0	40
11	Periyar Tiger Reserve	PTR	Wildlife	1969	Idukki	Periyar	30	20	50
12	Ezhimala Naval Academy	ENA	Defence	1983	Kannur	Ezhimala	33	6	39
13	Bakel Tourism Project	BTP	Tourism	1990	Kasargode	Bakel	13	17	30
14	Nedumbassery Airport	NIA	Airport	1994	Ernakulam	Nedumbassery	67	0	67
15	Muvattupuzha Valley Irrigation	MVP	Irrigation	1977	Kottayam	Muvattupuzha	30	0	30
						TOTAL	580	115	695

The details are presented in Chapter 5. To summarise it, the minimum age of the respondents was fixed as 18, at the time of displacement. All age groups were represented. An attempt was made to follow the pattern of equal representation of males and female respondents. We succeeded in getting 46 per cent women which is a higher proportion compared to the Goa and Orissa studies. In our case, males could interview women unlike in some states where custom does not permit this. Caste-wise, we obtained a fair representation of respondents from ST, SC, OBC and forward communities. The size or extent of landholding was also taken into consideration. A majority of projects did not have a Resettlement and Rehabilitation (R & R) scheme. Consequently, the affected people had to have recourse to self-resettlement. So, the proportion of the self-resettled is high in our sample.

Tools of Data Collection

Separate schedules were used for each of the three stages of data collection.

(1) Gazette Data

For the gazette, two types of schedules were used, one for below 5 hectares and another for five hectares and above. The latter had more details. In order to account for the large number of cancellations and corrections, we prepared a cancellation and correction list too.

(2) Secondary Data

An elaborate schedule was used for the collection of secondary data. Though a large and a short version were prepared, we used the larger version for all our data collection. The questions were predominantly closed ended with appropriate open-ended ones as well. The major areas studied were:

1. General information: project identification, location, support facilities, ownership, funding etc.

2. Nature and type of the project.
3. Construction details: number of units, year of starting and ending work, cost, capacity, installation and production.
4. Details of land acquisition: year of notification, taluk and number of villages affected, area and type of land acquired, process of take-over etc.
5. Details of persons displaced or deprived of livelihood or land.
6. Compensation and Resettlement: amount, type, nature, process, stages, present situation of those not resettled etc.
7. Other information.

(3) Primary Data

The group discussion schedule formed the first step in the process of primary data collection. The major areas covered were:

1. The administrative units like village, panchayat, taluk, district before and after displacement.
2. The socio-economic structure of the village: number of households in the village by caste/tribe, the educational status of the villagers and emerging social and political formations.
3. Economic profile including the pattern of land ownership and occupation of the people.
4. The process of displacement such as peoples' reaction to the announcement of land take-over and the co-operation of the project authorities, local leaders and people.
5. Compensation: the amount paid, its adequacy, the mode of payment and of spending it.
6. Resettlement and rehabilitation: the problems faced by the people in this process.
7. The impact of displacement and resettlement: mostly in the area of occupational change.
8. Its health and environmental impact, affecting water sources and air pollution etc.
9. Social and cultural changes after displacement with regard to the customs and practices affecting, particularly women, children and youth.

10. Overall evaluation of the displacement and rehabilitation process examining the advantages/disadvantages accruing to the affected people.

(4) Primary Data: Individual Interview Schedule

This schedule had other components over and above the pattern of the group discussion schedule. The questions were mostly closed ended with a sufficient number of open-ended type too. They inquired into the situation of the respondents before and after displacement.

1. Identification details: village, panchayat, taluk, etc.
2. Demographic data on the respondent and family.
3. Economic profile: land, occupation and crops grown.
4. The process of displacement: reaction to the announcement, co-operation of the leaders.
5. The process of land take-over and compensation: amount received, its adequacy, mode of payment and spending.
6. Resettlement and rehabilitation: by whom, manner, cost and time lag.
7. Impact of displacement and resettlement: change of job and amenities before and after displacement.
8. Health and environment: incidence of diseases, drinking water facilities etc.
9. Social and cultural impact: change in the behaviour patterns of women, youth etc.
10. Overall evaluation of rehabilitation officials: positive and negative points.
11. Additional information.

All the schedules were pre-coded and the investigators were thoroughly trained to make the entries according to instructions.

Data Processing

After carefully editing all the schedules used for data collection and checking their lacunae with the field investigators where needed, all the data were computerised with the help of technical experts and the latest software facilities. Tabulation was done correlating the variables we had identified earlier for the whole study, and in particular, on the basis of the five key variables of age, sex and caste/tribe of the respondents, the type of the project and the district of its location. Primary data were analysed from the demographic, social and economic points of view.

Socio-Economic Status (SES) Class Division

Based on these variables, the respondents were divided into five socio-economic status (SES) classes. We took for it some of the more important social and economic parameters and assigned points to them. They are land ownership, education, family income, job, cattle ownership and poultry ownership. The points assigned were:

1. *Land ownership*: 1 point for every 1 acre of land subject to a maximum of 20 points.
2. *Education*: 1 point for each grade, subject to a maximum of 10 points.
   Illiterate = 0, Literate = 1, 4th = 2, 7th = 3, 10th = 4, PDC = 5, DC = 6, P.G. = 7,
   Semi-Professional degree = 8, Professional degree = 10.
3. *Family income*: 2 points for those below the poverty line and a maximum of 10 points to those having 4 times that of poverty line (annual family income is calculated including agricultural income). The points are: Below Rs.11,000 = 2; 11,001-22,000 =4; 22,001-33,000=6; 33,001-44,000=8; More than 44,000=10.
4. *Job*: points for each category as follows upto a maximum of 20. Farm labour/unskilled = 2, Other labour = 4, Semi-skilled = 6, Animal husbandry = 8, Petty-business/Agriculture = 10, Artisan = 12, Skilled = 14, Government employee = 16, Doctors/Engineers/Lawyers/P.G. Teachers = 20.
5. *Cattle ownership*: 1 point per head, but if it is goats/pigs then 0.5 points per head, maximum of 5.
6. *Poultry ownership*: 1 point for every 30 numbers -maximum 5.
   Lower Lower Class (LLC) -Below 15 points

Lower Class (LC) -15 - 24
Middle Class (MC) - 25 - 34
Upper Middle Class (UMC) - 35 - 44
Upper Class (UC) - 45 +

Report Writing

Report Writing was a joint effort of the core team. While the report incorporates all the findings of the Kerala study, it also draws much inspiration and material from other studies done earlier. With a view to consolidating the major findings of the regional studies done in various States of India into a national report, we have followed a common format for the design of this study for the procedure followed, the schedules and the final report. While following a common format, when necessary we have adapted it to the local situation. The following is the structure of the report:

PART I

Chapter 1 : Displacement in India: Issues and Methodology

Chapter 2 : An Overview of Kerala

Chapter 3 : The Extent of Land Acquired

Chapter 4 : Displacement, Deprival, Resettlement and Compensation

PART II

Chapter 5 : Profile of Projects and the Respondents

Chapter 6 : The Process of Land Take-over

Chapter 7 : Compensation

Chapter 8 : Resettlement and Rehabilitation

PART III

Chapter 9 : Towards a Humane Policy of Land Acquisition, Displacement and Rehabilitation

Limitations of the Study

As mentioned in the section on the second phase of the study, the major constraint we experienced in this project was non-availability of records and files regarding the actual implementation of the projects, especially in the 1950s, 60s and 70s. It limited our efforts to create a comprehensive database, especially concerning the number and nature of persons displaced, the total area of land acquired and the details of their resettlement and rehabilitation. We also experienced a lack of co-operation from some government officials, both in the Ministries concerned and Departments as well as in the Collectorates. We could make up for these deficiencies through collateral sources and extrapolation. The near total absence of studies in these areas made our search more difficult. In the area of the total land acquired, we had to depend mostly on gazette data. In other cases, we got much information from knowledgeable persons.

McDowell (1996) in his volume on 'Understanding Impoverishment' remarks that it is often seen that whole large scale displacement gets attention, small scale displacement which is equally devastating in its effects seldom get noticed. This is much more true of Kerala than of any other state. It creates a problem for the researcher. The small numbers that get displaced are not often tracked. It is difficult to get accurate data on them. Nevertheless, we have tried to put together all the information available at the time of the study from the sources we explored. Therefore, we consider this study a pioneering effort in an area which has been little explored by researchers in Kerala.

Conclusion

Since the ultimate objective of this study is advocacy, our focus is mainly on professionals, the media, legal activists and the people affected by the projects. Hence, the report has taken a professional and popular form. Advocacy becomes important, because of a lack of national consciousness concerning those who are paying the price of development. A sign of lack of consciousness is the fact that 50 years after independence the country does not have a rehabilitation policy, leave alone a law. The State has to be pressurised to evolve new policies. This is true particularly in the context of liberalisation, because it is assumed that more land than in the past is needed, and consequently, much more displacement should be expected.

We consider this study important, because its primary objective is mobilising public opinion, promoting advocacy and lobbying. The methodology is geared to this objective. Its secondary objective is people's mobilisation. This study also raises questions on creative research and the role of ideology.

2

An Overview of Kerala

Tucked away in the southwest corner of India, Kerala is a strip of land between the Arabian Sea and the Western Ghats. It is situated between 8°-18 and 12°-48 north and longitudes between 74°-52 and 72°-22 east. The oldest legend on Kerala is that it is the land reclaimed by Parasuram, an incarnation of Vishnu, by throwing his axe with magical powers into the Arabian Sea. The legend continues to say that Parasuram gifted this land to his Brahmin devotees.

This charming land is like a green shawl spread out in the gleaming sunshine with its coconut groves which is the etymological source of the very name Kerala (Keram = coconut palms), the land of coconut palms. The lush green valleys, the idyllic lakes and lagoons, meandering waterways, the gentle-blowing rivers, vast expanse of paddy fields undulating in the gentle caress of the ever-flowing midland breeze, and the long coastal line -- all make Kerala a paradise to visitors and natives who enjoy the tranquilising lullabies of nature.

History tells us that people from the far off lands like the Phoenicians, Romans, Arabs and Chinese had found their way to Kerala coast even before Vasco da Gama set his foot in Calicut in 1498. Being a centre of spices and a transshipment point, the Dutch, the French and the British who followed the Portuguese for trade established their colonies on the Kerala coast.

The Land

The state of Kerala was formed on 1 November 1956 under the reorganisation of states of India on linguistic lines, bringing together the princely states of Travancore-Cochin and the Malabar region of the erstwhile Madras Presidency. As a result, Kerala became then the smallest state in India with a geographical area of 38,855 square kilometers equivalent to a mere 1.18 per cent of the total landmass of India.

Kerala can be divided broadly into three physiographical zones, namely (1) High land (2) Mid-land, and (3) the Coastal Region. Geographically and strategically, these three zones are important. The 590 kilometer long coastal line, the crops growing in the mid land; the forest and plantation areas of the hill terrain combined with a generally moderate temperature between 22° and 34° Celsius; and the socio-cultural backdrop make Kerala very endearing. The state is divided into 14 revenue districts, 61 taluks, 992 panchayats, 1,452 villages, 53 municipalities and five corporations (Government of Kerala, 2001).

Land Use Pattern

Kerala being a thickly populated state, one of the scarcest resources in the state is land. In the context of the displacement due to land acquisition, the existing land use pattern assumes greater importance. As of 1998, around 58 per cent of the land was being utilised for agricultural purposes. One significant legislation that facilitated increase in agricultural land in the erstwhile Travancore region of Kerala was the *Kuthakapattom Act of 1940*, giving exclusive right to the tenant for cultivation of food crops in forest land. This in practice marked the beginning of the encroachment of the forest land and the consequent depletion of forest wealth. However, over the last two decades, there has been a substantial change in the cropping pattern from food crops to cash crops. The present land use pattern has evolved due to the influence and interaction of a host of factors, historical, economic, technological, social and political (Nair, 1998: 11).

The Kerala Land Reforms Act 1970 was intended to end the exploitation of the peasantry and to increase productivity of the land. Whereas the Act enabled landless households to become owners of land, the fragmentation of land into smaller units affected its productivity adversely. According to Sen (1975: 10-11), a viable unit of farm should have been 10 acres, whereas Minhas (1996: 76-77) thinks 20 acres is the ideal size. By the implementation of this Act, eight lakh acres of land were distributed to 30 lakh tenants at an average extent of 27 cents each. The findings of the Land Reform Survey 1966-67 reported that out of the 19 lakh acres of land distributed to the tenants, more than one third was in the category of wet land (Nair, 1998: IE, 8 Dec. p.11). The fragmentation of agricultural land, the escalation of the cost of seeds, fertilisers, pesticides and labour brought down the area of land under cultivation in Kerala. Absentee landlords encouraged a shift from food crops to cash crops and other farmers followed suit.

Table 2.1

Land Use Pattern (1995-96)

	Classification of Land	*Area (ha.)*	*Per cent*
1.	Forest	1081509	27.83
2.	Land put to non agricultural uses	313131	8.06
3.	Barren and uncultivated land	43154	1.11
4.	Permanent pastures and grazing land	1170	0.03
5.	Land under miscellaneous tree crops not included in net area sown	26852	0.69
6.	Cultivated waste land	74382	1.91
7.	Fallow other than current fallow	29143	0.75
8.	Current fallow	51314	1.32
9.	Net area sown	2264842	58.29
	Total Geographical Area	38,85,497	100.00

Source: State Planning Board, 1998:27

The decline in the workforce in the primary sector is due to the shift in the cropping pattern in the state from paddy to coconut and rubber which demands more male workers than female labour (Gulati, et al., 1994).

The People

According to the 1991 census, Kerala had a population of 2,90,98,518 which is 3.41 per cent of the total population of India. Scheduled Castes and Schedules Tribes numbered 28.87 lakhs (9.92%) and 3.21 lakhs (1.10%), respectively. In the last decade (1981-91), the proportion of SCs had gone down slightly, while that of STs increased. Out of the 2.91 crores of Kerala's population, 26.39 per cent live in its 53 municipal towns and five corporations, which together cover a mere 9.13 per cent of the geographical area of the state. Kerala recorded a population growth of 14.32 per cent during the decade 1981--1991 which is the lowest in India. The average size of a household is 5.3 as against the Indian average of 5.6. The density of population is 749 per sq km as against the national average of 267, placing the state as the second most densely populated in India. Among the 14 districts, the most thickly populated is Alappuzha with 1,415 persons per square kilometer, followed by Thiruvananthapuram (1,344), Ernakulam (1,170) and Kozhikode (1,118). The most thinly populated district is Idukki (215) followed by Wayanad (315). These two districts are part of the highland.

The sex ratio is in favour of women, i.e. 1036 women per 1000 men. Thrissur has the highest sex ratio (1085) followed by Pathanamthitta (1062), Palakkad (1061) and Malapuram (1053). However, the scenario of Wayanad (966) and Idukki (975) is far from the realities of the State. Apart from the lowest density of population, these districts have the highest concentration of Scheduled Tribes. Wayanad district has nearly 36 per cent of its population belonging to ST, whereas Idukki's Tribal population is 16 per cent. In the development process of the State, the water resource projects have displaced a large section of the Tribal population in these two districts.

In the field of literacy, Kerala has made great strides and has become one of the foremost among the Indian states with a literacy rate of 89.81 per cent, while the all India average is 52.21 per cent. The male literacy rate is 93.62 per cent and that of female is 86.17 per cent (64.13% and 39.29% are the corresponding figures for India). Kerala's female literacy rate is far ahead of any other Indian states. This is a very significant parameter of social development.

Table 2.2

District-wise Distribution of Population and Density

District	*Population*			*Density*	*% of SCs*	*% of STs*
	Male	*Female*	*Total*			
Thiruvananthapuram	1447594	1499056	2946650	1344	11.66	0.55
Kollam	1182810	1224756	2407866	967	12.70	0.16
Pathanamthitta	576176	612156	1188332	450	13.3	0.58
Alappuzha	975885	1025332	2001217	1415	9.51	0.14
Kottayam	912860	915411	1828271	830	7.43	0.98
Idukki	545872	532194	1078066	215	14.56	4.66
Ernakulam	1408649	1408587	2817236	1170	8.58	0.18
Thrissur	1312683	1424628	2737311	903	12.22	0.15
Palakkad	1155822	1226413	2382235	532	15.89	1.49
Malapuram	1508280	1588050	3096330	872	8.26	0.34
Kozhikode	1292765	1327176	2619941	1118	7.05	0.21
Wayanad	341958	330170	672128	315	4.14	17.11
Kannur	1098838	1152889	2251727	759	4.05	0.87
Kasargod	528803	542705	1071508	538	7.65	2.73
State	1,42,88,995	1,48,09,523	2,90,98,518	749	9.92	1.10

Source: Registrar General and Census Commissioner, 1991.

There has been a gradual decline in school enrolment. The State Planning Board's estimates indicate that by 2001, the school age group population will be 52.92 lakhs (as compared to 58.69 lakhs in 1993 and 59.07 lakhs in 1992). This points to the declining birth rate in Kerala and people's adherence to the small family norm.

The Aged

The population aged 60 years and above has been increasing rapidly in our country from 56 million in 1991 to 70 million in 1998 and is expected to be 177 million by 2025 (Sandhu, 1999: 15). According to the 1991 census, the aged constitute 8.77 per cent of Kerala's population which is the highest among all the States and Union Territories in India. As the life expectancy of females is high in Kerala, the proportion of women is higher among the senior citizens (9.23% females and 8.29% males).

Over the last four decades, successive governments in Kerala introduced a number of social security schemes. The three major pension schemes being implemented in Kerala are (1) the Kerala Agricultural Workers pension scheme (2) Kerala Destitute pension scheme and (3) special pension scheme for the Handicapped. On the whole, the major pension schemes benefited about 6 lakh persons which is about 25 per cent of the 60 plus population. Institutional care is also provided by Government and voluntary agencies to the aged, infirm, destitutes and others. At present, these institutions are providing care for 4,721 aged and infirm (State Planning Board, 1997: 121).

Communities in Kerala

Kerala being a state where caste and community play a major role in the socio-cultural and political life of the people, some basic understanding of Kerala's communities along the caste-religion lines may be useful. However, since 1931 caste enumeration has been removed from the census, all we have is limited to estimates linking them with religion. The major religions in Kerala are Hinduism, Islam and Christianity. According to the 1991 Census, 58 per cent are Hindus, 23 per cent Muslims and 19 per cent Christians. Hindus belong to the major castes such as Ezhavas, Nairs, Thiyyas, Nadars, Brahmins, and most of the Scheduled Castes and a number of Scheduled Tribes. The estimates of Thomas (1997) show that Ezhavas form the largest group among the Hindus (30%), while Nairs come second (15%), SC/STs form 8 per cent and Brahmins 5 per cent. Christians are broadly grouped into Catholics and Non-Catholics. Catholics include Latin Catholics who belong to the OBC category, Syro-Malankara and Syro-Malabar Catholics who belong to the forward category. The Non-Catholics comprise Marthoma, CSI, Orthodox, and Jacobites. Christians of Syrian affiliation are considered to be forward communities. These castes and communities are distributed all over Kerala. Nevertheless, one does find a concentration of Christians in the central districts of Alappuzha, Kottayam, Ernakulam, and Thrissur, and that of Muslims in the northern districts of Malapuram, Kozhikode, Kasaragod, Kannur and Wayanad. The proportion of Hindus is high in the districts of Kasaragod, Kannur, Kozhikode, Wayanad, Palakkad, Thrissur, Alappuzha, Kollam, and Thiruvananthapuram.

The Scheduled Castes

In the caste-ridden India, the untouchables of the pre-independence era were grouped into Scheduled Castes in 1935. After independence, this schedule was revised twice in 1950 and 1976. According to the list of Scheduled Castes (SCs) published in 1976, Kerala had 68 communities under this category. The population of SCs in Kerala grew from 8.5 per cent of the total population in 1961 to 10.02 per cent in 1981 (25.49 lakhs). In the following decade, it has come down slightly to 10 per cent (Registrar General & Census Commissioner, 1991). Their urban proportion too was as low as 12 per cent, as against 19 per cent of the general population.

The Scheduled Caste population is concentrated considerably in the districts of Palakkad followed by Thiruvananthapuram, Thrissur and Kollam. It is quite smaller in Wayanad and a nominal representation of SCs in Kasargod. In both these districts, their gender ratio is the lowest, 946 and 990 respectively. Gender-wise, Idukki too is on the lower side (Ibid).

Prior to the creation of Kerala in 1956, the welfare of the SCs was taken care of by the rulers in the Travancore-Cochin and Malabar regions. With the creation of the State of Kerala, a directorate for the welfare of the SCs was formed to promote their educational and economic development. Under a special scheme, free education is provided upto any level. An annual grant to the tune of Rs. 2.50 crores is set apart for the benefit of SC students in the form of lump sum grant, stipend and fees.

Table 2.3

District-wise SC Population in Kerala

District	*Males*	*Females*	*Total*	*% to total SC Population*
Thiruvananthapuram	167251	176188	343439	11.9
Kollam	150894	154833	305727	10.59
Pathanamthitta	77821	80212	158033	5.48
Alappuzha	93926	96429	190355	6.59
Kottayam	67675	38201	135876	4.71
Idukki	78607	78315	156922	5.44
Ernakulam	120194	121525	241719	8.37
Thrissur	162962	171562	334524	11.59
Palakkad	184850	193698	378548	13.11
Malapuram	126097	129634	255731	8.86
Kozhikode	91547	93073	184620	6.40
Wayanad	14192	13643	27835	0.96
Kannur	45418	45805	91223	3.16
Kasargod	41180	40790	81970	2.84
State	14,22,614	14,63,908	28,86,522	100

Source: Registrar General and Census Commissioner, 1991.

Other socio-economic schemes made available to the SCs are training in technical skills, coaching for entrance tests, housing schemes for the homeless, site and house to the landless, and rehabilitation programmes for those staying in unauthorised locations.

Although the programmes for the SCs are galore on paper, many of the schemes are not properly implemented. As a result, large sections of SCs are deprived of these benefits. Consequently, the SCs continue to be the weakest section along with the STs in the State. More than 58 per cent of the SCs are agricultural labourers, whereas 25 per cent are cultivators, 4 per cent industrial workers and 36 per cent dependent on other sectors. SC women workers form more than one-third of the women agricultural labour force in the state.

Tribal Communities

There are 35 scheduled Tribal communities in Kerala comprising 3.21 lakhs of people. Of these, 22.4 per cent live in forests. The progress achieved by Tribals in Kerala is not encouraging even though the state is well known for its achievements in human development. Sex ratio among the Scheduled Tribes is 996 as against the corresponding figure of 1036 in the general population.

Table 2.4

District-wise Population of STs in Kerala

District	*Males*	*Females*	*Total*	*% to total ST Population*
Thiruvananthapuram	7860	8321	16181	5.04
Kollam	1943	1941	3884	1.21
Pathanamthitta	3459	3463	6922	2.16
Alappuzha	1407	1394	2801	0.87
Kottayam	8902	9094	17996	5.61
Idukki	25512	24757	50269	15.66
Ernakulam	2551	2390	4941	1.54
Thrissur	1990	2061	4051	1.26
Palakkad	17927	17538	35465	11.05
Malapuram	5213	5342	10555	3.29
Kozhikode	2654	2753	5407	1.69
Wayanad	57386	57583	114969	35.82
Kannur	9167	9076	18243	5.68
Kasargod	14841	14442	29283	9.12
State	1,60,812	1,60,155	3,20,967	100.00

Source: Registrar General and Census Commissioner, 1991.

Experts in the fields of Tribal studies point out many reasons for the lower sex ratio among the Tribals in Kerala. One reason is the influence of the neighbouring state of Tamil Nadu, where the gender bias is prevalent. Absence of prenatal and postnatal care, malnutrition of mother and child, the practice of purity-pollution, low literacy level, non-accessibility to public distribution system and imitation of upper castes seem to be other reasons.

In Kerala, the Tribal literacy rate is only 57.22 per cent as against the general literacy rate of 90 per cent. According to a family survey conducted by the Rural Development Department in 1992, 33,664 scheduled tribe families (48.48%) have been living below the poverty line (Government of Kerala, 1998:4). Even after spending huge amounts of money and manpower by the government, most of the problems like illiteracy, poverty, land alienation, indebtedness, unemployment, alcoholism, sexual exploitation, malnutrition, diseases and so on, still persist among the Tribals of Kerala. After poverty and hunger, alcohol menace remains the biggest scourge in the lives of the Tribals (Thekkekara, 1993: 26).

An official level inquiry conducted by the state Government on instructions from the Supreme Court has confirmed the existence of bonded labour in Palakkad, Wayanad and Pathanamthitta districts (Prabhakaran, 1996). In addition to the socio economic problems, the most serious danger seems to be the threat to their cultural identity. Many of the Tribal communities are apparently demoralised and are looking towards the government for continued assistance and support.

Alienation of land is a crucial problem faced by the Tribals in Kerala. "Tribal land is increasingly usurped by the non-Tribal settlers from other parts of Kerala who have political clout and as a result, the Tribals are reduced to the level of sub-humans" (Kunhaman, 1990: 133). As per the details collected by the Revenue Department, 80,590 ha. of Tribal land have been alienated up to 31.10.96. Out of this, 440 ha. have been restored (Government of Kerala, 1998: 4). In 1975, the State Government passed an Act restricting the transfer of land by members of the Scheduled Tribes and for the restoration of land alienated from them. However, the government could not implement this Act till date due to pressure from the non-Tribal settlers who are the present owners of much of the Tribal land. To offset this, the Kerala Assembly unanimously passed the 'Kerala Restriction on Transfer by and

Restoration of Lands to Scheduled Tribes Bill, 1999' on February 23, 1999. According to this Act, the Tribals who had lost their land will be entitled to restoration of equal extent of land by way of allotment from the Government. This provision is applicable, subject to certain conditions, to those Tribals who had effected the transfer of land owned by them to persons other than STs between January 1, 1960 and January 24, 1986. The bill got the assent of the Governor on March 11, 1999. On 10th July 1999, the Chief Minister of Kerala inaugurated the distribution of land to the landless Tribals as per the provisions of the latest Act. However, on completion of the hearing on the writ petition filed by Dr. Nallathampy Thera, People's Union for Civil Liberties and Niyamavedi Kochi, Kerala High Court struck down three important sections (sections 5, sub-section 1 and sections 6 and 222) defeating the very purpose of the Act, on 24 August 2000. The Sate Government is now pondering on appealing to the Supreme Court.

The forest policy followed by the Union Government in the post-independence period had a devastating effect on the Tribal culture and economy. The Government failed in understanding the culture of the Tribals and their relationship with forest while formulating the forest policy. After the implementation of the laws pertaining to forest, the Tribals realised that the forest was no more theirs and that external forces had secured total control over their homeland. "The Government started the gradual extension of its authority in the national interest and thus the process of reserving and protecting the forest areas by the government resulted in reducing the customary Tribal control over them to mere concessions" (Mathur, 1975: 193).

The close relationship of the Tribals to land and forest must be respected and they must be allowed to develop on the lines of their own skills and tradition. The present development strategy, which creates more dependencies on welfare bureaucracy and middlemen, must be suitably remedied so as to help the already marginalised to stand on their own feet. According to AR Desai (1981: 518), "the problems of the masses including the intensely oppressed Tribal population arise from the very character of the social order that is existing and is furthered in our country. Their solutions can be found only when a non-exploitative social order is established".

Human Development Indicators

In a country like India where millions of people live in conditions of appalling deprivation, where hunger, ill-health, homelessness, and illiteracy take a heavy toll, Kerala stands out as a state apart from all others, because of its accomplishments in the social, political and cultural fields in spite of the low levels of income. The quality of life indices of Kerala such as life expectancy, educational attainment, reduction of infant and maternal mortality etc., are at par with those of several developed countries. Development literature is replete with the social achievements of Kerala (United Nations, 1997; Sen, 1994; Dreze and Sen, 1995).

Health

The significant achievements of Kerala in the health front have been made possible with a combination of social factors like wider network of health and educational infrastructure and access to services particularly women's education, housing, general health consciousness, and availability of safe drinking water and clean health habits of the people. Kerala has succeeded in reducing Infant Mortality Rate to 13, whereas the all India average is 73. The prenatal mortality rate and neonatal mortality rate are also considerably lower in Kerala (Soman, 1998: 102)

Table 2.5

Important Health Indicators

Indicators	*Kerala*	*India*	*China*	*Russia*	*America*
Infant Mortality Rate	13	73	34	18	8
Crude Death Rate	6	9.2	8.5	NA	<5
Life Expectancy	73	59	69	65	77
Maternal Mortality Rate	<100	400	115	50	<25

Source: Soman, 1998:102

The development of an extensive health care infrastructure in both Government and private sectors in Kerala has facilitated greater access to the general population to health care services. The state has five general hospitals, 11 district hospitals, 42 taluk hospitals, 69 intermediary hospitals, eight mother and child hospitals, five medical college hospitals, three leprosy hospitals, three TB hospitals and three mental hospitals. Besides, there are 108 Ayurveda hospitals and 31 Homeopathy hospitals promoted by the state government (State Planning Board, 1999).

Private medical institutions play an important role in providing medical services in Kerala. According to a survey conducted in 1995 by the Department of Economics and Statistics, there were 4,288 private allopathic medical institutions with 67,517 beds in the State (Ibid.).

The family welfare programmes in Kerala are being implemented through a network of 956 primary health centres (PHC) and 5094 sub centres. Every PHC serves on an average 43 square kilometers covering a population of 30,346. However, at the national level, a PHC, on an average, serves an area of 155 sq. k.m. and a population of 38,618 (State Planing Board, 1997: 102). Kerala's achievements in the family welfare front have been impressive and are clearly proved by various demographic indices. The most direct evidence of the effectiveness of the programme is provided by the percentage of couples effectively protected by various methods of family planning.

Another sign of success is the low fertility rates in Kerala. This is associated with a higher age at marriage among the women in Kerala. The all-India average, which was 18.3 years in 1981, was notably lower than the Kerala average, 21.8 years. The present couple protection rate in Kerala is 64.3 as against the national average of 45.8. The total fertility rate in the state showed a declining trend from 4.1 in 1971 to 2.1 in 1990.

Improved child health and higher levels of education, particularly female education, are among the most important reasons for Kerala's low and declining birth rate and the general acceptance of a small family norm (Ramachandran, 1998: 227-28).

Kerala has achieved another landmark by attaining almost cent per cent institutional deliveries. Out of an estimated 6 lakh deliveries per year in Kerala, 97 per cent are institutional as against the all India average of about 60 per cent. In the field of immunisation too, the coverage in Kerala has been near total.

Education

As in the case of Health, Kerala has made rapid strides in the educational field. The male literacy rate is 93.62 per cent and that of female is 86.17 per cent (64.13% and 39.29% are the corresponding figures for India). It can be seen that Kerala's female literacy rate is far ahead of any other Indian state, as this is a very significant parameter of social development. Estimates made in 1995 showed that as much as 40 per cent of total budgetary expenditure of the State was set apart for social services, of which about 25 per cent was earmarked for education. Both in terms of female literacy and general literacy levels, Kerala has been far ahead of most other states in India.

The contribution made by Christian missionaries and the native intellectuals in the past centuries laid the foundation for modern education in Kerala. The indigenous school system was a major factor that laid the foundations of the educational achievement. Another set of factors that contributed to the phenomenal educational growth is the structural changes in the economy in the 19th and 20th century. Changes in the land tenure, along with the changes in religious and political practices, administrative and social reforms, growth and diversification of infrastructural facilities, the commercialisation of the economy brought about and the resultant demand for literacy. Changes in the social structure, government initiatives, the grants-in-aid schemes, stipulation of qualification for government jobs, emergence of strong and powerful pressure groups among the Nairs, Ezhavas and the Syrian Christian, various social reform movements and the ready acceptance of political ideologies further strengthened educational achievement of the State (Nair, 1978; Mathew, 1987; Tharakan, 1984).

The campaign-oriented movement for basic literacy during the pre-independence period gathered momentum in Kerala with the *Granthasala (library) Movement* led by P.N. Panicker. Along with the promotion of adult education programmes, the *Granthasala Movement* provided the much needed spurt for post-literacy and continuing education. The role of Non-governmental organisations, particularly the Kerala Sasthra Sahitya Parishad (KSSP) has been quite significant. The initiatives of the Left Democratic Front and the wholehearted co-operation of non-governmental agencies made it possible for Kerala to be declared as a 'totally literate' state in 1991.

But, all is not well with the educational scenario. The school system is in a crisis. The number of uneconomic schools is increasing and the number of private unaided English medium schools is multiplying rapidly. Out of the 5.70 lakhs students presented for the SSLC examination in 1999, only 50 per cent passed, even with moderation. Out of the 2.75 lakh students who pass the SSLC examination, nearly 1.50 lakhs get enrolled in the 174 arts and science higher secondary schools and 186 vocational higher secondary schools. After a rather prolonged political and academic warfare, the state Government de-linked pre-degree from regular colleges and transferred it to Higher Secondary schools. The process was, however, riddled with academic and administrative hassles.

The technical education infrastructure is woefully inadequate to cater to the needs of the State. In 1997, Kerala had only eight engineering colleges, 32 polytechnics, 47 technical high schools, five medical colleges, two dental colleges and three nursing colleges. As a result, large number of students went out of the state in search of professional courses paying huge amounts as donation. The universities in the state are: Kerala University, Mahatma Gandhi University, Cochin University of Science and Technology, Calicut University, and Kannur University. The Kerala Agricultural University specialises in Agriculture and Veterinary Sciences, whereas Sree Sankaracharya Sanskrit University specialises in Sanskrit, Indology, Indian Philosophy and Indian languages.

Impressive as the infrastructural facilities and the literacy levels may sound, the reality indeed is quite different. Both at the school and the university level, a vast majority of the students secure only an education of poor quality. A study on the elementary schools in Thiruvananthapuram revealed that 34 per cent of the pupils could not write their names in their mother tongue correctly. Another study by KSSP showed that a similar percentage of 4-7 standard students were illiterate in Thiruvananthapuram and Pathanamthitta districts (Mary John, 1993).

The percentage of pass in the SSLC examination raises the much-debated question of quality, whether it is in the minimum levels of learning (MLL) or in the basic necessities like drinking water and toilets, which are of prime importance. The educational authorities do not seem to be sufficiently creative at curriculum development and methodological improvement. The much-heralded District Primary Education Programme (DPEP), financed by the World Bank, has become a point of serious dissension between its proponents who think of it as the panacea for improving quality and opponents proclaiming it as the death-knell of even the little education that was being given. Politicisation and governmental intrusion have played havoc with the system. An eminent educator-cum-administrator went to the point of saying, 'Universities in Kerala are on the road to disaster' (Jayachandran, 1995). Lack of a clear vision, definite policy and political will, account for most of the ills in the educational sector.

Status of Women in Kerala

The place and role of women in Kerala's development achievements are worth emphasising. The women in Kerala have made more outstanding contributions in the fields of education and healthcare than any other states of India. Kerala's achievements in the field of health would have been impossible without female literacy and an enlightened and positive social attitude towards girl children and women. The female life expectancy at birth is 74 years in Kerala. This is 15 years higher than the Indian average and 6 years above the corresponding figure for men in Kerala. In taking to education and professional work in

Kerala, women have not been far behind men (Gulati, 1994: 49). The role of women in development as manifested in Kerala's experiences is the best example of the role women can play in advancing social and economic development of a society (Ramachandran, 1998: 317). According to Saradamony (1999: 504), the customary constraints against female education have practically disappeared in Kerala. However, the leadership, be it in the social reform movement or in the trade union in organised industrial sector has remained predominantly with the males. But, according to Ramachandran (1998: 317), women in Kerala have been important participants in the trade union movement, in the peasant and agricultural labour movements and the movements for land reforms and food.

On the other hand, the achievements of women are superficial with regard to work participation. The rates of unemployment being very high, the gender differentials in the labour market persist across caste, income and educational categories. A substantial number of women is engaged in traditional occupations like coir, cashew processing, and bamboo work. Leela Gulati (1994: 49) found that women's participation in politics in Kerala is very low and not different from that in the rest of the country. Their participation is limited to casting votes in the elections. In the 11th State Assembly of Kerala constituted in 2001 with 140 seats, women members form only 5.7 per cent, whereas it was 5.8 per cent in 1957. Out of the 20 elected representatives from the state to the Lok Sabha, there was only one woman, in the 13th Parliament, which means a meager five per cent representation. But, there is no dearth of organisations of women functioning in Kerala. In 1987, Kerala was reported to have 50,000 mahila samajams.

Saradamony (1999: 505) is of the opinion that women are losing their individuality and freedom by accepting to be protected. She argues that Kerala has the essential ingredients of what we have always believed necessary for women's emancipation viz. literacy and education, freedom from inhibitions against women's education and employment, right to own property and to have savings in one's own name. But, Kerala's women are far from being emancipated. The main reason she points out for this situation is the way in which Kerala society is changing primarily as a result of official development policies in which the regional identity, resources, needs and culture never got ingrained.

Unemployment

Unemployment is the most crucial social problem in Kerala. Leela Gulati (1994: 32) observed that unemployment, especially of the educated in Kerala, has been high and increasing among both men and women. Ninety one per cent of the unemployed are literate and two thirds are beyond primary school level. Nearly 8 per cent of the unemployed have a qualification of SSLC or above, while 12 per cent are Pre-Degree holders, 6.8 per cent are graduates and 1.2 per cent are post graduates (State Planning Board, 1997: 13). Another significant feature of Kerala's unemployment is that it is the highest in the 15-29 age group. Forty five per cent of women in this age group in the rural areas and 58 per cent in the urban areas are unemployed. The number of unemployed job seekers in the live registers of employment exchanges has increased from 32.87 lakhs in 1996 to 35.19 lakhs in 1997, registering an increase of 7.1 per cent. Among them, women outnumber men with 19.2 lakhs (54.5%) as against 16 lakhs (45.5%) men (Ibid.)

The high rate of educated unemployment has led to large-scale migration both within and outside the country. Much of the out migration has been to the Gulf countries. As per the survey conducted by the state department of economics and statistics in 1992-93, the estimate of migration from Kerala has been as follows.

Table 2.6

Migration from Kerala

Country	*Number*	*Percentage*
Gulf Countries	641387	53.79
Other Foreign Countries	27480	2.30
Other States and UTs	523456	43.91
Total	1192323	100.00

Source: State Planning Board, 1997:14

The inflow of large amount of Gulf remittances and its spending has resulted in unprecedented economic changes since the mid 1970s in Kerala. The Gulf migration has helped the migrant households attain higher levels of income, consumption, and acquisition of assets, and in turn helped to reduce to some extent poverty and unemployment in Kerala. Introduction of vocational education and training for skills is another positive change attributed to migration. But, the remittances have pushed up the prices of land and construction materials, consumer goods and charges on services in the fields of health, education, transport and labour charges. This price hike has adversely affected the non-migrant people belonging to poor, middle class and fixed income groups. Even though migration improved employment opportunities, it has led to the shortage of construction workers in Kerala, encouraging their migration from the neighbouring states to Kerala, a phenomenon of "migration due to migration". But, the re-absorption of returnee migrants in the labour market poses a serious problem.

An analysis of the utilisation of remittances of Gulf migrants for 1982-86 revealed that 21 per cent of the total amount was spent for purchasing or improving land, 36 per cent for constructing houses, purchasing or improving buildings, which are non-productive investments. It was found that expenditure on gold ornaments, repayment of loans and education accounted for 21 per cent. "It is significant to note that only a small portion of Gulf remittance was spent for starting business" (Prakash, 1998: 3212) and other productive investments. Only eight per cent was reported to be invested in banks and other financial institutions.

Consumerism

Kerala is widely known for its consumerism. Gulf remittance may be one of its causes. The rate of consumption in Kerala is above the national level even though its annual economic growth rate is below that of the national average (The 1999 Economic Survey claims that the State average has gone above the national). The phenomenon of consumerism emerged during the latter part of the 1970s. Now, it has become part of the life of an average Keralite irrespective of the class to which he belongs. Consumption has turned out to be the accepted label of recognition and reputation. When consumption became the sole criterion of social prestige and standing, Keralites opted for consumption either to enhance or retain social prestige (Sooryamoorthy, 1997: 73).

Despite the stagnation in per-capita domestic income, per-capita consumption expenditure registered a steady increase, 1.16 per cent from 1960-61 to 1971-72 and 1.81 per cent from 1972-73 to 1989-90 (Krishnan, 1994). Krishnan estimated that if the same rate of growth was maintained after 1990, real per-capita consumption in Kerala in 1994 would have been approximately double the per-capita consumption level of 1960-61 (cited in Ramachandran, 1998: 329).

Social Reform Movements

In response to the Christian missionary work and western education, a series of social reform movements had started at the beginning of the 19th century. They took the form of many caste-based organisations in Kerala. In 1903, Sree Nayana Guru organised a movement of Ezhavas with the objective of emancipating this marginalised community. The movement got established as Sree Narayana Dharma Paripalana Sangham (SNDP). It helped in changing the status of Ezhavas *from untouchables* to OBCs. Imbibing the spirit of SNDP, Ayyankali organised the Pulayas (SCs) under Sadhu Jana Paripalana Yogam in 1907 and it helped in the upward social mobility of Pulayas. Now, they have Pulaya Maha Sabha to fight for their rights. Nadar caste had Nadar Mahajan Sangam. Nair Service Society (NSS) was established in 1914, under the leadership of Mannathu Padmanabhan. They became a powerful community exerting considerable influence in the social and economic spheres in Kerala (Thomas, 1997: 31-34).

The experiences from the Mappila Riot (Mappila Lahala) and Khilafat Movement showed the need for an organised movement for Muslims. In 1926, Young Members Muslim Association was formed. Then, in 1930, Muslim Majlis was established to unite all Muslim organisations under one umbrella. In 1964, P.K. Abdul Gafoor formed the Muslim Educational Society (MES) which plays a crucial role in the socio-cultural development of the community.

Occupation

Kerala is predominantly an agricultural state with a total cropped area of 58.29 per cent of its land. The vast majority of the population (74%) residing in rural areas substantiate this perception. Kerala has a labour force of 9.15 million out of its 29 million population, according to the 1991 census. This workforce consists of 8.3 million people who work for 183 days or more a year and 0.85 million marginal workers who are under employed. The number of women workers is only 2.35 million, which works out to 345 female workers per 1000 male workers. In the context of the Kerala population having a high sex ratio, this female worker ratio is much lower than the national ratio of 409. It points to the acute unemployment problem among women in the state.

Table 2.7

Worker Participation Rate by Gender for Kerala and India (in per cent)

Year	*Kerala*			*India*		
	Person	*Male*	*Female*	*Person*	*Male*	*Female*
1971	29.79	45.22	14.60	34.17	52.75	14.22
1981	30.53	44.89	16.61	36.70	52.62	19.67
1991	31.43	47.58	15.85	37.68	51.56	22.73

Source: Registrar General &Census Commissioner, 1991.

The overall worker participation rate (WPR) in Kerala in 1991 was 31.43 for a total population of 29 million. The WPR of females is 15.85 per cent which is just about one third of the male WPR of 47.58 per cent. In fact, there has been a decline in the female WPR, from 16.61 per cent in 1981 to 15.85 per cent in 1991.

Table 2.7 gives the major shifts in the sectors over the last two decades. The shift in the cropping pattern in Kerala and the presence of large number of women above 15 years in the academic institutions seem to answer this phenomenon. Another reason is the introduction of mechanisation in the agricultural sector which brings down the number of farm labour. While the working class as a whole is adversely affected by the policy of mechanisation, women of the working class are special victims. The woman is pushed more and more into the homebound reproductive role. The alienation resulting from this is on the increase and the immediate danger is the threat that the mechanisation poses to the woman's role as a worker (Sen, 1992: 392). There seems to be some reluctance on the part of women to operate machinery that are used in the agricultural sector, influenced by the socio-cultural system. This establishes a clear link between high female literacy and the land use pattern and low WPR and mechanisation in Kerala vis-à-vis the higher WPR at the national level. It also substantiates the statements of Gulati (1994) that despite high literacy, women's status has not changed much.

Table 2.8

Sectoral Distribution of Main Workers by Gender (in %)

Sector	*Male*			*Female*		
	1991	*1981*	*Changes*	*1991*	*1981*	*Changes*
Primary	47.84	50.51	(-)2.67	48.61	55.25	(-)6.64
Secondary	17.14	18.19	(-)1.05	21.65	20.97	0.68
Tertiary	35.01	31.30	3.71	29.74	23.78	5.96
	100.00	100.00		100.00	100.00	

Source: Registrar General &Census Commissioner, 1991

What is more evident is the general trend of decline in the labour force of both male and female in the primary sector. This trend continues in the secondary sector of the male workforce, whereas there has been a marginal increase in the female workforce as Kerala is backward in industry. However, in the tertiary sector, there has been a significant increase among the female workforce over the last one decade.

Kerala Model of Development

The pre-eminent position of Kerala in respect of the key indicators of social development, in spite of its low economic achievement, has been the subject of many a debate. Kerala has emerged from within the third world, as a model of development by achieving many significant social indications, in spite of its failure to attain proportionate economic growth. Franke and Chasin (2000: 17) defined Kerala model as "a set of high material quality-of-life indicators coinciding with low per capita incomes, both distributed across nearly the entire population of Kerala". A number of factors contributed towards this spectacular growth. The most important process which accelerated the Kerala Model was the high levels of political participation and social activism among the ordinary people within a democratic ambience, supported by dedicated leaders at all the levels. This led to a number of legislations towards redistribution of wealth and resources through the Kerala Land Reforms Act, 1970 and other social welfare programmes focussed on the weaker and marginal sections. This political, social and cultural awakening was hastened evidently by the mass literacy movement. Thus, the most important lesson learned from the Kerala Model is that public action by popular movements and governmental intervention in and through democratic process can transform a society radically.

The development strategy in the state has helped to narrow down the gap between the urban and rural areas. "It is difficult to distinguish a village from a town in Kerala and in appearance, villages resemble an urban continuum and this is a unique feature" (Registrar General & Census Commissioner, 1991: 9). Every village in Kerala is connected with motorable roads and according to the Kerala State Electricity Board (KSEB 1995), all the villages of Kerala are electrified. The shortcomings of the power generation and distribution have led to a gradual deterioration in the power supply position of the state. Although electricity had reached all the villages in Kerala by 1979, only 60 per cent of the households have been electrified so far.

Table 2.9
Indicators of Human Development

	Indicators	*Kerala*	*India*	*Source*
1.	Literacy (%) (1991)	89.81	52.1	Registrar General & Census Commissioner, 1991
2.	Population growth (1981-91)	14.32	23.85	Do
3.	Density of population/sq km (1991)	749	274	Do
4.	Sex ratio (1991)	1036	927	Do
5.	Urbanisation (%) (1991)	26.39	25.73	Do
6.	Per capita Income (Rs./year)	4485	5778	Abusaleh Shariff, 1999
8.	Forest area (%) (1995-96)	27.83	21.9 (1989-90)	State Planning Board, 1998 and Fernandes, 1995.
9.	Worker Participation Rate (%)	31.43	37.68	Leela Gulati,1994
10.	Cultivated Area (%)	70.41 (1995)	59.5 (1983-84)	State Land Use Board, 1995 and Fernandes, 1995.
12.	Net Irrigated area (lakhs ha.)(1997)	4.19	—	State Planning Board, 1998
13.	Per capita power Consumption (KWH), (1996-97)	198	380	KSEB,1997
14.	Percentage of villages electrified (1996-97)	100	80.2 (1983-84)	KSEB,1997 and Fernandes, 1995.
15.	Population below poverty line (%)	30	39	Abusaleh Shariff, 1999
16.	Per cent ST population below poverty line (1995)	48.48	—	Rural Information Bureau, 1996
17.	Per cent SC population below poverty line (1995)	45.6*	—	Meenakshi, 2000
18.	Expectation of life at birth (1992)	68.8	59.0	Ramachandran, 1998
19.	Birth rate/1000 (1992)	18.5	29.5	Do
20.	Death rate/1000 (1992)	6.1	9.8	Do

* in rural areas

A power surplus state till 1987, when the state was in a position to supply power to the neighboring states, Kerala now faces a reversal of the situation with power shortages of varying magnitudes, depending on the intensity and vagaries of the monsoons. The resulting power cuts have been applied mainly on the industrial sector. The only local commercial energy resource endowment in Kerala is its hydro potential which is theoretically significant. However, reliance exclusively on a single source of power has made the Kerala power system depend heavily on the Central sector power grids and to some extent on assistance from neighbouring states. Kerala has been well below the all-India figure in per capita energy consumption. The growth rate of energy consumption in the state's industrial sector has also been much lower than the national figure.

The performance of the Kerala economy in terms of commodity producing sectors has been very poor compared to the Indian economy. The growth rates of State Domestic Products (SDP) are declining sharply. Per capita income which was very close to the national average in 1971, had declined to Rs. 4,485 in 1988-89, which is 70 per cent of the national average. The share of primary and secondary sectors has decreased in the economy while that of the tertiary sector has increased. Industrial and agricultural sectors are performing dismally. Thus, the Kerala economy is heading fast towards a crisis, because of its poor performance in commodity producing sectors. Unemployment has increased. Consequently, one-thirds of its population remains below poverty line. These are some of the symptoms of the crisis that are in the Kerala model. In the last two decades or so, the Kerala model of development has been encountering a severe crisis on many fronts. Stagnation in agricultural and industrial production, widespread reduction in productivity levels, acute power shortage, out-migration of industries and labour, all round deterioration in the quality of services and a debilitating fiscal crisis of the state are some of the manifestations of this development crisis (State Planning Board, 1998: 5).

According to Saradamony (1998: 508), every forward and progressive step that Kerala has taken has thrown up problems before the state. No serious attempt has been made to understand them in their totality. What is happening is not that Kerala has become a model, but that Kerala has accepted and even internalised other models. She also points out that striking problems like increasing number of old people, single person households, migration, female headed households etc., have not received the attention they warrant.

People's Campaign: The Search for a Solution

As a solution to this problem, People's Campaign on planning initiated in Kerala is a unique and pioneering effort of decentralisation in which the people at the grassroots level are involved in the decision-making process concerning the development plans. It is aimed at actualising Gandhiji's dream of '*Gramswaraj*' through devolution of powers to people under Panchayat Raj institutions. The 73rd and 74th Constitutional Amendment Act, 1992, which came into force from 24th April 1993 laid a strong foundation to Panchayat Raj institutions in the country. People's Campaign "is a system of multilevel planning where the lowest unit is allowed to plan and implement everything that can be performed most effectively at that level. It is a People's movement to establish their rightful role in decision-making by empowering themselves and local governments as opposed to the usual apologetic propaganda to manufacture popular consent for what the state does from above" (State Planning Board, 1998: 3).

People's Campaign is an attempt to conceptualise, operationalise and institutionalise the system of multilevel, people-centered planning process, suitable to the regional specificities of Kerala. This is expected to help the state to overcome its contemporary development crisis. The campaign has contributed towards strengthening people's unity in development action and generated a new developmental consciousness in the state with emphasis on production and quality of services with sensitivity to gender, environmental and poverty concerns (Issac, 1997: 41). But, the People's Campaign like the Kerala Model of Development is under a cloud now. The general complaint is that corruption too is being 'de-centralised' through People's Campaign. As per the study conducted by Sahayi (1998), the major complaints regarding the Campaign are political hijacking, increase of corruption, incompetence of the functionaries and non-co-operation of bureaucrats.

Increase in Suicide

One of the vexing social problems in Kerala is the tragic increase in suicide rate which is the highest in India. As against the national average of 9.9 per one lakh population in 1994, Kerala had 28 per lakh. It was almost 50 per cent more than that of Karnataka (19.1), which is the second highest in the country. The proportion of suicides in the below 30 years category is well below the national average, while those among 30-50 and above 50 years are higher than the national average.

The National Crime Records Bureau (NCRB) (Murphy, 1998: 2342) ascribes the motivating factors for suicide in Kerala as the same as in the rest of the country. The commonest among them are dreadful diseases, quarrel with spouse and quarrel with parents-in-law. James Vadakanchery, a criminologist, maintains that the reasons for suicide in Kerala are intoxication, quarrels, immorality, family conflict and tensions, lack of parental love, deviant family relations, poor quality of parent-child, sibling-sibling, husband-wife relationships... and, the influence of visual media particularly films and T.V. serials. A K Jayasree, an epidemiologist, suggested the precipitating factors such as debt, mental problems and failure in examinations. Kumar, a psychiatrist, points out the low frustration tolerance among Keralites as one of the main factors. Murphy (1998) concludes that poverty was rarely a factor and unemployment was not a factor at all. He suggests that underemployment may turn out to be the crucial factor influencing the suicide rate in Kerala. According to him, one aspect of Kerala's development success that may relate to its suicide rate is education, because people are unable to find jobs commensurate with their education and expectations.

II

Projects Under Various Categories

In this section, an attempt is made to identify the various categories of development projects which induced social, cultural, environmental and economic changes in Kerala with far reaching consequences in the behaviour of the people affected. The major ones are dams, industries, mines, defence establishments, environment protection projects, tourism, farms and fisheries, harbours, roads and railways etc.

Water Resources Schemes

Kerala has a total of 50 large dams constructed in 10 districts, each with a height ranging from 10 to 60 meters and above, the highest number in one category being 12 (24%) within the range of 10-20 meters. Pathanamthitta has three of these dams. After these come, 11 dams with a height of 30-40 meters. Palakkad district has five of these. Dams with 50-60 and above 60 meters high are seven each. Idukki district has five in the above 60 meter category. It is also significant that Idukki has a total of 15 dams in all the six categories. Table 3.1 in Chapter 3 gives the details of irrigation projects both completed and ongoing.

Table 2.10

Large Dams in Kerala

District	*Height (in Metres) from the lowest Foundation*						
	10-20	*20-30*	*30-40*	*40-50*	*50-60*	*60+*	*Total*
1. Thiruvananthapuram	0	0	0	1	1	0	2
2. Kollam	0	0	0	0	0	1	1
3. Pathanamthitta	3	2	1	0	0	0	6
4. Alappuzha	0	0	0	0	0	0	0
5. Kottayam	0	0	0	0	0	0	0
6. Idukki	2	2	2	1	3	5	15
7. Ernakulam	0	2	0	0	0	1	3
8. Thrissur	2	2	2	0	1	0	7
9. Palakkad	1	0	5	0	2	0	8
10. Malapuram	0	0	0	0	0	0	0
11. Kozhikode	0	1	1	1	0	0	3
12. Wayanad	4	0	0	0	0	0	4
13. Kannur	0	1	0	0	0	0	1
14. Kasargod	0	0	0	0	0	0	0
Total	12	10	11	3	7	7	50

Source: National Register of Large Dams, 1995.

Table 3.1 in Chapter 3 gives the details of irrigation projects both completed and ongoing.

Industries

Kerala is an industrially backward state in spite of its abundant human and natural resources. The main reasons adduced are shortage of power, militancy of trade unions, increased labour problems, high cost of labour and scarcity of land. However, in the existing units, the measures of total factor productivity as well as partial productivity have been declining over the years (George, 1994: 7). As a result, Kerala's industrialists prefer to set up their units in the neighbouring states. According to George, the low productivity of industries in Kerala is due to low capacity utilisation. He highlights the reasons for the flight of industry to the nearby states as absence of workers' commitment, demand for high wages, the existence of 'attimary' (militancy of head-load workers) and general unrest.

Table 2.11

Industries in Kerala (sector-wise)

	District	*Central*	*State*	*Private*	*Co-operative*	*Joint*	*Total*	*Per cent*
1.	Thiruvananthapuram	2	20	27	1	5	55	10.78
2.	Kollam	2	10	17	2	0	31	6.07
3.	Pathanamthitta	0	1	5	1	1	8	1.56
4.	Alappuzha	1	8	22	2	3	36	7.05
5.	Kottayam	1	2	16	3	0	22	4.31
6.	Idukki	0	0	8	1	1	10	1.96
7.	Ernakulam	11	9	124	1	4	149	29.21
8.	Thrissur	2	5	32	1	7	47	9.21
9.	Palakkad	2	3	53	3	6	67	13.13
10.	Malapuram	0	4	15	1	2	22	4.31
11.	Kozhikode	0	7	27	1	1	36	7.05
12.	Wayanad	0	0	3	0	0	3	0.58
13.	Kannur	1	7	11	2	0	21	4.11
14.	Kasargod	0	2	1	0	0	3	0.58
	Total	22	78	361	19	30	510	100
	Per cent	4.31	15.29	70.78	3.72	5.88	100	

Source: KSIDC, 1998.

Information technology (IT), the world's fastest growing industry is of special significance to Kerala since its resource endowment, especially the educated and skilled human power, is well matched with its requirements. There are significant developments in the fields of telecommunications. Internet and e-mail facilities are well established and are in the stage of development with a wider network. Internet is becoming widespread and popular at a fast pace and electronic commerce is going to be the way, the world will do business in future (State Planning Board, 1997: 82).

Power Supply

The acute scarcity of power in Kerala for over a decade affected its industry as well as agriculture. However, several new measures have been taken by the Government to improve the power generation and distribution in the state.

Table 2.12 gives a list of hydel and other projects commissioned as early as 1940 to the recently commissioned Kayamkulam Thermal Power Plant by NTPC in 1999. Realising that the hydro potential of the state is not sufficient to meet all the future energy requirements, the Government has turned its attention recently on the thermal sector. The Kayamkulam power project was started in October 1996 by NTPC in the Central sector exclusively for the benefit of Kerala. This 350 MW combined cycle power project was inaugurated in January 1999.

The annual demand for power is 16,264 million KW, whereas the availability is only 12,268 million KW. Various measures have been initiated to overcome this crisis. Among them, the involvement of the private sector was prominent. The government is now importing power from the neighbouring states to fill the deficit. The state government is now taking steps to complete and start other thermal power projects and mini hydel projects in the private and joint sectors, as well. There are four hydel and five thermal projects in the private sector under various stages of implementation with an expected installed capacity of 1533 MW.

In addition to this, an agreement has been signed with Hangshon International Centre, China for implementing 18 small hydel projects (State Planning Board, 1999: 97 and 102). From 1st November, 2000, the state government has withdrawn the power cut and it is claimed that the state has attained self-reliance in power generation. It is doubtful whether even these measures would satisfy the industrial requirements of the state.

Table 2.12

Power Projects in Kerala

Sl. No.	*Name of Station*	*Date of Commissioning*	*Capacity (MW)*	*Firm Power (MW)*	*Firm Annual Generation Capacity(MU)*
	HYDEL				
1.	Pallivasal	19-3-40	37.5	32.5	284
2.	Sengulam	1-5-54	48.0	20.8	182
3.	Neriamangalam	27-1-61	45.0	27.0	237
4.	Panniar	29-12-63	30.0	17.0	158
5.	Poringalkuthu	6-3-57	32.0	19.6	170
6.	Sholayar	9-5-66	54.0	26.6	233
7.	Sabarigiri	18-4-66	300.0	138.5	1338
8.	Kuttiyadi	11-9-72	75.0	28.0	268
9.	Idukki	12-2-76	780	230	2398
10.	Idamalayar	3-2-87	75	36.5	380
11.	Kallada	5-9-94	15	6.05	65
12.	Peppara	15-6-96	3.0	—	—
13.	Maniyar (Private)	31-3-94	12	4.1	36
	WINDFARM				
14.	Kanjikode	18-5-95	2.0	—	—
	THERMAL				
15.	Kayamkulam	17-1-99	350	—	—
	DIESEL				
16.	Brahmapuram	06-5-97	106.6	—	—
17.	Nallalam	06-12-99	128	—	—
	Total		1978.5	583	5713

Source: For 1 to 14, KSEB, 1996-7:11-12 and for 15, *Indian Express* dated 17-1-99.

Mines

Kerala does not feature prominently in the mineral map of India. The total mining area in the state is limited to 5496 ha. (Indian Bureau of Mines, 1998), which is 0.14 per cent of the total landmass. The major deposits are limeshell and silica sand. However, it has not made any significant impact on the economy of the state. KMML and IRE in Chavara are the projects which have displaced some of the marginalised fishing community.

Defence Establishments

The major defence units in Kerala are the military camp at Pangode, Naval Academy at Ezhimala, Naval Depot at Cochin, and the CRPF camp at Pallippuram. Among these, the Ezhimala Naval Academy and Naval Depot acquired private land. The land occupied by CRPF at Pallippuram was a gift from the King of Travancore and Mendez family. The Military camp at Pangode was established before 1951.

Environment Protection

Fourteen Wildlife Sanctuaries were established between 1950 and 1984. The total area earmarked for these projects was 2,315.44 square kilometers. The displaced and the project affected, invariably are the Tribals who live on minor forest produce. About 21 per cent of the forest area and 5.96 per cent of the state landmass is under wildlife sanctuaries, whereas in a state like Orissa, wildlife sanctuaries occupy only 3.96 per cent of state's geographical area and 10.36 per cent of its forest area (Fernandes, 1995). Thus, Kerala has allotted a higher proportion of its land to the wildlife sanctuaries than many other states. It is close to six per cent which is considered the ideal.

Tourism

Kerala is an extremely beautiful state with its rivers, backwaters, mountains, hills and valleys. Hence, the tourism potential of Kerala is abundant and today it is recognised as an industry in the State. One important feature of this fast-growing industry is that it

Table 2.13

Area Under Mining Leases in Kerala (in ha.)

District	Bauxite	China Clay	Fire Clay	Graphite	Iron Ore	Lime Shell	Lime stone	Magnesite	Quartz	Silica Sand	Sillimanite	Total
Thiruvananthapuram	0.00	142.22	—	0.59	—	—	—	—	—	0.61	—	143.42
Kollam	0.65	29.67	0.39	—	—	—	—	—	—	—	260.41	290.73
Pathanamthitta	—	—	—	—	—	—	—	—	—	—	—	—
Alappuzha	—	—	—	—	—	1446.04	—	—	—	1172.99	—	2619.03
Kottayam	—	—	—	—	—	1916.81	—	—	—	—	—	1916.81
Idukki	—	—	—	—	—	—	—	—	—	—	—	—
Ernakulam	—	6.82	—	—	—	—	—	—	—	—	—	6.82
Thrissur	—	—	0.65	—	—	—	—	—	—	—	—	0.65
Palakkad	—	—	—	—	—	—	247.5	0.81	—	—	—	248.31
Malapuram	—	—	—	—	—	20.23	—	—	—	—	—	20.23
Kozhikode	—	—	—	—	86.54	63.21	—	—	—	—	—	149.75
Wayanad	—	—	—	—	—	—	—	—	5.49	—	—	5.49
Kannur	—	84.14	—	—	—	7.53	—	—	—	—	—	91.67
Kasargod	—	2.65	—	—	—	—	—	—	—	—	—	2.65
Total	0.65	265.5	1.04	0.59	86.54	3453.82	247.5	0.81	5.49	1173.6	260.41	5495.95

Source: Indian Bureau of Mines, Nagpur, 1998.

can employ a large number of persons directly and indirectly. The employment opportunity figure in this sector is 1:2.36, i.e. the direct employment of one person in tourism creates jobs for 2.36 persons in related sectors of the economy.

Table 2.14

Wildlife Sanctuaries and National Parks in Kerala

	Sanctuary	*Area (sq km)*	*Year of Formation*
1.	Neyyar	125.00	1958
2.	Peppara	53.00	1983
3.	Shentharuni	100.32	1984
4.	Periyar	777.54	1950
5.	Chinnar	90.44	1984
6.	Idukki	70.00	1976
7.	Chimoni	75.00	1984
8.	Peechi-Vazhani	125.00	1958
9.	Parambikulam	285.00	1962
10.	Wayanad	344.46	1973
11.	Aralam	55.00	1984
12.	Silent Valley (National Park)	89.52	1984
13.	Eravikulam (National Park)	97.00	1978
14.	Thattekad (Bird Sanctuary)	25.16	1983
	Total	2,315.44	

Source: Kerala State Land Use Board, 1995: 238

The state's contribution to tourism sector has increased in the 1990s to about seven per cent of the Indian tourist market. Earnings from tourism showed an increase by 11 per cent in 1996 over the previous year. The share of expenditure on tourism was 0.52 per cent of the total plan expenditure in 1994-95 which has increased to 0.88 per cent in 1995-96 and to 1.28 per cent in 1996-97. The corresponding figures at the national level are 0.18 per cent, 0.21 per cent and 0.26 per cent respectively. The labour capital ratio is far higher in tourism (47.5) compared to manufacturing (12.7), railways (0.9), transport (13.8), mining and quarrying (2.6). The Department of Tourism and Kerala Tourism Development Council (KTDC) are the main agencies which undertake tourism development activities in Kerala. Bakel Resorts Development Corporation Kerala Ltd., and Tourism Resorts Development Kerala (TRKL) -- a subsidiary of KTDC help in facilitating the implementation of tourism projects in the state.

The Housing Scenario

The housing sector in Kerala has recorded an unprecedented growth in the last three decades (1960-90). During this period, the housing stock in the state has increased from 2.8 million to 5.5 million, virtually doubling the number. As per the 1991 census, there were 54.59 lakh houses and 55.13 lakh households in Kerala.

Table 2.15

Housing Available in Kerala and in India by Type

Type of Structure	*Percentage of Dwelling (Rural)*	
	Kerala	*India*
Pucca (Permanent)	53.43	37.72
Semi-Pucca	22.06	29.77
Kutcha (Thatched)	24.51	32.51

Source: State Planning Board, 1997:107

The factors that contributed to the substantial increase in the housing stock are grant of ownership to the hutment dwellers, gulf migration, the changing notion of family and organisation of domestic space. The growth of housing outpaced even the population growth. The Rural Development Department, SC/ST Department, Kerala State Housing Board and Kerala State Co-operative Housing Federation are some of the government and quasi-government agencies involved in implementing the housing programmes in Kerala. 'Maithri' is the major housing scheme for the economically weaker sections in Kerala.

Farms and Fisheries

Agricultural research and education in the state are exclusively the responsibility of the Kerala Agricultural University (KAU). With the introduction of National Agricultural Research Project

(NARP), the research activities in the state have been restructured and classified on the basis of five agro-climatic zones, viz., Northern, Central, Southern, Special and High Range. These Regional Agricultural Research Stations are located at Pilicode, Pattambi, Vellayani, Kumarakom and Ambalavayal respectively. During the Eighth Plan period, the University released 38 high yielding crop varieties, a high yielding oyster mushroom strain, one commercial layer of poultry, and another layer suitable for backyard system of rearing. It also developed a coconut-dehusking device. Research capability of the University has been strengthened with the starting of tissue culture laboratories at four regional centres. Thrust has been given to the development of hybrid and scented rice varieties, export oriented vegetables, mushrooms, tuber crops, spices, cash crops and cut flower varieties, integrated pest and disease management studies, organic farming and bio-fertilizers.

Table 2.16

Farms in Kerala

	District	*State Seed Farms*	*Special Farms*	*District Agricultural Farms*	*Coconut Nurseries*	*Total*
1.	Thiruvananthapuram	2	1	1	2	6
2.	Kollam	2	1	1	1	5
3.	Pathanamthitta	2	1	-	-	3
4.	Alappuzha	2	-	1	-	3
5.	Kottayam	2	-	1	-	3
6.	Idukki	1	1	1	-	3
7.	Ernakulam	2	-	1	1	4
8.	Thrissur	6	-	1	1	8
9.	Palakkad	5	4	-	-	9
10.	Malapuram	3	1	1	1	6
11.	Kozhikode	2	-	1	1	4
12.	Wayanad	-	-	-	-	-
13.	Kannur	2	-	1	1	4
14.	Kasargod	2	1	-	-	3
	Total	33	10	10	8	61

Source: Spices Board, 1999.

The geographical location of Kerala allows her to exploit the marine resources. Trends in fish production in Kerala for the last one and half decades show that it was stagnating at around 3.3 lakh tonnes per annum during the 1980s. In the 1990s, marine fish production increased to 5.7 lakh tonnes. This increase could, perhaps partly, be attributed to the resource conservation measures, namely ban on monsoon trawling introduced by the State Government since 1989 (State Planning Board, 1997: 43). It could also be attributed to the overexploitation of marine resource by the mechanised sector.

Table 2.17

Fishing Harbours under Harbour Engineering Department

	Project	*Original Cost (in Lakhs)*	*Year of Completion*
1.	Vizhinjam	173	1980
2.	Vizhinjam-II	704	Ongoing
3.	Neendakara	370	1988
4.	Thankassery	1411	1994
5.	Munambam	710	1994
6.	Puthiappa	527	1992
7.	Chombal	556	Ongoing
8.	Mopla Bay	564	Ongoing
9.	Kayamkulam	624	Ongoing

Source: State Planning Board, 1998: S73

The traditional fishermen who operate country-craft and traditional fishing gear have been threatened by the innumerable local and national forces who operate trawlers with international linkages. With competition running high, conflicts among fishermen have become endemic. This disrupted social life and triggered violence in the coastal areas. The traditional fish workers' trade union became active in the 1980s in Kerala. They put pressure on the Government to regulate the spread of fishing technologies inappropriate to the ecological conditions of the tropical waters and to ban trawler operations during the monsoon season, that is, in the months of June, July, and August as well as a total ban of purse-seiner operations. Finally in 1989, the State

Government enforced a ban on monsoon trawling in the months of June and July after receiving the recommendations from Balakrishnan Nair Committee, which studied this issue.

Though the Government thinks that fishing harbours are the lifeline for the marginalised, the fishing community in the state who ventures into the rough sea for a living think otherwise. Nearly 56 per cent of these projects have been completed between 1980 and 1994. The remaining are being implemented.

Transport

Kerala has a fairly well developed transport and communications system. The transport infrastructure includes roads, railways, airways, major and minor ports, and navigable waterways. The road net work of Kerala extends over 1,10,480 kms. It accounts for 3.65 per cent of the total road length in the country (State Planning Board, 1999: 139).

Table 2.18

Category-wise Length of Roads in Kerala

	Category	*Length (in kms)*	*Percentage*
1.	National Highways(NH)	1350.10	5.80
2.	State Highways(SH)	4123.72	17.70
3.	Major District Roads	10936.54	46.96
4.	Other District Roads	4880.48	20.96
5.	Village Roads	1997.02	8.58
	Total	23287.86	100

Source: State Planning Board, 1999: 139

The total railway route length in 1997 was 1,053 kms, of which 936 kms are Broad Gauge and 117 kms Meter Gauge.

There has been substantial development in air transport in Kerala. Nedumbassery airport has already started functioning as the third international airport in Kerala. A fifth airport at Kannur is under the consideration of the government. The expansion work of Thiruvananthapuram airport is pending due to land acquisition issues.

Table 2.19

Length of Railways in Southern States (in kms)

State	Broad Gauge	Meter Gauge	Total
Kerala	936	117	1053
Tamil Nadu	1516	2469	3985
Pondicherry	—	11	11
Andhra Pradesh	251	—	251
Karnataka	1201	434	1635
Total	3904	3031	6935

Source: Mathrubhoomi, 1999: 4

Kochi is one of the major seaports in the country. Besides Cochin/Kochi, there are 13 intermediate and minor ports in Kerala. Inland waterways consist of navigable rivers, backwaters lagoons and cross canals. Out of these, 205 kms have been declared as National Waterway.

Educational Institutions

Kerala has an effective infrastructure for education, particularly for school education. With 6,755 lower primary schools, 2,966 upper primary schools and 2,585 high schools, Kerala serves 94 per cent of its habitations and 96.2 per cent of its population, with the facilities of an upper primary school within a distance of 3 km. Out of 12,182 schools, 7,694 are in the private sector, and 4,488 under the government, which highlights the role of NGO sector in promoting education within the state.

There are 19 Teachers Training Institutes of which four are under government, the remaining 15 are in the aided category. There were eight government and five private aided, six self financing engineering colleges, one regional engineering college, and a model engineering college in Kerala (State Planning Board, 1999). The polytechnics number 54.

Rehabilitation in Kerala

Kerala does not have a rehabilitation policy for the people affected by development projects. In the case of most of the projects, the

Table 2.20

Category-wise Details of Schools and Colleges in Kerala

District	*Schools*				*Arts and Science Colleges*			
	Government	*Private-Aided*	*Private-Unaided*	*Total*	*Government*	*Private-Aided*	*Private-Unaided*	*Total*
1. Thiruvananthapuram	521	377	58	956	8	12	4	24
2. Kollam	413	456	34	903	1	12	2	15
3. Pathanamthitta	255	439	35	729	0	9	0	9
4. Alappuzha	319	401	23	743	0	12	1	13
5. Kottayam	296	569	46	911	1	20	3	24
6. Idukki	173	274	19	466	2	6	1	9
7. Ernakulam	361	548	72	981	4	21	3	28
8. Thrissur	318	703	37	1058	3	17	1	21
9. Palakkad	308	586	39	933	3	9	4	16
10. Malapuram	540	781	52	1373	3	7	2	12
11. Kozhikode	328	870	33	1231	6	8	2	16
12. Wayanad	138	114	13	265	2	4	0	6
13. Kannur	272	969	31	1272	2	9	2	13
14. Kasargod	280	220	20	520	3	2	0	5
Total	4,522	7,307	512	12,341	38	148	26	212

Source: State Planning Board, 1997.

Government pays compensation for the land acquired and is no more concerned about rehabilitation or post-displacement life. This is the situation in most projects. It is evident from the comment made by a senior official that the Government is giving handsome compensation for the land acquired. Moreover, many of the senior Government officials hold the view that displacement is not a serious issue in Kerala. Nonetheless, projects like IRE, Chavara, Nedumbassery airport, VSSC Thumba, Vizhinjam Harbour, and Bakel Tourism have their own resettlement schemes. NTPC Kayamkulam does have a rehabilitation policy mainly, because of the World Bank's compulsion. The rehabilitation schemes of these projects include a house for the displaced, land, provision of jobs, self-employment schemes, and provision of loan facilities. Their adequacy is questionable.

Conclusion

Although Kerala is a model of development for others, and the state has achieved certain targets in specific areas of development, it is plagued with manifold problems of underdevelopment. Among the many areas that need immediate attention is the formulation of a comprehensive policy and a master plan, which would give top priority to human beings, thus, lending development a human face. The absence of political determination combined with the petty squabbles of political parties often throw to the winds the objectives of democracy, equity and social justice.

In a state like Kerala with its dense population having predominantly small land holdings, the impact of development induced displacement is quite serious. The displaced and the project affected have been invariably the poor and the marginalised. The following chapters will substantiate this perception in detail.

3

Extent of Land Acquired

This chapter focuses on the extent of land acquired for development projects implemented during the period 1951-95. The data gathered are secondary in nature and their main source is the Gazette of the State Government. A serious effort was made to peruse the project records, government reports, research studies, and documents to substantiate, supplement and validate the data from the Gazette. But, the outcome was disappointing since we did not get adequate information from district authorities. However, this was a worthwhile exercise as it helped us to identify the extent of land acquired for development purposes. Besides, from official and research sources, we managed to garner information on a representative set of projects which made extrapolation possible.

Our presentation follows the categories identified earlier, namely water resources, industry, power, mining, defence, environment protection, tourism, urban development, farms and fisheries, transport, educational institutions, social welfare and others. An attempt was also made to study the extent of land required for the proposed projects in Kerala.

Water Resources Projects

In this category, we have included land acquired for irrigation, hydel projects, canals and distributaries and all other infrastructure facilities provided under the same project. According to the Irrigation Research Development Bureau (IRDB), there are 14 major and 14 medium projects in Kerala. First, we shall present a brief profile of each of the projects, followed by a schematic presentation of decade-wise land acquisition by the water resource projects in Kerala. The number of projects presented in Table 3.1 is less than the number of dams presented in Table 2.10 of Chapter 2, because some projects have many dams. For example, Idukki project has three dams, namely Cheruthony, Idukki and Kulamavu. What we present in Table 3.1 is the number of projects.

Table 3.1

Water Resource Projects in Kerala

Category	*Type*	*Completed*	*Ongoing*	*Total*
Irrigation	Major	7	0	7
	Medium	6	6	12
Hydel		11	10	21
Multipurpose	Major	4	3	7
	Medium	—	—	—
Total		28	19	47

Note: Net irrigat.d area: This is the total area irrigated, counting, an area irrigated more than once on the same land in an agricultural year, only once.

Gross irrigated area: This is the total of irrigated area under various groups during the year, being the sum of net irrigated area and area irrigated more than once in the same year (Department of Irrigation, 2000).

Sources: *for completed irrigation and multipurpose projects-Office of the Chief Engineer, Investigation, Vikas Bhavan, Thiruvananthapuram.

*for ongoing irrigation and multipurpose projects-Office of the Executive Engineer, Planning Section, Public Office, Thiruvananthapuram.

*for hydel projects-Office of the Assistant Executive Engineer, Vydhuthi Bhavan, Thiruvananthapuram.

Irrigation projects are classified into three categories: Major, Medium and Minor.

Major: All surface water schemes having a Cultivable Command Area (CCA) of more than 10,000 hectares.

Medium: All surface water schemes having a CCA of less than 10,000 hectares, but more than 1,600 hectares.

Minor: The classification of irrigation schemes as minor introduced since the beginning of planning era has been based on different criteria. The criteria adopted for the purpose during different periods are as indicated below.

(a) *Pre-Plan period*: Pre-Plan schemes irrigating individually 1600 hectares or less.
(b) *Beginning of First Five Year Plan to March 1965*: Schemes individually costing less than Rs. 10 lakhs.
(c) *April 1965 to March 1970*: Schemes individually costing less than Rs. 25 lakhs in the plain area and less than Rs. 30 lakhs in the hill areas.
(d) *Now recommended*: Schemes having a CCA of 2,000 hectares or less.

Gross Command Area (GCA): The total area (including uncultivable area under habitation, roads, tanks, water lands etc.,) covered by a specific irrigation project.

Cultivable Command Area (CCA): This represents the cultivable area in the gross command area (Department of Irrigation, 2000)

Major Irrigation Projects

(1) *Kuttiady Project*: The dam for this project is built across the Kuttiady river at Peruvannamuzhi in Kozhikode district. It was taken up in 1962 and was planned to irrigate 14,500 ha. in Kozhikode, Vadakara and Koyilandy Taluks. Both the left and the right bank canals have a length of 37.20 kms each. The branch canals total up to 172 kms with 600 kms of distributaries. For power generation there is a hydroelectric scheme, with a separate dam up stream in the river, which is to conserve 1200 mc. ft. of water. Its ultimate benefit is 31,400 ha. (gross)/15700 ha. (net). Water is being distributed to 34,815 ha. (gross) (Planning Board, 1999).

(2) *Pazhassi Project*: Started in 1961, this was the first major scheme conceived for supplying irrigation water to the paddy fields of Thalassery and Thalipparambu taluks of Kannur district. This project was intended to benefit about 16,110 ha. The dam is constructed across the Valapattanam river at Kuyilur. The length of the main canals is 46 kms and that of the distributaries and field boothies 720 kms. Its ultimate benefit is

for 17,873 ha. (gross)/11,525 ha. (net). Water is distributed to 12,696 ha. (gross)/6,348 ha. (net) (Planning Board, 1999).

(3) *Malampuzha*: This project was started during the first Five-Year Plan period (1951-56) to utilise the water potential of Bharathapuzha in Palakkad district. The project was completed in 1955 and commissioned in 1964. It irrigates an area of 20,553 ha. The construction of the right bank canal is in progress. A hydel scheme was expected to be completed by the end of 2000.

(4) *Chitturpuzha*: This is another project in Palakkad district which was started in 1964 and completed in 1992. The dam was constructed across the river *Chitturpuzha*. The length of the main canal is 85.70 km and that of the distributaries 179.2 kms. Of the 15,700 ha. of physical plan, 13,748 ha. have been achieved (IRDB). Its ultimate benefit goes to 31,400 ha. (gross)/15,700 ha. (net). Water is being distributed to 29,950 ha. (gross)/14,975 ha. (net) of land (Planning Board, 1999).

(5) *Kanjirappuzha*: This dam constructed on the river Kanjirappuzha in Palakkad district was taken up in 1961. It consists of a total of 71.19 kms of canals and 169.97 kms of distributaries with a net irrigated area of 9,713 ha. The project was completed in 1995 and the estimate for the second phase of the project, namely Trippanal Irrigation Project has already been submitted for approval. An area of 21,854 ha. (gross)/9,713 ha. (net) benefits from it. Water is distributed to 16,349 ha. (gross)/7,266 ha. (net) of land (Planning Board, 1999)

(6) *Chimoni*: This is a multipurpose project in Thrissur district. It was started in 1976. The dam is located at Echippara across the Chimoni River. It was supposed to irrigate 1,300 ha. of land. The project is also intended for power generation (2500 KW) and supply of drinking water to the neighbouring villages. Water is let out to the entire ayacut of 26,000 ha. (gross benefit is for 2,997 ha.)/1,391 ha. (net) (Planning Board, 1999).

(7) *Kallada*: Kallada is a World Bank assisted multipurpose project in Kollam district, started in 1961. The project was intended to

irrigate Pathanapuram, Kottarakkara, Kunnathur and Karunagappally taluks of Kollam district; Kozhencherry taluk of Pathanamthitta district, Mavelikkara and Karthikappally taluks of Alappuzha district with an expected irrigated area of 92,800 ha. (gross)/61630 ha. (net). A small hydroelectric project is also functioning with an installed power generating capacity of 15 MW. The project has served 23 villages.

The major components of the project are the main dam at Parappar, saddle dam at Pallamvetty, a control vier at Ottakal, left and right bank canals (125.67 kms) and distributaries (812.8 kms). The project was completed in 1994. Water is distributed to 45,798 ha. (gross)/30,415 ha. (net) (Planning Board, 1999).

(8) *Pampa*: This project was planned to irrigate 49,456 ha. in Ranni, Kozhencherry and Thiruvalla Taluks of Pathanamthitta district, as well as Chengannur, Mavelikara, and Karthikappally Taluks of Alappuzha district. The dam is on the Kakad river. The length of the canals is 67.38 kms and that of distributaries, 1020 kms. The project was transferred to Command Area Development Authority (CADA) in 1994. It benefits 49,456 ha. (gross)/32,800 ha. (net). Water is being distributed to 48,480 ha. (gross)/20,718 ha. (net) (Planning Board, 1999).

(9) *Idamalayar*: This project in Ernakulam district was conceived in 1966-67, commenced in 1981 (IRDB) and commissioned in 1987 (*The Hindu*,11-11-99, p-4). This project was expected to irrigate 14,394 ha. in Idukki and Ernakulam districts using the water from Periyar and Chalakudy rivers. A major portion of the main canal is passing through the forest. Hence, 161 ha. of forest land had to be made available for the project. The total catchment area is 380.79 sq kms. The dam is located at Bhoothathankettu and the powerhouse is at Makarachaal.

This project is in the initial stages of execution. Ultimate benefit goes to 29,036 ha. (gross)/14,394 ha. (net) (Planning Board, 1999).

(10) *Muvatupuzha Valley*: This project, started in 1974, was aimed at irrigating an area of 17,737 ha. by using the water from

Moolamattam powerhouse of Idukki hydroelectric project. The dam of this project is on the river Moovatupuzha. The main areas benefited are Thodupuzha, Kothamangalam, Muvattupuzha, Vaikom and Kottayam taluks which are located in the Idukki, Ernakulam and Kottayam districts. The canals of this project have a total length of 66.20 kms and the distributaries are 143 kms long. This project also provides 700 cusecs of water for Hindustan Newsprint factory, Vellore and 65 cusecs of water for drinking purpose and industrial use.
It is expected to benefit 34,773 ha. (gross)/17,787 ha. (net) when completed (Planning Board, 1999).

(11) *Periyar Valley*: This project was taken up during the Second Five-Year Plan. The dam is across the Periyar river in Ernakulam district. The project was planned to irrigate 32,800 ha. of double crop paddy land and 20,000 ha. of puncha (wet) land in Kothamangalam, Muvattupuzha, Kunnathunad, Kanayannur, Aluva and Paravur taluks. The total length of the canals is 45.1 kms and of the distributaries 461.47 kms. It benefits 85,600 ha. (gross)/32,800 ha. (net). Water is distributed to 79,280 ha. (gross)/30,378 ha. (net) (Planning Board, 1999).

(12) *Neyyar*: Neyyar Irrigation project in Thiruvananthapuram district was started in 1952 and was completed in 1964. This project has a cultivable command area (CCA) of 15,380 ha., of which 3,725 ha. are in Tamil Nadu State. This project has benefited 22 villages in the Thiruvananthapuram district.

(13) *Peechi*: This project was partially commissioned in 1953 and completed in 1959. The storage dam is across *Manali* river, a tributary of *Karavannur* river. The reservoir capacity is 108 million cubic meters and the net area 17,555 ha. with 224 kms of canals, branches, and distributaries. The irrigated area is 15,236 ha. in Mukundapuram and Thrissur taluks (State Land Use Board, 1981a).

(14) *Chalakudy River Diversion Scheme*: This scheme consists of a diversion vier across *Chalakudy* river at Thumburmuzhi. The two major hydel schemes, namely Poringalkuth and Sholayar are situated in the upper reaches of this river. The command

area of this scheme lies in the Thrissur and Ernakulam districts. It has two stages - the first stage was expected to cater to 11,445 ha. of wet land, and the second phase, completed in 1966 to add 8,155 ha. Thus, the total command area is 19,600 ha., but it actually irrigates only 13,530 ha. The right bank canal irrigates 15 villages in Mukundapuram; the left bank canal five villages in Mukundapuram and six villages in Aluva taluks (State Land Use Board, 1981b).

Medium Irrigation Projects

(1) *Karappuzha*: Karappuzha is a scheme for constructing an earthern dam across Karappuzha at Vazhavettu and a storage reservoir, and a canal system to irrigate an area of 9,300 ha. (gross) in Wayanad district. The project was expected to be commissioned at the end of the IX Five-Year Plan. The construction work is still in progress.

Ultimate benefit is expected to go to 8,721 ha. (gross)/5,221 ha. (net) (Planning Board, 1999).

(2) *Attappady*: The project envisages construction of a masonry dam at Chittur in Attappady and a canal system to irrigate a gross area of 8,378 ha. of land in Palakkad district. The work had commenced in 1975. Ultimate benefit would go to 8,378 ha. (gross)/4,347 ha. (net). Execution of this project was stopped due to an inter-state problem. Government has decided to restart the work (Planning Board, 1999).

(3) *Banasurasagar*: This project consists of a dam across Karamanathode, a tributary of Panamaram river, and construction of a canal system to irrigate an area of 4,800 ha. (gross) in Wayanad. The work was started in 1979.

Investigation and land acquisition of the main canal has been completed and that of the branch canals and distributaries is in progress. Ultimate benefit would reach 4,740 ha. (gross)/2,800 ha. (net) (Planning Board, 1999).

(4) *Bridge cum-regulator at Chamaravattom*: This scheme is to construct a bridge-cum-regulator at Chamaravattom across Bharathappuzha to irrigate 8,660 ha. (gross). The aims of the

projects were: (1) to provide water for lift irrigation so as to stabilise the second crop in the project area and to raise an additional third crop in an area of 400 ha., (2) to prevent intrusion of saline water upstream and (3) to supply drinking water to the coastal towns of Ponnani and Tirur in Malapuram district. The project was expected to be completed by the end of the IX Plan. Preliminary works are completed. Ultimate benefit is expected to be 9,559 ha. (gross) (Planning Board, 1999).

(5) *Kuriarkutty-Karappara*: This project was planned to irrigate an area of 23,472 ha. (gross) in the drought prone areas of Palakkad district. It utilises the tailrace water from Kuriarkutty hydroelectric scheme. The total area to be benefited by the project is 18,688 ha. This project is in the initial stages of execution.

Modified project report is under preparation. The initial work had started, but is at a standstill due to a vigilance case. Ultimate benefit will go to 34,976 ha. (gross) (Planning Board, 1999).

(6) *Kakkadavu*: This project envisages to irrigate an area of 41,760 ha. (gross) in Kannur and Kasargod districts by constructing a dam at Kakkadavu across the Kariyangode river. Preliminary work was started in 1979, but could not be continued due to the objection of the affected people. An expert committee appointed to conduct a study in this regard has submitted its report. The project has not yet been approved by the Central Water Commission.

Mangalam, Gayathri, Pothundy, Cheerakuzhy, Walayar and Vazhani are the other completed medium projects. No data are available as these projects were started as long ago as in 1950s.

Hydel Projects

There are 13 completed hydroelectric projects with an installed capacity of 1508.50 MW. Of these, Pallivasal, Sengulam, Neriamangalam, Idukki and Panniar are in Idukki district. The remaining projects are Poringalkuth and Sholayar (Thrissur dist.),

Sabarigiri (Pathanamthitta dist.), Idamalayar (Ernakulam district), Kuttiady (Kozhikode dist.) and Kallada mini Project (Kollam district). There are 14 ongoing projects (State Planning Board, 1999: S79). Many of the water resource projects are multipurpose. The details are given in Table 2.12 in Chapter 2.

Minor Irrigation Schemes

Minor irrigation schemes in Kerala can be broadly classified into surface flow irrigation schemes, surface lift irrigation schemes, and ground water based schemes. The Table 3.2 is self-explanatory.

Table 3.2

Area Irrigated by Minor Irrigation Schemes in Kerala (in ha.)

District	*Surface Flow Schemes*	*Surface Lift Schemes*	*Dug Well Schemes*	*Total*
Thiruvananthapuram	21072	1325	5582	27979
Kollam	13026	2129	1330	16485
Pathanamthitta	13263	4384	819	18466
Alappuzha	28006	944	325	29275
Kottayam	11681	4923	2870	19474
Idukki	3727	1932	1920	7579
Ernakulam	13298	45320	7830	66448
Thrissur	27867	34751	8850	71468
Palakkad	10757	30016	10400	51173
Malapuram	12084	19373	4665	36122
Kozhikode	2063	3958	2086	8107
Wayanad	5083	10276	550	15909
Kannur	9852	400	2332	12584
Kasargod	4927	4895	5488	15310
Total	1,76,706	1,64,626	55,047	3,96,379

Source: CWRDM, 1995: 33

Land Acquisition: Water Resources

Our study reveals that 27,995.9782 hectares or 53.98 per cent of the total area acquired as per the Gazette notifications was for water resources development. This proves beyond any doubt that water resources development projects are the largest land acquisition agents in Kerala as in the rest of the country. Irrigation projects are predominant among all the schemes under water resource category.

Decade-wise analysis of land acquisition shows that more than half of the land acquired was during the period of 1971-81. This decade includes the last three years of the Fourth Five Year Plan, the whole of the Fifth Plan and the early years of the Sixth Plan in addition to the annual plan of 1979-80. The major schemes during this period were Kallada, Muvatupuzha Valley, Pampa, Periyar Valley, Attappady, Kanjirappuzha, Kutiadi, Karappuzha and Pazhassi. During this decade 1971-81, Kozhikode district recorded the largest land acquisition which accounts for more than half of the water resources projects, 55.20 per cent. Palakkad district comes next with about 10 per cent of land acquired under the scheme, because of the irrigation facilities created in the district for agriculture and allied services. Palakkad is the main rice bowl of Kerala in spite of the latest trends in shifting from paddy cultivation to cash crops.

Project-wise data on private land acquisition for water resource projects are available only for a few. Hence, we have no other alternative, but to extrapolate from the available data. As per the estimate of the Planning Commission, every hectare of land acquired for the construction of a dam and reservoir, canals and distributaries and other infrastructure facilities would irrigate five hectares of land (1:5). But, for extrapolation of the land acquired by irrigation projects, we use the norm of 1:10. This is to avoid any exaggeration in the estimates made.

We have data on private land regarding four major irrigation/multipurpose projects. They are Kanjirappuzha (1,160 ha.), Kutiadi (404.86 ha.), Kallada (284.68 ha.) and Muvatupuzha valley (713.81 ha.). The total area acquired for these four projects comes to 2,563.35 ha. Estimated area acquired by other major irrigation/multipurpose projects by using the extrapolation criterion of 1:10 gives 5,377.53 ha.

Table 3.3

Decade-wise Land Acquisition for Water Resources (area in hectares)

District	1951-61	1961-71	1971-81	1981-91	1991-95	N.A	Total
Thiruvananthapuram	140.6116	635.0872	194.9713	22.8904	31.8447	0.3622	1025.7672
Kollam	74.5616	996.7074	959.7996	263.3711	16.3802	1.1852	2312.0051
Pathanamthitta	94.6758	278.6143	188.2683	35.5314	2.0692	0.0380	599.1969
Alappuzha	3.5423	144.7854	607.1988	52.4602	0.0121	1.6327	809.6314
Kottayam	19.3192	21.8435	3.0436	3.0311	41.8782	0.2983	89.4138
Idukki	0.3521	246.4032	702.9715	17.4397	6.5193	0.0000	973.6858
Ernakulam	257.6565	1334.2439	757.9276	214.2567	105.2675	146.3920	2815.7444
Thrissur	960.2535	203.4844	235.9988	137.6766	23.6989	67.5330	1628.6451
Palakkad	1231.944	1429.0780	1531.223	314.0572	13.0094	3.4898	4522.79877
Malapuram	24.1415	317.5696	79.1372	28.4876	3.1679	0.0000	452.5038
Kozhikode	26.3428	1523.4525	8534.2597	18.1582	1.0134	282.9820	10386.1086
Wayanad	0.0498	26.6523	637.8620	142.4501	129.1778	9.8886	946.08051
Kannur	5.3888	200.3848	995.3820	163.4448	5.2781	4.0474	1373.9258
Kasargod	1.4933	8.4606	21.5120	0.5057	0.0040	0.0000	31.9756
N.A.	3.4112	10.4237	10.6553	1.1450	0.3055	2.5546	28.4953
Total	2843.7438	7377.1906	15460.208	1414.8057	379.6262	520.4039	27,995.9782
Percentage	(10.15)	(26.35)	(55.22)	(5.05)	(1.36)	(1.85)	(100)

Source: Kerala Gazette (1951-95)

For medium projects, we have data only on five out of 12 projects. The average area of the three projects, namely Karappara, Chamravattom and Attapady is 485.33 ha. We take this average as the base for extrapolating the area of land used by remaining six medium projects (2,914.98 ha.). Since Chamravattom project is not yet completed, we take only 50 per cent of the area as already acquired and the remaining area will be counted in the category for future requirements. Thus, the total for medium projects will be 6,245.6965 ha.

For hydel projects, we have data about private land only for Idukki project (15.58 ha.). Taking this as a representative figure, the total private land acquired by 13 hydel projects would come to 202.54 ha. The information from many officials substantiate our hypothesis that the hydel projects in Kerala used minimum private land and most of them used forest land as the dams are constructed in the forest area. So, this 202.54 ha. seems to be a reliable estimate of land acquired for hydel schemes in Kerala.

Area irrigated by minor irrigation projects is 3,96,379 ha., of which 2,19,673 ha. is irrigated by surface flow and dug well schemes. Since these two schemes do not require much land, we consider only the area used for surface flow schemes in the minor irrigation projects. By taking the norm 1: 10, the area acquired for irrigating 1,76,706 ha. is estimated to be 17,670 ha. However for a more realistic assessment we take only half of this area, namely, 8835 ha. Thus, the total extent of land used for irrigation will be 22,821.8770 ha.

Hence, the total private land used by water resources projects worked out through extrapolation amounts to 23,244.4170 ha. But, Gazette notifications give an area of 27,995.9782 ha. of private land acquired for this category. So, we take this gazette data (32,079.417 ha.) for calculating the total land acquired. As per the estimates of Karunakaran (1995: 162), the total forest land used for irrigation, hydel and water supply projects is 21,226.65 ha. We have data on 349.8 ha. of common land used for water resources projects. When we add these figures of private land, forest land and common land, we arrive at the total of 49,572.4282 ha. as acquired for water resource projects.

Proposed Water Resource Projects

Mananthavady Multipurpose Project

This project proposes to construct a dam in the river Mananthavady at Pallivathukal near Valat. The area to be submerged is 3,900 ha. including 650 ha. of forest land. About 11,000 families will be displaced by this project and majority of them are Tribals (FEDINA, Sulthan Bathery). The installed capacity proposed for the hydel scheme is 225 (5 × 45) MW (Solidarity, 2000).

Pandiar Punnappuzha Project

This is a multipurpose project in Wayanad district which envisages generation of 150 MW power. The project also aims at irrigating an area of 91,093.12 ha. and to supply water to about 10 lakh people. The area of land required for this project is 1,779.1377 ha., of which 1,417 ha. is forest land. This project is estimated to displace 4,000 families (FEDINA, 2000).

Kallampathy Irrigation Project

The dam for this project is planned to be constructed in the river *Chuzhalippuzha* in Meppady village. An area of 540 ha. will be submerged. This project will displace 5,000 families including 1,200 tribal (FEDINA, 2000).

Chundelipuzha Project

This project proposes to irrigate an area of 2,647 ha. The dam of this project will be on the river Chundelipuzha at Mylambady. The area to be submerged is 2,000 ha. and it will displace 2,000 families of which 500 are Tribal (FEDINA, 2000).

Meenachil

This project is meant to irrigate an area of 9950 ha. (net) in Meenachil and Changanassery taluks in Kottayam district by constructing a masonry straight gravity dam across Teekoy River, one of the tributaries of the Meenachil River. The length of the main canal is 44 km, with 949 kms of branch canals and 101 kms of distributaries. The investigation work is at a standstill though the project officially started in 1980.

Vamanapuram

The project is intended to construct a dam across *Kallar*, a tributary of *Vamanapuram* river in Thiruvananthapuram district. The project proposes to irrigate an area of 11,673 ha. (gross). It has acquired 5.34 ha. so far. The investigation work of the revised project is in progress. The total area to be submerged is 365 ha. This project is expected to displace 447 families. The total expense for the project would be 315 crores (*Malayala Manorama*, 1-3-2000).

Chaliyar

This project is meant to irrigate 50,200 ha. of land in Malapuram and Kozhikode districts. The proposed reservoir would emerge by the construction of a dam at Ambuttampetty (Chief Engineer Investigation, Irrigation Dept., 1998). It would require 1, 430 ha. (Supt. Engr, Kozhikode).

These projects except Meenachil require an area of 10,014.1377 ha. Let us take the area required for Meenachil project as 995 ha. (for irrigating 9,950 ha.). The area required for Kakkadavu project is estimated to be 2,088 ha. Since Chamravattom project is in its initial stages, we have already counted half of the area. The remaining stage would require 216.5 ha.

So, the total land required for the proposed water resource projects would be 13,313.638 ha. This is 26.86 per cent of the area already acquired by this category in the 45 years since 1951. Among these water resources schemes Mananthavady, Pandiar, Punnappuzha, Kallampathy and Chundelippuzha are in the Wayanad district. Social activists question the rationale for constructing so many dams in such a small district (2131 sq kms of area), which is situated 2,700 feet above the mean sea level, since there are already two major schemes (Karappuzha and Banasurasagar) in this district.

Table 3.4
Major Industries in Kerala

Sl. No.	Sector/name of unit	Location/taluk/district	Line of production
1	Balmer Lawrie & Co. Ltd.	Cherthala, Alappuzha	Margine freight containers
2	Cochin Refineries Ltd.	Kunnathunadu, Ernakulam	Petrolium products asphalt drums
3	Cochin Refineries Balmer Lawrie Ltd.	Kunnathunadu, Ernakulam	Polyisobutene
4	Cochin Shipyard Ltd.	Kochi, Ernakulam	Ship building
5	The Fertilizers & Chemicals Travancore Ltd.	Eloor, Udayamandal	
5.1	The Udyogamandal Division	Aluva, Ernakulam	Ammonium sulphate/phosphate, caprolactum etc.
5.2	The Cochin Division	Kunnathunadu, Ernakulam	Sulphuric acid, urea etc.
5.3	Fact Engineering Works	Kochi, Ernakulam	Penstock & allied products
6	Hindustan Latex Ltd.	Thiruvananthapuran	Rubber contraceptives
7	Hindustan Newsprint Ltd.	Vaikom, Kottayam	Newsprint
8	Western India Plywoods Ltd.	Kanayannur, Ernakulam	Plywood, hardboard etc.
9	Tata Oil Mills Co.Ltd./Hindustan Lever Ltd.	Ernakulam, Ernakulam,	
10	Tata Tea Ltd.	Devikulam, Idduki	Instant tea
11	Travancore Chemicals & Mfd. Co. Ltd.	Kalamassery, Ernakulam,	
12	Premier Tyres Ltd.	Kanayannur, Ernakulam	Automobile tyres and tubes
13	Malayala Manorama Co. Ltd.	Kottayam	Printing press
14	M R F Ltd.	Kottayam	Automobile tubes Tread rubber
15	Carborundum Universal Ltd.	Kalamassery, Ernakulam,	

Contd...

Contd...

16	Indian Aluminium Co. Ltd.	Kanayannur, Ernakulam	Aluminium ingots (Billets Aluminium Laboratories Ltd., Extruded products)
17	Indian Express Pvt. Ltd.	Ernakulam	Printing press
18	Apollo Tyres Ltd.	Mukundapuram, Thrissur	Mild steel ingots
19	The Kerala Dinesh Beedi Workers Central Co-Operative Society Ltd.	Kannur	Beedi
20	Milma	Thiruvananthapuram	Milk and Milk products
21	HMT Ltd.	Kanayannur, Ernakulam	Machine tools, lathes printing machine
22	Indian Rare Earths Ltd.	Mumbai	—
22.1	Rare Earths Division	Parur, Ernakulam	Rare earths chloride, trisodium phosphate
22.2	Minerals Division	Karunagappally, Kollam	Ilmenite, etc.
23	Hindustan Organic Chemicals Ltd.	Kanayannur, Ernakulam	Phenol, acetone
24	Kerala Minerals And Metals	Karunagappally, Kollam	Ilmenite, monozite zircon, rutile etc & titanium dioxide
25	Kerala State Cashew Development Corporation Ltd.	Kollam	Processing of raw cashew nuts
26	Malabar Cements Ltd.	Palakkad	Portland cement
27	Travancore Cements	Kottayam	White cement and cement paint
28	*Travancore –Cochin Chemicals Ltd.	Parur, Ernakulam	Caustic soda, sodium hydrosulphite, sodium sulphide.
29	Travancore Titanium Products Ltd.	Thiruvananthapuram	Titanium dioxide Sulphuric acid
30	Units Under Kerala State Electronics Development Corporation Ltd. Thiruvananthapuram	—	—
31	Kerala Electrical & Allied Engg. Co. Ltd.	—	—
32	Steel Industrials Kerala Ltd. (SIKL)	Certhala, Alappuzha	Steel Fabricants, Steel Castings

Source: Kerala State Industrial Development Corporation, 2000.

Industry

Industrial Estates/Plots/Areas

Industrial plots are meant for small scale industries. The land and 50 per cent of the infrastructure are provided by the Industries Department. The parties concerned have to meet the remaining expenses. Industrial Areas require a minimum of 202.43 ha. Here, small, medium and large scale industries are allowed. Land for industrial areas is provided by Industries Department. This land could be either purchased or leased by the department. Industrial Growth Centres are established in collaboration with Kerala State Industries Development Corporation (KSIDC). They require a minimum of 101 ha.

Most of the Mini Industrial Estates acquired have an area of about one acre each. In Kerala, there are12 Industrial Development Areas, 16 Development Plots, 16 Conventional Estates and 100 Mini Industrial Estates (Directorate of Industries and Commerce, 1998).

A close look at these projects shows that many of the units are lying vacant. For instance, in the Kanjikode Industrial Development Area, Palakkad, started in 1994, there are only 42 operating units as against the space provided for 221 (*Malayala Manorama*, 22-24 July, 1999). Similarly, out of the 52 units in the Pudussery Industrial Development Area, Palakkad, only 43 are functioning. The land acquisition for this project was done in 1983. Again in the Veli industrial area of Thiruvananthapuram district, 37 per cent of the 138 units continues to remain vacant. The amount of land acquired in 1963 was 70.94 ha. In the Mini Industrial Estates at Chavara in Kollam district, vacant units rose up to 50 per cent of the total 10 and in Perinad, it went up to 57 per cent (DIC, Kollam, 1999). In this context, it is important to question the present pattern of acquiring a larger area than required, without utilising it effectively and causing dislocation of people. The studies in other states too revealed the same trend of acquiring a larger area of land than actually required (Fernandes and Asif, 1997; Fernandes and Naik, 1999).

Table 3.5

Land Acquisition for Representative Projects

Sl. No.	District	Year	Taluk	Village	Area (ha.)
Industrial Estates					
1	Kollam	1961	Kollam	Thrikovilvattom	13.77
2	Alappuzha	1957	Mavelikara	Thekkekara	13.22
3	Thrissur	NA	Thrissur	Edakkurissi	15.50
4	Palakkad	1962	Ottappalam	Shornur	6.20
5	Alappuzha (Chemical Estate)	1966	Cherthala	Aroor	6.39
6	Kasargod	NA	Kasargod	Thekkil	11.36
7	Thiruvananthapuram	NA	Thiruvananthapuram	Pappanamcode	6.89
Industrial Plots					
8	Thiruvananthapuram	1975	Thiruvananthapuram	Attipra	11.33
9	Kollam	NA	Kollam	Eravipuram	6.94
10	Kollam	1970	Kollam	Mundakkal	8.36
11	Thrissur	1994	Thrissur	Ayyanthole, Chiyaram	89.21
12	Kannur	NA	Kannur	Muzhipilangadi	22.16

Contd...

Contd...

Industrial Areas					
13	Thiruvananthapuram	NA	Thiruvananthapuram	Kadakampally	70.94
14	Ernakulam	NA	Paravur	Kodungallur	180.07
15	Alappuzha	1966	Cherthala	Aroor	24.80
16	Palakkad	1972	Palakkad	Pudussery West, Pudussery Central	199.34
17	Kasargod	NA	Kasargod	Ananthapuram	42.13
18	Kasargod	NA	Kasargod	Urathamchal	43.72
19	Kannur	NA	Thaliparamba	Anthur	24.01
20	Alappuzha	1983	Mavelikara, Cherthala	Chengannur	6.28
21	Alappuzha	1972	Ambalappzha	Punnapra	23.19
22	Alappuzha	1976	Ambalappzha	Kottakadavu	19.09
Industrial Development Centres					
23	Kollam	1967	Kollam	Eravipuram	6.00
Industrial Township					
24	Palakkad	1994	Palakkad	Pudusssery Central	279.94

Contd...

Contd...

Industrial Growth Centres					
25	Malapuram	1995	Eranad	Panakad	105.43
26	Kozhikode	1994	Kozhikode	Eangappuzha	101.22
27	Kannur	1994	Thalassery	Cheruvamchery	101.17
Coir Park					
28	Alappuzha	NA	Cherthala	Cherthala	16.78
Export Promotion Industrial Park					
29	Ernakulam	1995	Kanayannur	Kakanadu	72.87
Technopark					
30	Thiruvananthapuram	1993	Thiruvananthapuram	Kariavattom	92.99
				Total	1621.3

Sources: For items 5, 6, 17 to 22, and 28 - DIC of the concerned districts,
For 7 - DGM, SIDCO, Thiruvananthapuram,
For 29 - Asst. Engineer, KINFRA, Kakkanadu,
For 30 - Administrative Office, Technopark,
For all others - Kerala Gazette (1951-95).

Kerala being an industrially backward state, the extent of land acquired for industries is comparatively small, 5,061.50 ha. This constitutes only 9.75 per cent of the total land acquired for development projects (based on government gazette). This includes the area acquired for industrial plots, estates, and other such schemes listed in Table 3.5 above, through the gazette notifications.

FACT, one of the leading Government of India enterprises, located in the industrial belt of Cochin, acquired 850 ha. of land in 1964. The Precision Instrument Factory at Kanjicode of Palakkad District is the manufacturer of precision pressure valves. It acquired an area of 324.24 ha. in 1963. Mavoor Gwalior Rayons of the Birla group, which is now known as the Grasim Industries, in Kozhikode district acquired 166.06 ha. of land in 1959. The Hindustan Newsprint factory at Vellore in Kottayam district acquired land from the Idukki district too.

A good proportion of the land acquisition for industries took place during the 1961-71 decade (58.04%). Ernakulam, the industrially forward district of Kerala, stands first in the extent of area acquired (55.05%) followed by Palakkad (18.83%) in that period. The Third Five Year Plan, the early years of the Fourth Plan and the annual plan of 1966-69 were in this decade. It is also worth noting that Wayanad district carved out of Kannur and Kozhikode in 1980 has acquired only a negligible area of land specifically for industry, although agro-based estates and a few industries flourish there in the private sector. Tourism is the growing industry of Wayanad district.

Out of the 19 Central Government industries, we have data on nine. One of the units is in the industrial development area at Aroor. Area occupied by these nine units amounts to 2,005.829 ha. For calculating the area utilised for the remaining ten units, we take the average of 174.046 ha. Thus, calculated the total for the remaining nine comes to 156.914 ha. Therefore, the total area acquired for central Government industries would be 3572.243 ha.

We have data on 13 out of the 62 (State Planning Board, 1999: S94) State Government undertakings. The area used by these 13 units is 759.337 ha. By taking the average of 67.0812 for

Table 3.6

Decade-wise Land Acquisition for Industries (area in hectares)

District	*1951-61*	*1961-71*	*1971-81*	*1981-91*	*1991-95*	*N.A*	*Total*
Thiruvananthapuram	3.4728	265.2400	16.8175	1.9050	126.7310	0.0000	414.1662
Kollam	1.1089	34.1514	121.0631	18.0955	2.0443	0.0000	176.4631
Pathanamthitta	17.9494	28.9892	0.0000	0.0000	0.0000	0.0000	46.9386
Alappuzha	21.0586	164.0978	80.5050	0.3642	0.0000	0.0000	266.0255
Kottayam	0.0000	23.3270	344.7148	19.8120	0.4655	0.0000	388.3193
Idukki	0.0000	0.0000	20.8314	0.0000	0.0000	0.0000	20.8314
Ernakulam	45.2543	1617.1978	22.3125	8.2326	52.4895	0.0000	1745.4867
Thrissur	10.9046	56.0205	52.6202	1.4040	82.5476	1.4470	204.9439
Palakkad	2.1772	553.2611	38.8673	216.0651	283.8660	0.0000	1094.2367
Malapuram	0.0000	35.9647	14.7722	0.0000	105.4950	0.0000	156.2319
Kozhikode	58.2511	115.5121	80.3574	0.0000	101.2150	0.0000	355.3355
Wayanad	0.0000	0.0890	0.4047	0.0000	0.0000	0.0000	0.4937
Kannur	10.8457	43.7256	2.3111	13.9711	101.1725	0.0000	172.0259
Kasargod	12.2130	0.0150	7.7620	0.0000	0.0202	0.0000	20.0102
Total	183.2355	2937.591	803.3390	279.845	856.0465	1.4470	5061.5086
Percentage	(3.62)	(58.04)	(15.87)	(5.52)	(16.91)	(0.00)	(100)

Source: Kerala Gazette (1951-95)

extrapolation, we arrived at a total of 3219.8976 ha. for the remaining 48 units (one unit is in Cochin Export Promotion Industrial Zone - CEPZ). Accordingly, the total land used by State Government units would be at least 3979.2346 ha.

Table 3.7

Land Acquired for Central Government Industries

	Name of the Company	*Area Acquired (in ha.)*
1.	Cochin refineries Ltd., Ernakulam	141.73
2.	Hindustan Newsprint, Vellore	277.34
3.	Indian Telephone Industries, Palakkad	40.34
4.	Instrumentation Ltd., Palakkad	242.91
5.	Hindustan Latex Ltd., Thiruvananthapuram	4.66
6.	Hindustan Machine Tools Ltd., Kalamassery	316.1943
7.	FACT, Udyogamandal	944.1273
8.	Hindustan Insecticides Ltd., Ernakulam	25.7638
9.	Kerala Lekshmi Mills, Pullazhi	12.7636
	Total	2005.829

Source: Kerala Gazettes.

Table 3.8

Land Acquired for State Government Industries

	Name of the Company	*Area acquired (in ha.)*
1.	Steel Industries Kerala Ltd., Cherthala	48.00
2.	Malabar Cements Ltd., Walayar	339.00
3.	Kerala Ceramics Ltd., Kannur	102.82
4.	Perumon Special Refractories, Perumon	12.15
5.	Steel Complex, Kozhikode	17.80
6.	Kerala Minerals and Metals Ltd., Chavara	117.4089
7.	Traco Cables, Thiruvalla	14.57
8.	Travancore Titanium Products Ltd., Thiruvananthapuram	30.47
9.	Travancore Cochin Chemicals, Eloor	36.7071
10.	Metal Industries, Shornur	13.9551
11.	Kerala Electrical and Allied Co. Ltd., Chemmanad	5.5812
12.	Carbon and Chemicals Factory, Chemmanad	12.1405
13.	KELTRON, Thiruvananthapuram	8.7342
	Total	759.337

Source: Kerala Gazettes.

Out of the 385 private units, we have data on four, which amounts to 158.5955 ha. Thirty three private sector units are in CEPZ and 39 in different IDAs, IDPs etc. Five units are in Technopark. On the basis of estimate for the average (12.6478 ha.) of this category, the area for the remaining 304 private undertakings would be around 3844.916 ha. Thus, the total land acquired for private industries would be 4003.5115 ha.

Table 3.9

Land Acquired for Private Industries

	Name of the Company	*Area Acquired (ha.)*
1.	English Indian Clays Ltd., Veli	78.15
2.	Automobile Tyre Factory, Perabra	13.09
3.	Gwaliyor Rayons, Mavoor	55.15
4.	Switch Gear Factory, Munnar	12.2055
	Total	158.5955

Source: Kerala Gazettes.

Data about only two out of the 16 industries in the co-operative sector are available. These two occupy an area of 72.6317 ha. The total area for the remaining 14 industries based on extrapolation from the average of 36.3159 ha. works out to 508.4219 ha. Thus, the total for co-operative sector industries comes to 581.0536 ha.

For the estimate of the area used by the joint sector industries, we take the average area used by private sector units as base (12.6478 ha.). This works out to 3543.1384 ha. for 28 units. One of the joint sector units is in CEPZ.

Thus, the total for all the five sectors of industries together comes up to an area of 12,490.181 ha. of land.

By taking the average from the data available, the area acquired for 16 Industrial Plots is estimated to be 313.01 ha. Similarly, the area acquired by 16 Industrial Estates would be 146.66 ha. All the 100 Mini Industrial Estates together occupy an area of 40.49 ha., because mini industrial estates acquired one acre each approximately. When we add the 92.99 ha. of area acquired by Technopark and 72.87 ha. of land by the Export Promotion Park at Kakanadu, the total for industries other than individual industries like HMT, Titanium etc., would be 666.02 ha.

In sum, through extrapolation we have identified the following.

Table 3.10

Sector-wise Land Acquisition for Industries

	Sector	*Area (ha.)*
1.	Central	3572.243
2.	State	3979.2346
3.	Private	4003.5115
4.	Co-operative	581.0536
5.	Joint	354.1384
6.	Industrial Plots	313.0100
7.	Industrial Estates	146.600
8.	Mini Estates	40.4900
9.	Technopark	92.9900
10.	Export Promotion Industrial Park	72.8700
	Total	13156.1411

This total includes the land acquired for large and medium industries.

Our Gazette search had revealed that the Industrial Growth Centres acquired 307.82 ha., Industrial Development Areas 833.38 ha., Industrial Township 279.94 ha. and Industrial Development Centres 6.00 ha., thus totally 1422.14 ha. This total represents combination of medium, large and small scale industries. Our other estimation included the medium and large industries. It is not possible to separate small scale industries from large and medium from this total, due to lack of differentiated data. Hence, we decided to leave this data out in calculating the total land acquired for industries, for fear of duplication of data.

Thus, the total area of land under industries in Kerala is estimated to be 13156.1411 ha. This includes 368.65 ha. of forest land used by Malabar Cements Ltd., Walayar and 17.64 ha. by Kerala Wood Industries Ltd., Nilambur and 131.1829 ha. of common land.

Proposed Industrial Projects

The proposed industrial projects require an area of 314.54 ha. of land.

Mines

Mining in Kerala can hardly be considered in the context of development activities due to the limited mineral deposits, except the rare ones found in the sandy beaches. Our study depended mostly on Indian Bureau of Mines (IBM). The two major industries exploiting these resources are IRE and KMML at Chavara.

The total mining leases in Kerala occupy an area of 5,495.95 ha. Of these, only 107.6308 ha. were acquired through Gazette notifications. Most of the rest is on lease. Mining for lime shell is the largest operation in Kerala, limited to Kottayam and Alappuzha districts, because of the proximity to backwaters. Silica sand has the second place monopolised by Alappuzha (IBM 1998).

Non-hydel Power

We have already accounted for the hydel projects in the water resource category. So, here we deal with only the other power projects, namely thermal, wind farm and diesel power projects. In addition to NTPC project at Kayamkulam, there are two diesel power plants at Brahmapuram and in Nallalam in Kozhikode. We have also included the land acquired for power stations and substations connected with electricity generation and transmission under the category of non--hydel power projects. The Gazette records show that only 1.70 per cent of the total area acquired for development projects was exclusively for this category. The biggest number of acquisitions for these power projects was done during the decade 1961-71. Nearly fifty eight per cent of the area acquired during this period was from Ernakulam district.

NTPC project in Kayamkulam acquired 485.83 ha. of land of which 364.37 ha. is Government owned *Kayal farm.*

Substations also occupy land. There is only one substation of 400 KV. The number of 220 KV substations is ten. In addition to

Table 3.11

Proposed Projects of Kerala Industrial Infrastructure Development Corporation (KINFRA)

	Project	*District*	*Location*	*Area (ha.)*	*Remarks*
1.	International Apparel Park	Thiruvananthapuram	Menamkulam	16.19	Construction in progress
2.	Integrated Infrastructure Development Centre	Thiruvananthapuram	Menamkulam	16.19	Construction in progress
3.	Film And Video Park	Thiruvananthapuram	Kazhakuttam	30.36	Land acquisition is over
4.	Marine Products Infrastructure	Alappuzha	Aroor	—	Procedure not started
5.	Rubber Park	Ernakulam	Perumbavoor	44.13	Acquisition in progress
6.	Export Promotion Industrial Park	Ernakulam	Kakkanadu	68.82	Construction in the final stage
7.	Techno Industrial Park	Malapuram	Thenhippalam	29.1376	Acquisition in progress
8.	Integrated Infrastructure Development Centre	Kannur	Eranholi	20.24	Pre-acquisition stage
9.	Integrated Infrastructure Development Centre	Wayanad	Meenangadi	—	Acquisition in dispute
10.	NA	Kasaragod	NA	89.47	Acquisition in progress
	Total	—	—	314.54	

Source: KINFRA parks-strategic locations, a brochure by KINFRA, 1999.

Table 3.12

Major Mining Leases in Kerala

	Lessee	*District*	*Taluk*	*Villages*	*Date of Execution*	*Area (ha.)*	*Mineral*
1.	Kerala Clays & Ceramics Products Ltd., Pappinassery.	Kannur, Kasargod	Kannur, Hosdurg	Madai, Kannapuram, Udukaai	1981	11.8807	Chinaclay
2.	Kerala Ceramics Ltd., Kundra.	Kollam	Kollam	Mulavana.	1983	4.222	China Clay, Ball Clay, Fire Clay.
3.	English Indian Clays Ltd., TVM.	Thiruvananthapuram	Thiruvananthapuram	Melethonnakal, Pallipuram, Andoorkonam	1987	14.733	Chinaclay
4.	Mrs. Suhra Beevi	Thiruvananthapuram	Thiruvananthapuram	Melethonnakal	1994	644.00	China clay
5.	Radha Clay Pattom	Thiruvananthapuram	Thiruvananthapuram	Veiloor	1996	11.5680	China Clay
6.	Travancore Cements Ltd., Kottayam.	Kottayam, Alappuzha.	Kottayam, Vaikom Cherthala	Kumarakom, Vaikom Pallipuram Thanneermukam(S) Vaduthala Madathil Bhagam	1985	486.25	Limeshell

Contd...

Contd...

7.	Travancore Electro Chemicals Ltd. (TECIL), Chingavanam.	Kottayam Alappuzha, Wayanadu	Kottayam, Vaikom, Cherthala, S.Bathery, Mananthavady.	Kumarakom, Vaikom, Naduvila, Pallipuram, Nenmani, Thrissilassery	1992	200.2155	Limeshell
8.	Vaikom Limeshell Co-operative Society, Vaikom.	Kottayam	Vaikom.	Vaikom.	1996	94.5	Limeshell
9.	Vaikom Taluk White Limeshell Co-operative Society, Vaikom	Kottayam	Kottayam	Kumarakom	1995	500.00	Limeshell
10.	Malabar Cements Ltd., Palakad	Palakad	Palakad	Pudussery East	1985	157.64	Mineral sand
11.	Kerala Minerals & Metals Ltd., Chavara	Kollam, Alappuzha	Karunagapally Karthikapally	Chavara, Thekkum Bhagam, Kulasekarapuram, Panamana, Pudupaaly	1985	127.64	Mineral sand
12.	Indian Rare Earths Ltd.	Kollam	Karunagappally	Chavara Thekumbhagam, Panamana	1995	62.202	Mineral Sand
13.	Kerala Chemicals Co., Punnapra	Alappuzha	Cherthala	Pallipuram	1991	3.2537	Silica Sand
					Total	2,318.1049	

Source: Department of Mining and Geology, Government of Kerala 1999.

Table 3.13

Decade-wise Acquisition for Non-Hydel Power Projects (area in Hectares)

District	*1951-61*	*1961-71*	*1971-81*	*1981-91*	*1991-95*	*N.A*	*Total*
Thiruvananthapuram	0.0379	7.8305	7.4199	9.9850	1.0000	1.0312	27.3046
Kollam	0.1255	5.0594	15.7619	1.4202	0.1700	0.0000	22.5369
Pathanamthitta	0.0000	1.4176	27.8210	3.1553	0.1920	0.0000	32.5859
Alappuzha	3.8557	21.6324	9.7457	5.5018	4.1590	0.0000	44.8946
Kottayam	7.8024	6.3731	11.0952	2.6587	6.0326	1.2586	35.2206
Idukki	0.0000	19.6372	8.2536	0.2125	0.3338	0.0000	28.4371
Ernakulam	21.9544	129.6898	83.1877	83.6188	0.5335	0.0000	318.984
Thrissur	2.3897	8.1715	9.5910	1.1306	3.9878	0.0000	25.2706
Palakkad	3.9498	5.0930	11.5584	5.8150	24.9239	0.0000	51.3400
Malapuram	0.0000	0.0020	5.8900	3.7078	6.2560	0.0000	15.8558
Kozhikode	0.1831	18.3034	0.9580	13.4906	18.8508	0.0000	51.7859
Wayanad	0.0000	1.0100	0.0260	0.4195	0.3200	0.0000	1.7755
Kannur	0.0000	1.3435	3.2658	8.2433	0.4603	0.0000	13.3129
Kasargod	0.0000	0.0000	0.0000	0.0436	60.7386	0.0000	60.7822
N.A.	0.0000	0.0000	0.0000	0.0000	1.8839	0.0000	1.8839
Total	40.2985	225.5635	194.5743	139.4026	129.8422	2.2898	731.9708
Percentage	(5.51)	(30.81)	(26.58)	(19.04)	(17.73)	(0.31)	(100)

Source: Kerala Gazette (1951-95)

this, there are 25 substations of 110 KV, and 102 substations of 66 KV. On an average, 220 KV substations occupy an area of 14 ha. each and 66 KV substations require 0.2024 ha. each. Thus, the total area for 220 KV substations would be 136.15 ha. and for 66 KV substations, 20.6477 ha. Of the 25 substations of 110 KV, we have data on three which amount to 6.225 ha. According to the KSEB officials, 110 KV substations on an average occupy an area of one acre of land each. So, for the remaining 22, the total area will be 8.9049 ha. The total for 110 KV substations is 15.1302 ha. Since we have no data on the 400 KV substations, we are taking the area of this as 14 ha. (same as 220 KV). Thus, the total area under substations in Kerala would amount to 185.9247 ha.

When we add the 597.785 ha. of forest land used for transmission lines (Karunakaran 1995: 162), and 364.37 ha. of common land to the 731.9708 ha. of area acquired through Gazette notifications, the total area of land under this category comes up to 1,694.1258 ha.

The Kannur power project is a future scheme under the consideration of the state government. Negotiations are in progress. This project has acquired 71.255 ha. (176 acres) of land in Kalyassery and Pappinassery villages. This project intends to generate power using naphta (The Mathrubhoomi Daily, 1999).

Defence Establishments

Most acquisitions for defence units were during the 1961-71 decade (52.97%). Of the area acquired during this period for defence units, 74.27 per cent was from Ernakulam district. Through secondary sources, we came to gather that 1862.1458 ha. were acquired for the Cochin Naval Depot and the Ezhimala Naval Academy. Of these, 850 ha. (LAO II, Kannur) were acquired for the Ezhimala Naval Academy, Kannur and 1012.1458 ha. for the Cochin Naval Depot.

But, Gazette notifications give only 359.1733 ha. This discrepancy by source is either because a part of the land was acquired before 1951 or because some was transferred from one Government department to another. We could not collect further details due to security reasons.

Table 3.14

Decade-wise Land Acquisition for Defence Units (area in hectares)

District	*1951-61*	*1961-71*	*1971-81*	*1981-91*	*1991-95*	*N.A*	*Total*
Thiruvananthapuram	1.2597	27.6704	13.7593	5.1120	0.2914	0.0000	48.0928
Kollam	1.2667	2.8124	0.1000	1.5137	0.0000	4.6529	10.3457
Pathanamthitta	0.2966	0.0000	0.0000	31.6000	3.1121	5.0627	40.0713
Alappuzha	0.5463	6.5668	1.7321	3.7133	0.0000	11.9265	24.4850
Kottayam	10.7492	0.5162	2.7952	1.6863	0.3025	0.0000	16.0494
Idukki	0.0000	0.6151	0.0000	1.9044	0.0000	1.2141	3.7336
Ernakulam	1.7645	141.2956	0.7446	2.6822	0.0000	0.0000	146.4868
Thrissur	9.6974	1.1857	0.2064	2.1706	0.0000	0.0000	13.2601
Palakkad	0.0000	3.0752	0.1994	1.2363	0.5200	0.0000	5.0309
Malapuram	0.0000	0.7689	0.0234	0.0190	0.0000	0.0000	0.8113
Kozhikode	0.0000	3.3427	0.2023	0.1902	0.0000	0.0000	3.7352
Wayanad	0.0000	0.5261	0.0000	0.2929	0.0000	0.0000	0.8190
Kannur	0.0000	1.8655	0.0000	34.2576	7.2573	0.0000	43.3804
Kasargod	0.0000	0.0000	0.0000	2.3878	0.4838	0.0000	2.8716
Total	25.5803	190.2407	19.7627	88.7663	11.9671	22.8562	359.1733
Percentage	(7.12)	(52.97)	(5.50)	(24.71)	(3.33)	(6.36)	(100)

Source: Kerala Gazette (1951-95)

When we add the 183.6201 ha. land acquired by Gazette notifications, the total area acquired for the defence establishments would be 2,045.7659 ha.

Environment Protection

Land acquired for wildlife sanctuaries and national parks is included in this category. According to Gazette notifications, the years between 1991 and 1995 account for about 96 per cent of the acquisitions for environment protection. This may be due to the heightened awareness created in India about the importance of environment protection by the Earth Summit in Rio de Janeiro, Brazil in 1992 (Rao, 1998).

Table 3.15

Decade-wise Land Acquisition for Environment Protection
(area in hectares)

District	*1951-61*	*1961-71*	*1971-81*	*1981-91*	*1991-95*	*Total*
Thiruvananthapuram	0.0000	0.0000	0.0000	0.0090	0.0000	0.0090
Kollam	0.0000	1.4300	0.0000	0.0000	0.0000	1.4300
Pathanamthitta	0.0000	0.0000	0.0000	0.0000	0.0000	0.0000
Alappuzha	0.0000	0.0000	0.0000	0.0000	68.0149	68.0149
Kottayam	0.0000	0.0000	0.0000	0.0000	0.0000	0.0000
Idukki	0.0000	7.9009	0.0000	0.2549	2.4360	10.5918
Ernakulam	0.2711	0.0000	0.0000	0.4341	0.0000	0.7052
Thrissur	0.0000	0.3683	0.0000	0.0000	0.0000	0.3683
Palakkad	3.5775	0.0000	13.0389	0.0000	0.0000	16.6164
Malapuram	0.0000	7.4285	0.0000	0.0000	470.7756	478.2041
Kozhikode	0.0000	0.0000	0.0000	9.8401	0.0000	9.8401
Wayanad	0.0000	0.0000	0.0000	0.0000	408.1540	408.1540
Kannur	0.0000	0.0000	0.0000	0.0000	60.0000	60.0000
Kasargod	0.0000	0.8094	0.0000	0.0000	0.0000	0.8094
Total	3.8486	17.9370	13.0389	10.5381	1009.3805	1054.7431
(Percentage)	(0.36)	(1.70)	(1.24)	(0.99)	(95.69)	(100)

Source: Kerala Gazette (1951-95)

Forty seven per cent of the acquisition during this period was from Malapuram district and 40.44 per cent from Wayanad. The total presented here is very small compared to the actual area under environment protection, because most wildlife sanctuaries and National Parks are on forest or other government land. So, the area was only notified as a sanctuary without any land acquisition. Most of the sanctuaries in Kerala are notified as per the provisions of the Kerala Forest Act, 1971 and the Wildlife Protection Act of 1972. The area in Table 3.12 is over and above the area notified by the Government through these laws. Area acquired in this category was 1,054.7431 ha. which accounts for 2.04 per cent of the total land acquired for this purpose in Kerala, during the period 1951-95 through Gazette notifications.

Tourism

The extent of land acquired for tourism is very little, even though Kerala has many tourist centres. The main reason is that the tourism schemes were developed within the existing projects themselves. That is, many of the tourist places in Kerala are linked more or less to existing development projects such as dams and sanctuaries. For example, Neyyar dam in the Thiruvananthapuram district and Malampuzha dam in Palakkad district are tourist centres. Similarly, the Thekady tourist centre forms a part of the Periyar Wildlife area, in the Idukki district. This would be much clearer when one looks at the extent of land acquired for tourism. Wayanad district with the most tourism potential in Kerala does not feature in the Gazette notification on land acquisition for tourism projects. At present, Kerala has 32 tourist resorts (KTDC, Thiruvananthapuram).

The total area acquired for tourism through Gazette notifications was 147.809 ha. Of these, two-thirds were acquired during the period 1991-95, distributed in Kasargod, Thiruvananthapuram and Idukki districts. The secondary data in this regard have not provided any significant insight, as information is available only about Bakel Tourism Development Project, which has acquired an area of 59.51 ha. of land. Almost all the tourist resorts in Kerala are in the private sector without the government acquiring and transferring the land to them and it is very difficult to get these details. Hence, we limit ourselves to the Gazette data of land acquisition of 147.809 ha. for this category.

Table 3.16

Decade-wise Acquisition for Tourism (area in hectares)

District	*1951-61*	*1961-71*	*1971-81*	*1981-91*	*1991-95*	*Total*
Thiruvananthapuram	0.2023	12.1481	2.1504	2.7712	6.4912	23.7632
Kollam	0.0000	0.6291	0.3066	0.0000	0.0000	0.9356
Pathanamthitta	0.0000	0.3025	0.0000	0.0000	0.0000	0.3025
Alappuzha	0.5342	1.2710	0.0000	0.0300	0.0000	1.8352
Kottayam	0.0405	0.4269	0.0000	0.0000	0.0000	0.4673
Idukki	0.0000	1.2060	0.4047	0.0000	0.4100	2.0207
Ernakulam	10.9165	1.1455	0.0000	0.7970	0.0000	12.8559
Thrissur	0.1012	2.0376	0.0000	0.0000	0.0000	2.1388
Palakkad	0.0000	2.7762	0.0000	0.0000	0.0000	2.7762
Malapuram	0.0000	0.5099	0.0000	0.0000	0.0000	0.5099
Kozhikode	0.0809	1.9950	1.2303	3.0833	0.0000	6.3896
Wayanad	0.0000	0.0000	0.0000	0.0000	0.0000	0.0000
Kannur	0.0000	1.3315	0.0000	0.0000	0.0000	1.3314
Kasargod	0.0000	0.0000	0.0000	0.7988	91.5676	92.3664
N.A.	0.0000	0.0000	0.0000	0.0000	0.1133	0.1133
Total	11.8756	25.7791	4.0919	7.4803	98.5821	147.8090
(Percentage)	(8.03)	(17.44)	(2.77)	(5.06)	(66.87)	(100)

Source: Kerala Gazette (1951-95)

Rural/Urban Development

Land acquired for housing schemes, office complexes, stadia, commercial centres, public markets, hospitals and playgrounds were included under this category. It was during the 1971-81 decade that more land for urban/rural development was acquired (45.35%). Twenty four per cent of the land acquisition during this period was from the Ernakulam district, 22.57 per cent from Malapuram and 13.99 per cent from Thiruvananthapuram district. The Gazette data give the impression that 9.01 per cent of the total land acquisition was for this category. An area of 4674.39 ha. was acquired for this purpose.

Table 3.17

Decade-wise Acquisition for Urban/Rural Development (area in hectares)

District	1951-61	1961-71	1971-81	1981-91	1991-95	NA	Total
Thiruvananthapuram	19.1100	196.2989	296.4730	155.8277	25.5193	11.9446	705.1736
Kollam	20.7532	108.5224	56.5940	41.6534	2.7439	0.0000	230.2668
Pathanamthitta	5.7627	11.8254	10.2268	23.7634	12.0844	0.0000	63.6628
Alappuzha	11.5870	70.7650	97.2853	39.5802	1.4421	0.0000	220.6596
Kottayam	13.6314	211.6987	89.4741	36.5580	3.8959	0.0000	355.2581
Idukki	2.2414	15.5326	5.4807	7.7077	3.9983	0.0000	34.9607
Ernakulam	78.3879	338.3078	499.1092	91.2022	50.8123	2.8820	1060.7013
Thrissur	71.3824	66.0275	190.2658	52.5879	6.2894	2.6871	389.2401
Palakkad	29.4798	127.3778	89.0124	59.1919	2.1422	0.5622	307.7662
Malapuram	2.6588	66.0918	478.4924	35.2496	3.8887	0.6190	587.0002
Kozhikode	19.7807	149.6440	188.4541	53.4131	13.7790	0.0000	425.0709
Wayanad	0.0000	18.4782	29.8388	6.2471	6.7899	1.6950	63.0489
Kannur	9.1985	77.0739	74.5138	29.6732	2.6580	0.0000	193.1173
Kasargod	0.0445	7.3896	14.1927	3.5895	1.5792	0.0000	26.7955
NA	0.0000	2.5334	0.2185	1.2713	7.6464	0.0000	11.6696
Total	284.0183	1467.5668	2119.6315	637.5162	145.2691	20.3899	4674.3917
Percentage	(6.07)	(31.39)	(45.35)	(13.64)	(3.107)	(0.44)	(100)

Source: Kerala Gazette (1951-95).

Since we have no data from other sources, we depend fully on Gazette data for land acquisition for urban/rural development which is 4,674.3917 ha.

Farms and Fisheries

Under farms and fisheries, we have included central and state farms, fisheries, plantations, dairy farms and agricultural farms of all categories. Palakkad district stands first in the extent of land acquired for this category in Kerala, with an area of 338.698 ha., followed by Kannur district with 179.71 ha. and Thiruvananthapuram district (174.8955 ha.).

Table 3.18

Decade-wise Acquisition for Farms and Fisheries (area in hectares)

District	*1951-61*	*1961-71*	*1971-81*	*1981-91*	*1991-95*	*Total*
Thiruvananthapuram	7.2035	90.9792	65.1686	2.8738	8.6704	174.8955
Kollam	8.5369	14.6111	1.6187	10.6343	4.1939	39.5949
Pathanamthitta	9.3569	4.3267	1.0614	0.9526	0.0000	15.6975
Alappuzha	1.0724	69.1290	0.0800	3.0971	0.2024	73.5809
Kottayam	33.4916	30.6331	31.7536	0.3886	0.0000	96.2669
Idukki	4.9696	0.4125	9.7700	6.6975	0.0000	21.8496
Ernakulam	0.3480	53.7131	31.2672	0.3389	4.2441	89.9114
Thrissur	3.9197	49.6017	28.6006	7.4389	0.0000	89.5609
Palakkad	15.2366	263.0631	55.5730	4.8261	0.0000	338.6988
Malapuram	46.7053	73.3056	13.6832	0.0000	0.0000	133.6940
Kozhikode	5.1234	18.9558	18.2752	0.0000	2.4594	44.8138
Wayanad	0.1293	0.1538	0.0000	0.0000	0.0000	0.2831
Kannur	29.8297	142.9225	4.6459	2.3136	0.0000	179.7117
Kasargod	0.0000	44.8510	4.0792	0.0000	0.0000	48.9302
Total	165.9229	856.6580	265.5766	39.5615	19.7702	1347.4891
Percentage	(12.31)	(63.57)	(19.71)	(2.94)	(1.47)	(100)

Source: Kerala Gazette (1951-95)

Most of the acquisitions for farms and fisheries were during the 1961-71 period (63.57%). Thirty one per cent of the acquisitions during this period were from Palakkad district, 16.8 per cent from

Kannur and 10.62 per cent from Thiruvananthapuram. Only 2.59 per cent of the total area acquired was for farms and fisheries which constitutes an area of 1,347.49 ha. The emphasis given to agriculture by the governments concerned in their respective Five Year Plans explains the rationale for such projects.

There are 33 State Seed Farms in Kerala occupying an area of 355.017 ha. In addition, there are 10 special farms, 10 district agriculture farms and eight coconut nurseries. The area of land used by Special Farms is 1,120.192 ha., district agriculture farms 576.805 ha., and by coconut nurseries 30.994 ha. Thus, the total area under agricultural farms amounts to 2,052.014 ha. of which, 372.55 ha. were taken over before 1951. Hence, the total area acquired during the 1951-95 period is 1,679.464 ha. The Gazette gives the information only on 1,347.4891 ha. of private land. So, the remaining 331.9749 ha. should be common land.

When we include the 11,709.754 ha. of forest land under the Plantations Corporation of Kerala, 3,645.640 ha. under Oil Palm India Ltd., 2,265.218 ha. under State Farming Corporation, 121.340 ha. of Tropical Botanical Gardens at Palode, 299.019 ha. under Rubber Board at Kottayam, 39.15 ha. occupied by the Indo-Swiss project at Mattuppetty, and 116.24 ha. under the Coffee Board, the total of forest land under farms comes to 18,197.361 ha. (Karunakaran 1995:162). Hence, the total area under farms and fisheries works out to 19,875.825 ha.

Transport

Within this section we have included land acquisition for roads, railways, airports and harbours. An area of 5,112.406 ha. was acquired for transport through Gazette notifications.

A very large area of land was acquired in this category from Ernakulam district i.e., 1,051.19 ha. followed by Kozhikode with an area of 534.94 ha. Of the acquisitions for the category of transport, 42.78 per cent was during the 1961-71 period. Ernakulam is the district, from which the largest area of land was acquired for this purpose during this period (16.16%) followed by Alappuzha (12.22%) and Kozhikode (12.01%).

Table 3.19

Decade-wise Acquisition for Transport (area in hectares)

District	*1951-61*	*1961-71*	*1971-81*	*1981-91*	*1991-95*	*NA*	*Total*
Thiruvananthapuram	23.1983	105.9216	118.7445	113.5944	26.7241	0.0683	388.2512
Kollam	23.1272	183.3784	176.9284	11.2429	6.8429	0.4735	401.9933
Pathanamthitta	56.6485	75.9100	97.1126	23.8349	18.7036	0.0000	272.2096
Alappuzha	114.6799	267.2453	111.3647	24.6398	3.4046	1.8275	523.1618
Kottayam	59.1681	71.5657	55.9530	25.8489	36.3647	0.3402	249.2407
Idukki	6.1063	52.9007	26.0870	31.5781	0.2681	0.0081	116.9482
Ernakulam	188.7421	353.4822	138.9627	58.5137	309.3701	2.1223	1051.1931
Thrissur	81.0156	141.1802	48.8606	20.8665	4.8516	7.2215	303.9959
Palakkad	56.1529	204.6758	143.7301	35.1479	1.6548	1.1596	442.5211
Malapuram	61.8622	261.3723	69.4205	29.6911	12.3151	3.8956	438.5568
Kozhikode	44.6425	262.6329	151.6202	48.2224	27.5195	0.2615	534.8990
Wayanad	0.1336	12.8041	9.6711	19.5706	16.1595	0.0000	58.3388
Kannur	28.9468	97.5590	31.4990	28.5916	3.6293	0.9888	191.2145
Kasargod	9.0124	88.3064	11.4158	11.4075	2.2780	0.0000	122.4201
NA	6.1786	8.6362	1.5000	0.0000	0.0000	1.1468	17.4616
Total	759.6151	2187.5708	1192.8701	482.7503	470.0858	19.5137	5112.4057
Percentage	(14.85)	(42.78)	(23.33)	(9.44)	(9.19)	(0.38)	(100)

Source: Kerala Gazette (1951-95)

An area of 932.56 ha. was acquired for the three airports in Kerala. Of these, 222.67 ha. were acquired for the Thiruvananthapuram airport. As per the data available, Karipur airport in the Kozhikode district acquired 45.96 ha. But, this is far below the requirement for an airport. An area of 487.22 ha. was acquired for the Nedumbassery airport in the Ernakulam district.

In the initial stages, the land for most of the village roads was gifted by the local people. Gradually these roads were taken over by the PWD, which started the expansion process for which more land was acquired. No official records provide any estimate of the area of land donated by the people. Hence, the data presented here include both acquired and donated land. Therefore, one may count 50 per cent of the total area under the roads to estimate the area acquired for roads during the study period. The total length of roads in Kerala is 23,318.951 kms. This includes national highways, state highways, major district roads and village roads. The area under roads works out to 40,183.2685 ha. (see Table 3.20).

Table 3.20

Details of Land Use for Roads in Kerala

Sl. No	*Category*	*Dimension*		*Area (Ha.)*
		Length	*Width*	
1	National Highway	1047.20 km	0.03 km	3142
2	State Highway	3769.00 km	0.03 km	11306.9
3	District Roads	5124.00 km	0.015 km	7686
4	District Roads other categories	10994.14 km	0.008 km	15741.2
5	Village Roads	2884.691 km	0.008 km	2307
	Total			40183.26

Source: Office of the Chief Engineer-PWD, Thiruvananthapuram.

For railways, land is acquired mainly by notifying only in newspapers and not in the Gazette. So we present the area under railways through extrapolation. Of the present 1,320 kms of railway lines in Kerala (including 267 kms of double lines), 678 kms were built prior to Independence, and 642 kms after (Prasad, 1999). There were no new lines except the restoration of the 67 km of Shornur-Nilambur line between Independence (1947) and the Reorganisation of the States (1956). The average area of land required to construct one km of rail track is estimated to be 8.0972 ha. (Fernandes and Asif, 1997: 83). Hence, the area under railway lines for the period after 1956 works out to 5,198.4024 ha. We have no reliable data to say how much of it were acquired from private parties.

There are eight harbours in Kerala, which together acquired 96.6318 ha. Vizhinjam harbour (40.16 ha.), Mattanchery fishing harbour (8.0936 ha.), and Azheekode fishing harbour (8.0412 ha.) (Kerala Gazette). Taking the average area of 8.0674 ha. per harbour, the total area for the remaining five would be 40.337 ha. If we add up all these, the total for transport would come up to 46405.7566 ha.

The proposed Kannur airport requires an area of 517.23 ha. (Madhyamam Weekly, 1998). The total area of land proposed to be acquired for the expansion of Thiruvananthapuram airport is 28.34 ha. For the expansion of the Vizhinjam harbour, 202.4292 ha. of land is required. The proposed Kerala State Road Transport Project of PWD requires an area of 5.43 ha. (Debnath, 2001). Hence, the total area for the proposed projects in the category of transport would be 753.4292 ha.

Educational Institutions

Since Kerala is an educationally forward state, there are many institutions both in the private and Government sectors. We have included research centres, university campuses, colleges and schools and professional institutions like engineering colleges, polytechnics and medical colleges in this category.

The majority of the area acquired for this category through Gazette is from Thiruvananthapuram district, 1,245.377 ha. constituting 31.34 per cent of the total acquisition. The actual area under educational institutions in Kerala is likely to be higher, because a good number of them are in the private sector.

About 70 per cent of the acquisition for educational institutions was during 1961-71 decade. Nearly thirty eight per

Table 3.21

Decade-wise Acquisition for Educational Institution (area in hectares)

District	*1951-61*	*1961-71*	*1971-81*	*1981-91*	*1991-95*	*NA*	*Total*
Thiruvananthapuram	72.4579	1067.8699	81.6391	16.6041	6.1302	0.6809	1245.3821
Kollam	27.4973	56.1726	116.7990	10.8179	0.1100	0.1214	211.5181
Pathanamthitta	3.5354	72.9058	4.8376	8.5771	0.0000	0.0000	89.8559
Alappuzha	18.3998	238.1052	7.4138	9.4703	23.5386	0.3976	297.3253
Kottayam	27.7836	171.8430	29.9444	9.6107	35.5185	0.0000	274.7002
Idukki	0.9065	6.6549	21.1451	4.5341	3.8866	0.0000	37.1273
Ernakulam	8.1806	81.7827	52.6653	29.9713	33.1483	0.0000	205.7481
Thrissur	41.6451	265.3670	57.9582	48.0823	0.0000	0.0000	413.0527
Palakkad	6.7745	179.1822	42.5923	32.3744	0.0000	0.0648	260.9882
Malapuram	1.9668	412.7691	72.9667	13.6349	9.8574	0.0000	511.1949
Kozhikode	36.9887	202.3443	49.7067	11.5880	1.8296	1.1533	303.6105
Wayanad	8.0938	4.7494	3.6105	13.2753	0.4208	0.0000	30.1497
Kannur	16.3819	32.1452	9.3393	7.8102	0.0810	0.0000	65.7576
Kasargod	16.4102	1.9370	0.6595	0.5665	0.4816	0.2509	20.3057
NA	0.5990	5.8051	0.0000	0.4047	0.0000	0.0000	6.8087
Total	287.6210	2799.6334	551.2775	217.3217	115.0026	2.6689	3,973.5251
Percentage	(7.23)	(70.46)	(13.87)	(5.46)	(2.89)	(0.06)	(100)

Source: Kerala Gazette (1951-95)

cent of the area acquired during this period was from Thiruvananthapuram district, 9.48 per cent from Thrissur and 8.50 from Alappuzha districts. A total area of 3,973.525 ha. was acquired for educational institutions in Kerala. This is 7.66 per cent of the total land acquired for development projects.

Table 3.22

Land Acquisition for Universities in Kerala

	Name of University	*Year*	*Location*	*Area in ha.*	*Source*
1.	University of Kerala	1961, 1962	Kariyavattom	209.2733	Kerala Gazette
2.	Sanskrit university	1963	Kalady	25.10	Office of the University, Kalady
3.	Mahathma Gandhi University	1989	Priyadarshini Hills	42.00	LAO-General, Kottayam
4.	Cochin University of Science and Technology	1965	Kalamassery	49.04	Office of the University, Kalamassery
5.	Calicut University	1964, 1970, 1972	Thenhippalam	272.7169	Kerala Gazette
6.	Agricultural University	1970	Vellanikara	379.6	Collectorate, Thrissur
	Total			977.7302	

Most of the schools and colleges in Kerala under private management, do not involve any acquisition of land. These agencies purchase land from individuals. The minimum area required for an Arts and Science College is 3.24 ha., Law College -- 2.83, Medical College -- 60.73 ha., Dental College, Nursing College, Homeo College and Pharmacy College -- 10.12 ha. each, Ayurveda College, Engineering College, and Physical Education College -- 20.24 ha. each, Training College -- 2.02 ha., Polytechnic -- 4.655 ha., Technical High School and High School -- 1.215 ha. each, UP School and LP School -- 0.4049 ha. each (University Statute, 1977).

Since the formation of the State was in 1956, the data on educational institutions prior to November 1956 was not available.

The statistics in 1961 are available and we depend on them for extrapolation. In 1961-62, there were 629 high schools, 1985 UP schools, and 6745 LP schools. The corresponding numbers in 1998-99 were 2585, 2966 and 6755 respectively. The number of high schools started after 1961 was 1956 and the number of UP schools 981 and LP schools 10.

The area under Arts and Science colleges is 686.88 ha., Dental Colleges -- 20.14 ha., Nursing College -- 30.36 ha., Homeo Colleges -- 40.48 ha., Ayurveda Colleges -- 101.2 ha., Training Colleges -- 38.38 ha., Polytechnics -- 176.89, Technical High Schools -- 47.385, High Schools -- 2372.895 ha., UPS and LPS -- 401.2559 ha. These work out to a total of 3,915.8659 ha.

Thus, the total area occupied by the universities in Kerala comes up to 977.7302 ha.

Table 3.23

Land Acquisition for Professional Colleges in Kerala

Institution	*Year*	*Location*	*Area (in ha.)*
Medical College			
1. Alappuzha	1963, 1970, 1988, 1989, 1993	Punnapra	126.6217
2. Kottayam	1961, 1962	Athirampuzha	109.1854
3. Thrissur	1984	Thrissur	18.9488
4. Kozhikode	1958, 1961	Chevayur	11.481
Total Area for Medical Colleges			266.2369
Engineering College			
1. Thiruvananthapuram	1964	Monvila	23.4558
2. Thrissur	1959, 1960	Viyyur	10.7021
3. NSS Engineering College	1963, 1964, 1965	Akathethara	130.0671
4. Regional Engineering College	1961	Kozhikode	110.9660
Total Area for Engineering Colleges			275.191
Veterinary College			
1. Thrissur	1956	Ollurkara	11.4365
Agriculture College			
1. Thiruvananthapuram	1959	Vellayani	16.6894
Total			569.5538

Source: Kerala Gazette, 1951-95.

There is only one medical college in the co-operative sector, which is at Pariyaram in Kannur. The land occupied by this institution was an estate. The land for Thiruvananthapuram medical college was acquired prior to the present study period. Out of the 21 engineering colleges, we have data on four. They occupied an area of 275.191 ha. Taking the minimum area required for an engineering college as 20.24 (University of Kerala, Document), the remaining 17 engineering colleges might have used 344.8 ha. of land. Thus, the total area used by 21 engineering colleges adds up to 619.271 ha. and the total area acquired by all the professional colleges would come up to 914.3538 ha.

Of these, the land occupied by TBGRI is on lease from the forest department. CESS acquired and reused mining land. CDS purchased land from a private party.

Table 3.24

Land Acquisition for Major Research Institutes in Kerala

	Name of Institute	*Year*	*Location*	*Area (in ha.)*	*Source*
1.	Centre Tuber Crops Research Institute (CTCRI)	1961, 1974	Sreekaryam	58.9598	Kerala Gazette
2.	Central Plantations Crops Research Institute (CPCRI).	NA	Kasargod	121.96	Karunakaran, 1995
3.	Kerala Forest Research Institute (KFRI)	NA	Peechi	28.174	Karunakaran, 1995
4.	Centre for Development Studies (CDS)	1968	Ulloor	4.0486	Primary data
5.	Centre For Water Resource Development and Management (CWRDM)	1978	Kozhikode	63.62	Registrar, CWRDM.
6.	Coconut Research Station	NA	Pilicode	16.19	RDO, Kasargod
7.	Centre for Earth Sciences Studies (CESS), Akulam	NA	Akulam	18.00	
8.	Tropical Botanical Gardens Research Institute (TBGRI), Thiruvananthapuram	NA	Palode	121.340	Karunakaran, 1995
	Total			432.2924	

Thus, land acquired for universities (977.7302 ha.), major professional colleges (914.3538 ha.), and research institutes (432.2924 ha.) total up to 2,324.3764 ha.

CPCRI at Kasargod, KFRI at Peechi and VSSC at Valiayamala occupy 121.96 ha., 28.174 ha., and 115.4 ha. of forest land, respectively. So the total forest land under this category will be 265.534 ha. Cochin University occupies 44.99 ha. of common land. Therefore, the total land used for educational institutions adds up to 5,807.9499 ha.

Social/Welfare Centres

Land acquisition for rehabilitation centres, mother and child centres, old age homes and various other social welfare institutions is included in this category. Only 452.2146 ha. were acquired for this category through the Gazette. Much of the acquisition for this category was done during the 1961-71 decade. Thiruvananthapuram stands first among the districts in the extent of the land acquired for social welfare. Ten per cent of the acquisitions during this period were from Malapuram district. Since no supporting data are available regarding land acquisition for this category, we depend fully on the Gazette for calculating the area of land acquired for this purpose.

Miscellaneous Schemes

Land acquisition for other social needs such as post offices, temple development, burial grounds, drainage schemes and all other purposes, which are not included in the listed categories are brought together in Table 3.26.

The largest portion of the land for miscellaneous category was acquired during the decade 1961-71. Of this, 33.91 per cent was from Palakkad district, 13.71 from Malapuram and 9.27 from Ernakulam district. The total area acquired in the miscellaneous category was 796.99 ha. This constitutes only 1.15 per cent of the total land acquisition covered by the present study.

Table 3.25

Decade-wise Acquisition for Social Welfare (area in hectares)

District	*1951-61*	*1961-71*	*1971-81*	*1981-91*	*1991-95*	*NA*	*Total*
Thiruvananthapuram	20.3901	39.7770	18.7332	1.7462	0.1456	0.0000	80.7921
Kollam	17.4418	4.2421	7.3309	0.0121	15.2470	0.0000	44.2739
Pathanamthitta	0.1416	5.9096	0.3637	0.2820	0.0000	0.0000	6.6970
Alappuzha	8.6523	11.6450	4.2617	0.0000	0.0000	0.0000	24.5590
Kottayam	20.3041	11.5312	1.0564	0.0000	0.0000	0.0405	32.9322
Idukki	0.6070	0.0607	0.0000	4.0468	0.0000	0.0000	4.7145
Ernakulam	35.4350	17.2415	8.7077	3.5416	0.0000	0.1215	65.0473
Thrissur	35.2973	2.8308	13.3495	2.4051	0.0000	0.0405	53.9231
Palakkad	8.4944	14.2325	2.5819	0.7698	0.0000	0.0000	26.0786
Malapuram	1.8009	44.4971	2.8301	0.0000	0.0000	0.0000	49.1281
Kozhikode	0.0567	22.0730	0.8209	0.1214	0.0000	0.0000	23.0720
Wayanad	0.0000	0.0000	0.0000	0.0000	0.0000	0.0000	0.0000
Kannur	9.2876	22.6642	5.8534	1.2285	0.0405	0.0000	39.0742
Kasargod	0.0000	1.2141	0.3645	0.0000	0.0000	0.0000	1.5786
NA	0.3035	0.0000	0.0405	0.0000	0.0000	0.0000	0.3440
Total	158.2124	197.9188	66.2943	14.1536	15.4331	0.2025	452.2146
Percentage	(34.99)	(43.77)	(14.66)	(3.13)	(3.41)	(0.00)	(100)

Source: Kerala Gazette (1951-95).

Table 3.26

Decade-wise Acquisition for Miscellaneous Projects (area in Hectares)

District	*1951-61*	*1961-71*	*1971-81*	*1981-91*	*1991-95*	*NA*	*Total*
Thiruvananthapuram	24.0138	20.7187	38.5020	16.5985	23.7588	0.3663	123.9581
Kollam	1.2946	3.2323	2.6890	9.2011	27.0070	0.0000	43.4239
Pathanamthitta	0.0657	8.7424	0.7020	1.8683	0.0000	0.2024	11.5808
Alappuzha	2.6408	8.0194	2.8669	0.4322	0.0000	0.0000	13.9593
Kottayam	0.5300	7.7333	4.0909	0.4126	0.9027	0.0000	13.6694
Idukki	1.0954	2.4129	0.3427	0.6890	32.1092	0.0000	36.6492
Ernakulam	17.7985	25.7950	31.1673	13.4028	0.0000	0.5710	88.7345
Thrissur	49.6521	15.5913	11.6361	10.2463	4.9726	0.2243	92.3227
Palakkad	5.8742	94.3941	1.7756	4.4384	1.6188	0.0000	108.1001
Malapuram	0.2024	38.1653	5.3619	7.1622	0.0000	0.0000	50.8917
Kozhikode	7.0376	24.2720	129.1767	1.2315	0.0000	0.0000	161.7177
Wayanad	0.5423	5.3320	0.0000	0.2600	4.3796	0.0000	10.5139
Kannur	1.5941	23.1723	2.7750	2.1077	0.0810	0.0000	29.7301
Kasargod	0.0000	0.7746	0.3885	0.1100	10.4711	0.0000	11.7442
Total	112.3413	278.3554	231.4744	68.1606	105.3007	1.3640	796.9964
Percentage	(14.10)	(34.93)	(29.04)	(8.55)	(13.21)	(0.17)	(100.00)

Source: Kerala Gazette (1951-95)

Type of Land Acquired

Private Land Acquired

The following table (3.27) gives the district-wise distribution of projects with respective area acquired for development purposes during the last five decades. It comes to 51,862.8383 hectares which constitutes 1.33 per cent of the total geographical area of Kerala. But, this is based only on the information from the Gazette. We have also to look into other projects about which data were not available in the Gazette. For instance, we got data on only a portion of the land acquired for the railways, because it is published mostly in newspapers (Assistant Engineer, Railways). Similarly, the land acquired through the application of the urgency clause would not be notified in Gazette.

Most of the acquisition was made in the decade 1961-71. The first democratic state government of reconstituted Kerala was formed in 1957, with a communist ministry. This Government had influenced certain social and legislative reforms in the state. But, the ministry was dismissed in 1959 under pressure from various communities and political parties. Their opposition took the form of agitations against the educational policy of the ministry. The subsequent election and formation of ministries had to address the development needs of the state as enunciated by the Communist government. This period of 1961-71 also coincided with the Third and Fourth Five Year Plans of the country (Mrityunjay, 1981).

We shall first analyse the extent of private land acquired through the Gazette. Going by the extent of private land acquired for development purpose through the Gazette during the period under study from each of the 14 districts of Kerala, it becomes evident that the largest area acquired from one single district was 12,316.75 ha. in Kozhikode. Hence, it may appear that Kozhikode district had the highest share of development projects over the 45 years since 1951. Some of the schemes undertaken during this period are Kutiadi irrigation, Kuttiady hydel scheme, Rayons, Industrial Growth Centre, Medical College, and Nallalam Diesel

Table 3.27

Private Land Acquired (in Hectares) through Gazette - District and Category-wise

District	*Thiruvananthapuram*	*Kollam*	*Pathanamthitta*	*Alappuzha*	*Kottayam*	*Idukki*	*Ernakulam*	*Total*
Category								
Water resources	1025.7672	2312.0051	599.1969	809.6314	89.4138	973.6858	2815.7443	8625.4445
Industries	414.1662	176.4631	46.9386	266.0255	388.319	20.8313	1745.4866	3058.2303
Non-hydel power	27.3045	22.5369	32.5858	44.8945	35.2286	28.437	318.9841	509.9714
Mine	2.2660	53.8920	3.7595	0.2300	0.1396	0.0000	0.0161	60.3032
Defence	48.0927	10.3457	40.0713	24.4850	16.0494	3.7336	146.4868	289.2645
Environment protection	0.0090	1.4300	0.0000	68.0149	0.0000	10.5917	0.7052	80.7508
Tourism	23.7632	0.9356	0.3025	1.8352	0.4673	2.0206	12.8589	42.1833
Urban Development	705.1735	230.2668	63.6628	220.6596	355.2581	34.9607	1060.7012	2670.6827
Farms & fisheries	174.8954	39.5949	15.6975	73.5808	96.2669	21.8495	89.9113	511.7963
Transport	388.2512	401.9932	272.2096	523.1617	249.2406	116.9482	1051.1930	3002.9975
Educational Institutions	1245.3821	211.5181	89.8558	297.3253	274.7002	37.1272	205.7481	2361.6568
Social welfare centres	80.7920	44.2739	6.6970	24.5590	32.9322	4.7145	65.0473	259.0159
Others	123.9581	43.4238	11.5807	13.9592	13.6694	36.6492	88.7345	331.9749
Not available	0.0000	0.5220	0.0855	2.2660	0.4194	1.4123	1.1141	5.8193
Total	4259.8215	3549.2015	1182.6441	2370.6285	1552.0971	1292.9622	7602.7323	21,810.0914
	(8.21)	(6.84)	(2.28)	(4.57)	(2.99)	(2.49)	(14.66)	(42.05)

Contd...

Contd...

District / Category	Thrissur	Palakkad	Malapuram	Kozhikode	Wayanad	Kannur	Kasargod	NA	Total	Grand total
Water resources	1628.6450	4522.7987	452.5038	10386.1085	946.0805	1373.9258	31.9755	28.4953	19370.5331	27995.9782 (53.98)
Industries	204.9439	1094.2366	156.2318	355.3355	0.4937	172.0259	20.0102	0.0000	2003.2776	5061.5085 (9.75)
Non-hydel power	25.2706	51.3400	15.8558	51.7859	1.7755	13.3129	60.7822	1.8839	222.0068	731.9707 (1.41)
Mine	26.9734	5.9230	0.000	7.2800	0.0243	0.000	7.1267	0.000	47.3274	107.6308 (0.21)
Defence	13.2601	5.0308	0.8113	3.7352	0.8190	43.3804	2.8716	0.000	69.9084	359.1732 (0.69)
Environment protection	0.3682	16.6163	478.2040	9.8401	408.1540	60.000	0.8093	0.0000	973.9919	1054.7431 (2.03)
Tourism	2.1387	2.7761	0.5098	6.3895	0.0000	1.3314	92.3664	0.1133	105.6252	147.8898 (0.28)
Urban Development	389.2401	307.7661	587.0002	425.0708	63.0489	193.1172	26.7955	11.6696	2003.7084	4674.3916 (9.01)
Farms & fisheries	89.5609	338.6987	133.6940	44.8137	0.2831	179.7116	48.9302	0.0000	835.6922	1347.4891 (2.59)
Transport	303.9959	442.5211	438.5567	534.8990	58.3387	191.2144	122.4200	17.4616	2109.4074	5112.4057 (9.86)
Educational Institutions	413.0526	260.9882	511.1948	303.6105	30.1497	65.7575	20.3056	6.8087	1611.8676	3973.5250 (7.66)
Social welfare centres	53.9231	26.0785	49.1288	23.0719	0.0000	39.0742	1.5785	0.3440	193.199	452.2146 (0.87)
Others	92.3226	108.1009	50.8916	161.7176	10.5138	29.7300	11.7441	0.0000	465.0206	796.9963 (1.15)
Not available	1.5729	4.1732	31.1776	3.0898	0.0000	1.1536	0.0000	0.0096	41.1767	46.9964 (0.09)
Total	3245.2685	7187.049	2905.7600	12316.7485	1519.684	2363.733	447.7163	66.7860	30,052.7423	51,862.8383
	(6.25)	(13.86)	(5.60)	(23.75)	(2.93)	(4.56)	(0.86)	(0.128)	(57.94)	(100)

Source: Kerala Gazette, 1951-1995.

Power Plant. Conversely, the lowest area acquired during the same period was from Pathanamthitta district (1,182.64 ha.).

Forest and Common Land

About 91 per cent of the land used by farms was forest. Another major category which used the forest land was water resource projects (43%). Most of the dams in Kerala are constructed in the forest area. Forest land was also used for power transmission lines, two industries and three research institutes.

We do not have the full details of common land acquired for development projects. Available data show that farms and fisheries are the major categories occupying common land. The main acquisition of common land was the 364.37 ha. for NTPC project at Kayamkulam. Water resources and industries are the other categories which acquired common land, though in small plots.

Magnitude of Land Acquisition in Kerala

We have so far analysed the extent of land acquired for different categories of projects. Now, we shall attempt to present the total picture of the land acquired for all categories. What we present is not the exact figures, but a conservative estimate. Since it was difficult to collect the exact data on the acquisition of land for many projects, we depended on extrapolation through which we arrived at this conservative estimate. This includes all the land currently occupied by the projects.

Since the year and type of land for this is not available, we have not included in the table the 2,31,544 ha. of area under sanctuaries and parks.

Data for this table come from a variety of sources. Gazette gave primarily data on private land. Other secondary sources have not given us full details of common land acquired. Hence, we have restricted ourselves to the available data.

The total area of land acquired/used for development projects in Kerala during the period 1951-95 works out to 1,55,263.5200 ha. which is 4.00 per cent of the total geographical area of the state.

Table 3.28

Type of Land Acquired for a Representative Set of Projects

Name of Project	Private	Common	Forest	Total	Source
Water Resources					
1. Chulliar Dam	NA	NA	NA	165	Project report, Revamping and Consolidation Programme, Gayathri Project Stage I& II, 1998
2. Idukki Hydro Electric Project	15.58	00	5463.84	5479.43	Revenue divisional office, File no. 766/78, Idukki.
3. Kallada Irrigation Project	284.68	00	2144.32	2429	Chief engineer, KIP, Kottarakara, 1998.
4. Karappuzha Irrigation Project	809.7165	NA	NA	1174	Report by Kayal, Nellarachal.
5. Kutiadi Irrigation Project	404.86	NA	NA	1052.63	Project report, Kutiadi irrigation, 1998
6. Kutiadi Augmentation (Banasurusager)	7.69	00	1277.00	1284.69	Project report, PWD, irrigation.
7. Meenkara Irrigation	NA	NA	NA	250	Office of the Asst. Exe. Engineer, Meenkara Irrigation Project.
8. Muvattupuzha Valley Irrigation Project	713.81	00	1.79	715.40	Office of the Exe. Engr., MVIP, Thodupuzha.
9. Pothundy Dam	NA	NA	NA	982.82	Project report from Irrigation office, Nemmara, 1967.
10. Neriamangalam Hydro Electric (HE)	00	64.80	32.06	96.86	Office of the Asst. Exe. Engr., Civil Division, Kallarkuty, Adimali.
11. Sengulam	00	00	29.1	29.1	Do
12. Panniar HE (Ponmudi, Anayirangal Dam)	00	5	764.4	769.40	Do
13. Idamalayar HE	00	00	2930	2930	Do
14. Poringalkuth HE	00	00	285	285	Do
15. Sholayar	00	00	870.5	870.5	Do
16. Sabarigiri	00	00	1951	1951	Do

Contd...

Contd...

Name of Project	Private	Common	Forest	Total	Source
17. Lower Periyar	00	00	44.5	44.5	Do
18. Chaliyar river valley (proposed)	545	245	640	1430	Office of the Superintending Engr., Information and Planning, Kozhikode.
19. Kanjirappuzha irrigation	1160	35	00	1195	Office of the Exe. Engr, Siruvani, Palakkad.
Total	3,941.34	349.8	17,989.51	24,690.33	
Industrial Projects					
1. Apparel Park At Menamkulam	31.34	13.73	00	45.07	Office of the KINFRA, Oral Information from Project Consultant, Vellayambalam
2. SIKL, Cherthala	NA	NA	00	48	Office of the Personnel Manager, SIKL, Cherthala
3. Chemical Industrial Estate & Development, Aroor	6.39	00	00	6.39	District Industries Center, Alappuzha.
4. Cochin Refineries Limited	141.73	00	00	141.73	LAO, Vytila, Cochin.
5. Coir Park 1 & 2, Cherthala	16.78	00	00	16.78	District Industries Center (DIC), Alappuzha.
6. Conventional Industrial Estate, Thekkil	00	11.36	00	11.36	DIC, Kasargod
7. Development Area, Ananthapuram.	00	42.13	00	42.13	DIC, Kasargod
8. Development Area,Urathamchal	00	43.72	00	43.72	DIC, Kasargod
9. Development Area and Development Plot, Anthur	24.01	00	00	24.01	DIC, Kannur.
10. English Indian Clays Ltd.	3.66	NA	00	78.15	Office of the Draftsman, English Indian Clays Ltd. Kochuveli.
11. Automobile Tyre Factory Appollo, Perambra	13.09	00	00	13.09	Collectorate, File No. 1477/75, Thrissur.

Contd...

Contd...

Name of Project	Private	Common	Forest	Total	Source
12. Export Promotion Industrial Park, Kakkanad	72.87	00	00	72.87	Office of the Asst. Engineer, KINFRA, Kakanad
13. Hindustan News Print Mill, Velloore	277.34	00	00	277.34	Personnel Officer, Hindustan Newsprint Mill, Velloore.
14. Hindustan Petroleum Corporation Ltd., Kanjikode	NA	NA	NA	9.29	LAO, LA register and Award File, 1990.
15. Indian Oil Corporation Ltd., Parippally	28.13	00	00	28.13	LA General, File no. LA_2-9295/92, Civil Station, Kollam.
16. Indian Telephone Industries Ltd., Pudussery	NA	NA	NA	40.34	LAO, LA and Award file, Kottaikokam, 1990.
17. Industrial Development Area, Pudussery	54.31	00	00	54.31	Manager, DIC, Palakkad.
18. Industrial Estate-Pappanamcode	NA	NA	00	6.89	Deputy General Manager, SIDCO, Thiruvananthapuram.
19. Industrial Growth Center., Kannur	105	00	00	105	LAO, Award Register, Thalassery.
20. Instrumentation Ltd., Pudussery	00	00	00	242.91	Administrative Office, Pudussery.
21. Kanjikode Industrial Township	299.59	00	00	299.59	LAO, Oral information from Clerk, Palakkad
22. Kerala Ceramics Company Ltd., Madayi.	NA	NA	00	102.82	Oral Information from a villager.
23. Malabar Cement, Walayar	00	00	339	339	Civil Engineer, Malabar Cements Ltd.
24. Mavoor Gwaliyor Rayons	55.15	00	00	55.15	Collectorate, Award No. 1/60, 1/64, 25/67, Kozhikode
25. Peruman Special Refractries	12.15	00	00	12.15	LAO- General, File No. A5-1015/89, Civil Station, Kollam.
26. Development Areas and Dev. Plots, Chengannur	6.28	00	00	6.28	DIC, Alappuzha.
27. Development Areas and Dev. Plots, Punnapra	23.19	00	00	23.19	DIC, Alappuzha.
28. Development Areas and Dev. Plots, Kottakadavu	19.09	00	00	19.09	DIC, Alappuzha.
29. Sidco, Nallavattanam.	3.44	00	00	3.44	Land Manager, SIDCO

Contd...

Contd...

Name of Project	*Private*	*Common*	*Forest*	*Total*	*Source*
30. Steel Complex, Chevayur	17.80	00	00	17.80	Works Manager, Steel Complex.
31. Sugar Factory, Menompara	NA	NA	NA	44.53	Manager, Administrative Office.
32. Technopark, Thiruvananthapuram	32.26	60.73?	00	92.99	Special Tahsildar, Addl. LA Unit, File no. A_2/379/92. Thiruvananthapuram AND
33. Traco Cables Company Ltd., Irumpanam	NA	NA	00	14.57	Personnel Manager, TRACO, Cochin.
34. FACT, Udyogamandal Division	20.2429	00	00	307.6923**	Estate Manager, FACT, Udyogamandal Division, Cochin.
35. FACT, Cochin Division	636.4372	00	00	636.4372	Estate Manager, File No.141-2, FACT, Cochin Division.
36. HMT Ltd., Kalamassery	316.1943	00	00	316.1943	Land Manager, HMT Ltd.
37. Travancore Titanium Products Ltd., Thiruvananthapuram.	NA	NA	00	30.47	Works Manager, Travancore Titanium Products Ltd.
38. Hindustan Latex Ltd., Peroorkada	NA	NA	NA	4.66	Primary data
Total	2216.41	171.67	339	3341.45	
Non-hydel power projects					
1. 120 Mega Watt Diesel Generator Power Plant, Nallalam.	10.85	00	00	10.85	Office of Exe. Engr.-thermal, Vydhuthi Bhavan, Pattom.
2. 66 KV Sub Station Of Puthencruz	1.82	00	00	1.82	Office of the Exe. Engr., Vydhuthi Bhavan, Pattom
3. 220 KV Substation, Andoorkonam	14	00	00	14	Exe. Engr., File No. 4593/82/LA_3, KSEB, Thiruvananthapuram, 1998.
4. 220-400 KV Switching Plant, Areecode	20.21	00	00	20.21	Vydhuthi Bhavan, Pattom.
5. K.S.E.B. Substation, Uduma	30.77	00	00	30.77	Asst. Engr., Oral Information, KSEB, Kasargod.

Contd...

Contd...

Name of Project	Private	Common	Forest	Total	Source
6. National Thermal Power Corporation	79.35	364.37	00	551.79	R & R office, Choolatheruvu.
7. 220 KV Substation, Kasargod	31.94	00	00	31.94	Special Deputy Collector, KSEB, Award Register Vol. I, Kozhikode
8. Wind Farm, Kanjikode	NA	NA	NA	21.58	Exe. Engr.- Thermal, Vydhuthi Bhavan, Pattom.
Total	188.94	364.37	—	682.96	
Defence Units					
1. Naval Academy, Ezhimala	NA	NA	NA	850	LAO-II, Correspondence file, Thalikkavu, Kannur.
2. Kerala Armed Police Camp, Pathanamthitta.	12.64	00	00	12.64	RDO, LA file, Adoor.
Total	12.64	—	—	862.64	
Environment Protection					
1. Elephant Project, Tahriyode	88.49	00	00	88.49	Collectorate, File No. B6-20048/92 dtd 7-4-1992, Wayanad
2. Elephant Project – Marayoor	NA	NA	NA	30.15	RDO, Devikulam
3. Periyar Tiger Reserve, Mlappara	NA	NA	NA	54.36	RDO, File No.4926/83, Devikulam
Total	88.49	—	—	137.00	
Tourism					
1. Bakel Resort Development Corporation	59.51	00	00	59.51	Manager, Bakel Resorts Devt. Corporation, Kasargod.
2. Veli Tourism	NA	NA	00	9.24	Collectorate, Thiruvananthapuram.
Total	59.51	—	00	68.75	
Urban/Rural Development					
1. Medical College, Trissur	18.96	00	00	18.96	Collectorate, File No. R Dis E_1-34708/84, R Dis 60051/83, Thrissur

Contd...

Contd...

Name of Project	Private	Common	Forest	Total	Source
2. District Town Planning Scheme For Elamkulam extension	47.63	NA	00	47.63	Town Planning Section, Greater Cochin Devt. Authority (GCDA), Cochin.
3. Medical College, Alappuzha	32.48	00	00	32.48	LAO- General, Alappuzha
4. Edappally Housing Accommodation Scheme	6.51	00	00	6.51	LAO, KSHB, Thiruvananthapuram.
5. Elamkulam West housing scheme	39.29	00	00	39.29	Town Planning Section, Greater Cochin Devt. Authority (GCDA), Cochin.
6. Housing Colony, Nadakavu	5.29	00	00	5.29	LAO, File No. 1064/82, Collectorate, Kozhikode.
7. Housing Accommodation, Chelavur	17.34	00	00	17.34	Chief Engineer, Oral Information, Housing Board, Kozhikode.
8. Municipal Stadium & Park Tiruvalla	6.08	00	00	6.08	RDO, File No. B_2. 107/87, Thiruvalla.
9. Thrikkakara Sub-Urban Accommodation	15.32	00	00	15.32	LAO, Panampally Nagar and Thiruvananthapuram File No. 1243/80, A-1243/80, 1243/87.
Total	349.54	—	—	1293.29	
Farms and Fisheries					
1. Attapadi Goat Farm, Agali, Palakkad	NA	NA	NA	6.92	LAO, LA Register and Award File, 1987, Kottaikakom
2. Fish Cultivation Farm, Pallippuram	12.24	00	00	12.24	Collectorate, File No. R Dis 3432/61, Thrissur.
3. Seed Farm, Edathuruthy	8.42	00	00	8.42	Collectorate, File No. R Dis 2746/61, Thrissur.
4. Seed Farm, Pazhayannur	9.84	00	00	9.84	Collectorate, Thrissur
5. Fish farm, Eranholi	NA	NA	NA	11.96	Office of the Fish Farm, Thalassery
6. Seed farm, Anakayam	NA	NA	NA	10.98	Office of the Seed Farm, Anakayam.
7. State Seed Farm, Eravattur	11.96	00	00	11.96	Office of the Seed Farm, Oral information from Clerk.

Contd...

Contd...

Name of Project	Private	Common	Forest	Total	Source
8. CTCRI, Sreekariyam	NA	NA	00	44.53	Oral information from a Villager
Total	42.46	—	—	116.85	
Transport					
1. Aroor–Cherthala Bye-Pass-NH 47	NA	NA	00	5.63	LAO- Highways, Alappuzha.
2. Ernakulam–Kayamkulam Broad gauge Railway	NA	NA	00	487.22	LAO-Railway, Alappuzha and Deputy Exe. Egnr., Railways, Ernakulam.
3. Ettumanoor-Eratupetta Road	4.45	00	00	4.45	Collectorate, LAO, Award Register No. G_5-50830/94, Vol. V to VIII and G_5. 30105/94, Vol. IV to VI, Kottayam
4. Kalpetta Bye – Pass	10.57	00	00	10.57	RDO, Wayanad.
5. Karipur Airport	45.96	00	00	45.96	LAO, Award Register No. 5/95 to19/95, Malapuram.
6. Nedumbassery International Airport, Cochin	489.29	00	00	489.29	LAO-I, II, and III, Ankamaly.
7. Needakara Fishing harbor	2.02	00	00	2.02	Exe. Egnr/- Fisheries, Kollam.
8. Thalassery-Mahe Bye Pass NH-47	35.06	00	00	35.06	LA-II, Kannur.
9. Thankassery harbor	NA	NA	00	1.21	Exe. Egnr- Fisheries, Oral Information, Kollam.
10. Thiruvananthapuram International Airport	10.53	00	00	10.53	Land Manager (Oral Information), Airport, Thiruvananthapuram.
11. Vizhinjam harbour	NA	NA	00	40.16	Collectorate, File No. A_{11}. 334/85, Thiruvananthapuram.
12. Calicut Bye-pass-17 (Mapuzha-Arapuzha)	NA	NA	NA	22.33	LAO-I, Award Register, B 128/83, Kozhikode.
Total	597.88	—	—	1154.43	

Contd...

Contd...

Name of Project	Private	Common	Forest	Total	Source
Educational Institutions					
1. Centre for Water Resource Development and Management, Kozhikode	NA	NA	NA	63.62	Registrar, CDWRDM
2. Cochin University of Science and Technology	4.05	44.99	00	49.04	Engineering Section, File No –44/E_4-4/65-66, Cochin University.
3. Coconut Research Station, Pilicode	16.19	00	00	16.19	RDO, File no. R. Dis. 2765/69 dtd 21-8-70, Kasargod
4. Government Polytechnic, Purakady	8.24	00	00	8.24	Collectorate, File No.B_6/19159/97, Wayanad
5. Expansion Of Govt. Polytechnic Kodumba	NA	NA	NA	8.29	LAO, LA Register and Award, Kottaikakom, 1986.
6. Kerala Agricultural University, Vellanikara	379.56	00	00	379.56	Collectorate, File No-E3 18498/70, Thrissur
7. Mahatma Gandhi University, Kottayam	NA	NA	00	42.51	LAO- general, Collectorate, Kottayam
8. NSS Engineering College, Akathethara, Palakkad	00	00	00	50.61	Civil section, NSS Engineering College, Akathethara.
9. Regional Agricultural Research Station (RARS), Kumarakom	NA	NA	00	44.76	Dept. of Economics, RARS, Kumarakom.
10. Sri.Sankaracharaya Sanskrit University	25.10	00	00	25.10	Dept. of Development, Sanskrit University, Kalady.
Total	433.14	—	—	687.92	
Social Welfare					
1. Punalur Rehabilitation Centre	4.01	00	00	4.01	LAO- General, File no.138/95 B, Civil station, Kollam.
Others					
1. Treatment Plant For Calicut Drainage	15.74	00	00	15.74	Collectorate, File No. 4869/76, Kozhikode, 1976.
GRAND TOTAL	8000.10	885.84	18328.51	33055.37	

Table 3.29

Total Land Used for Development Projects in Kerala by Category

	Category	Private	Common	Forest	Total	Percent
1.	Water Resources	32079.4170	349.8	21226.65	53655.8590	34.56
2.	Transport	5112.4057	NA	NA	46405.7566	29.89
3.	Farms and Fisheries	1347.4891	331.9749	18197.361	19875.8250	12.80
4.	Industries	12638.668	131.1829	386.29	13156.1411	8.47
5.	Educational Institutions	5497.4259	44.99	265.534	5807.9499	3.74
6.	Mine	NA	NA	00	5495.9500	3.54
7.	Urban Development	4674.3917	NA	00	4674.3917	3.01
8.	Defence	2045.7659	NA	00	2045.7659	1.32
9.	Non-hydel Power	731.9708	364.37	597.785	1694.1258	1.09
10.	Environment Protection	1054.7431	NA	*	1054.7431	0.68
11.	Others	796.9964	NA	NA	796.9964	0.51
12.	Social/Welfare Centres	452.2146	NA	00	452.2146	0.29
13.	Tourism	147.8090	NA	00	147.8090	0.10
	Total	6759.2480	1222.3178	40673.620	155263.5200	100
	Percentage	42.99	0.79	26.19	**100	

**The type of land for 30 per cent is not available

We do not have specific data regarding the type of land for 46,753.6691 ha. A major portion of this is under the roads and railways in the category of transport. Since no forest land has been acquired for railways after 1951, we presume that 75 per cent of it (35,065.2518 ha.) is private. Adding this to the area of private land presented in Table 3.28, the total private land comes to 1,01,824.50 ha. which is 65.58 per cent of the total area acquired. The percentage of the forest land is 26.19, while common land constitutes 0.79 per cent. The remaining 7.44 per cent (11,684.0913 ha.) is either common or private land. We do not have its exact category.

For example, in Orissa, the total land acquired for development-related projects during the period 1951-95 is estimated to be 9,56,353.0486 ha. which is 6.14 per cent of the total geographical area of the state. Of these, 41.81 per cent was private, 27.99 per cent common and 30.20 per cent forest land (Fernandes and Asif, 1997: 85). In Goa, 4.43 per cent of the State's landmass was acquired for development projects during the period 1965-95. Most of the land taken over for water resource projects was common or forest. Much of the land for transport and human resource development except universities and research institutes was private, while most of the land taken over for miscellaneous schemes was common (Fernandes and Naik, 1999: 46).

Conclusion

As revealed in the data presented in this chapter, Kerala has acquired four per cent of the landmass of the state for development projects. This is very significant for a small state like Kerala where the density of population is very high (749). Furthermore, Kerala has a large extent of forest land (27.83%) and very little common land. All these indicate that a small plot of land acquired is likely to affect many persons.

It is estimated that the proposed projects under various categories would require an area of 14452.86 ha. That would come to 9.31 per cent of the area acquired for development projects during the 1951-95 period. About 92 per cent of the area required for future projects would be for water resource projects. The remaining will be for the Kannur Airport, Kannur Power Project, expansion of Vizhinjam Harbour, expansion of Thiruvananthapuram Airport, Kerala State Transport Project and various Industrial Projects. So, one can expect many more people to be affected. We shall discuss the numbers of the displaced and those deprived of their livelihood and the impact of displacement and deprivation in the following chapter.

4

Displacement, Deprival, Resettlement and Compensation

In the preceding chapter, we presented a conservative estimate of the extent of land acquired for development projects during the four and half decades since 1951. We have seen that the area acquired is very significant for a state like Kerala where the density of population is high. That is, acquisition of a small extent of land is likely to deprive many people. So, in the present chapter, we shall attempt to analyse the extent of deprival of life and livelihood of people affected by these projects as a result of land acquisition. We shall also present the resettlement details of a certain number of projects and the amount of compensation paid to the affected people. Many projects did not have R & R schemes. Adequate data are not available even for projects having R & R schemes.

Families/Persons Displaced and Affected by Development Projects

Our desire to prepare a comprehensive and exhaustive database on the number of persons and families displaced and affected by the development projects in Kerala could not be fully realised, because of the lack of availability of reliable official sources and other constraints from the side of authorities we approached. However, we present the available information with the support of data gathered from respondents in the form of primary data and from some knowledgeable persons in the localities concerned. The number of people and families presented in the following tables include the estimates of both displaced and affected people of some representative projects from different categories.

Number of DPs of Water Resource Projects

Out of the seven projects presented in Table 4.1, Idukki, Kallada and Muvatupuzha are the major ones. A total of 1,394 families were affected by Idukki project which include many Tribals. By taking the average family size in Kerala (5.3), the total number of affected persons of Idukki project is estimated to be 7,388. But, as per the estimates of Ramachandran et al., the number of persons displaced is only 4,544. They concluded that three villages viz. Ayyappankoil, Kanjiyar and Vairamoni were blotted out. No figures are available about the Tribals, but their report acknowledges that there were settlements like Mattukota, Marikulam, and Thonithady around Ayyappankoil.

Kallada, located at the eastern part of Kollam district is a multipurpose project, which has displaced 410 families comprising 2,000 persons. The Muvattupuzha Valley Irrigation project has displaced 120 families and has affected around 474 families (Special Thahasildar, Elanji, 1999). But, according to data available from field (primary data), this project has displaced only 40 families who had been residing in *non-patta* land in puramboke area. If this is true, all the remaining 554 families would have been affected.

Of the 14 major irrigation and multipurpose projects, we have data on three. They have displaced 2,869 persons. Malampuzha and Chalakudy River Diversion were started in 1949 and hence, we did not include these two for calculating the displacement as the present study focuses on displacement after 1951. Also, Pamba Irrigation Project uses the tailrace water of Kakad hydroelectric project and has only a barrage. It acquired only 30 ha. of land adjacent to the river and forest (Project Report, Pampa Irrigation). Idamalayar project is in its initial stages. So, we need to extrapolate the number of DPs of the remaining seven projects only. Taking the average of multipurpose and major irrigation projects (excluding the extreme values) of 956 persons as a representative figure, the number of DPs of these seven projects would be 6692.

Table 4.1

Number of Families/Persons Displaced by Water Resource Projects

Name of the Project	*Type*	*Families*	*Persons*	*Source*
Asurankundu Reservoir Scheme	NA	31	164	Collectorate, File No. B_2- 1783/89, Thrissur.
Idukki Hydroelectric Project	Hydel	1394	7388	Revenue divisional office, File No. 766/78, Idukki.
Kallada Irrigation Project	Major	410	2000	Chief Engineer, KIP, Kottarakara
Kanjirapuzha Irrigation Project	Major	44	233	Executive Engineer, Kanjirappuzha irrigation, Oral Information.
Karappuzha Irrigation Project	Medium	322	1052	Report of 'Kayal', Nellarachal
Muvattupuzha Valley Irrigation Project	Major	120	636	Exe. Engr., MVIP, Thodupuzha.
Venganallur Reservoir Scheme	NA	45	238	Collectorate, File No. E_3 29228/78, and R Dis 29226/78, Thrissur
Pooyamkutty hydroelectric	Hydel	184	773	KFRI, Peechi
Total		2550	12,484	

Accordingly, leaving out the above four, *the ten major and multipurpose projects would have displaced 9561 persons.*

We have no data on the completed medium irrigation projects. Of the ten medium, six were completed projects which had started in the 1950s. Going by the estimate given by knowledgeable persons, a minimum of 500 persons would have been displaced by each medium irrigation project. Hence, these six projects would have displaced 3,000 persons.

The construction work of Karappuzha dam is not yet completed. The project had acquired land way back in 1970. The work of the Karappuzha project is in progress with the possible eviction of 1,052 persons. Of these, 530 people were already displaced and the rest continue to stay in the water spread area. They could be displaced at any time. The implementation of the project has drastically affected their livelihood, because they have lost the freedom to cultivate their own agricultural land (For details about the problems the Tribals faced after announcement, see Chapter 6). *Thus, the medium irrigation projects would have displaced 3,530 persons.*

Idukki and Pooyamkutty hydroelectric projects had displaced 8,161 persons. As per the information collected from the nearby villagers, the number of people displaced by Panniar hydroelectric project ranges from 300 to 500 families. They reported that there were many SCs and OBCs among the DPs. The local people at Sengulam hydel project revealed that nearly 500 families were displaced by this project. They told us that there were Tribals residing in the nearby places of the dam. But, none of the informants was sure about whether these Tribals were affected by the project. The number of families displaced by Neriamangalam hydel project was estimated to be between 100 and 200. The officials claimed that the Idamalayar project has no displacement (Office of the Exe. Engr, Kothamangalam). But, as per the information from a key informant, this project had displaced between 100 and 150 tribal families. For the purpose of calculating the number of DPs of these projects, we take the lower figure of 100 families (530 persons). Thus, the number of families of these four hydel projects comes to 1,000 (5,300 persons). For the sake of extrapolation of the DPs of the remaining four hydel projects viz. Poringalkuth, Sholayar, Sabarigiri, and Lower Periyar, even if we take the minimum number of families displaced per project as 100, these four projects would have 2,120 DPs. *Thus the total number of DPs of hydel projects would be 15,581.*

According to this calculation, the water resources projects must have displaced 28,672 persons.

Of the 773 people displaced by Pooyamkutty hydroelectric project, 62 per cent are Tribals. Most of the DPs of Idukki, Karappuzha and Idamalayar projects are Tribals. Since most of the dams were constructed in the forest areas, a good number of DPs of these projects were Tribals.

Of the remaining medium projects, Chamravattom, Attappady, Banasurasagar, Kuriarkutty-Karappara, and Kakkadavu irrigation project are in their initial stages. As per the information collected from the project office (Executive Engineer, Eswaramnagalam), these are not likely to displace any people. The work has not yet started. Kuriarkutty-Karappara project is in the investigation stage. According to experts, there are 300 tribal families in the water spread area of Banasurasagar project in the Kozhikode district. These people will be displaced in the near future when the dam will be completed.

PAPs of Water Resource Projects

Hydel projects, besides displacing people, also give rise to Tribal PAPs whose livelihood is affected by these projects. Since we have no specific data, we are not attempting to estimate the PAPs of hydel schemes. In the case of irrigation projects, we have to depend on the length of main canals, branch canals, and distributaries to estimate the number of PAPs. It is estimated that one km of main canal on an average requires an area of five acres (2.024 ha.). Similarly, one km of branch canal takes 2.5 acres (1.012 ha.) and one km of distributary, one acre (0.4049 ha.) (Assistant Executive Engineer, IRDB). Based on this area and the density of population of the corresponding district, we estimated the number of PAPs.

We have the length of canals and distributaries of eight major projects viz. Kuttiady, Pazhassi, Chitturpuzha, Kanjirappuzha, Kallada, Pampa, MVIP, and Periyar Valley. The number of PAPs of these projects based on the above criteria would be 24,379. Taking the average number of PAPs per project (3,047), the number of PAPs of the remaining six projects viz. Malampuzha, Chimoni, Neyyar, Chalakudy River Diversion, and Peechi would be 18,284. *Thus the number of PAPs from major irrigation and multipurpose projects will come to 42,663.*

The completed medium irrigation projects are Gayathri, Pothundy, Cheerakuzhy, Walayar, Mangalam and Vazhani. Since all these projects were started in the 1950s, no data on the length of canals and distributaries are available. So, we are unable to apply the above norm for extrapolation. Therefore, taking the ratio that ten ha. irrigated area require one ha. of land, the area used for canals and distributaries by Gayathri, Pothundy, Walayar and Manglam projects would be 546.5 ha., 546.5 ha., 323.8 ha., and 344 ha., respectively. Multiplying the area by density of the corresponding district, the total number of PAPs of these projects would be 9,367. Based on the average area (440.224 ha.) and average population density (547), the average number of PAPs per project would be 2,408. Therefore, the number of PAPs of the remaining two projects would be 4816. Hence, *the total number of PAPs of these six projects would be 14,183.*

Thus, the number of PAPs of major and medium irrigation projects together works out to 56,846.

The area covered by minor irrigation projects in Kerala is 8,835 ha. Taking the average of density of population for the period 1951-91 as 547, the PAPs of minor irrigation would be 48,328. When we take the three categories of projects together, namely major, medium, and minor, *the total number of PAPs of water resource projects works out be 1,05,174.* This means that about 19844 families have been affected by irrigation projects in Kerala. Obviously, this is a conservative estimate.

We have not included the PAPs of Attappady, Karappuzha, Banasurasagar, Chamravattom, Karappara, and Kakkadavu projects since they are in the initial stages of execution. They are included among the PAPs of the proposed water resource projects.

DPs of Proposed Water Resource Projects

The proposed water resource projects would displace 18,948 families involving *1,00,424 persons*. This is nearly four times the number of people displaced by water resource projects for the period 1951-95. We have no data on the DPs of Chamravattom, Attappady, Karappara and Kakkadavu projects. These projects are in their initial stage. Hence, we have not even attempted to estimate the DPs of these projects.

Table 4.2

Number of Families to be Displaced by the Proposed Water Resource Projects

Project	*Families*	*Persons*	*Source*
Mananthavady Multipurpose	11000	58300	Philipose, Fedina, Sulthan Bathery
Chundelipuzha	2000	10600	Do
Kallampathy	5000	26500	Do
Vamanapuram	438	2321	*Malayala Manorama*, 2000
Chaliyar	210	1113	Chief Engineer, Irrigation Department, 1998.
Banasurasagar	300	1590	Sukumaran Nair, KIRTADS, Kozhikode.
Total	18,948	1,00,424	

To calculate the number of persons who could be affected by the six proposed medium irrigation projects, we depended on the proportion between the area irrigated and the area acquired. Accordingly, the four medium irrigation projects viz. Attappady, Karappuzha, Banasurasagar, and Chamravattom together could affect 8,613 persons. Taking the PAPs of Banasurasagar as 882, the remaining two could affect 1,764 persons. Therefore, the total number of affected persons of proposed medium projects would amount to 10,377. According to experts, at least a half of this (5,189) would be DPs. *Thus, the number of DPs of the proposed water resource projects would come to 1,05,613 and the number of PAPs 5,189.*

One possible reason for this higher number of persons to be affected by the proposed water resource projects is the population growth and subsequent internal migration.

Families/Persons Affected By Industries

We present below the details of families and persons displaced and affected by 16 industrial projects in Table 4.3. Autocast Ltd. at Cherthala in Alappuzha district is a subsidiary of Steel Industries Kerala Ltd. (SIKL) which has affected 107 families. One can estimate the number of people affected by it as 567 taking 5.3 as the average family size in Kerala. Kanjikode Industrial Township is another major industrial project owned by KINFRA in Palakkad district. This project affected 180 families.

Table 4.3

Number of Families/Persons Displaced by Industries

Name of the Project	*Families*	*Persons*	*Source*
Displaced			
1. Autocast Ltd., Cherthala	107	567	Personnel Manager, SIKL, Cherthala
2. Kochi Refineries Limited	837	4436	LAO, Vytila.
3. Traco Cables Company Ltd., Thiruvalla	27	143	Personnel Manager, TRACO Ltd., Kochi.
4. Peruman Special Refractories, Kollam	203	1076	LAO- General, File No. A5-1015/89, Civil Station, Kollam.
5. Indian Oil Corporation Ltd. – Parippally	114	604	LA General, File No. LA_2-9295/92, Civil Station, Kollam.
6. Export promotion Industrial park, Kakkanad	38	197	Asst. Manager, KINFRA, Kochi.
7. FACT, Udyogamandal Division	150	795	Estate Manager, FACT Ltd.
8. FACT, Kochi Division.	775	3895	Estate Manager, FACT Ltd.
9. HMT Ltd., Kalamassery	300	1590	Land Manager, HMT Ltd.
10. Indian Rare Earths Ltd., Chavara	84	445	Primary data
11. Kerala Minerals and Metals Ltd., Chavara	17	90	Primary data
12. Kanjikode Industrial Township, Palakkad	124	657	Primary data
13. Technopark, Thiruvananthapuram	20	106	Primary data

Contd...

Contd...

14. Indian Telephone Industries, Palakkad	18	93	LAO, LA and Award File, Kottaikokam, 1990.
15. Industrial Development Area, Palakkad	120	636	Primary data.
16. PVS Petroleum Co., Chaliyam	75	308	MICTRA, Kozhikode.
Total	3009	15638	
Affected			
1. Mavoor Gwaliyor Rayons	60	305	Collectorate, Award No. 1/60, 1/64, 25/67, Kozhikode
2. Hindustan News Print Mill, Vellore	260	1378	LAO, Kochi refineries, Kochi.
3. Technopark, Thiruvananthapuram	68	362	Special Tahsildar, Addl. LA unit, File No. A2/379/92. Thiruvananthapuram.
4. Kerala Minerals & Metals Ltd., Kollam	416	2205	Administrative Office, Kerala Minerals and Metals Ltd.
5. Kanjikode Industrial Township, Palakkad	56	297	LAO, Oral information form clerk, Palakkad.
6. Traco Cables Company Ltd., Thiruvalla	22	116	Personnel Manager, TRACO Ltd., Kochi
Total	882	4663	
Grand Total	3891	20301	

We have data on displacement by 12 industries. The total number affected by these projects comes to 20,301. Besides, the number of DPs of four projects, namely Technopark, Export Promotion Park, Kanjikode Industrial Township and Industrial Development Area comes to 960.

Seventy nine out of the 499 units are located inside the IDAs, IDPs, Technopark or CEPZ. We take the average number 446 as a base (excluding the extreme values), the number of people affected by the remaining 420 industries would be 1,87,320.

Since industries usually acquire large area of land, the number of DPs will be much higher. We take for granted that three-fourths of these (1,40,490) are DPs. *Thus the total number of DPs of industries would come up to 1,56,128.*

Travancore Titanium Products Ltd., a chemical factory at Thiruvananthapuram causes acute environment problems in the form of water and air pollution. This has serious implications in the lives of thousands of fishermen in the coastal areas of Kochuveli, Kannanthura and Vettukad. According to knowledgeable persons, more than 2,000 families are adversely affected by the pollution of this factory. If we calculate the number of PAPs of this company, it would amount to 10,600. Thus, *the number of PAPs for all industries together would be 62,023.*

DP/PAPs of Environment Protection

There are 11 Wildlife Sanctuaries, two National Parks and one Bird Sanctuary in Kerala. The official version is that displacement in these projects is minimal though the authorities concerned acknowledge the possibility of displacing Tribals from the project area. The management plans of different sanctuaries give the impression that the forest department is planning to shift several persons from the sanctuaries to its fringes. This is an indication that these projects do intend to displace some people.

The situation in Periyar Tiger Reserve in Idukki district reveals that the project had many PAPs. As per the official estimates, the number of families displaced by Periyar Tiger Reserve was only 14. But, actually hundreds of Tribals employed in the cardamom estates as labourers lost their livelihood. This has resulted in bringing starvation to many of the affected people.

Table 4.4

Number of Families/Persons Displaced by Environment Protection

Name of the Project	*Families*	*Persons*	*Source*
Elephant Project, Thariyode.	40	212	Collectorate, File No. B6-20048/92 dt. 7-4-1992, Wayanadu.
Elephant Project, Marayoor	335	1775	RDO, File No.2036/94, Devikulam.
Periyar Tiger Reserve, Mlappara	14	74	RDO, File No.4926/83, Devikulam.
Total	389	2,061	

The statistics presented in the Table 4.5 comprise people seriously affected by the parks or sanctuaries. Several of these people had been depending on the forest for their livelihood including Non-Wood Forest Produce (NWFP) collection. They number 12,827 persons. We count them as PAPs.

Table 4.5

Population Inside Wildlife Sanctuaries and National Parks in Kerala

Name of the Sanctuary	*Area (sq km)*	*Population*		
		Male	*Female*	*Total*
1. Neyyar	128	601	729	1330
2. Sentharuny	100.32	NA	NA	212*
3. Peppara	53	334	350	684
4. Chinnar	90.44	549	647	1246
5. Idukki	70	752	742	1494
6. Eravikulam (N.P.)	97	70	51	121
7. Parambikulam	285	415	433	848
8. Thekkady (Periyar)	777.54	805	791	1596
9. Wayanadu	344.46	2165	2124	4289
10. Thattekad (B.S.)	25.16	NA	NA	NA
11. Peechi-Vazhani	125	NA	NA	689*
12. Chimoni	75	0	0	0
13. Silent Valley (N.P.)	89.52	0	0	0
14. Aralam	55	NA	NA	318*
Total	2,315.44			12,827

Sources: Forest statistics, Management Plan; Joy M S, Wildlife Sanctuaries in Kerala (Malayalam), 1997.

*only the totals are available

DPs/PAPs of Non-Hydel Power Projects

The combined cycle power project of NTPC at Kayamkulam is the first thermal power project in Kerala. Though the land acquired was largely Government owned, it did affect the livelihood of many. They belong to three categories, namely Kayal Farm workers (1,052), those who lost land (553) and a group of fishing families who lost their source of livelihood. The number of DPs of the project was estimated to be 63 (NTPC brochure). According to the estimates of Thomas (1995), a total of 1,510 families having 8,062 members were affected and 23.3 per cent of these were below 15 years of age. Eighty-six per cent belonged to OBC, 11 per cent SC and the remaining three per cent to forward communities and the total population was 3,632. There is a wide discrepancy between the data provided by the official sources (Table 4.6) and those obtained from research studies.

Table 4.6

Number of Families/Persons Displaced by Non-Hydel Power Projects

Name of the Project		*Families*	*Persons*	*Source*
National Thermal Power Corporation	Displaced	NA	63	NTPC (brochure), 1996
	Affected	NA	2181	
120 Mega Watt Diesel Generator Power Plant, Nallalam.		59	312	Office of Exe. Engr.-Thermal, Vydhuthi Bhavan, Pattom.
Total		—	2,556	

The diesel generator power plant at Kozhikode (Nallalam) is the first of its kind in Kerala. This is a new venture by the state government which has shifted its attention from hydel projects to diesel and thermal sources for power generation. This project has displaced 59 families.

So, the number of displaced from these two non-hydel projects is 375 and the number of PAPs 2,181. Most of the persons affected by both these projects belong to fishing community and OBCs.

DPs/PAPs by Defence Establishments

We have no information about the defence projects other than Ezhimala. The displaced persons include fishermen, SCs and OBCs.

Table 4.7

Number of Families/Persons Displaced by Defence Establishments

Name of the Project	*Families*	*Persons*	*Source*
Naval Academy, Ezhimala	340	1800	Knowledgeable Persons, Ezhimala.

DPs/PAPs by Transport

Airports and harbours cause large-scale displacement. This is true for Kerala too. The three airports together displaced 7,553 persons. Several of the DPs of Nedumbassery airport belong to Scheduled Castes. A good majority of the 300 families displaced from Thiruvananthapuram airport are fishermen.

We have data on three out of the eight harbours. These three had 6,010 DPs. Taking the minimum number of 74 for the purpose of extrapolation, the remaining five harbours would have 370 DPs. Thus, the total number of DPs of harbours comes to 6,380. Almost all the DPs are fisherfolk.

Table 4.8

Number of Families/Persons Displaced by Transport

	Name of the Project	*Families*	*Persons*	*Source*
1.	Kalpetta Bye-Pass	46	243	RDO, Wayanad
2.	Nedumbassery International Airport	820	4346	Dhanam, Feb.15-20, p.5
3.	Thiruvananthapuram International Airport*	300	1590	Land Manager, Airport.
4.	Karipur Airport, Kozhikode	305	1616	LAO, Award Register No. 5/95 to19/95, Malapuram.
5.	Neendakara Fishing Harbour, Kollam	50	265	Exe. Egnr-Fisheries, Oral information, Kollam.
6.	Vizhinjam Harbour	1070	5671	Collectorate, File No. A11. 334/85. Thiruvananthapuram.
7.	Thankassery Harbour, Kollam	14	74	Exe. Egnr-Fisheries, Oral information, Kollam.
	Total	2,605	13,805	

*as per the information from displaced people, the number of displaced families is 500.

The total area under roads in Kerala is 40,183.2085 ha. (For calculations, see data on land acquisition in Chapter 3). For the purpose of extrapolation, let us assume that half of this area had been acquired during the period 1951-95. It would amount to 20,091.63 ha. The average density of population per sq km during the period 1951-91 in Kerala was 547. Multiplying the area by density, the number of persons affected by roads would be

1,09,898. Similarly, the area acquired for railways after 1947 is estimated to be 5,148.4024 ha. By taking the average density of population, acquisition of this land would have affected 28,162 persons.

Airports and harbours mostly displace people, while railways and roads would create PAPs. From our calculations, we arrive at the number of persons displaced by transport to be 13,563. The number of PAPs is estimated to be 1,38,060.

The proposed Kannur airport would displace 700 persons. About 350 families (1,855 persons) in the nearby localities of Nedumbassery airport are under the threat of displacement (Jyothish, 1998). The expansion of Thiruvananthapuram airport is expected to displace 500 families (2,650 persons).

The proposed Kerala Transport Project of PWD would affect 7,133 families (37,804 persons). Of these, 141 families (747 persons) will be displaced (Debnath, 2001: 5).

Thus, the DPs of proposed projects in this category would be 5,952, the number of PAPs 37,057.

DPs/PAPs by Tourism

Since most of the 32 tourist resorts in Kerala are in the private sector, we take into account only the cases given by the official sources (343). The number of persons affected by tourist projects comes to 343 of which 94 are displaced. Most DPs of these two projects are fisher folk. According to the information collected from the officials, only these two projects acquired land for tourism purposes.

Table 4.9

Number of Families/Persons Displaced by Tourism

Name of the Project	*Families*	*Persons*	*Source*
1. Bakel resort development project	18	94	Manager, Bakel Resorts Dev. Corporation, Kasargod.
2. Veli Tourist village (affected).	47	249	Collectorate, File No. K4.70884/97. Veli Tourism. Thiruvananthapuram.
Total	65	343	

DPs/PAPs by Urban/Rural Development

Since from official sources we learnt that no other major rural/urban development schemes had displaced people, we limit our estimate of the number of persons displaced by this category to 1,003.

Table 4.10

Number of Families/Persons Displaced by Urban/Rural Development

Name of the Project	Families	Persons	Source
District Town Planning Scheme, Elamkulam	94	498	Town Planning section Greater Kochi Dev. Authority, Kochi.
Edappally Housing Accommodation Scheme	35	185	Town Planning section Greater Kochi Dev. Authority, Kochi.
Elamkulam West Extension	16	85	Town Planning section, Greater Kochi Dev. Authority, Kochi
Thrikkakara Sub-Urban Accommodation scheme	45	238	LAO, Housing Board, Thiruvananthapuram
Total	190	1,003	

DPS/PAPS by Farms and Fisheries

There are 61 agricultural farms in Kerala. Of these, we have data on five as shown in Table 4.11. They have displaced 503 persons. Taking the average of 100 DPs per project, the number of DPs of the remaining 56 would be 5,600. So, the total number of displaced by this category would be 6,161.

Table 4.11

Number of Families/Persons Displaced by Farms and Fisheries

Name of the Project	Families	Persons	Source
Anakayam Seed Farm	13	69	Oral information from a villager.
Seed Farm, Chavakad	19	100	Collectorate, Thrissur
Seed Farm, Thalappally	22	117	
Seed Farm, Edathuruthy	19	100	Collectorate, File No. R Dis 2746/61, Thrissur
Seed Farm, Pazhayannur.	22	117	Collectorate, Thrissur
Fish Cultivation Farm, Pallippuram.	11	58	Collectorate, File No. R Dis 3432/61, Thrissur.
Total	106	561	

DPs/PAPs by Educational and Research Institutions

The total area under various educational institutions is 3,915.8659 ha. Since most of them are under private management, they have their own land. We presume that only a third of this area was acquired or purchased. The proportion between Government and private educational institutions is 1:2 (see Table 2.20 in Chapter 2). For the purpose of calculating the number of persons affected by them, we shall take the area acquired by Government institutions multiplied by average density for the period (1951-91) as 547. This brings us to an estimate of 7,069 persons.

As the area required for an institution is relatively small, the number of displaced could also be small. Taking one fourth of the affected as DPs, the number of DPs would be 1,767 and the number of PAPs, 5,301.

Table 4.12

Number of Families/Persons Displaced/Affected Universities

Name of the University	*Families*	*Persons*	*Source*
Displaced			
Cochin University of Science and Technology	90	477	Engineering Section, File No - 44/E4-4/65-66, Cochin University.
Sri. Sankaracharya Sanskrit University	109	577	Dept. of Development, Sanskrit University.
University of Kerala	300	1590	Primary data
Affected			
Agricultural University, Vellanikara.	NA	31	Collectorate, File No - E3 18498/70, Thrissur
Mahatma Gandhi University, Kottayam.	178	943	Collectorate, LAO, File No. G2 - 46339/84, G2-3213/86, G2-22449/87, Kottayam.
Total	677	3,618	

Cochin University, University of Kerala and Sanskrit University together displaced 2,644 persons. According to the officials, Calicut University has not displaced anyone. The number of persons affected by the Agricultural University and Mahatma Gandhi University is 974. Since we do not have sufficient data on displacement, we presume that one-fourth of the affected is displaced. So, the number of DPs of these two universities comes to 244. Consequently, the total number displaced by the universities in Kerala would amount to 2,888. Thus, the number of PAPs of universities would be 731.

The total area occupied by engineering colleges in Kerala is 699.91 ha. (6.999 sq kms). Taking the average density of population during the 1951-95 period (547), the number of people affected by them would be 3,829. We presume that one fourth of them are displaced. So, the DPs are 957 and PAPs 2,872.

Based on the density of Kottayam district, Kottayam medical college would have affected 651 persons. We take for granted that one fourth of them are DPs, that is 163 persons, the remaining 488 are PAPs. We have no data about the DPs of Kozhikode medical college. But, taking 57 as the number of DPs (as that of the Thrissur Medical College) will not be an over estimation. Thiruvananthapuram medical college was established prior to Independence. Thus, the number of DPs of medical colleges would be 351 and the number of PAPs, 710. Professional colleges would have 1,308 DPs and the number of PAPs would be 3,582.

Table 4.13

Number of Families and Persons Displaced and Affected by Professional Colleges and Research Institutions

Name of the College	*Families*	*Persons*	*Source*
Displaced			
1. Medical College, Thrissur	26	57	Collectorate, File No., R Dis. 60051/83, Thrissur
2. V.S.S.C, Thumba	330	1716	Primary Data
Affected			
1. Medical College, Alappuzha	56	296	LAO-General, Alappuzha
Total	412	2,069	

Among the research institutions, VSSC project at Thumba displaced 1,716 fish workers. CTCRI at Sreekaryam has not displaced any one. There were no PAPs too. The land was a cashew orchard. Land occupied by the Centre for Earth Sciences Studies at Akulam is a reclaimed mining land used by English Indian Clays Ltd., KFRI at Peechi acquired forest land. CDS at Ulloor purchased land from a private party. The land occupied by TBGRI in Palode is on lease from the forest department. We have no data regarding displacement by CPCRI at Kasargod and CWRDM, Kozhikode. The major displacement by research institution is only by VSSC (1,716 persons).

Thus, the number of DPs of educational institutions comes to 5035. The number of PAPs would be 9,614.

DPs/PAPs by Social Welfare Institutions

According to official sources, the number of persons displaced by Punalur Rehabilitation Plantations Ltd., amounts to 42. Since no data were available regarding other projects in this category, we resorted to extrapolation. Thus, the number of persons affected based on the area acquired (452 ha.) for this category and the average density of population (547) for the period of 1951-95; the number of affected persons worked out to be 2,472. We count all these as PAPs since we have no parameters to estimate the number of DPs.

Displaced and Affected Persons in Kerala

In our estimate, the total number of persons affected by development projects in Kerala during the 1951-95 period is 5,52,233 which is 1.90 per cent of the total population in Kerala. Obviously, this is a conservative estimate.

Of the 5,52,233 persons affected by development projects, 40 per cent are displaced and the remaining, PAPs. In several projects, it was difficult to get caste-wise data regarding the number of persons affected. However, we can observe some trends. The Tribals in Kerala are located in specific districts like Wayanad, Idukki, Palakkad and Thiruvananthapuram. Forest land was acquired mainly for water resources and environment protection projects. A major share of the projects of these categories is located in these districts where Tribal population is relatively higher.

Hence, we can conclude that Tribals were affected mainly by water resources and environment protection projects in Kerala. Harbours generally affected fisher folk.

Industries in Kerala are usually located close to the towns or in rural areas with infrastructural facilities. Dams are in remote and forest areas. Hence, the number of persons affected by industries is relatively high, because of the high density of population evicted from urban or semi-urban areas, whereas it is relatively lower in water resource projects since these are located in relatively thinly populated areas.

The number of DPs of the proposed projects in different categories is 1,16,770 and that of PAPs is 42,246. Most of these are persons to be displaced by the proposed water resource projects. Thus, the total number of persons to be affected by the proposed projects is estimated to be 1,59,016. This constitutes 23.80 per cent of the total number of people affected by development projects during 1951-95 period.

Table 4.14

Number of Persons Displaced and Affected by Development Projects (1951-95): Category-wise

Category	*Displaced Persons*	*Project Affected Persons*	*Total*	*Percentage*
1. Industries	160791	62023	222814	40.34
2. Transport	13563	138060	151623	27.46
3. Water Resources	28672	105174	133846	24.23
4. Environment Protection	2061	12827	14888	2.70
5. Educational Institutions	5035	9614	14649	2.65
6. Farms and Fisheries	6161	NA	6161	1.11
7. Non-hydel Power	375	2181	2556	0.46
8. Social Welfare	NA	2472	2472	0.45
9. Defence Establishments	1800	NA	1800	0.33
10. Urban/Rural Development	1003	NA	1003	0.18
11. Tourism	94	249	343	0.06
12. Mines	78	NA	78	0.01
Total	219633	332600	552233	100
Percentage	39.77	60.23	100	

When we take the already affected together with the proposed, the number of affected persons would be 7,11,249 which constitutes 2.44 per cent of the total population of Kerala (Census of India, 1991).

On the other hand, a similar study in Goa shows that more than 60,000 families have been affected by development projects during the period of 1965-95 which constitutes 5.63 per cent of the state's population (Fernandes and Naik, 1999: 59). This includes both DPs and PAPs. In another study, Fernandes and Asif (1997:113) estimate the number of DPs of development projects in Orissa as 6,32,634 (2% of total population). Of these, 2,55,317 are Tribals, 73,620 Dalits and 3,03,697 other castes. According to them, the number of PAPs is 8,33,275 (2.63% of the state's population). Of these, 3,60,799 are Tribals, 1,04,822 Dalits and 3,67,654 others. The total number of persons affected by development projects in Orissa adds up to 14,65,909 which is 4.63 per cent of total population of the state.

Resettlement

This section focuses on the resettlement and rehabilitation schemes offered by different projects in Kerala. This is another area in which we had to face the constraints of the availability of data. Many of the officials do not know these details. Therefore, we had to depend on the local people to supply information on many projects. We present the resettlement and rehabilitation schemes of the major projects in the following table.

As per the available data, the number of families resettled in Kerala is 5,461. By taking the average family size in Kerala this come to 28,943 persons. That means only 13.18 per cent of the DPs in Kerala benefited by the resettlement offered by the project.

It is evident from the table that almost all the projects allotted land to the displaced. On an average, the extent of land varies from four to ten cents. The Idukki project is an exception in this general trend of giving a mere house plot, because some of the displaced from this project got three acres each. Allotment of a small plot of land will not compensate the trauma of involuntary displacement.

Table 4.15

Number of People Resettled/Rehabilitated in Kerala

	Name of Project	Year	Nature of resettlement/rehabilitation	No. of families resettled	Resettled as percentage of displaced	Source
1.	Bakel Tourism Project	1990	4 cents of land	3	16.67	Manager, Bakel Resorts Dev. Corporation.
2.	Diesel Power Plant, Nallalam, Kozhikode	1998	5 cents of land	59	100.00	Office of the Exe. Engr, Vydhyudi Bhavan, Pattom.
3.	Apparel Park, Menamkulam	1997	10.83 cents of Land and Rs.10,000 as shifting charge.	10	41.67	Office of the KINFRA, Thiruvananthapuram
4.	Technopark, Thiruvananthapuram	1993	Land	20	100.00	Draftsman, Technopark, Thiruvananthapuram
5.	Vizhinjam Harbour, Thiruvananthapuram	1982	4 cents of Land, House (Resettlement colony)	1052	98.32	Collectorate, Thiruvananthapuram
6.	Indian Telephone Industries, Palakkad	1990 awd	11.11 cents of Land	18	100.00	Land Acquisition Office, Kottakakom.
7.	Kanjikode Industrial Township	NA	Land	124	NA	Land Acquisition Office, Palakkad.
8.	FACT Ltd., Ernakulam	1965	10 cents of Land	775	78.68	Manager Estates, FACT Ltd.
9.	NTPC, Kayamkulam	I-1987	House plots/income generation schemes/self employment schemes	49	77.68	R&R office, Choolatheruvu
10.	SIKL Ltd., Cherthala.	1978	Job	65	60.75	Legal Officer/Personnel Manager, SIKL Ltd.

Contd...

Contd...

11.	Periyar Tiger Reserve, Thekady.	1969	Land	14	100.00	Office of the RDO, Devikulam.
	TOTAL			2189		
12.	Hindustan Newsprint Ltd, Velloore.	1974	Job as per Qualification	150	NA	Special Thahasildar, Land Acquisition, Hindustan Newsprint Ltd.
13.	Mahatma Gandhi University, Kottayam	NA	Land	178	100.00	LA General Office, Collectorate, Kottayam
14.	Muvattupuzha Valley Irrigation, Kottayam	I-1977	4 cents of land and financial assistance to build house	58	75.32	Exe. Engr, MVIP, Thodupuzha
15.	HMT Ltd, Kalamassery	1964	Land and unskilled temporary jobs	300	100.00	Manager Estates, HMT Ltd, Kalamassery.
16.	Centre for Water Resource Development and Management (CWRDM), Kozhikode	NA	Self employment scheme	18	NA	Registrar, CWRDM.
17.	Traco Cables Ltd., Kochi	1960	Job	57	NA	Manager (P & A), TRACO, Kochi.
18.	Indian Rare Earths Ltd., Chavara.	1965	5 to 8 cents of Land and Shifting Charge of Rs.300 to 10,000 (according to year of acquisition)	84	100.00	Villagers (Primary Data)
19.	Kerala Minerals and Metals Ltd., Chavara.	1972	10 cents of land, and Rs. 9,000 as shifting charge.	17	100.00	Do
20.	Idukki hydroelectric project	1967	1 to 3 acres of Land	NA	100.00	Primary Data
21.	Karappuzha Irrigation, Wayanad	1970	—	NA	—	—

Contd...

Contd...

22.	Industrial Development Area, Pudussery	1985	5 to 10 cents as per the area lost	120	100.00	Do
	Total			982		
23.	Mavoor Gwaliyor Rayons, Kozhikode	1958	—	NA	—	Primary Data
24.	VSSC, Thumba.	1961	10 cents of Land, Job, House (Resettlement colony)	220	66.67	Do
25.	Naval Academy, Ezhimala	1983	10 cents to 1 acre (1 acre for SCs) of Land	340	100.00	Do
26.	Nedumbassery Airport, Angamaly.	1994	Land, Shifting charge, Money for constructing new house (Resettlement colony)	820	100.00	Do
27.	Kallada Irrigation Project	1966	House Plots	410	NA	Office of the Exe. Engr, Kallada Irrigation, Kottarakara.
28.	Thiruvananthapuram Airport	1986	10 cents to 1 acre of land	500	100.00	Primary data
	Total			2290		
	Grand Total			5461		

It requires a planned rehabilitation scheme to start life anew. This is the aspect that needs much attention from the part of the authorities, because most of the project authorities equate rehabilitation with the allotment of a house plot. It also points to the fact that most of the projects in Kerala provide only resettlement and not rehabilitation.

Only Vizhinjam, VSSC and Nedumbassery projects provided resettlement colony to the displaced. Apparel Park at Menamkulam, IRE, KMML and Nedumbassery projects offered shifting charges also to the displaced. Hindustan Newsprint at Vellore, SIKL, Alappuzha, VSSC, Thumba, HMT Ltd., at Kalamassery, and Traco Cables Ltd., Kochi projects offered jobs also to the displaced. NTPC project at Kayamkulam offered house plots, income generation schemes and self-employment schemes to the affected people depending on the category they belonged to (the details are given in Chapter 8).

IRE project in 1975-76 provided each evicted family with eight cents of land and Rs.300 as shifting charges. But, in 1987-88 and 1993-94, the size of the house plot was reduced to 5 cents and the shifting charges were raised to Rs.10,000.

One of the resettlement areas of IRE project is in Kozhikode, an island-like village, surrounded by rivers. The Company made arrangements for boat services to ferry people and goods from and to this resettlement place. Crossing the river is very difficult, especially when people have to depend entirely on the ferry, which has a limited service. Drinking water, electricity and toilet facilities were absent in the new village.

Among the other projects, the resettlement package varied from a small house plot of 6 cents to 10 cents of land as reported in Bakel, IDA, MVIP, IRE and KMML projects. Among this, only IRE, KMML, NTPC and Nedumbassery were the four projects that promised some basic facilities like drinking water, road and electricity in the resettlement colony. But, in most of these cases, the promises were not kept. This caused serious problems to the displaced.

The Nedumbassery project acquired 36 acres of paddy fields at Akaparambu for the resettlement of 300 evicted households. Rather than filling the low lying slushy field with red earth to raise the land by one meter, the earth filling was limited to less than one foot which hardly covered the grass that grew in the fields. A very light rain was sufficient to flood the area. Infrastructural facilities such as water, electricity and road were not provided although these were part of the deal with the people. Each household was allotted six cents of this land. The official report said that all the displaced were resettled. People had to build their own houses at the new sites after they were evicted. All building materials had to be transported by head-loads, as there were no roads on which vehicles could ply to reach the resettlement area. Besides the payment of compensation fixed by the Tahsildar, the resettlement package meant six cents of land in a housing colony and a sum of Rs. 10,000/- as relocation cost.

The Bakel tourism Project in Kasargod district disposed of the displaced with a small house plot of five cents each. The five displaced families in this project had to mobilise their own resources for resettlement in the newly allotted site. This meant shifting their belongings to the new place, putting up a new house, seeking new job opportunities, getting acquainted with the new place and people, apart from the psychological trauma experienced by all in the family including children.

The Industrial Development Area (IDA) projects were not any better than the Bakel tourism project in resettling the displaced. The only difference was that the IDA offered six cents of land instead of the five cents provided by Bakel as house site. A visit to these locations helped our team members to understand the predicament of the displaced. The following case studies illustrate the problems of the ill-fated victims.

In the case of Ezhimala Naval Academy project in Kannur district, the displaced households were provided with a plot of land at Chorichal and Paruthicaud, varying from 10 cents to one acre. Here again, the DPs have the same problems as those of Bakel and IDA projects.

Some of the evicted families from Idukki project area were given one acre of land at Amaravathy and ten khajans of coconut palm leaves.

The Karappuzha project is another example of injustice meted out to the displaced. Almost all of them were Tribals. The R & R officials made an estimate of a value for the house the displaced were living in and made a payment to the family. It was left to the displaced to identify a place, buy the land and build a house of their own.

Displacement in Chaliyam

Chaliyam is a coastal village located near Beypore port in the Kadalundi panchayat of Kozhikode district. The main occupation of the villagers is fishing and related activities. There are about 1,200 families residing in this small island.

It was in 1995 that the government acquired 19.43 ha. (48 acres) of land and handed it over to a private party for establishing PeeVees Petroleum company. The families residing there had 10 to 40 cents of land each. The company displaced 76 families. Among the 144 families in the resettlement site (RWS & ES project, 2000), 65 with 308 persons belong to fishing community. Among them 70 are men, 74 women, 84 boys and 80 girls. The remaining 11 families had no other alternative, but to depend on their relatives. Since the land was pattaless, it was easy for the authorities to displace them. As the people protested against their displacement, the government officials and local leaders initiated discussion with them. The agreement was to provide four cents of land and a thatched house for the displaced. Those who had only land before displacement were provided with four cents of land and Rs.7,500 each. Six acres of acquired land were set apart for resettlement.

The house provided for resettlement was 10 feet long and six feet broad. Most of the huts perished within two years, because of poor quality. So, the people had to spend additional amounts to repair and maintain them. This resulted in indebtedness. The authorities promised patta for the land, toilet facilities, well, drinking water and ration card. But, none of these promises were fulfilled. Moreover, the place of resettlement is within the range of Coastal Zone Protection Act and these poor families are still waiting for the patta for the land.

(MICTRA, Document)

The state of homelessness attached a stigma to the poor and people reacted negatively. Such reactions and stigma caused social distance of the poor. It also suggests that they face discrimination in social relations, employment and housing which will contribute to the perpetuation of their homeless condition and the public may not support policies that would improve their situation (Phelan et al., 1997: 335). Further, having lost the means of livelihood by their eviction from their original settlement and without any hope for a job, which does not come easily in their new settlement, the project would have done justice had they offered jobs to the displaced. KMML, VSSC, SIKL, NTPC and Nedumbassery were the few projects that offered some jobs to the displaced or created job opportunities for them. The Tiger Project was the worst. The Tribals were not given any resettlement package and they had nowhere to go. All these clearly show that a vast majority of the projects do not have a proper resettlement scheme.

Irrigation and hydel projects are the large scale displacement agents in Kerala. But, the information on resettlement and rehabilitation of most of them is not available. We presume that most of them gave only compensation for the land acquired. Idukki and Kallada projects are exceptions among the water resource projects as they have offered land to the displaced.

Wildlife Sanctuaries and Resettlement

Out of the 11 wildlife sanctuaries in Kerala, we have obtained some information on resettlement of the affected from the respective management plans of Parambikulam, Neyyar, Peppara and Chinnar projects. These plans speak of one Tribal colony inside Parambikulam (Management Plan, 1990: 18), 14 Tribal settlements inside Neyyar (Management Plan, 1990: 26), and 12 tribal settlements in Peppara sanctuary. The Management Plan (1990: 8-9) of Chinnar Sanctuary acknowledges the presence of Tribals of Muthuvan and Hill Pulaya communities. This report also speaks about the need for resettling them. But, any such schemes are yet to be implemented. The relocation scheme of Peppara envisages payment of compensation for standing crops, monitory assistance

Rehabilitation Scheme of a Proposed Project

Chaliyar irrigation project is proposed to irrigate 50,200 ha. of land in Malapuram and Kozhikode districts. The proposed reservoir would be created by the construction of a dam at Ambuttampetty. It requires 1430 ha. of land (Supt. Engr., Kozhikode). The reservoir will submerge about 210 tribal families in 12 colonies in the catchment area of *Chaliyar* river.

Irrigation Department, Government of Kerala, in line with the recommendations of the Central Water Commission has prepared a rehabilitation plan costing Rs. 610 lakhs for the DPs of this project. The salient features of this rehabilitation plan are given below.

Table 4.16

Proposed Compensation

Item		*Amount*
1.	Land	Rs.2.47 Lakhs/ha
2.	Crops	Rs. 1.95 Lakhs/year
3.	Pucca house	Rs. 25,000
4.	Semi Pucca house	Rs. 18,000
5.	Kacha house	Rs. 8,000
6.	Cow	Rs. 3,000
7.	Goat	Rs. 533.33
8.	Poultry	Rs. 53.33
9.	Honey Collecting Can	Rs. 200
10.	Well	Rs. 5091
11.	Cot	Rs. 500
12.	Chair	Rs. 100
13.	Table	Rs. 200
14.	Bench	Rs. 284.37
15.	Radio	Rs. 733
16.	Temple	Rs. 7,500

Land and House: The cost of 210 ha. of forest land for rehabilitating the displaced is estimated to be Rs. 2.50 crores. Each family will be given about 10 cents of land with a model residential building including latrine and bathroom. The total estimated cost for this scheme is Rs. 73.50 lakhs.

Facilities: A new road to the colony from the main road, electrical lines to the colony, bore well and an overhead tank with pump set for water supply will also be given. A Solar lamp may be provided to each house and a solar street light in the colony.

Recreation Centre with a Community hall: A community hall and a recreation centre with a Television set will be provided.

Co-operative Society: A tribal farming co-operative society is proposed with a view to administer the cultivation of land available in the colony.

Land for Cultivation: Forty hectares of land each may be set apart for cultivation of teak, coconut, arecanut with pepper and rubber.

Collection centre for Minor Forest Produce (MFP): Facilities will be provided at the farming co-operative society for collection of MFP.

Model Dairy Unit: Twenty model dairying units are proposed, each consisting of two milk animals and a cattle shed.

Other Facilities Proposed: Twenty bio-gas plants are also proposed to be given to these beneficiaries who get benefits under model dairy units. Five anganwady/balawady buildings for the welfare of women and children, a medical institution, tribal school up-gradation, pre-metric hostels, common worshipping places, pension schemes for those above 60 years of age (Rs. 100 per mensem), tribal voluntary services, and a burial ground are the other facilities proposed for the displaced.

Source: Chief Engineer Investigation, Irrigation Department, February, 1998.

for construction of buildings in the new site, shifting charges, construction of approach roads, provision of drinking water facilities and self employment schemes (Management Plan, 1990: 22).

The above mentioned documents of the forest department are ample evidence to disprove the official version that the sanctuaries in Kerala have not affected any people. Further, these areas have been notified as sanctuaries in the early 70s or 80s and the officials are still in the stage of planning to resettle the displaced even after decades. This proves beyond doubt the official apathy in resettling the Tribals whose livelihood has been jeopardised by the creation of wildlife sanctuaries.

The proposed scheme sounds very idealistic. If it is implemented, it will do real good to the displaced. Personal visits and discussions with key informants and *gramapanchayat* members reveal that this project is not likely to take off. Therefore, the proposed scheme is of no practical value and it may be treated as a routine exercise of the department concerned.

Experiences elsewhere in India show that fairly good resettlement schemes were offered to the DPs, mainly because of three factors viz. agitation, pressure from the World Bank, and the initiative of a good administrator. For example, in Rourkela, it was under the initiative of a good administrator, the T. N. Singh Formula of giving one job per displaced family was evolved. The T. N. Singh Formula was in force from 1961-86. However, in Kerala we did not come across any evidence of it being applied during this period. Also, we see better R & R schemes for the World Bank projects, because they have a policy on resettlement and rehabilitation.

In Kerala, agitations seem to be a predominant factor in the fight to get good resettlement. As mentioned earlier, VSSC, Idukki, Nedumbassery and NTPC are the projects which offered relatively better resettlement package. In Idukki, Nedumbassery and VSSC projects, it was because of the agitations. The Communist party had taken the initiative in Idukki project and the local church leaders in VSSC project, whereas the organised movement in Nedumbassery project was by social activists. It was at the insistence of the World Bank that the NTPC project at Kayamkulam offered an R & R scheme. But, in Kerala, we did not find any scheme that evolved a resettlement package at the initiative of a good administrator.

Compensation

Compensation includes the value of the land and all the immovable assets therein. However, in agricultural land compensation is calculated in addition to the value of the land taking into account the annual productivity and the life span of the perennial crops.

An attempt is made in this section to analyse the amount paid as compensation for the land and other assets. To understand its impact, it suffices to have data from a set of representative projects from all the categories. That is what we have given in Table 4.16.

From the available information, we calculated the average compensation per hectare for a project in a given year. To illustrate it, let us take the case of Idukki project.

The area of land taken over for Idukki hydroelectric project (given in Table 4.17) was 15.5849 ha., whereas the total land acquired for this project is much higher. The information on the amount of compensation pertains to the area of land mentioned in the table. From these data, we calculated the average compensation per hectare. The same procedure is followed for calculating the average amount of compensation per hectare for each project.

The compensation paid in the 1980s and 1990s would be far higher than what was paid in the earlier decades, because of the inflationary factor intervening in the course of time. Therefore, we have converted the amount of compensation paid in different years to the current price (1999 base).

Similarly, the value of land varies in accordance with the type of land and the location (site value). Along with these, we have also taken into account the land value and price escalation depending on the density of population and demand for land.

The compensation paid per hectare varies from Rs. 6,467.65 to Rs. 1,76,45,382. Unlike in other states, no marked district-wise difference in payment can be found in Kerala. But, a significant difference can be seen with regard to the different locations/sites. For example, the lowest amount quoted in our study was for Kuttiadi Irrigation project which is located in the remote part of Kozhikode, whereas the highest compensation was paid for the land acquired for Thiruvananthapuram International Airport which is in the state capital. The second highest amount was paid for the Nallalam Diesel Power Plant in Kozhikode. In the mid 90s, the land value in Kerala was at its peak. It was during this period that acquisition for this project was made which explains the inflationary rate of compensation paid. Hindustan Petroleum

Table 4.17

Compensation Paid by a Representative Set of Projects in Kerala

Name of the Project	Land (ha.) Acquired	District	Year *	Compen-sation given	Rs. per Hectare.	Rs. in Current prices (1999)	Source
WATER RESOURCES							
1. Kuttiadi Irrigation Project	1052.631	Kozhi-kode	Wb-1960	2956000.00	2808.20	6467.65	Project report (I) of KIP, PWD.
2. Karappuzha Irrigation Project	512	Wayanad	1961	31029321.00	60604.14	134007.72	Office of the Executive Engineer, Kalpetta.
3. Idukki hydroelectric Project	15.5849	Idukki	I-1963	235873.99	15134.77	31796	Office of the Deputy Collector, KSEB, File No. LA_2-1139/61, Thiruvananthapuram.
4. Pathazhakundu Reservoir Scheme	8.4696	Thrissur	I-1964	103563.59	12227.68	22982.14	Collectorate, File No. R Dis. 6685/64, Thrissur.
5. Muvattupuzha Valley Irrigation Project	714.3887	Kottayam	I-1976	95811366.00	134116.58	797523.86	Office of the Exe. Egnr., MVIP and LAO, Elanji.
6. Venganallur Reservoir Scheme	12.6870	Thrissur	I-1978	306104.99	24127.45	15398.27	Collectorate, File No. E_3 29228/78, Thrissur
7. Kuttiadi Augmentation (Banasurasagar)	7.6923	Wayanad	1981	388447.33	50498.20	232099.87	Office of the Deputy Collector, Award Register, KSEB, Kozhikode.
INDUSTRIES							
8. Traco Cables Company Ltd, Irumpanam	14.5748	Ernakulam	1960	309086.18	21206.88	48842.18	Manager(P&A), Traco Cables.

Contd...

Contd...

9.	Sugar Factory, Menampra	44.5344	Palakkad	Wb-1964	500000.00	11227.27	21101.85	Manager, Administrative Office.
10.	Chemical Industrial Estate & Development Area, Aroor.	6.3967	Alappuzha	Wb-1966	2900000.00	453358.76	709024.81	DIC, Alappuzha.
11.	Steel Complex, Chevayur.	17.8016	Kozhikode	Awd-1972	842517.81	47328.20	54801.27	Collectorate, Kozhikode, 1972.
12.	Automobile Tyre Factory (Appollo), Kodakara	13.0850	Thrissur	Awd-1975	318173.14	24315.87	51084.20	Collectorate, File No. 1477/75, Thrissur.
13.	Autokast, Cherthala	48	Alappuzha	1980	20000000.0	416666.67	2046163.30	Manager Personnel, SIKL, Cherthala.
14.	Industrial Development Area, Pudussery.	54.3117	Palakkad	I-1983	12046687	221806.48	855157.42	DIC, Palakkad.
15.	Hindustan Petroleum Corporation Ltd., Palakkad.	9.2915	Palakkad	Wb-1990	117092122.0	1260206.86	3063292.1	LAO, LA Register and Award File, 1990.
16.	Indian Telephone Industries Ltd., Palakkad	40.3360	Palakkad	Awd-1990	20098000.0	498264.57	1211174.2	LAO, LA and Award File, Kottakakom, 1990.
17.	Technopark, Kazhakkuttom	32.26	Thiruvanantha-puram	1993	21481224.0	665877.99	1281273.4	Special Tahsildar, Addl. LA unit, File No. A_2/379/92. Thiruvananthapuram
18.	Cochin Refineries Limited, Ernakulam	141.7328		I-1994	160333887.0	1131240.52	1763947.5	LAO, Vytila.
19.	Kanjikode Industrial Township	299.5951	Palakkad	1997	82288487.0	274665.66	317685.55	LAO, Oral information from Clerk, Palakkad
20.	Apparel Park, Menamkulam	45.0728	Thiruvanantha-puram	1997	14804963.0	328467.79	379914.51	Office of the KINFRA, Project Consultant, Vellayambalam

Contd...

Contd...

POWER								
21.	K.S.E.B. Substation, Uduma	30.7692	Kasargod	Wb-1984	7600000	247000.24	855180.63	Office of the Asst. Engr, KSEB, Thiruvanantha-puram.
22.	National Thermal Power Corporation, Kayamkulam	108.0728	Alappuzha	I-1989	60147745.0	556548.40	1421805.6	LAO, Harippad.
23.	120 Mega Watt Diesel Generator Power Plant	10.8502	Kozhikode	1998	44220000.0	4075500.91	4435974.1	Office of Exe. Engr.- Thermal, Vyduthi Bhavan, Pattom.
MINES								
24.	Mining of Granite Stones, Palavayal.	3.2960	Palakkad	1991	124837.43	37875.43	59322.96	Collectorate, LAO, Award No. 1/91 dtd 4-2-91, Palakkad.
DEFENCE								
25.	Kerala Armed Police Camp.	12.6397	Pathanamthitta	I-1983	3657093.00	289333.84	1115503.8	RDO, LA file, Adoor.
ENVIRONMENT PROTECTION								
26.	Elephant Project, Thariyode.	88.4979	Wayanad	1994	9956000	112499.85	175421.59	Collectorate, File No. B6-20048/92 dtd 7-4-1992, Wayanad
27.	Elephant Project – Marayoor	30.1538	Idukki	1995	6540980.00	216920.58	302404.53	RDO, Devikulam.
TOURISM								
28.	Veli Tourist Village.	9.2388	Thiruvanantha-puram	II-1988	2597800	281183.70	718335.63	LAO, Collectorate, Thiruvananthapuram.
29.	Bakel Tourism, Kasaragod.	59.5141	Kasargod	1997	154000000	2587622.09	2992911.9	Bakel Development, Corporation, Kasargod.
URBAN DEVELOPMENT								
30.	Edappally Housing Accommodation Scheme	6.5101	Ernakulam	I- 1979	3213566.40	493627.80	2935356.3	Kerala State Housing Board, Thiruvananthapuram.

Contd...

Contd...

No.	Project	Area	District	Year				Source
31.	Housing Colony, Nadakkavu.	5.28744	Kozhikode	1986	4483026	847863.23	2624710.3	LAO, File No. 1064/82, Collectorate, Kozhikode.
32.	Municipal Stadium & Park Tiruvalla	6.07692	Pathanamthitta	Awd-1988	758073.91	124746.66	318688.35	RDO, File No. B2. 107/87, Tiruvalla.
33.	Medical College, Thrissur.	10.8677	Thrissur	Awd-1989	2863808.00	263515.55	673199.08	Collectorate, File No. R Dis E1-34708/84, R Dis 60051/83, Thrissur
	FARMS AND FISHERIES							
34.	Seed Farm, Edathuruthy.	8.4170	Thrissur	I-1961	76273.20	9061.80	20037.43	Collectorate, File No. R Dis 2746/61, Thrissur
35.	Seed Farm, Pazhayannur.	9.8380	Kozhikode	I-1961	114182.28	11606.24	25663.69	Office of the State Seed Farm, Perambra.
36.	Fish Cultivation Farm, Pallippuram	12.2380	Thrissur	I- 1980	297413.84	24302.41	119344.08	Collectorate, File No. R Dis 3432/61, Thrissur.
37.	Attappadi Goat Farm, Agali	6.9190	Palakkad	1980	91164.04	13175.89	64704.05	LAO, LA Register and Award File, 1987, Kottakakom.
	TRANSPORT							
38.	Thiruvananthapuram International Airport	10.5263	Thiruvananthapuram	Wb- 1986	60000000.00	5700008.55	17645382	Office of the Land Manager,) Airport.
39.	Ernakulam Kayamkulam Broad-guage Railway	487.2227		1993	180000000.00	369440.91	710873.2	LAO, Alappuzha.
40.	Cochin International Airport, Nedumbassey	489.2914	Ernakulam	1994	595206999.0	1216467.32	1896842	LAO, Angamaly.
41.	Kalpetta Bye – Pass	10.5708		1996	12773394	1208365.87	1397627.8	RDO, Wayanad.
42.	Karipur Airport	45.95.95	Malapuram	Awd-1995	126327847.0	2748677.55	3831874.9	LAO, Award Register No. 5/95 to19/95, Malapuram.

Contd...

Contd...

EDUCATIONAL INSTITUTIONS								
43.	Cochin University of Science and Technology	49.0405	Ernakulam	Awd-1965	222105.31	4529.01	7763.71	Engineering Section, File No - 44/E_4 - 4/6 5-66, Cochin University.
44.	Kerala Agricultural University, Vellanikara.	379.5615	Thrissur	Awd-1974	2882070.99	7593.15	15952.13	Collectorate, File No - E3 18498/70, Thrissur.
45.	Mahatma Gandhi University, Kottayam	42.5061	Kottayam	Awd-1989	26663074.04	627276.41	1602493.3	Collectorate, LAO, File No-G_2 - 46339/84, G_2 -3213/86, G_2 - 22449/87, Kottayam.
46.	Government Polytechnic, Purakady	8.2389	Wayanad	1991	2553310.75	309909.18	485399.86	Collectorate, File No.B_6/19159/97, Wayanad
47.	Sri.Sankaracharaya Sanskrit University, Kalady.	25.1012	Ernakulam	Awd-1994	29320000.0	1168071.64	1821378.4	Department of Development, Sanskrit University, Kalady.
OTHERS								
48.	Punalur Rehabilitation Plantations	4.0121	Kollam	I-1994	2031004.00	506219.69	789350.24	LAO-General, File No.138/95 B, Civil Station, Kollamr

*The year of land take over is given in this column, but in many cases this was not available. So we have given any one among the following 1. Year of first notification (I), 2. Second notification (II), 3. Award (Awd) or 4. the year of work begun (Wb).

Corporation at Palakkad ranks third in the amount paid. Bakel Tourism Resorts in Kasargod district, which is relatively backward, ranks fourth in the amount paid as compensation. One possible reason for this higher amount of compensation paid is that this was a location attracting tourists, because of its historical importance even prior to the acquisition.

In Kerala, the rate of compensation awarded (market value) for the land acquired is approximately one-third of the real value of the land. It should be appreciated that the assets in the land also got paid based on the returns from it. This is somewhat positive compared to other states. But, in this process, there is possibility of corruption creeping in. In practice, it is left to the discretion of the officer in charge to make the assessment. In reality, the people get only about one-third of the replacement value of the land. The findings of the present study also substantiate the inadequacy of compensation as a good number of respondents complained.

Studies in Orissa conducted by Fernandes and Raj (1992:92) revealed that there was a substantial difference in the amount of compensation in different districts and regions. It depended on the extent of peoples' exposure to the external economy, the type of resistance they put up, their negotiating power and the perceived backwardness of the area. They concluded that even within a given project, the amount received differed from village to village, depending on the power relations. For instance, the DPs/PAPs of coastal districts, most of whom belong to the middle castes, got a higher compensation than their counterparts in the administratively backward districts (Fernandes and Asif, 1997: 116).

Similar is the situation in Goa (Fernandes and Naik, 1999: 65). The compensation paid to landowners in the advanced *talukas* is not very low, but it is low in the administratively neglected regions. As such it was totally inadequate for the affected people to start life anew. For instance, the amount paid per hectare of land acquired for the Rock Garden in the urban area of Mapusa was Rs. 30,000 only (Ibid: 64).

Conclusion

It is evident that most of the persons affected by development projects in Kerala belong to the marginalised communities like small farmers, fisher folk, Tribals and other backward communities. The mere fact of absence of reliable data regarding the number and type of people affected and displaced by the projects, even in the offices concerned, proves the lack of human consideration for these victims of development. Absence of policy for rehabilitation of the affected population adds to their miseries as the projects limit their schemes to mere monetary compensation. The amount of compensation paid for the land acquired is far below the replacement value. Many projects offered only resettlement facilities in place of proper rehabilitation.

In Kerala where the achievements in the field of social development in terms of literacy, health, life expectancy and better opportunities for women are outstanding, the sensitivity of the Government to the problems of development-induced displacement is far below expectation. In the context of economic development, the state often denies social justice to the affected. This is very evident from the absence of a rehabilitation policy in the state. This might eventually grow into a threat to the achievements of the State in the field of social development.

5

Profile of Projects and Respondents

In the previous chapters, we presented the extent of land acquired and the magnitude of displacement consequent upon it. This chapter gives a brief picture of the projects selected for detailed study and the demographic, social, and economic profile of the respondents. An attempt is also made to compare these parameters with some of the other states in the country.

I
Profile of the Projects

1. Indian Rare Earths Ltd. (IRE)

Indian Rare Earths Ltd. is a government of India undertaking located at Chavara in Karunagappally taluk of Kollam district. The company produces Ilminite, Routile etc., from mineral sand. The mining of the raw materials is done in the nearby area. IRE started production in the year 1970.

2. Kerala Minerals and Metals Ltd. (KMML)

This company is located at Sankaramangalam in the Karunagappally taluk of Kollam district. It is owned by the government of Kerala. Work on this project started in 1979. The products of KMML are Titanium Tetra Chloride, Illmenite, Monozite, Zircon, Sillimanite, Leucoxene and Titanium Dioxide Pigment (Rutile). These are processed from mineral sands. KMML also manufactures Ironoxide bricks used for building purposes.

The factory has its own mines in the nearby villages in the coastal area of Chavara.

3. Idukki Hydro Electric Project (IHP)

Idukki Hydro Electric Project, a Canadian aided project conceived in 1961, is the biggest hydel project in Kerala. It is the second highest dam in India. This project was envisaged to harness the power potential of the river *Periyar*. It comprises three dams viz. Idukki, Cheruthoni and Kulamavu and an underground power station at Moolamattam. The Idukki dam and powerhouse are 43 kms apart. The installed capacity of the powerhouse is 1080 MW consisting of 6 units of 180 MW each.

The inaugural run was on October 4, 1975. Commercial operation of the powerhouse commenced in February 1976. The first stage was completed by the end of 1976 at a total cost of Rs.87.6 crores. The cost of the second stage was Rs. 59 crores and it was completed in 1987. The third stage was completed in 1991 at a cost of Rs.16.5 crores. The total cost of the project is estimated to be at Rs.309.7 Crores (Brochure of KSEB on Idukki Hydro Electric Project). A good number of the people displaced by this project are Tribals.

4. Karappuzha Irrigation Project (KIP)

The Karappuzha Irrigation Project, originally proposed by the British Government, was undertaken by the Government of Kerala in 1972. The construction work of an earthern dam across the river Karappuzha is going on at Vazhavetta in Wayanad district. The project was envisaged to irrigate an area of 9300 ha. (gross). The original estimated cost of the project was Rs. 7.60 crores and the revised cost in 1986 came to Rs. 40.66 crores. The project was expected to be commissioned at the end of the ninth five-year plan.

5. Industrial Development Area (IDA)

The Industrial Development Area is situated in Pudussery village of Palakkad district, one of the leading industrial districts in

Kerala. 303.64 ha. of land was acquired for this project in 1985, displacing 137 families.

6. Steel Industries Kerala Limited (SIKL)

Steel Industries Kerala Ltd. is a state government undertaking, located at S.N. Puram in Cherthala taluk, Alappuzha district. It has two units viz. Autocast, which produces steel castings with an installed capacity of 23,000 M.T., and a steel fabrication unit with an installed capacity of 3,000 M.T. (State Planning Board, 1997: s123-124). The corporate office of the company is located at Athani in Thrissur district (KSIDC, 1998).

7. Kayamkulam Combined Cycle Power Project (NTP)

This is the only thermal power project in Kerala. It is owned by the National Thermal Power Corporation and is located at Choolatheruvu, and extends to five villages viz. Arattupuzha, Muthukulam, Cheppad, Chingoli, and Pallipad of Karthikappally and Mavelikkara taluks in Alappuzha district. The main plant package funded by the World Bank for this project was Rs. 1,310.58 crores. The installed capacity is 350 MW. The project uses Naphtha and/or Natural gas as fuel. The first unit of the project started functioning in 1999. The work on the remaining units is in progress (*The Power to Care*, a brochure by NTPC, 2000).

8. Vikram Sarabhai Space·Centre (VSSC)

The Thumba Equitorial Rocket Launching Station (TERLS) was the first initiative for building and test firing rockets in India. It required the facilities of land and sea. It started functioning in 1963. This endeavour was later expanded to include missiles, satellites and other strategic and defence related research centres under the name of Indian Space Research Organisation (ISRO) with its units in different states. Honouring its founder, Vikram Sarabhai, the three units set up in Kerala at Thumba, Vattiyurkavu and Valiamala in the suburbs of Thiruvananthapuram were renamed Vikram Sarabhai Space Centre (VSSC). For the project at Thumba, a portion of Veli and the whole of Pallithura village in Attipra Panchayat of Thiruvananthapuram taluk were acquired. The acquired area stretched from Veli bridge to the Thumba Fathima Church and from T.S. Canal to the Arabian Sea. It displaced about a thousand families at different stages of acquisition. A vast majority of the evicted were from the fishing community of the coastal belt of Pallithura and Veli.

9. Mavoor Gwaliyor Rayons (MGR)

The Mavoor Gwaliyor Rayons factory widely known as Grasim Industries is the largest private sector industrial unit in Kerala and is located at Mavoor, 25 kms east of Kozhikode under the ownership of the Birla group. The company started manufacturing pulp and staple fibre from bamboo and wood in 1963. Its manufacturing process has been creating severe environmental problems by endangering the lives of thousands of villagers in its neighbourhood.

10. Vizhinjam Fishing Harbour (VZM)

Vizhinjam is one of the fishing harbours of Kerala located 15 kms south of Thiruvananthapuram, the capital. Majority of the inhabitants of this project area are fisher folk. There is also a 'war watching station' and 'signal station' for navigational communications of vessels anchored offshore to give weather signals to sea vessels and fishing crafts attached to the harbour. Vizhinjam port has been declared as a customs port.

11. Periyar Tiger Reserve (PTR)

The Periyar Tiger Reserve lies on the high ranges of the Western Ghats in Idukki district. The forests around the Periyar river were declared Reserved forests in 1899. These forests were turned into the Nellikkampathy Sanctuary in 1934, and taken by the forest department in 1966. It was declared a Tiger Reserve in 1978 under the scheme 'Project Tiger'. The total area under the sanctuary is 777.54 sq kms (77,754 ha.) (*Periyar Tiger Reserve*, A brochure by the wildlife wing of Kerala Forest Dept.)

12. Ezhimala Naval Academy (ENA)

Ezhimala is one of the major defence units in Kerala, situated at Ramanthali village of Taliparambu taluk in Kannur district. An area of 1012.15 ha. of land was taken over for this project in 1983, displacing about 1,800 people.

13. Bakel Tourism Project (BTP)

The project area spreads over four panchayats, namely Chemmanadu, Vallikkara, Uduma and Ajasoor in Kasargod district. The project envisages the development of Beach Resorts in the Bakel Fort area. The proposal for this project was submitted to the government in 1995 by a study team appointed for collecting details of the area. The Bakel Resorts Development Corporation is the agency entrusted with the management of this project. The land required for the project was 277.33 Ha.

14. Nedumbassery International Airport (NIA)

This is the fourth airport in Kerala and was conceived in collaboration with Non Resident Indians (NRIs) from 30 countries. The location selected for this airport was Nedumbassery, a village 14 kms north-east of Cochin. The project with an estimate of Rs.230 crores was prepared in 1992 and the Cochin International Airport Authority was formed in 1993. The airport started functioning in June 1999. An area of 526.32 ha. of land was acquired for the project by displacing about 1,200 families.

15. Muvattupuzha Valley Irrigation Project (MVIP)

This project started in 1974 was meant to irrigate an area of 17,737 ha. in Idukki, Ernakulam and Kottayam districts by channeling the water from the Moolamattam power house of Idukki Hydroelectric Project. The dam of this project is on the river Muvattupuzha at Malankara.

II
Profile of the Respondents

The focus of this section is the demographic, social and economic characteristics of the respondents. It is important to analyse these factors, because the impact of displacement and resettlement is felt differentially by different categories such as caste/tribe, age, gender and the socio-economic status.

Age of the Respondents

The age of the respondents is a crucial factor while gathering data about displacement, because the person who shares the information about the process and impact of displacement should be one who can remember the trauma of involuntary displacement. In principle, those belonging to the higher age groups can be expected to be more knowledgeable about the problem under study. That is why we chose a larger proportion belonging to the higher age groups in all the categories.

More than three fourths (75.83%) of the total respondents belong to the above 40 age group, the highest concentration is in the 60 and above age group. There are two respondents in the below 20 age group and another two of twenty years. They belong to Rayons and NTPC projects. The reason for their inclusion in the sample is because NTPC is a recent project and Rayons project became problematic, because of the excessive environmental pollution created by the company, which evoked large-scale protest from the people in the locality in recent times. We felt that it was important to get a representation of the younger generation in these two areas who would be more sensitive to the issues around these projects. The prevalence of larger number of respondents in the 40 and above age group is because of the higher age of projects selected for the study.

Caste-wise, more than a half of STs and general category are in the 50 and above age group, while a higher concentration of the SCs and OBCs is in the 40-49 age bracket. Thus, the age composition of respondents shows that the vast majority of all categories are knowledgeable to offer us valid information regarding the problems related to displacement. Males outnumber females in all the age groups except in 30-39, whereas the percentage of females is 52.53. The reason for this will be explained in section on marital status.

Religion and Caste of Respondents

The major religions in Kerala are Hinduism, Islam and Christianity. In the religion-wise classification, we have included 'Tribals' as a separate religion, because some of the Tribes in Kerala have their own religious practices, and they do not belong to any of the organised religious traditions. But, in general many of the Tribes are Hindus. With regard to the caste-wise classification, we have followed the standardised categorisation of government, namely Scheduled Tribes (STs), Scheduled Caste (SCs), Other Backward Classes (OBCs) and Forward Class (GN).

Fifty three per cent of the total respondents are Hindus, 30 per cent Christians, 12.37 per cent Muslims and 4.75 per cent Tribals. Among the STs, 46 per cent are Hindus, 24 per cent Christians, and 30 per cent Tribals. Except one Christian, all SCs belong to Hindu religion. One half of the OBCs are Hindus, 31 per cent Christian and 20 per cent Muslims. Among the forward castes, nearly 50 per cent are Hindus, 38 per cent Christians. Twelve per cent (from Ezhimala) claimed that they belong to the forward caste. Project-wise, the highest concentration of STs was found in the Idukki Tiger project, and Karappuzha Irrigation Project.

The percentage of SCs found in the sample is only 7.19 as against the state proportion of 9.92. This is because SC population is widely scattered all over the state and their concentration is more in the agricultural sector. Three of the projects in our study, namely Nedumbassery, MVIP and Ezhimala have a higher concentration of SCs, because they acquired agricultural land. We find a higher proportion of OBCs in VSSC, Vizhinjam and IRE projects, which are located in the coastal areas where all the affected persons belong to the fish-workers community. In three projects, viz. Rayons, NTPC and SIKL, more than two third of the respondents belong to the forward caste. MVIP come close to these with 53 per cent of forward caste.

Marital Status of the Respondents

About 80 per cent of the respondents are married, of whom 62 per cent are males. The percentage of the widowed is 14 and that of the unmarried is 6. Two each of the respondents are divorced or separated. More than three-fourth of SCs, OBCs and forward castes are married, while their proportion among the SCs is 92. Among the widowed, nearly 60 per cent are found in OBC category and 25 per cent among the forward castes.

Widowhood is prevalent in the 60 and above age group. All the two divorced and one of the separated respondents belong to the age group of 40-49 and the other one of the separated is in 30-39 age group. The proportion of widowed is found to be 5 per cent in STs, 18 per cent in SCs, 19 per cent in OBCs and 10 per cent in the forward castes. In all the castes, more than 80 per cent of the widowed are females. This perfectly agrees with the general pattern in Kerala society where the life expectancy of females is higher than that of males. Also, all the divorced and separated respondents were females.

Fifty six per cent of the respondents are males. Our aim was to get an equal proportion of respondents from both sexes (Sex was another criterion for sample selection). However, we could not ensure this fully. There were many reasons for this difference in male-female ratio. In the case of the tribal respondents, women hesitate to come forward for interview in the presence of men. This is an indication of male domination among these Tribals. This may be due to closer contact of Tribals with other communities from whose value system they also imbibe the upper caste culture of male domination. The data give a clear picture of the males' over representation in the projects which have a dominance of ST population, namely Idukki Tiger project and Karappuzha Irrigation Project. In the case of KMML and Bakel projects, a majority of the respondents are OBCs, the percentage of males was 71 and 70 respectively.

The ratio of females in our sample is higher in IRE, NTPC, IDA and Vizhinjam projects, because the men were out of their house for work during daytime. This is particularly true of fishing communities in IRE and Vizhinjam projects where men are out in the sea for most part of the day and even in night.

Sex Ratio in the Respondents' Families

Though the sex ratio in Kerala is 1036 which is in favour of females, our sample gives the opposite picture (954). This difference is substantial in some age groups. In the below four age group, there are only 74 girls against 106 boys. That means the sex ratio is 698. Generally, the number of boys under the age of 5 is higher than girls. But, they balance off in the higher ages, because of the lower survival rate of the boys. Except in the age groups of 15-17 and 25-29 where the sex ratio is 827 and 877 respectively, in all the other age groups there is no substantial difference in the number of males and females.

Compared to the Kerala average, the sex ratio among the STs, OBCs and forward castes in our sample was found to be lower -- 858, 937, and 998 respectively. Only among SCs, it is higher (1099). The sex ratio of STs in Kerala is 996, while that of SCs is 1029. Some studies reveal that the sex ratio among fisher-folk and STs is lower in Kerala (Pushpangadhan and Murugan, 1999).

Nearly a third of the respondents in our sample belongs to the lower classes/castes, among whom some signs of discrimination against the female child were found. According to experts in the field of tribal studies, the possible reasons for lower sex ratio among the Tribals include influence of Tamil culture where gender discrimination is practised, absence of prenatal care, lack of proper care during pregnancy, the practice of purity and pollution, neglect of the girl child and practices to imitate upper caste customs.

A similar study done in Goa shows that the males outnumber in the 0-9 and 18-24 age groups. The reason for this seems to be the female infant and child mortality in the early age group and high maternal mortality in the 18-24 age group. In the above 60 age group, the higher number of females is due to the prevalence of widowhood (Fernandes and Naik, 1999:71).

In IRE and MVIP projects, the number of women and men in the respondents' families is almost equal. In the case of Rayons project, the number of men is slightly higher. In the VSSC project, all the respondents belonged to a fishing community where females outnumber males; whereas in Vizhinjam, another fisher-folk community, the number of men is higher (175 men against 134 women). Male dominance can be seen again in NTPC, IDA, Karappuzha and Bakel projects, while females outnumber males in Nedumbassery and Tiger projects.

Members in the Respondents' Families

The average family size in Kerala is 5.3. With regard to our sample, it is 4.89. Though the family size in our sample is lower than the general population, this is not an indicator of planned population control, but due to extraneous factors. It may be attributed to factors such as low nutritional level, greater poverty, non-accessibility of proper medical care, poor sanitation and infrastructure facilities, and low literacy among the weaker sections. This finding is similar to the findings of Orissa study where the family size among Tribals was found to be 5.25 which is lower than the state average (Fernandes and Raj, 1992).

Table 5.1

Number of Members in Respondents' Families

Project	*1*	*2*	*3*	*4*	*5*	*5+*	*Total*
IRE	0	2	4	8	13	16	43
KML	2	0	3	2	8	2	17
IHP	2	7	16	14	18	13	70
KIP	0	1	2	16	17	26	62
IDA	1	1	2	10	17	14	45
SIKL	0	0	3	10	13	4	30
NTP	0	3	10	17	15	26	71
VSC	2	7	12	12	11	16	60
MGR	1	4	7	9	8	12	41
VZM	0	0	0	1	6	33	40
PTR	3	10	11	18	3	5	50
ENA	1	3	2	4	12	17	39
BTR	2	1	3	5	6	13	30
NIA	0	8	12	24	17	6	67
MVP	0	2	8	10	6	4	30
Total	14	49	95	160	170	207	695
Percentage	2.0	7.0	14	23.0	24.0	30.0	100

But, in the case of Vizhinjam project area, 82 per cent of the families have more than 5 members and several of them exceed the Kerala average. This may be attributed to the extreme social and economic backwardness of this region and probably also due to the influence of religious norms on population and fertility.

Education of Respondents

The percentage of the illiterate in the sample is 22. This is a significant finding in a state like Kerala which is supposed to be totally literate. Majority of the respondents of the present study came from remote rural and tribal areas in Kerala where literacy still remains low. This may be one of the reasons for such a large number of illiterate persons. For instance, 76 per cent of the respondents from the Tiger project who are Tribals and 63 per cent of fishermen respondents from Vizhinjam are illiterate. Also a higher proportion of illiterates can be found in the STs and SCs. About 45 per cent of the STs and 30 per cent of the SCs are illiterate. The corresponding percentages for OBCs and forward castes are 18.46 and 12.82, respectively.

Forty three per cent of the total respondents can barely read and write or have only primary school education. Those who passed 7th or 10th standards are 13 per cent each. Only one of the respondents has a professional degree in Engineering. He is from the SIKL project area at Cherthala. Nearly three per cent of the respondents have semi professional qualifications like ITI, diploma and TTC. Almost six per cent have college education.

Unlike other states of India, no sex-wise difference was found in the educational status of the respondents. But, 30 per cent of females as against 15 per cent of males were illiterates. However, the percentage of illiterate females is lower (42) among the Tribals of the Tiger project and higher (79) in Vizhinjam project, which are the two projects having more illiterate people.

About 39 per cent of ST males, 26 per cent of SC males, 10 per cent of OBC males and 7 per cent of males from forward castes are illiterate. The corresponding percentages for females are 58, 35.48, 28.35 and 20.38, respectively.

Land Ownership Before and After Displacement

We have considered both patta and non-patta land for the calculation of land ownership. Before displacement, 37 per cent of the Idukki project respondents had more than 10 acres of land each. 66 per cent of Nedumbassery had only less than one acre each. 45 per cent of the respondents had an ownership of less than 50 cents of land each. 78 per cent of Vizhinjam project respondents and 54 per cent of IRE, both from fishing communities, had no land before displacement. This shows that a good proportion of the displaced people were poor agricultural labourers.

Caste-wise 92 per cent of SCs, 56 per cent of forward castes, 55 per cent of OBCs and 37 per cent of STs had an area of less than one acre each before displacement.

It is important to note that the percentage of landless people decreased from 12 to one after displacement. On the one hand, the percentage of people having an area of land less than 50 cents had increased notably from 45 to 70 after displacement. On the other hand, the percentage of people having an area of land between 1-2.5 acres had slightly decreased and those with an area of more than five acres had decreased considerably after displacement. However, those having an area of land between 2.51 and 5 acres had slightly increased from 9 to 12 per cent.

The trend emerging from these data shows that more people became legal owners of land after displacement. Secondly, the area owned by the displaced persons increased in the lower categories and decreased in the higher categories. Those who had agricultural land were reduced to mere homestead. This affected their occupation and source of livelihood. One of the possible reasons for this change could be that the amount received as compensation was utilised for purchasing land and constructing house, and a variety of social needs. Since the criterion for fixing compensation is market value, the people could not purchase an equal measure of land with the compensation received.

All the respondents of KMML, Nedumbassery, MVIP projects, and all except one of IRE project, over 90 per cent of respondents from IDA, NTPC, VSSC, Vizhinjam, and Ezhimala projects, and over 80 per cent of respondents from Tiger Project and SIKL became owners of less than one acre of land each. Caste-wise, all except one SC, 85 per cent of OBCs, 78 per cent of forward castes and 51 per cent of STs belong to this category.

Some of the recent policies declared by the government of Kerala are favourable to the people who are now living in non-patta land. The declaration of the then Revenue Minister that all the VSSC project DPs who were then living in non-patta land would be given pattas was a recognition of the rights of VSSC project DPs (*Manorama*, 1999). But, they have been living on this non-patta land since 1961 and it took 38 years for the government to take such a humane decision. The recent land policy of the government to give land to all the landless Tribals is another turning point in this regard which will help the Tiger Project DPs living on non-patta land to become owners of land.

Income Distribution: Before and After Displacement

In calculating the income of the households of the respondents, we used a method in which the incomes from agricultural products and wage employment were added. When we assessed the economic position of the respondents before and after the displacement, we took into consideration the inflationary factor by converting the pre-displacement income in terms of prices in 1999.

Examining the economic consequence of displacement on the respondents, we find that the category of those who belong to less than Rs.5,000 annual income decreased considerably from nine to 2.45 per cent. This has brought about an improvement in the economic condition of three per cent of those who belong to lowest income group. On the other hand, there is a considerable increase in the number of persons with an annual income of Rs. 5,000-10,000 category. The change is from 41 to 67 per cent.

There is a consistent lowering of proportion of the respondents belonging to the higher income groups from

Rs.10,000 to 50,000. This is because about six per cent of the lowest category were able to climb up to this category, while 19.69 per cent of those who belong to higher income groups came down. However, there is hardly any change in the proportion of those who belong to above Rs.50,000 income group. The ratio of those who lost out in this process to those who gained is 3:1. The net outcome is that the percentage of those who were below the poverty line was 50 before displacement rose to 70 (when we take an annual income of Rs.10,000 as the cut-off point) after displacement.

Examining the situation caste-wise, we find that the general trend is reflected in all the categories. Among SCs and STs, we find no one in the below 5,000 rupees category, whereas their proportion increased in the Rs.5,000-10,000 category after displacement which is explained in terms of those who rose up from the lowest category. However, SCs seem to have lost out most among all categories after displacement. Ninety per cent of those who belong to above Rs. 10,000 category have fallen down to Rs. 5,000-10,000 after displacement. In OBC and general categories, there has not been much improvement in the case of those who belong to the lowest categories. Though there is a considerable increase in the Rs.5,000-10,000 category, most of them are those who have lost out from higher categories.

The deterioration of economic condition of the general category is most visible in MVIP and IDA projects. One third of the Tribals in KIP project were able to rise from the two lower categories to higher income groups, whereas the same trend is not seen among the respondents of PTR and IHP projects. All the 16 households who belong to general category in MVIP project had a steep fall from Rs.35,000-50,000 category to Rs.5,000-10,000.

Occupation of Respondents: Before and After Displacement

A fourth of the total respondents were labourers before displacement, while 22.16 per cent depended on agriculture for their livelihood. One-thirds of the respondents were jobless, whereas the percentage of salaried class is only 3.74. All the females coming under "No" category are housewives, whereas the males in this category are jobless. About 11 per cent of the respondents depended on fishing for their livelihood. All the respondents coming under "NP" were students at the time of displacement.

Project-wise, 88.57 per cent of Idukki and 60 per cent of Karappuzha respondents were cultivators before displacement. Nearly 60 per cent each of the IRE and Vizhinjam project respondents, 58.54 per cent of Rayons, 38.03 per cent of NTPC, and 22.39 per cent of Nedumbassery project respondents had no job before displacement. About 64 per cent of IDA, 52.24 per cent of Nedumbassery, 35.2 per cent of NTPC, and 26 per cent of Tiger respondents were labourers before displacement. Thirty five per cent each of IRE and VSSC projects, and 32 per cent of Vizhinjam respondents had fishing as their occupation before displacement. All of them were men, because in Kerala, women do not go out for fishing.

About 49 per cent of STs were cultivators and 84 per cent of SCs labourers, while 35.57 per cent of OBCs and 35.89 per cent of forward caste respondents were jobless before displacement.

Before displacement, 33.95 per cent of males and 8.23 per cent of females depended on agriculture or animal husbandry. About 8.42 per cent of males and 61.26 per cent of females were jobless.

The proportion of cultivators decreased from 22.16 per cent to 15.11, while the percentage of jobless increased from 31.22 to 39.71 after the displacement. The change in the percentage of labourers is from 24.17 to 22.3, and those who depended on fishing for their livelihood had slightly decreased from 10.94 to 9.06 per cent. The percentage of salaried class, petty business, unskilled, and skilled decreased slightly after displacement.

Only 37 per cent of the STs had agriculture as livelihood after displacement, whereas it was 49 before.

About 22 per cent of men and nine per cent of women depended on agriculture or animal husbandry after displacement and 16 per cent of men and 70 per cent of women remained unemployed.

The percentage of housewives increased from 48 to 55 after displacement. This increase is due to loss of labour opportunities for women who worked earlier as agricultural and manual labourers. The percentage of the jobless men doubled after displacement. This is because of loss of their labour opportunities in agriculture, and the inability to find new jobs in the resettlement area. Though there has been an increase in the rate of unemployment in both the sexes, the increase among men (9.47%) is higher compared to that of women (7.71%).

Socio-economic Class of the Respondents After Displacement

Nearly 78 per cent of the respondents belonged to the Lower Lower Class (LLC) and 19 per cent to the Lower Class (LC) indicating that a majority of the affected population belong to the weaker sections. About three per cent among the respondents are of the Middle Class (MC). Only one of the respondents belonged to the Upper Middle Class (UMC) and one to the Upper Class (UC). All the respondents of KMML, MVIP and Tiger Projects, over 90 per cent of those of VSSC, IDA, and NTPC projects, about 85 per cent of those of Nedumbassery, IRE, and Ezhimala projects, and 68 per cent of Rayons were from LLC. Around 77 per cent of Idukki project and 48 per cent of those of Karappuzha project were LC. The only one in UC is from Bakel and the UMC from the Karappuzha project. This clearly substantiates the hypothesis that a majority of the DPs/PAPs belong to the marginalised groups.

Caste-wise all except one of the SCs, 65 per cent of STs, 85 per cent of OBCs and 71 per cent of the forward castes belong to the LLC. The percentages of LC among the STs, OBCs and forward castes were 35, 12 and 24, respectively. One UMC respondent belonged to the ST and another one-UC to the OBC.

Educational Status by Class After Displacement

Twenty-seven per cent of LLC had passed IV standard, while 27.22 per cent were illiterate and 15.56 per cent just literate. More than one-fifth of the respondents of LC had studied up to X standard. The only one MC respondent was a post graduate and the one UC respondent had an engineering degree. About 30 per cent of LLC

Table 5.2
Education with Socio-Economic Class

Class	Caste	Illiterate		Literate		4th class		7th class		10th class		PDC		DC		PG		Semi pro-fessional		Total			Grand Total
		M	F	M	F	M	F	M	F	M	F	M	F	M	F	M	F	M	F	M	F	Total	
LLC	ST	29	19	8	2	8	0	2	1	0	2	1	1	0	0	0	0	0	0	48	25	73	540
	SC	5	11	4	4	8	9	1	3	1	2	0	1	0	0	0	0	0	0	19	30	49	
	OBC	16	37	22	20	41	39	19	19	19	11	5	0	0	1	0	0	1	2	123	129	252	
	GN	9	21	10	14	22	22	12	13	17	9	1	5	1	2	0	2	2	4	74	92	166	
LC	ST	0	3	6	0	10	5	4	2	5	2	1	0	1	0	0	0	0	0	27	12	39	133
	SC	0	0	0	0	0	0	0	0	0	0	0	0	0	0	0	0	0	1	0	1	1	
	OBC	0	1	9	0	6	0	5	0	5	1	4	1	2	0	0	0	2	1	33	4	37	
	GN	0	0	5	1	15	3	7	1	14	3	3	0	1	0	0	0	3	0	48	8	56	
MC	ST	0	0	0	0	0	0	0	0	0	0	0	0	0	0	0	0	0	0	0	0	0	20
	SC	0	0	0	0	0	0	0	0	0	0	0	0	0	0	0	0	0	0	0	0	0	
	OBC	1	0	0	0	2	0	1	0	1	1	0	0	1	0	1	0	0	0	7	1	8	
	GN	0	0	1	0	2	0	1	1	0	1	0	1	2	0	0	0	2	0	9	3	12	
UMC	ST	0	0	0	0	0	1	0	0	0	0	0	0	0	0	0	0	0	0	0	1	1	1
	SC	0	0	0	0	0	0	0	0	0	0	0	0	0	0	0	0	0	0	0	0	0	
	OBC	0	0	0	0	0	0	0	0	0	0	0	0	0	0	0	0	0	0	0	0	0	

Contd...

Contd...

	GN	0	0	0	0	0	0	0	0	0	0	0	0	0	0	0	0	0	0	0	0	0	
UC	ST	0	0	0	0	0	0	0	0	0	0	0	0	0	0	0	0	0	0	0	0	0	1
	SC	0	0	0	0	0	0	0	0	0	0	0	0	0	0	0	0	0	0	0	0	0	
	OBC	0	0	0	0	0	0	0	0	0	0	0	0	0	0	1	0	0	0	1	0	1	
	GN	0	0	0	0	0	0	0	0	0	0	0	0	0	0	0	0	0	0	0	0	0	
Total	ST	29	22	14	2	18	6	6	3	5	4	2	1	1	0	0	0	0	0	75	38	113	695
	SC	5	11	4	4	8	9	1	3	1	2	0	1	0	0	0	0	0	1	19	31	50	
	OBC	17	38	31	20	49	39	25	19	25	13	9	1	3	1	2	0	3	3	164	134	298	
	GN	9	21	16	15	39	25	20	15	31	13	4	6	4	2	0	2	7	4	131	103	234	
	Total	60	92	65	41	114	79	52	40	62	32	15	9	8	3	2	2	10	8	389	306	695	
Grand Total			152		106		193		92		94		24		11		4		18		695*		
Percentage			21.87		15.52		27.77		13.24		13.53		3.45		1.58		0.56		2.59		100		

*Note: We have not included in this table one respondent who has a professional degree in engineering because there is only one (male) in this category.

males and 25.36 per cent of LLC females had primary education (Table 5.2).

Land Ownership by Class-After Displacement

About 91 per cent of the LLC respondents owned less than 50 cents of land, whereas 45 per cent of LC owned between 2.51 and 5 acres. Both the UMC and UC respondents had more than 10 acres of land.

Table 5.3
Land Ownership with Socio-Economic Class

Class	*Caste*	*None*	*0.01 - 1*	*1.01 - 2.5*	*2.51 - 5*	*5.01 - 10*	*10+*	*Total*
LLC	ST	2	53	9	8	1	0	73
	SC	0	49	0	0	0	0	49
	OBC	2	235	7	6	2	0	252
	GN	2	153	6	5	0	0	166
LC	ST	0	5	9	22	2	1	39
	SC	0	0	0	0	0	1	1
	OBC	0	16	3	15	2	1	37
	GN	0	23	5	23	5	0	56
MC	ST	0	0	0	0	0	0	0
	SC	0	0	0	0	0	0	0
	OBC	1	2	2	2	0	1	8
	GN	0	6	1	2	1	2	12
UMC	ST	0	0	0	0	0	1	1
	SC	0	0	0	0	0	0	0
	OBC	0	0	0	0	0	0	0
	GN	0	0	0	0	0	0	0
UC	ST	0	0	0	0	0	0	0
	SC	0	0	0	0	0	0	0
	OBC	0	0	0	0	0	1	1
	GN	0	0	0	0	0	0	0
Total	ST	2	58	18	30	3	2	113
	SC	0	49	0	0	0	1	50
	OBC	3	253	12	23	4	3	298
	GN	2	182	12	30	6	2	234
Grand Total		7	542	42	83	13	8	695
Percentage		1.0	77.98	6.04	11.94	1.87	1.15	100

About 79 per cent of the respondents belonged to the two lowest classes possessing an area of less than one acre of land (Table 5.3).

Occupation by Socio Economic Class After Displacement

About 27 per cent of the LLC respondents are wage labourers, whereas four per cent are agriculturists and 49 per cent jobless. Among the LC respondents, 57 per cent depend on agriculture. Nine out of 20 MC respondents are skilled workers. About three fourth of the LLC females are jobless, while 17 per cent are labourers. About 38 per cent of the LLC males are labourers, whereas 24 per cent depend on fishing. More than two-thirds of the LC males are agriculturists.

Excluding the unemployed, we find that 44 per cent of the two lowest classes are employed in agriculture, animal husbandry, fishing and casual labour. Besides, all those employed in fishing are found in the LLC.

Income Distribution by Socio-Economic Class After Displacement

The increase in LCC can be attributed to the reduced land ownership, decreased returns from the land and increased unemployment.

Seventy one per cent of the LLC and 61 per cent of LC respondents have an annual family income between Rs.5,001 and Rs. 10,000 after displacement. Eleven per cent of the LLC and 13 per cent of LC have a higher income of Rs.10,001 to 15,000. Nearly five per cent of the LLC belong to the income group of Rs.15,001-20,000, four per cent to Rs.20,001-30,000, and 3.89 per cent to Rs.30,001-50,000 income groups.

In the two lowest socio-economic classes, we find the concentration of 81 per cent of the respondents in the category of below Rs.15,000 income group. The remaining 20 per cent are distributed along the higher income groups.

Table 5.4
Annual Income After Displacement with Socio-Economic Class

Class	*Caste*	*Less than 5,000*	*5,001- 10,000*	*10,001- 15,000*	*15,001- 20,000*	*20,001- 30,000*	*30,001- 50,000*	*50,000+*	*Total*
LLC	ST	0	62	6	2	2	1	0	73
	SC	0	41	6	0	2	0	0	49
	OBC	13	157	25	22	15	15	5	252
	GN	3	125	21	4	5	5	3	166
LC	ST	0	30	4	1	2	1	1	39
	SC	0	1	0	0	0	0	0	1
	OBC	0	15	8	5	2	4	3	37
	GN	1	35	5	2	5	6	2	56
MC	ST	0	0	0	0	0	0	0	0
	SC	0	0	0	0	0	0	0	0
	OBC	0	0	0	2	0	1	5	8
	GN	0	1	2	0	1	3	5	12
UMC	ST	0	1	0	0	0	0	0	1
	SC	0	0	0	0	0	0	0	0
	OBC	0	0	0	0	0	0	0	0
	GN	0	0	0	0	0	0	0	0
UC	ST	0	0	0	0	0	0	0	0
	SC	0	0	0	0	0	0	0	0
	OBC	0	0	0	0	0	0	1	1
	GN	0	0	0	0	0	0	0	0
Total	ST	0	93	10	3	4	2	1	113
	SC	0	42	6	0	2	0	0	50
	OBC	13	172	33	29	17	20	14	298
	GN	4	161	28	6	11	4	10	234
Grand Total		17	468	77	38	34	26	25	695
Percentage		2.45	67.34	11.08	5.47	4.9	3.74	3.6	100

Conclusion

A majority of the respondents belong to the higher age groups and are married. Fifty three per cent of the total respondents are Hindus, 30 per cent Christians and 12.37 per cent Muslims. A vast number of the respondents are from weaker sections such as SCs, STs and OBCs. The ratio of females in respondent's families is significantly less in the age groups of below 5, 15-17 and 25-29. Forty three per cent of the displaced are mere literate or only passed 4th standard and 22.45 per cent are illiterate. For 11 per cent of the respondents, the pattern of land ownership improved as they obtained at least a homestead after the displacement, whereas they had nothing before. Land holding has come down for 15 per cent of the respondents.

The percentage of respondents having an annual income between Rs. 5,000-10,000 increased from 41 to 67.34 after displacement, whereas those belonging to the less than 5,000 income group decreased from 8.92 to 2.45. At the same time, the respondents who belong to Rs. 45,000-50,000 had increased slightly from 2.59 per cent to 3.17 per cent. The percentage of respondents belonging to all other income groups decreased after displacement. There was a significant increase in the Rs. 5,000-10,000 group among the SCs from 3.54 to 84 per cent. There was no tribal respondent with an annual income of less than Rs. 5,000 after the displacement, but their percentage was 21.24 before the displacement.

The major changes in the pattern of occupation after the displacement are the increase in unskilled labourers and decrease in the number of persons who depended on agriculture. About 90 per cent of the DPs belong to Lower Lower Class indicating that the present socio-economic condition of the DPs/PAPs is extremely poor.

6

The Process of Land Takeover

The problem of displacement starts with the procedure the government adopts to acquire land for a project. This chapter deals with the various stages in the process of land takeover, like how people came to know about the project, what was their first reaction, problems faced immediately after announcement, reaction of local leaders, promises made by officials and their fulfillment, and attitude of officials towards the DPs. The entire analysis here deals with the real agony DPs undergo during the process of the displacement.

Mode of Information About the Project

How the people of an area came to know about a development project is very significant as this is the stage at which the local people form their own perceptions regarding the scheme. This can be considered as the initial stage of a long process during which the project is coming into the life of the people as a reality, quite unexpectedly, with the potential to change their lives for better or worse. At this stage, there are chances of rumour mongering by persons with vested interests and subsequent generation of misunderstanding and suspicion about the project and its impact on the people. In many cases, the rumours are the first source of information.

For our respondents four major sources of information were project and other government officials (50.44%), other villagers (26.25%), Notification (25.76%) and radio or newspaper (22.58%).

Often the officials tend to give 'glittering promises' in the beginning to ensure the cooperation of the people. Past experiences prove that usually most of these promises were broken later by the same people who made them.

Besides, it also shows that the local people receive the information at a much later period. In a highly literate state like Kerala, they should have obtained the information from the newspapers or radio much earlier. Of course, only 22.58 per cent of the respondents came to know about the project in this manner. Still it is a small number and indicative of the inefficiency of mass media to give such information to the people concerned. When information is not received at the appropriate time, the people may not get enough time to understand the problems involved in a project and mobilise a common stand among the villagers through adequate discussion. The data also show that government notification on the project is not very effective in giving the information to the target group. The chances of getting information on development projects from government notification and gazette are very limited as people rarely read them. A similar study conducted in the equally literate state of Goa shows that only a very few of the respondents got information through notifications (Fernandes and Naik, 1999:74).

Other villagers constitute another major source of information (26.25%). This is quite natural since the implementation of a project in a place is part of the development of the whole locality and therefore, people will be much interested in discussing the matter with their peer groups or neighbours. This can help the community to form a public opinion regarding the project. In the VSSC project, 40 per cent of the respondents got the information from church leaders.

Political and other local leaders had very little role in passing on the information about the project to the people. In an educationally forward and politically conscious state like Kerala, this passive nature of the local leadership at a time of critical developments in their lives is quite strange. Only in NTPC and Nedumbassery Projects, a few respondents reported that they had received the information from the political leaders. Incidentally, these are recent projects. Besides, a majority of the respondents (69.01%) of NTPC belongs to the general category. In Nedumbassery too 44.77 per cent were from forward communities.

Among the Tribal respondents, 58.4 per cent came to know about the project from project or other government officials and 36.28 per cent from other villagers. The main source of information about the project for the SC respondents was other villagers. Project or other government officials constituted the major source for 60.35 per cent of OBCs. About 46 per cent of them got information through the notification and another 20.8 per cent through radio or newspapers. A majority of the forward caste respondents had project or other government officials as major sources of information, while 31.62 per cent got it through radio or newspapers.

There is a marked difference between males and females in the mode of getting information. While for 102 males (26.22%) radio or newspaper was the source of information, it was truc only for 52 females (17%). Among the women, 21 per cent of SC, 39 per cent of OBC and 40 per cent of the general category received the information through the media. On the other hand, no Tribal woman got the information from radio or newspaper.

Similarly, when 195 males (50.12%) obtained information from project and government officials, only 149 females (48.69%) came in this category. However, no such difference among sexes was noticeable for sources like from notification and other villagers.

When we compare this situation with some other states, we notice some variations. Unlike in Kerala, in Orissa, the political leaders at the national and local levels played an important role in informing the people about the project (Fernandes and Raj, 1992:70). The Prime Minister and Chief Minister of that time announced some of the major projects. When such eminent persons make announcements, the people accept them more easily. The leaders always present a project as national development that is beneficial to everyone, including the DPs or PAPs. In Orissa, it has happened that the local political leaders themselves announced the project even before the publication of the notification. A similar study conducted in Goa also showed that no attempt was made to inform the people about the project at an early stage. Most of them came to know about it from the village leaders or from other villagers. In Goa too, the political leaders had not played any role in informing the people about the project. A good number of the DPs came to hear about the project from project and government officials (Fernandes and Naik, 1999:73).

First Reaction to the Announcement

The people living in a locality come to hear the announcement of a project all on a sudden. Of course, in many cases, they might have heard some rumours regarding the implementation of a project. For most cases, the announcement reached them at a time when they least expected it. They may not even know the gravity of the changes that would be brought about by the project. So, the people are forced to react to such a vital issue without any forethought. The response of a sizable number of people (45%) to the announcement of land acquisition was one of fear of losing land and house. To them, their land and house meant everything. That is where the family had lived for generations. The land and building may have been ancestral property to which they have emotional attachment. Their relationship to the local community, their social network system, all play very crucial roles in their life. Depriving them of all the belongings, all on a sudden with an uncertain future evoked fear, a sense of helplessness and despair among a large section of the respondents. This response was predominant in the case of five projects, namely Idukki (all respondents), VSSC (54 out of 60), Ezhimala (32 out of 39), MVIP (20 out of 30) and IDA (26 out of 45).

About a fifth of the respondents had positive reactions, such as happiness and opportunity to sacrifice for national development. While 60 males (15.42%) had this optimism, only 31 females (10.13%) expressed such a feeling. Thirty two OBC males (19.51%) were happy and considered it an opportunity to sacrifice for national development. Twenty OBC women (14.92%) also had a similar reaction. Among the general category, 25 men (19.08%) and nine women (8.73%) responded in this manner. On the other hand, only a negligible number of SC and ST respondents had this reaction.

Helplessness or fear of losing house or land was the immediate reaction of 82.69 per cent of the respondents and 30.83 per cent felt either anger or despair. Gender-wise analysis shows that 178 men were afraid (45.75%) of losing their land in comparison with 128 women (41.83%). The difference is very conspicuous among STs and SCs. When 37 Tribal men (49.33%) had this reaction, only nine women (23.68%) had such a response. The situation is quite opposite among SCs, where only two men have this fear, while 17 women were afraid of losing their land. The other major reaction is helplessness. It was reported by 135 men (34.70%) and 112 women (36.60%). The difference is sharper in the general category. Here, when 24 men reported this, only 12 women said so. While considering other reactions, 118 men (30.33%) had a feeling of anger and despair, whereas only 89 women (29.08%) felt this.

In Idukki, all the respondents had the fear of losing land and house. As majority of them were Tribals, they did not have an existence without land to cultivate. They cannot think of other occupations, because of their socio-economic backwardness. However, there was a marked difference in the reaction of the respondents of the IRE project where 32 out of 43 were happy with land acquisition. Here, the displaced people were living on the beach without any legal ownership of their land. The proximity to the sea made the location of their houses very unsafe, especially during the monsoon. They were happy to be evicted as they expected to get land of their own and a relatively better and new house in the resettlement colony. At the same time, 24 respondents of IRE project expressed a feeling of helplessness. This shows the uncertainty in their mind till the process of displacement and resettlement is completed.

The reaction of the people displaced by the Thekkady Tiger Project was more or less equally divided into two opposites. While half of them had the feeling of helplessness, the other half had hope of a better life. Only 14 families were displaced by this project, while many of the people who depended on the forest for their livelihood lost their lifeline. A majority of the affected people were Tribals belonging to Mannan and Paliyan communities. These poor, unorganised Tribals found themselves in a helpless situation when they heard about the project. They also believed the promises made by the authorities and the leaders that they would get a job in the project.

Only 8.94 per cent of the respondents had the hope of a better life by securing new jobs. However, their hopes were shortlived. Even when they were made by the project officials and leaders, they turned out to be blatant lies or gimmicks. They got this information mainly from other villagers and project or other government officials. Thirty-four (30 General and 4 SC) respondents out of 71 from NTPC Kayamkulam had expected jobs. But, it was a game played by the project authorities and political leaders to get the support of the local people. Data show that a large number of the affected people had faith in this promise. Only a negligible number of them were influenced by noble ideals like an opportunity to sacrifice for national development though political leaders always try to teach the citizens the need to have such attitudes towards development. On the whole, it is clear that the most prominent reactions are fear and helplessness. While 37.83 per cent of the respondents had a feeling of helplessness, 75.69 per cent expressed negative reactions like anger, fear, despair and fatalism. This is quite natural as all the affected people are faced with a threat, which is beyond their capacity to cope with.

Nearly 44 per cent of Tribals, 38 per cent of SCs, 49.82 per cent of OBCs and 50.43 per cent of forward castes felt helpless. Fear of losing house or land was the feeling of 40.7 per cent of STs, 38 per cent of SCs and 42.81 per cent of OBC respondents. Helplessness and fear of loss of house or land was the predominant feeling among all the castes.

Problems Faced Immediately After Announcement

Most of the respondents did not face any specific problem immediately after the announcement of the project. Project authorities allowed them to stay in their own houses and continue their occupation. So, the announcement did not bring any noticeable change in their lives. However, the data show that there are some variations from this general trend in the case of certain projects. Thirty five males (8.99%) and nine females (2.94%) reported that all the development projects were stopped in their villages immediately after the announcement of the project. Among the men, nearly half were Tribals and all except one of them were from Idukki. This definitely affected the life of the people, especially when the time gap between the announcement of the project and land takeover became very long. In the case of IHP (Idukki), 33 out of 70 respondents experienced this problem.

A little over a fourth of the respondents revealed that the project officials prevented them from cultivating their land. This constitutes 29 Tribals (25.66% of total STs), 11 SCs (22% of total SCs), 81 OBCs (27.18% of total OBCs), and 57 respondents of general category (24.35% of total forward caste). One hundred and sixteen men (37.53%) and 72 women (23.52%) stated this problem. About 43 (out of 62) of the respondents of Karappuzha project reported that they had to stop cultivation immediately after the announcement of the project. Almost all the Tribal women from Karappuzha project reported this issue, whereas only 50 per cent of the Tribal men had a similar view. In the Bakel project, all except one respondent reported this problem. They constitute 20 men and nine women out of a total sample of 30. In Nedumbassery project too, 20 men (54.05) and 15 women (50%) experienced this problem.

As their major occupation is agriculture, this had serious implications for their lives. They generally do not have any income other than from agriculture and this decision of the officials adversely affected them. In certain cases, the time gap between the project announcement and land takeover was very long. It is true in the case of Karappuzha Irrigation Project where the land was acquired 29 years ago and the project has not yet been implemented. So, the poor people in the project area find themselves as refugees in their own homeland. Their life is sacrificed for the sake of 'National Development', which is yet to materialise. A considerable number of people in NTPC Kayamkulam (22.53%) and MVIP (36.67%) projects had to confront this problem of rumour mongering by antisocial elements to scare the affected people. As the affected people are in a confused state of mind after they hear about the project, they are very susceptible to such rumours. The people who are behind the rumours spread them in order to exploit the local people further. The strained relationship that exists between the project officials and the villagers generally prevents the latter from approaching the officials for explanations in order to check the validity of these rumours. Rumour mongers have a definite objective to buy the assets.

A small size of the population studied reported that some outsiders tried to buy their assets at a very low price. This problem is not as acute as in other states like Orissa since the people are more informed in comparison with their counterparts in other states. Hence, it is not that easy to cheat them. But, a few did face this problem. None of the respondents faced the problem of people stealing others' property.

A good number of the respondents from all the communities, viz. STs (48.6%), SCs (62%), OBCs (64.91%) and forward castes (51.7%) said that they did not face any serious problems immediately after the announcement of the project.

Reactions of Local Leaders

It is important to examine the reaction of the local leaders towards the development projects. The local leaders can play an effective rôle in generating public opinion either for or against the project. The degree of threat to life and livelihood is a major factor in the reaction to the project. The greater the threat to life, greater will be the agitation and unity among the local community.

According to 44.87 per cent of the respondents, the local leaders who are supposed to be the representatives of the common people did nothing to help the people even after the announcement of the project. Of these, 52.67 per cent were women. The local leaders did not seem to have taken seriously into account the impact of the project on the life of the people. Many of the respondents consider this attitude of the leaders as irresponsible or as dereliction of duty. Another finding is that according to 16.13 per cent of the respondents, their leaders openly supported the project. Of these, 44.54 per cent were women. Furthermore, 1.9 per cent of the respondents revealed that their leaders became dalals of the project. Of those respondents, more than half were women. On the other hand, 21.11 per cent said that their leaders called people's meetings in order to intimate and discuss the information on the project. Of these, 34.72 per cent were women. A silver line in this not so encouraging scenario is that none of the respondents except one SC woman from Nedumbassery project thought that the leaders misled the people by giving false information.

On the positive side, 32 respondents (out of 71) displaced from Idukki project pointed out that their leaders with the best interest of the people tried to unite them against the project. In this group, 23.53 per cent were women. The respondents of Ezhimala and Nedumbassery projects also had the same experience. In the case of NTPC in Kayamkulam and Hydro electric Projects in Idukki, 33 (out of 71) and 28 (out of 62) of the respondents respectively opined that their leaders discussed the matter among themselves without sharing their views with the people. The percentage of women with this response is 72.73 and 21.43, respectively. This reaction of the leaders was inadequate in helping the affected people. Some respondents from Nedumbassery project reported that their leaders approach them only during the elections. According to them, these leaders support the rich and the influential people in order to get favours from them. In VSSC project, 15 (out of 60) respondents said that their leaders called people's meetings to discuss the matter. All of them were men belonging to the OBC category.

In the case of Vizhinjam Harbour, the local church leadership organised group meetings, made the people aware of their rights, the impact of the project and the need to remain united to get justice from the authorities concerned. However, other local leaders did nothing. In the coastal areas, normally the church leadership is very strong. Here, the church leaders organised the local people to demand their rehabilitation rights. They come under the category of 'others'.

According to 48.67 per cent of STs, 52.28 per cent of OBCs, and 35.89 per cent of the Forward Castes, the local leaders did nothing. The response of, 18.58 per cent of STs, 22 per cent of SCs, 25.96 per cent of OBCs and 16.24 per cent of forward castes was that the leaders called people's meeting. Only 18 per cent of the SCs, 11.53 per cent of the forward castes, 16.81 per cent of STs and 9.1 per cent of OBCs said that the leaders tried to unite people against the project. According to 16.14 per cent of OBCs, 18.37 per cent of forward castes and 38 per cent of SCs, the leaders supported the project.

Unlike in Orissa in most of the projects, leaders did not play a negative role.

Time Lag Between Demarcation and Displacement

The period of time taken between demarcation and displacement has great significance while analysing the problems of the displaced people. If the time taken for displacement is very short, then the affected people may not be ready to face the consequences of this traumatic experience. On the other hand, if people are not displaced even two years after demarcation, they are bound to face numerous uncertainties. They may be in a totally confused state of mind as they are obliged to live in the land over which they cannot exercise their ownership. As majority of the people displaced and affected by projects in Kerala are either small and marginal farmers or agricultural labourers, they find it extremely difficult to manage their life without any freedom to cultivate their land. At the same

KARAPPUZHA PROJECT

The erstwhile British Government proposed the Karappuzha Irrigation project in Wayanad in the pre-independent era. But, it was only in 1972 that the state government undertook this project. The project was expected to be completed by 2000 AD. One thousand and five hundred acres of land was acquired from Ambalavayal and Thomotuchal villages of Sultan Bathery Taluk displacing about 1300 people including 217 tribals. At the very beginning, a sum of rupees 70 lakh was set apart for the resettlement and rehabilitation of the evicted. But, nothing was done in this respect. It is estimated that millions of rupees were wasted in the process of implementing the project. Land acquired for the project about 20 years ago was kept unutilised, and the loss on this account is estimated to be to the tune of rupees 80 crores. According to financial experts, cash crops worth 200 crores of rupees could have been raised from this land, a year. And no development activities were undertaken in this area, since then, as the saying goes "ploughing bulls seldom sow". But, the project report said that an additional 1500 tons of cash crops would be produced annually by the implementation of the project. The people opined that due to the commencement of project, their employment opportunities were lost and their livelihood became very bleak. Moreover their cultural heritage was also wreaked.

The blasting of rocks with dynamite for construction works in 1987 made cracks on the walls and foundations of the houses and a chapel in the vicinity causing extensive damages. The people got no compensation for the damages from the project. The project authorities denied them compensation claming that the damage was due to defective materials used and faulty construction of the buildings. Some people who could influence the revenue officers got adequate compensation for their land. Whereas the majority of people in the area who were farm labourers and small and marginal farmers were left out high and dry.

A group of 217 tribal families belonging to Paniyan, Naikan, Chettiyar, and Kuruma were resettled in six colonies each for a particular tribe.

A common well was constructed in each of these colonies. But, acute scarcity of water is the perennial problem they face. Some tribals were spend-thrift with the compensation amount and became debtors and beggars. The people who eventually became kudikidappu (tenants) were exploited by other classes and castes. Lack of toilets in the area force the people to defecate in the open space. This causes serious health and environment problems.

time, they could not move to a new place, as a majority of them had not received compensation or resettlement facilities soon after demarcation. It comes only after displacement. Consequently they are like refugees in their own homeland. The Karappuzha Irrigation project is a typical example in this context where land was acquired 29 years ago, but the construction work of the dam is still going on. Only a few families have been displaced from here for undertaking some initial construction work. The remaining people are living on their land and waiting to be displaced at any time. They have no sense of security in their own homeland and cannot even construct a good house or cultivate some cash crops, because of the threat of eviction hanging over them like the sword of Damocles.

Table 6.1

Time Lag Between Demarcation and Displacement

Project	*Less than one month*	*Less than 6 months*	*6 months - 1year*	*1-2 years*	*2-3 years*	*3 years and above*	*NA*	*NP*	*Total*
IRE	0	0	30	0	12	0	0	1	43
KML	1	0	16	0	0	0	0	0	17
IHP	0	0	1	43	26	0	0	0	70
KIP	0	0	8	3	2	1	0	48	62
IDA	9	5	25	4	0	0	1	1	45
SIKL	0	0	16	10	2	1	0	1	30
NTP	0	0	0	6	5	15	0	45	71
VSC	0	1	38	12	4	1	3	1	60
MGR	2	1	14	0	0	2	7	15	41
VZM	0	0	39	0	0	0	0	1	40
PTR	0	0	3	21	0	0	0	26	50
ENA	0	35	4	0	0	0	0	0	39
BTP	0	1	2	0	0	0	0	27	30
NIA	21	3	42	1	0	0	0	0	67
MVP	0	0	10	20	0	0	0	0	30
Total	33	46	248	120	51	20	11	166	695
Percentage	6.2	8.7	48.89	22.68	9.64	3.75	2.07		

About 48 per cent of the people were displaced within a period of six months to one year. For a majority of DPs (70.7%), the time lag between demarcation and displacement was six months to two years. At the same time, the period between demarcation and displacement was too short for 14.9 per cent of the respondents who got less than six months before being thrown out. They were forced to make immediate adjustments facing a number of hostile conditions. Very often such sudden changes result in mal-adjustments in their life. This was a serious problem, especially for 21 out of 67 of Nedumbassery project respondents and 35 out of 39 of Ezhimala project DPs.

On the other hand, 13.8 per cent of the respondents had to lead an uncertain life without getting displaced even after two years in projects like IHP, IRE and NTPC. As mentioned above, their social and economic activities were totally disrupted due to this uncertain existence. On the whole, while considering the agony of land acquisition and displacement, it is imperative that the authorities give due attention to the time lag between demarcation and displacement.

Promises Made by the Officials

Making promises is a significant strategy in the long process of land takeover. After the decision to takeover the land for a specific project, the authorities concerned, either of the government or the project officials or both approach the affected people to seek their co-operation. They are supposed to implement the project with least resistance from the people. So, they usually allure the people with many promises as a strategy to minimise the resistance from them and to make the process smooth. This has a special implication in the Kerala context, where the number and intensity of agitations are much higher. In almost all the projects we studied, there were organised movements against the project (the details will be presented in the Chapter 7).

The nature and type of these promises include house, job, land for land, better compensation and better facilities. Since unemployment is a crucial problem in Kerala, a majority of the projects (9 out of 15) promised employment to the affected people. Jobs were the only promise made by the NTPC, SIKL, and the IDA projects. But, closer observation reveals that only a few of the projects have, in fact, given jobs for its DPs. This promise was fulfilled only by SIKL project. The reason given for the non-compliance with this promise is lack of qualified persons among the displaced. But, the people deny this. For example, in Nedumbassery, the qualification prescribed for the post of taxi driver is P.D.C. and they restricted people even for unskilled jobs based on age. Those above 35 were not given jobs. The affected people questioned the rationale behind this. The authorities also denied jobs on the basis of some aviation laws which restrict the appointment of unqualified hands. The people cannot check the truth of it, as they are ignorant about such laws. The authorities of VSSC project agreed to give land and job for three generations of DPs. There was collective demand for the same. However, many respondents said that the promised jobs were not given to them. In NTPC project too, jobs were offered to the DPs at the time of land acquisition. NTPC is the only project which offered rehabilitation to the displaced people. But, later the officials refused to give them jobs saying that the local candidates did not have the required technical qualification.

Houses were promised in VSSC and Vizhinjam projects which are relatively old projects located in the coastal area. As a majority of the DPs are poor fisherfolk, constructing a house was very difficult for them. While considering the relationship between the nature of the promises made and type of the project, it is clear that jobs were mainly offered in industries, airport and power projects. Such promises were not generally made in hydel, mining, harbour, defence, wildlife sanctuary and tourism projects. However, no specific relationship was found between the age of the project and the promises made.

Another set of promises concerned better living conditions and facilities in the resettlement site. But, there were several complaints about lack of such facilities. For example, in IRE the officials offered to provide road, electricity and water facilities in the resettlement sites. But, they have given these only in one of the three resettlement sites. This is true also for the Industrial Development Area and the Karappuzha projects. In the Vizhinjam Project, the Christian DPs did not occupy the houses given at the resettlement site, because of lack of facilities such as drinking water and toilets. They gave the houses at the resettlement site to others for rent. Here too, the officials had promised to give 'better facilities'. In Nedumbassery project, the situation is comparatively better as they have provided road, electricity and water. (see Table 6.2 for the promises made)

We have not taken the usual compensation for land acquired as part of the promise. The term better compensation means compensation given for trees, other assets and loss of cultivation etc. Better facilities refer to basic facilities such as roads, electricity, drinking water etc. The data show that among the various promises made by the officials, three were very prominent. They were promised job (38.41%), land (29.78%), and houses (15.3%). Actually these promises are related to the most fundamental needs of any community. Without the satisfaction of these needs, people will not be able to lead a decent life. Widespread complaints against displacement and rehabilitation could have been avoided by fulfilling these promises. Such an honest action could create a positive attitude towards development in the affected community as well as among the general public when a project is being implemented.

Attitude of Project Officials

The attitude of project officials at various stages of displacement was another aspect we looked into. This is one of the many factors which contribute to the alleviation or accentuation of the hardships of the DPs. We discuss the attitudes under four heads, namely helpful, condescending, indifferent, and unhelpful. Nearly 43 per cent of the respondents found the project authorities indifferent to their plight, while 28.5 per cent perceived them as even unhelpful. For a small group of about 10 per cent, the officials showed themselves to be condescending. Only about 15 per cent said that they were helpful.

Table 6.2

Promises Made by the Officials

Project	Land	House	Road	Drinking water	Electricity	All Facilities #	Job	Relocation cost	Better compensation	Compensation for crops	Rehabilitation	Self employment
IRE	34	0	11	7	5	7	9	25	11	0	0	0
KML	14	0	0	0	0	9	17	1	0	0	0	0
IHP	23	0	1	1	2	0	0	0	19	0	0	0
KIP	29	3	0	0	1	1	2	0	22	5	0	0
IDA	5	0	2	1	1	3	9	0	2	0	0	0
SIKL	0	0	0	0	0	0	28	0	1	0	0	0
NTP	2	4	0	0	0	0	55	0	0	0	6	2
VSC	40	41	0	0	0	0	56	0	2	0	0	0
MGR	0	0	0	0	0	0	19	0	0	0	0	0
VZM	9	27	0	5	6	0	6	0	0	0	0	0
PTR	0	0	0	0	0	0	0	0	0	0	0	*All No
ENA	10	3	2	5	3	3	8	0	6	0	0	0
BTP	6	1	0	0	0	0	6	6	10	0	0	0
NIA	35	1	0	0	0	13	42	1	35	0	0	0
MVP	0	0	0	0	0	0	0	0	0	0	0	*All No
Total	207	80	12	17	20	38	267	19	93	5	6	2
Percentage	29.78	11.51	1.63	2.45	2.88	5.47	38.42	2.73	13.38	0.72	0.86	0.28

#Note: The question regarding the promises was of descriptive type. The column headings are on the basis of the descriptive answers.

Helpful

While analysing the helpful attitude of the officials, some variations can be observed among different categories. More OBCs (58 out of 298) have reported that the attitude of the project authorities was helpful. On the other hand, only a very small number of SCs (2 out of 50) held this opinion. Tribals and the general category come in between these two extremes, 13 out of 113 and 31 out of 234, respectively. It is clear that only a minority of the total respondents in each group considered the attitude of the authorities as helpful. The vast majority had one or other type of negative feelings regarding the attitude of the authorities. This is a serious issue to be dealt with in the process of land take over to give a better treatment to the DPs. A helpful attitude of the officials can reduce considerably the agony of the affected people during the period of displacement and resettlement.

Data on the difference between sexes show some complex features. Among the OBCs, no difference exists, while the situation in the remaining groups shows different patterns. Among the SC and general categories, more women perceived the attitude of the authorities as helpful. Not a single man from the SC community had this opinion. But, the difference between sexes in the general category appeared to be quite significant. When 18.44 per cent of women said that the attitude of the officials was helpful, only 9.16 per cent of men had a similar opinion. On the other hand, among the Tribals a reversal of this trend was visible. Here, a considerable number of men reported that the project authorities were helpful towards them, while the number of women holding the same view was much less.

Condescending

Regarding the condescending attitude of the officials, only a small number of the respondents of different categories expressed any serious concern. While more DPs from the general category reported this issue (29 out of 234) compared to the OBCs (29 out of 298), the same has least significance among the Tribals (6 out of 113) and the SCs (4 out of 50). This phenomenon was more visible in NTPC, IHP, MVIP projects. On the whole, the data do not give any clear difference between the various categories.

In all categories, the males have experienced this problem more than the females. The difference between sex is fairly uniform among SC, OBC and general categories. But, no such difference is noticed in the Tribal community.

Indifferent

Caste-wise and sex-wise analysis of the data was carried out in order to understand whether any variation exists among different categories of respondents. Out of the total number of Tribal DPs, 44.2 per cent reported that the attitude of the project authorities was indifferent. This group constituted 31 males and 19 females. That means that 41.33 per cent of the Tribal males and 50 per cent of females perceived an attitude of indifference in the project officials. Forty two per cent of SC respondents reported the same, where more females (14, i.e. 45.16%) than males (7, i.e. 36.84%) held this opinion. One third of the males and females in the OBCs also held the same view, whereas more than half the number of males and females in the general category too had the same impression.

The results of the investigation show that members of the general category are more aware of their status and express more self-esteem. They seem to expect a better deal from the project authorities. They consider that when they sacrifice for the nation, it is their right to get a decent treatment from the officials concerned. The difference in opinion across sexes is more pronounced among the SCs and STs. In all categories, except in the general, more women said that the officials were indifferent. Women in the socio-economically backward groups were more vocal against the negative attitude of the officials, because they had greater stakes than men in experiencing deprivation.

Unhelpful

In comparison with others, a larger number of SCs (40%) said that the project authorities had an unhelpful attitude towards them.

Many respondents reported that the officials did not even hear their complaints patiently, but tried to impose decisions on them. The response of the Tribals and OBCs show similar tendency. More than one-third of the DPs of these groups reported this. However, only 13.67 per cent from the general category faced this problem. On the whole, the socio-economically backward groups had more complaints about the unhelpful attitude of the project officials.

Analysis on the basis of sex shows that except among the Tribals, more men experienced this problem than women seemingly because the officials responded more sympathetically to the women than men. On the other hand, there is a marked difference in this aspect in the general category. While 17.55 per cent of the males reported this issue, only 8.73 per cent of females did so. Among the SCs and OBCs, the difference is very little.

On the whole, the SCs seem to be most worried about the attitude of the authorities as majority of them had negative experiences from them. On the other hand, the OBCs were able to develop a relatively better rapport with the project officials.

After examining all these responses, it may be concluded that the project authorities have failed to establish a healthy relationship with the affected people. All the different sections of the DPs had predominantly negative feelings regarding their attitude. Being a serious issue, the vast majority of the DPs had a clear-cut opinion on this matter. Much patience and empathy are required to handle the process of displacement and resettlement. The officials are uncertain about the response of the people and generally anticipate a hostile reaction from them. So, without proper consultation with the affected people, the officials very often try to impose their decisions on them, which often create negative feelings in them. Many of the officials are not equipped to handle this type of a harrowing situation and may not have any previous experience in this field. At the same time, they have official compulsions to carry out the project within a stipulated period of time.

NEDUMBASSERY INTERNATIONAL AIRPORT

Nedumbassery international airport was one of the development dreams of Central Kerala. This became a reality when the Non-Resident Indians (NRIs) of 30 countries 10,000 shareholders, Commercial Banks, HUDCO and Air India joined hands with the Government of Kerala. The project estimated to be of Rs.230 crores was prepared in 1992 and the Cochin International Airport Authority was formed in 1993. The project required 1500 acres of land, out of which 600 acres were meant for the aerodrome, 100 acres for the cargo complex, 300 acres for hotels and the remaining 500 acres for establishing trade and commerce centres.

The lot fell on Nedumbassery, a village 25 kilometers north-east of Ernakulam, with an expanse of paddy fields and coconut palms, dotted by medium and small houses occupied by farmers and agricultural labourers. The first estimates showed that while acquiring 1500 acres of land, only 200 households would be evicted. This was proved to be a complete underestimate. A total of 820 families were evicted (Dhanam, Feb. 15-20, P. 5) while acquiring 1300 acres of land. Among the DPs, the families were with three cents to three acres of land holdings, which means majority of the evicted were agricultural labourers and marginal farmers.

According to the special Tahsildar, Land Acquisition, Office Kochi, 605.15 hectares land were acquired from 4 villages, Nedumbassery, Vadakumbhagam, Chowara and Angamali displacing 1937 families. First notification was issued in 1993 followed by the second notification in 1994 and the Award was given in 1996. Besides, payment of the compensation fixed by the Tahsildar, the resettlement package meant 6 cents of land in a housing colony and a sum of Rs. 10,000/- as relocation cost.

Eviction was a traumatic experience for the victims. Those who accepted the compensation were allowed to move out from the place with 80 per cent of the compensation amount. Those who resisted the land acquisition or appealed for higher compensation were forcefully evicted by battering the houses by bulldozers, destroying everything the family stored within the house, and without providing the 6 cents of land and the relocation charges (Cfs.OP No. 7380/1997-C in the High Court of Kerala, Ernakulam). Peoples Union for Civil Liberties (PUCL), Kerala Unit, appointed a commission under its President Justice (Rtd.) T. Chandrasekhara Menon and four others to make an on the spot study of eviction process, the resettlement and rehabilitation. They confirmed demolition of 13 houses using bulldozers even when the owners pleaded for a few hours to remove the valuables. However, the official report is that the owners salvaged the reusable materials. Land acquisition was based on the invocation of emergency clause of the Land Acquisition Act.

The commission also visited the resettlement area, which is lower than the roads in the neighbourhood, and gets flooded in the monsoon. The Commission confirmed that the undated eviction notice had the date seal/stamp of the sorting office of Chowara Post Office, which read 8.12.1997. Ironically, on the same day bulldozers battered those 13 houses down after the inhabitants were arrested and removed by the police. They pleaded with the project officials and the police for a few hours to let them salvage whatever they could, but to no avail. This is a blatant violation of fundamental rights guaranteed by the constitution of India, all in the name of development. These displaced people, when released by the police, had no where to go. They were neither paid compensation nor allotted the 6-cent house plot along with the Rs. 10,000/- as relocation charges. This is how the displaced pay the price for the development process of the country.

Rastra Deepika, Malayala Manorama, Madhyamam, Malayalam, all reported the news on forced eviction highlighting heinous crimes of the project officials against the hapless victims of development. Having been evicted from the land, which they had nourished and cherished for years and perhaps generations where did these people go? The official report held that they were all resettled. Jyothish (1998) of the Malayalam weekly reported on a colony of six cents per family at Akaparambu, covering 36 acres of paddy fields were acquired by the project for resettlement. About 300 families were allotted land here. Rather than filling the low lying slushy field with red earth to raise the land by one meter, the earth filling was limited to less than one food which hardly covered the grass that grew in the fields. A very light rain would be sufficient to flood the area including the houses. Although the project is expected to provide safe drinking water, electricity and road, none of these is provided. All building materials had to be transported by head-loads, as there were no roads on which vehicles could ply. For drinking water, people depended heavily on the water holes dug by some in their own premises. Unfortunately, the single pit latrine and the well are very near to each other. This makes contamination easy when the area gets flooded with a single rain.

The "resettled" are not given pattas of the land distributed. Without pattas they are unable to take loans to construct houses to live in. Many who started house construction were constrained to discontinue or abandon altogether their dream of a new house. So, most of the families had to do with shanties and hutments made of palm leaves, which do not last beyond one monsoon. The slushy surrounding moist floor, lack of safe drinking water and mosquito breeding, all made life miserable for people, especially for women and children who need special care and attention.

There is another darker side of the land acquisition story. This concerns families with alcoholics, drug addicts or gamblers. When these families got the compensation, they had their field day letting flow the compensation to the drain. They were forced to limit themselves within the 6 cents of land provided by the project in a shed made of palm leaves. Their future appears very bleak. Similarly, there are scores of households who utilised the compensation amount for marrying off their daughters and end up in debt trap. Many such families seem to be contemplating family suicide, a wave that is on the rise in Kerala. If emergency relief does not reach these people, these resettlement colonies would become death yard or cemetery for many families.

(Jyothish V. R., *Malayalam Weekly*, 17-4-98, p-22)

Analysing this situation from the perspective of the DPs, the findings are not at all encouraging. The people are very unsettled and are filled with mental strain during the process of displacement. The significant persons dealing with them on this occasion are the project officials. A harmonious relation between them and the DPs could have been very helpful to reduce the tension and pain of this critical situation. As the people do not want to leave their place in most of the projects, they have a tendency to respond to the authorities in a hostile manner. Due to various reasons mentioned above, the officials too commit mistakes endangering mutual trust. This is one of the major aspects of displacement which is neglected by the government and the project authorities.

Conclusion

The issues discussed in this chapter deal with some of the vital problems faced by the DPs after the announcement of a project and before the actual displacement. It also looks into the time lag between demarcation and displacement. The study shows that even today, most of the concerned people are ignorant about a project in its early stages as notification is found to be an ineffective tool to pass on the information. Only a small number of the Tribals and SCs got the information through notification. Another finding of the study is that the people, irrespective of caste, experience fear and helplessness after the announcement of a project. They are quite uncertain about their future and have to face many economic problems to start life anew. The response of the local leaders has been far from encouraging and in many cases, they did nothing to help the affected people. The time lag between demarcation and displacement seems to be reasonable for a good number of respondents. However, no uniformity is noticed among the various projects. Many people are evicted either within a short period or not displaced even after two years. Finally, many attractive promises were made by the officials which remained unfulfilled. It is clear from the responses of the affected people that the project authorities had failed to establish a healthy relationship with them. These findings can be helpful for the officials concerned and for the government to develop a better understanding of the problems of displaced people.

7

Compensation

This chapter focuses on various issues related to the payment of compensation, such as the mode of payment of compensation, amount and nature of expenses incurred by the DPs/PAPs in the process of getting compensation, its adequacy, awareness regarding the fixation of the amount, delay in getting compensation, the mode of spending it, and the nature and outcome of protests.

There are many issues around compensation. The discourse on the concept of compensation has been dominated by its equation with the market value or the notional value in the market. This treats the displaced person as a willing seller. It does not account for the part coercion plays in the law of acquisition, though compulsion is tempered by a solatium of 30 per cent (Ramanathan, 1996:1488). Smithu Kothari (1996:1480) observes that very few resettlement programmes in India have adequately compensated all those who were dispossessed. Kothari points out that the way of life of displaced persons in the post-displacement period has been a matter of lowest concern for the project planners and in a majority of cases the Land Acquisition Act (LAA) is used to pay an insultingly low cash payment that is grossly inadequate to restore and enhance the standard of living.

Usha Ramanathan describes many significant omissions in the law for computing compensation. First of all, it does not hold the agency acquiring the land responsible for providing for the replacement value of the land and rights lost. Secondly, mass displacement often affects populations whose lives are not constructed around formal legal rights, making market value an irrelevant criterion. She says:

> "It is of significance that having spoken to the possible poverty of displaced populations, and to the public purpose involved in providing for them, it is *not a right to compensation, but a discretion to care* that has been prescribed." (Ramanathan, 1996: 1489).

Fernandes and Naik (1999: 64) maintain that only legal obligation is taken into consideration while fixing compensation. People's livelihood and their right to life with dignity are ignored. The law treats land only as a market commodity, but the market forces alone cannot determine the right of every citizen to life with dignity which is a fundamental right (Article 21). But, it does not seem to be a concern of the decision-makers when compensation is fixed. Keeping these issues in mind, let us now move on to the realities of the process of payment of compensation to the affected people in Kerala.

Mode of Payment of Compensation

According to 95 per cent of the respondents, the mode of payment was fully through the bank. All the respondents of the KMML, Nedumbassery and SIKL projects received the compensation in this manner. More than 98 per cent of Karappuzha project, 97.72 per cent of IDA project, 96.67 per cent of Bakel project, 96.65 per cent of VSSC project and 94.87 per cent of Ezhimala project received the compensation through a bank account. This channel is more reliable than cash. Only in IRE project, 16 out of 43 respondents received the compensation in cash.

All the STs, 98.81 per cent of the forward castes, 92 per cent of the SCs, and 91.11 per cent of OBC respondents received compensation fully through a bank account. Revenue officials paid the compensation fully in cash only to two respondents who happened to be women.

More than a fifth of the respondents have not received any compensation. All respondents in the Tiger project and 46 out of 71 respondents in the NTPC project are in this category. In the

Tiger project, the authorities denied compensation, because the DPs had no *patta* for the land. Many respondents in the NTPC project are PAPs who were working in the Government owned *Kayal farm*. They were provided with some resettlement schemes depending on the category they belonged to (for details, see Chapter 8 on Resettlement and Rehabilitation).

In Kerala, compensation is paid fully through bank and this ensures that it reaches the people concerned with minimal exploitation by middlemen. Only 3.36 per cent of the respondents received the compensation fully in cash.

Studies in Orissa also show that compensation given in cash directly to people is appropriated by merchants and middlemen or frittered away. The DPs are left with only trinkets and often become indebted. The case of the DPs of Hirakud and Upper Kolab are examples (Fernandes and Asif, 1997: 116).

Time Lag between Award and Compensation

One of the problems, which adversely affect post-displacement life, is the delay in getting compensation. The people who lost their land, house and livelihood require money for meeting their immediate needs such as purchasing land, construction of house, cost of transportation of household materials and other necessities to start a new life. Any delay in it aggravates the problems of the affected who are already impoverished. The present study reveals that the experience of Kerala DPs/PAPs is somewhat different from most other states. The displaced persons in Kerala got the compensation without much delay.

It is noteworthy that 20 per cent of the respondents received the amount immediately after the award. About 58 per cent of the respondents of the IDA project belong to this category. About 93 per cent of the respondents in the VSSC project got the compensation before land takeover. Only 15.67 per cent of the total respondents received the amount one year or more after the demarcation. Ninety per cent of the respondents of the SIKL project belong to this category.

About 41 per cent of the total respondents received the compensation immediately after land takeover. All the respondents in KMML project, 63 per cent of those of IRE project, 95 per cent of those of Ezhimala project and 66 per cent of those of Nedumbassery project fall in this category. About 59 per cent of the displaced people from Bakel project and 42 per cent from Karappuzha project received the compensation more than a year after land takeover.

Caste-wise analysis shows that 68 per cent of SCs, 47 per cent of forward castes, 38 per cent of STs and a third of the OBC respondents received compensation more than a year after land takeover. About 28 per cent of STs, a fifth each of SCs and OBCs and 16 per cent of forward caste respondents received the compensation immediately after the award. At the same time, a fifth of the OBCs and 16 per cent of forward caste respondents got the amount a year after demarcation.

On the whole, 80.58 per cent of the respondents received the compensation immediately after land takeover or even before that.

Expenses Incurred for Getting Compensation

Two main constraints, the displaced people had to confront to get the compensation amount were bribing of officials and involvement of middlemen. But, the overall experience of DPs in Kerala has been tolerable. Only a minority had to spend small sums to get the amount released. About 23 per cent of the respondents had to spend an amount of Rs. 500 to 2500 for this purpose. All the respondents of KMML project also spent an amount in this range.

At the same time, 38 per cent of the respondents did not have to spend any money to get compensation. Eighty four per cent of respondents in NTPC project and 96 per cent in VSSC project too received what was due to them without any payment. None of the respondents of Idukki project spent any amount for getting compensation.

In brief, the payment of compensation was properly done and involvement of middlemen was the least in Kerala. Though some

Table 7.1

Expenses Involved in Getting Compensation

Project	< 500	500 to 2500	2501 to 4500	4501 to 6500	6501 to 8500	8501 to 10500	10501 to 50000	50001 upto one lakh	One lakh & above	NO	NA/ Don't know	NP	Total
IRE	5	14	2	0	0	0	0	0	0	0	22	0	43
KML	0	17	0	0	0	0	0	0	0	0	0	0	17
IHP	0	0	0	0	0	0	0	0	0	59	1	10	70
KIP	1	7	7	13	4	3	10	2	0	12	1	1	62
IDA	2	21	5	4	0	2	3	0	0	4	4	0	45
SIKL	0	5	1	5	0	0	3	0	0	7	11	0	30
NTP	0	2	2	0	0	0	0	0	0	21	0	46	71
VSC	0	2	0	0	0	0	0	0	0	55	1	2	60
MGR	6	3	0	0	0	1	6	1	0	1	10	13	41
VZM	6	7	0	1	0	0	0	0	0	0	3	23	40
PTR	0	0	0	0	0	0	0	0	0	0	0	50	50
ENA	2	5	0	1	0	0	1	0	0	18	12	0	39
BTP	5	5	2	9	0	1	4	2	1	1	0	0	30
NIA	9	33	2	2	1	2	0	1	1	10	5	1	67
MVP	0	0	0	0	0	0	0	0	0	13	4	13	30
Total	36	121	21	35	5	9	27	6	2	201	74	159	695
Percentage	6.72	22.57	3.91	6.52	0.93	1.67	5.04	1.12	0.37	37.5	13.81		

of the respondents had to spend money for court expenses, the procedure of payment seems to have been transparent. In spite of this, we cannot ignore the fact that 27 respondents spent more than Rs.10,500 and six persons, an amount of more than Rs.50,000 and two persons, an amount of more than one lakh each for court expenses.

Nature of Expenses for Getting Compensation

According to 78 per cent of those who spent money to get compensation, their cases are still pending with the court. Consequently, they spent a lot of money for constant travel and court expenses. They are forced to visit various offices several times in order to receive the compensation. The study reveals that 13.73 per cent of the affected persons had to bribe the officials and 1.27 per cent had to bribe the middlemen. Here, the experience of the DPs of Karappuzha project must be specially mentioned that 25 (out of 62) had to bribe the officials to get the compensation. It is to be noted that more than half of the respondents of this project are Tribals. This proves that the poor, illiterate Tribals are exploited and harassed by the officials.

Court expenses had to be met by 27.47 per cent of respondents, showing that only a minority of the people are taking the issue of compensation to the courts of law. Majority of the respondents tried to get the amount through other channels.

All respondents of the KMML project and 10 out of 43 respondents of IRE project told that the major expense was for preparing documents.

Mode of Spending Compensation

Most DPs/PAPs have utilised the money they received as compensation for creation of assets. Only a few have spent it wastefully or to purchase consumer goods and ornaments. Also, a small number of them spent the money on social functions like wedding, while some others used it to repay loans. Similarly, only a negligible number of respondents used the money on livestock purchase or to start a business which could improve the economic status of their family. Some utilised the compensation fully for constructing a house. On the whole, it is seen that the major share of the compensation was spent on land purchase (28%) and house construction (62%). These two are the immediate necessities of the displaced. So, naturally, the compensation they received was spent for the most basic and essential needs. This has serious economical implications, as they could not spend the money on productive investments like purchasing livestock or starting a business. If they were provided with a resettlement package of land and house, they could have spent the compensation in a more productive manner. However, 15 respondents of Bakel project deposited the money in Banks, two spent it for the education of children, while one each for the marriage of a daughter or shared it among the family members. Four respondents of the Bakel project used the compensation for pilgrimage to Mecca.

Overall, the respondents in Kerala used the compensation more fruitfully compared to their counter parts in Orissa where a good number of DPs, majority of them Tribals, spent the money for consumer goods and social functions. The Tribals from Koraput and Keonjhar districts were exploited by merchants and money lenders who control the trade in household and consumer goods. Lack of experience on the part of the Tribals in handling cash made this possible (Fernandes and Raj, 1992: 99).

About a half of the Tribal respondents in Kerala spent the compensation amount for building house, while 28.30 per cent spent it for purchasing land. The percentage of Tribals who spent the money for developing land was 24.52. Repayment of loan was the priority for 15.09 per cent. None of the Tribals spent the money for consumer goods, household articles, livestock purchase, ornaments and starting business.

More than 90 per cent of SC respondents used the compensation for building house. Nearly a third of them used part of the amount for purchasing household articles. Not a single SC family wasted the money or spent it on consumer goods, social functions, ornaments etc.. This may be due to the fact that nothing was left after constructing a house. At the same time, none of them invested the money productively by starting a business or purchasing livestock.

A half of the OBC respondents spent the compensation amount for house building, whereas purchase of land was the priority for 23.34 per cent. Another 15 per cent of the OBCs spent the amount for purchasing household articles. None of the OBC respondents spent the money for consumer goods and other lavish means.

In the case of forward castes, majority (80.85%) spent the money for house building. Forty seven per cent of this category had also purchased land with the amount.

However, many of the respondents in IRE and KMML projects received land for land and therefore, they spent the amount of compensation on constructing house. IRE project provided an area of 5 to 10 cents of land and KMML project provided an area of 10 cents each to the displaced families.

Many respondents said that they have been living in houses without any amenities like a good kitchen or bathroom before displacement. Even though they had great desire to construct a good house they did not have the required funds. On receiving the compensation, they decided to construct the house, but were unable to complete it due to lack of proper estimates and sufficient funds.

Decision Regarding Utilisation of Compensation

The decision regarding spending the amount is as important as the mode of spending it. If the decision in this regard is not taken in keeping with the priority needs of the family, it can add to their impoverishment. At the same time, the involvement of the whole family does not guarantee that the money will not be squandered away.

In 36.75 per cent of the cases who received compensation, the whole family was involved in decision-making. In the case of 29.66 per cent of the respondents, the husband took the decision independently and in 25.74 per cent, both wife and husband took the decision together. In the context of Kerala society, joint decision-making either by the couple or by the whole family seems to be the prevailing pattern.

Women taking decision independently in this regard is rare and in the case of 11 projects, not a single case was found of wife alone taking decision regarding the spending of the compensation received, while some husbands enjoyed such a privilege in all except two projects. When men alone take decisions regarding the utilisation of compensation, there is more possibility of spending it for status improvement.

The experience in Orissa is somewhat different where caste-wise difference among the DPs seems to be more prevalent (Fernandes and Raj, 1992: 101-02). In the middle caste dominated districts, the decision regarding spending compensation was taken by men, while in the Tribal communities it was men in consultation with wife or even by the two together. This difference substantiates the findings of other studies that women have a higher status among the Tribals and Dalits than among the middle and higher castes.

Whereas 30 per cent of the respondents in Kerala reported that the husband alone made the decision in spending the compensation, there was only a single wife, an OBC from Idukki project, who took an independent decision about the utilisation of compensation. Thus, gender inequalities are very well reflected in this issue.

Among the Tribals in Kerala, there was no case of wife taking decisions independently regarding the utilisation of compensation. The whole family was involved in decision-making in 22 out of 113 ST families. Seventeen ST respondents said that husband alone took the decisions, while 16 DPs reported that both husband and wife had taken the decision together. Children and relatives had no significant role in the decision-making process.

The fact that in the fishing communities, the husband has clear advantage in decision-making is supported by the data of IRE, KMML, and Vizhinjam projects. On the contrary, in the case of VSSC project, we noticed a healthy decision-making process in which the whole family was involved in 29 cases. Both the husband

and wife together made the decisions in 14 cases. This is a reflection of the empowerment of women among fisherfolk.

Only in eight cases, the husband made the decision independently regarding the manner of spending compensation among the 50 SC families. However, the wife had no such authority to take decisions by herself. But, the decision was taken by both husband and wife or the whole family together in 20 cases each. Neither the relatives nor the children took decision independently in this regard.

The situation is somewhat different among the other backward classes (OBCs). Here, husbands exercised more freedom in decision-making. Husbands alone took decisions in 96 cases out of 298, while only five wives enjoyed similar freedom. However, both husband and wife had taken the decision jointly in 57 families. The entire family was involved in this process in 73 cases. The relatives of husband or wife had no role in taking decisions. Only in eight families, the children took the decision independently concerning the use of compensation.

The whole family had a significant role in decision-making among the general (forward) category. In 82 (of the 169) cases, the entire family was involved in this process and in 45 families, both husband and wife together took the decision. However, husbands enjoyed this freedom independently in 38 (27.33%) families. The most prominent feature is that in no case did the wife in the forward community have the authority to take this decision by herself. Children and relatives played no role in this regard. The literacy level combined with the exposure to the mass media and participatory role of women in the planning process of community based organisations (Neighbourhood Groups, Self Help Groups) did have great influence in empowering women in participating in the family decision-making process.

On the whole, the analysis by caste shows the dominance of patriarchal values in Kerala society. In all the four categories, husbands alone enjoyed the privilege of decision-making in a considerable number of cases. This dominance is more pronounced among OBCs. A deeper analysis reveals that the dominance of husbands among SCs is noticed only in one project i.e., Nedumbassery. In the same manner, in the Tribal communities, the husbands had taken decisions independently only in the Karappuzha project. Among the OBCs, male domination in taking decision was obvious in 10 projects. For instance, their dominance was very pronounced in the case of IRE project. Male dominance can be treated as a general tendency in OBCs and forward castes.

This finding raises some questions about the status of women in Kerala. Even though there is a popular impression that women irrespective of caste or community enjoy a higher status here, the study reveals that the most common ways of decision-making are the whole family together (36.75%), husbands alone (29.66%) and husband and wife together (25.74%).

About one third of the men and 27 per cent of women told that husband alone took the decision. According to 38 per cent of the men and 35 per cent of the women, the whole family together involved in the decision-making process.

Knowledge of Criteria for Compensation

The knowledge about the criteria for fixing the compensation is an important aspect which influences the perception of the adequacy of compensation. Our analysis shows that 51.51 per cent of the total respondents were ignorant of the criteria, while 40.43 per cent were not even aware of it. Project-wise, all the respondents of Ezhimala, most of those of MVIP (96.67%), VSSC (96.66%) followed by Tiger (92%) project, and a majority of those of Idukki (67.147%) followed by NTPC (54.92%), and Nedumbassery (52.23%) were unaware of it. In contrast to this, all the respondents of IRE, KMML and Bakel projects expressed awareness of the criteria. Even though a good number of respondents said that they were aware of the criteria, only a few of them knew how the authorities fixed the amount. Most of them knew only the percentage of compensation they received. For some others, the criteria for the fixation of compensation were the type of land and the mode of cultivating it.

Similar is the situation in Orissa and Goa where very few of the DPs/PAPs had any knowledge of the criteria fixed by the project authorities to determine compensation. Most of them knew only what they had received and not the manner in which it was worked out. Also, the major difference in awareness of the criteria was not based on the district, Caste or Tribe of the DPs/PAPs, but on the extent of agitation and negotiations that preceded the decision (Fernandes and Raj, 1992: 94).

The age of the project did seem to have some direct association with the level of knowledge regarding the criteria for compensation. For instance, when 52.23 per cent respondents of the Nedumbassery project (1994) remained ignorant of this, all the respondents of KMML (1980) which was established much earlier were knowledgeable about the same.

In a state like Kerala which is considered as forward in terms of social awareness, political consciousness and literacy, this finding seems to be an anomaly. The local leaders and project officials did not seem to have played a creative role in imparting such knowledge to the ordinary people. Availability of correct information can clear the doubts of the local community.

Adequacy of Compensation

Most DPs considered the compensation they received inadequate. During the data collection, the investigators noticed that this was one of the major complaints identified by the respondents. Almost everywhere, there was a feeling that the authorities cheated them on this account. The people had a number of reasons to justify their complaints. Most of these issues were closely related to their economic and social well being. About 64 per cent of the respondents felt that the compensation was inadequate, while 12 per cent thought that it was adequate.

Reasons for Inadequacy of Compensation

About two-thirds of the respondents thought that the land they had lost was fertile and the compensation received was inadequate in comparison with its real value. Among these, 67.67 per cent

Table 7.2
Awareness of Criteria for Compensation

Project	*Aware*	*Not Aware*	*NA*	*NP*	*Total*
IRE	43	0	0	0	43
KML	17	0	0	0	17
IHP	23	47	0	0	70
KIP	31	30	0	1	62
IDA	25	18	0	2	45
SIKL	16	14	0	0	30
NTP	11	39	0	21	71
VSC	1	58	0	1	60
MGR	21	3	4	13	41
VZM	33	0	7	0	40
PTR	0	46	0	4	50
ENA	0	39	0	0	39
BTP	30	0	0	0	30
NIA	30	35	2	0	67
MVP	0	29	0	1	30
Total	281	358	13	43	695
Percentage	40.43	51.51	1.87	6.18	100

were males. Many people said that their old land was really good for cultivating a variety of crops. It was a great economic support to the family since a majority of respondents were farmers. Their whole life was shattered after losing it. This complaint is quite widespread since a sizable number of respondents from eight projects have raised this issue. Forty-three per cent of STs, 28 per cent of SCs, 33.22 per cent of OBCs and 44.44 per cent of forward caste respondents had this complaint. Most of these respondents purchased some land after displacement which happened to be barren and less in area.

Also, the second major reason for the inadequacy of compensation is related to land. According to 38 per cent of the respondents, an equal measure of land costs much more. About 92 per cent of respondents of Bakel, 89 per cent of those of Rayons, 68 per cent of those of IDA and 57 per cent of those of Karappuzha projects found that the compensation they received was inadequate to replace the land and assets they lost.

Another land related complaint was the site value of the land they lost, i.e., the land occupied by them was on the roadside and naturally they could get higher prices if it was sold in the open market. The location of the land is decisive in fixing its value. Many respondents said that the excess money they had received for the land on the roadside was not at all commensurate with its market price. Thus, all three major complaints are related to land and are interdependent in nature. The DPs in general felt that while fixing compensation, the quality, replacement value and site value of the land lost were not estimated properly by the authorities concerned.

A serious economic problem was identified by 17.5 per cent of the respondents. According to them, the compensation did not replace the income they obtained from the assets owned before displacement. This was reported by 88.33 per cent of the respondents of Idukki project. It was already explained that the DPs were unable to purchase an equal area of land with the compensation they received. Naturally, the income from the land is lost or reduced. Some respondents who were living near the public road, small towns etc., were earning some money through petty business like pan shop, tea shop and so on. After displacement, as the DPs were shifted to interior areas, they had to give up such activities, thus reducing their income. The location of the land and other property is very important in this context.

Another problem is related to housing. Like land, a house is another fundamental need for human existence. Twenty per cent of the respondents held that they could not rebuild their house with the compensation received. Many could not even make an estimate of the value of their old house, because of emotional attachment to it. Besides, even in economic terms, the compensation received does not enable the DPs to construct a new house with somewhat similar conveniences. In projects like IDA (72.09%) and Nedumbassery (40.98%), some could not complete their house construction due to shortage of funds.

Some respondents (14.32%) pointed out that the compensation was inadequate as they had many dependents. As most of the DPs were economically backward, they were in real trouble due to land takeover. The money received was not sufficient to resettle the family in a new place. Many families spent money to support themselves between displacement and resettlement. The economic problems in the family got aggravated in many cases where the head of the household or other earning members had lost their jobs after displacement.

DRIFT FROM RICHES TO POVERTY

Mr. Kunj (name disguised) is one of the displaced persons from the recently inaugurated Nedumbassery airport project. He had lost nine acres of land for the project, of these six acres were paddy fields. He owned two brick making units. That was his major source of livelihood. He lost his two-story house. He filed a case against the acquisition of his house. He was arrested and was in jail for one month for resisting the authorities while dismantling the house. On his return from jail, nothing was left for him in the place of his house. He received Rs. 5 lakhs as compensation, but the authorities denied him the six cents free land eligible to the DPs. The compensation he received was spent mainly on court expenses (Source: *The Newstitle*, September 2, 1999:13).

Expected Amount of Compensation

We have seen that a majority of the DPs/PAPs were not satisfied with the compensation. The enquiry regarding the expectations of respondents about the amount of compensation showed that 44 per cent expected an amount more than four times they actually received. This includes 96.42 per cent respondents of Rayons, 70.18 per cent of those of Karappuzha, 60.45 per cent of those of IDA, 50 per cent of those of Bakel, 46.6 per cent of those of SIKL, 44.44 per cent of those of VSSC, and 42.42 per cent of those of Ezhimala. More than a fifth of the respondents expected double the amount. Among them, 64.58 per cent were females. Nearly 18 per cent of the respondents expected more than three times the amount. The implication is that the compensation paid to the DPs/PAPs was far below their expectation. We have to look into the type, nature and extent of land, to verify whether these expectations were reasonable or not.

It is already understood that the very process of displacement is not acceptable for a majority of the respondents with the exception of some in IRE project. In this context of frustration and uncertainty, the people cannot even make rational judgements regarding the amount of compensation. Most of them consider their earlier possessions precious and no compensation can really satisfy them. As many of them are ignorant about the criteria for compensation, they cannot even calculate the amount they are eligible. Besides, some individuals may not even be knowledgeable about the nature of compensation, but spread rumours about the possibility of getting very high amounts. That always creates uncertainty and frustration in the mind of the people.

Protest Against the Project

Lodging protests against the project seems to be a unique characteristic in the process of land takeover in Kerala. One form of protest is organised movements against the project or against inadequate compensation and resettlement. Usually, the media give good coverage to such issues. This is either under the initiative of a political party or by the local leaders. For example, it was the communist party which organised mass movements in Idukki for better resettlement of the displaced. In VSSC, the church leaders took the initiative for the negotiation with the project authorities and they succeeded in getting a resettlement colony.

Another form of protest is lodging complaints individually. Usually, people demand better compensation from the project or revenue officials. The upper class people would directly go to the court to get justice in the payment of compensation. About 45 per cent of the people had lodged protest against inadequate compensation, on the other hand 35 per cent did not lodge any protest.

People who did not have legal documents (non-patta landholders) also lodged complaints either individually or collectively for redressal of their grievances against eviction.

All the respondents from KMML and SIKL projects; all those, except one, of IRE; 91.11 per cent of those of IDA, 74.11 per cent of those of Karappuzha and 70 per cent of those of Bakel project lodged their protest.

IDUKKI – HYDRO ELECTRIC PROJECT (IHEP)

Under the impact of the post World War II famine in Kerala, the then Diwan Sir C.P.Ramaswamy Iyer allotted marshy land within the dense forests of Moovattupuzha to agricultural labourers of Travancore-Kochi in 1947-48 under the "Grow more food programme" on condition that they paid the annual cess and would not construct any house, but only sheds to live in. On implementation of the Land Reforms Act (1959), pattas were awarded to those tillers under Moovzttupuzha RDO. The price they had to pay later for their sweat and toil was eviction under the label of IHEP.

For the implementation of IHEP under the Indo-Canadian collaboration, the villages of Pothumattam, Kulamavu, Koodavara, Muthikandam, Churuli, Venganamchal, Kanakayam, Nadavayal, Vairamani, Nediyani, Mayynna, Kannampadi, Muttampadi – (Thodupuzha Taluk), Ayyappan Covil, and Upputhara (Peerumedu Taluk) were acquired in 1961 evicting hundreds of families. Key informants reported that thousands of people were displaced by the project. The manner in which land was acquired and people were evicted was very cruel. The evicted were given one acre of land at Amaravathy and ten pieces of coconut palm leaves.

The Malanadu Karshaka Union, formed by Fr. Joseph Vadakkan and his colleagues, came to the rescue of the evictees who put up a resistance. The former M.P., A.K.Gopalan's indefinite fast unto death and the flow of memoranda to the then Prime Minister, Mr. Nehru, helped in obtaining a stay on the eviction till 1969. Finally in 1969, each of the evicted families was allotted 3 acres of land elsewhere (irrespective of the amount of land they owned) and a cash compensation for their assets to facilitate resettlement.

Those families displaced from Mayanna were resettled at Chettikulangara (Chalakudy); Manjapara (Aluva) and the five families from Nadukani were given land at Bhumiaramkulam. The displaced families of Kudavara, Muthukandam, and Vairamani had to go to Ranni, Marumaruti, Madatharuvi, Neeretukavu, Pallikkale and Athikayam, whereas Ponnambra, Vairamani people were sent to Kaliyar, Vannapuram, Chelachuvadu, Thallakkanam, and Kanjikuzhi. Representatives of those families when interviewed reported that they were exploited by the authorities by extracting money from the evictees. About 18 officers were suspended on charges of corruption. Majority of the resettled people sold off their newly allotted land and moved to far off places for the reason that they had no sufficient money and materials to settle down and develop the land and plant cash crops which would take at least five years before they could get any income. They did not know any occupation other than agriculture and the meager resettlement package was inadequate for their rehabilitation.

On the contrary, none of the respondents of Idukki and MVIP had protested. We cannot assume that their passivity was due to better compensation and resettlement packages. In MVIP, majority of the DPs were residing in *puramboke* and they got 4 cents of free patta land, because of the project. Thus, they considered themselves fortunate in getting the benefits accrued to them through the intervention of the project.

Because of the characteristic of socio-political atmosphere in Kerala, the people do not accept any development project easily. They have a critical attitude towards the motives behind. As the media give good coverage to the problems and prospects of each project, people always consider that they have the right to demand a good compensation. Experiences of displaced people of earlier

Table 7.3

Number of People Who Lodged a Protest Against Compensation

Project	*Lodged Protest*	*Not Lodged any Protest*	*NA*	*NP*	*Total*
IRE	42	1	0	0	43
KML	17	0	0	0	17
IHP	0	60	0	10	70
KIP	46	15	0	1	62
IDA	41	2	1	1	45
SIKL	30	0	0	0	30
NTP	27	13	0	31	71
VSC	21	37	0	2	60
MGR	3	24	1	13	41
VZM	22	0	1	17	40
PTR	0	0	0	50	50
ENA	15	24	0	0	39
BTP	21	9	0	0	30
NIA	27	39	0	1	67
MVP	0	17	0	13	30
Total	312	241	3	139	695
Percentage	44.89	34.68	0.5	20.72	100

projects teach them how to manage to get a better compensation. In Nedumbassery, some respondents revealed that all those who protested got more benefits in comparison with others who vacated their land peacefully. Therefore, to lodge protest against compensation becomes quite natural and often inevitable for the affected people.

Nearly 23 per cent of the respondents received no response to the complaints from the authorities. This shows the negative attitude of officials in terms of their concern for the affected people. This may possibly be related to red tapism and corruption. Sometimes, the protest may be lodged by occupants of non-patta land. In such cases, the officials may not take any interest favourably due to legal constraints.

Houses of 17 respondents of IRE got transferred. The extent of land given as resettlement for 15 respondents of Nedumbassery had increased as a result of the protest. Seven respondents in KMML got temporary jobs.

The state of Kerala, which took the initiative for the social development of its people, has not shown a similar concern for the economic development of the people affected by development projects. This shows the ambivalence of the state government in dispensing its responsibility towards the socio-economic development of the victims of development. The neglect of the project-affected people in their economic crisis is a serious omission on the part of the government which has a tradition of a welfare approach.

Nature of Court Settlement

Besides the 16 per cent (113 out of 695) whose cases were referred to a court of law by the project authorities, another five per cent had direct recourse to the court. It is remarkable that two DPs of the Rayons project went even to the Supreme Court to obtain justice.

The information regarding the court settlement of the case is not very encouraging. The cases of 15.97 per cent of DPs were pending with the court at the time of the study. These people are

Table 7.4

Outcome of the Protest

Project	No response from authority	Contract job got	Referred to court	Permanent job	Compensation increased	Got land	Others*	NA	NP	Total
IRE	12	0	0	0	0	7	23	0	1	43
KML	0	0	0	0	0	9	8	0	0	17
IHP	0	0	0	0	0	0	0	0	70	70
KIP	23	0	20	0	0	1	1	0	17	62
IDA	5	0	16	0	0	12	8	1	3	45
SIKL	1	0	24	2	3	0	0	0	0	30
NTP	2	1	24	0	0	0	0	0	44	71
VSC	5	0	4	2	10	0	0	0	39	60
MGR	0	0	2	0	0	0	0	3	35	41
VZM	5	0	0	0	0	9	7	2	17	40
PTR	0	0	0	0	0	0	0	0	50	50
ENA	0	0	15	0	0	0	0	0	24	39
BTP	16	0	0	0	3	1	0	0	10	30
NIA	2	0	8	0	2	1	15	0	39	67
MVP	0	0	0	0	0	0	0	0	30	30
Total	71	1	113	4	18	40	62	6	379	695
Percentage	22.47	0.32	35.76	1.27	5.7	16.6	19.62	1.9		

leading their lives with uncertainty in their minds. The fact that the court has increased the compensation of 33 DPs (29.2% of 113 persons who approached the court) may motivate others to follow suit. However, the court had rejected the case of two respondents.

Conclusion

In a state like Kerala, which has achieved high social development, a corresponding concern is not seen towards the victims of development. The gross ignorance of more than a half of the respondents about the criteria for fixing the compensation shows that they were kept in the dark about the whole process of land acquisition and denied their right to demand adequate compensation for the sacrifices they made. This study reveals that out of 51 cases settled by the court, 33 were awarded higher amount of compensation. In other words, the compensation fixed by the project or state authorities was grossly inadequate and arbitrary. Whereas a section of those who are socio-economically forward seeks justice, a majority of the marginalised keep aloof from such means for want of awareness, social support, determination and money power. The experience of most of the respondents was that they were unable to purchase the same extent of assets they lost with the compensation received for them. This points to the faulty system of fixing compensation and lends weight to the demand that the criterion for compensation should be replacement value. This inherent weakness of the system gives rise to the situation where the rich people are getting a better deal in comparison with the poor and marginalised who are unable to utilise the assistance of the legal system. It is a blatant denial of the fundamental right to equality enshrined in the Constitution of India (Articles 14 to 18).

Another important finding is that the authorities equate compensation with resettlement. Whenever they talk of compensation, they affirm it as adequate. But, compensation cannot be treated as a substitute for resettlement, because it is the only price paid for the marketable assets. The resettlement and

Table 7.5

Status and Nature of Court Settlement

Project	Status				Nature				
	Settled	Not settled	NA	NP	Case Rejected	Increased Compensation	Case Pending	NA	NP
IRE	1	41	0	1	0	0	4	0	39
KML	0	16	0	1	0	0	0	0	17
IHP	0	0	0	70	0	0	0	0	70
KIP	7	40	0	15	1	5	24	5	27
IDA	1	43	1	0	0	1	35	1	8
SIKL	16	14	0	0	0	14	4	3	9
NTP	10	17	0	44	0	8	0	2	61
VSC	2	3	0	55	1	1	2	0	56
MGR	12	5	1	23	0	1	13	4	23
VZM	0	9	1	30	0	0	0	1	39
PTR	0	0	0	50	0	0	0	0	50
ENA	0	15	0	24	0	0	15	0	24
BTP	1	29	0	0	0	2	7	0	21
NIA	1	31	0	35	0	1	7	1	58
MVP	0	0	0	30	0	0	0	0	30
Total	51	263	3	378	2	33	111	17	532
Percentage	7.34	37.84	0.43	54.39	0.28	4.75	15.97	2.45	76.55

Note: The total in this table will not tally because we have integrated responses of two questions

rehabilitation is to help the deprived to restore the lost capabilities and congenial environment enjoyed by them before displacement and begin life anew.

For rehabilitation to be effective, compensation should not be viewed in its restrictive financial sense alone, but has to be understood as a crucial step in the process of helping the weakest to cope with displacement (Fernandes and Raj, 1992:109). The value of the land should be determined according to what it contributes to the people who depend on it. The criteria for compensation will go beyond material assets. It should take into account the food and other needs that the land met. It should also compensate for the trauma of displacement, the break up of community systems and other forms of attack on peoples' livelihood (Fernandes and Asif, 1997: 126).

To a great majority of the respondents (95%), the compensation was paid fully through the bank. More than a fifth of the respondents have not received any compensation. It is noteworthy that 19.59 per cent of the respondents received the amount immediately after the award itself. Nearly 41 per cent of the respondents received the compensation immediately after land takeover. Only 15.67 per cent of the total respondents received the amount one or more years after the demarcation. On the whole, a good majority (80.58%) of the respondents received the compensation immediately after land takeover or even before that. Some amount was spent for getting compensation by a minority.

About 38 per cent of the respondents had not spent any money to get compensation. At the same time, 23 per cent of respondents had to spend an amount of Rs.500 to 2,500 to get compensation. All the respondents of KMML spent an amount in this range. In brief, the payment of compensation was properly done and involvement of middlemen was the least in Kerala. Though some of the respondents had to spend money for court expenses, the procedure of payment seems to be transparent. But, we cannot ignore 27 respondents who had spent more than Rs.10,500 and 6 persons, an amount of more than Rs.50,000. Also, two persons spent an amount of more than a lakh each in order to get compensation that was due to them.

The case of 77.96 per cent of respondents is pending with the project and they have to travel constantly. They are forced to visit various offices several times in order to receive the compensation. Court expenses had to be met by 27.48 per cent of the respondents. Only a negligible number of respondents spent money as bribe to middlemen to get compensation amount. Nearly 14 per cent of the respondents had to bribe officials for getting compensation. Here, the experience of the DPs of Karappuzha project must be specially noted that 25 (out of 62) of them had to bribe the officials to get the compensation. More than half the respondents of this project are Tribals. This indicates that the poor, illiterate Tribals had to bribe the officials for receiving compensation. Majority of the DPs had to approach the court of law to get the amount of compensation.

The DPs have utilised the money they had received as compensation in a rather fruitful manner. Only a few people spent the compensation wastefully or to purchase consumer goods and ornaments. A few of them spent the money on social functions like wedding, while some others used it to repay loans. Some utilised the compensation fully for constructing a house. But, only negligible number of DPs used the money on livestock purchase or to start a business which could have improved the economic status of the family. On the whole, it is seen that the major share of the compensation was spent on land purchase and house construction. This has serious economical implications, as they could not spend the money on productive investments like purchasing livestock or starting a business. If they were provided with a resettlement package of land and house, they could have spent the compensation in more productive ways.

There is a marked gender difference among those who spent the compensation for building house. About 71 per cent among those who spent the money in this mode are men. No such difference can be found among those who purchased land. The gender difference can again be found among those who used the money for land development.

In the context of Kerala society, joint decision-making either by the couple or by the whole family seems to be the prevailing pattern. Women taking decision independently in this regard is rare and in the case of 11 projects, not a single wife had the opportunity to take decision regarding the spending of compensation, while the husbands did enjoy such a privilege except in two cases. On the whole, the caste-wise analysis shows the dominance of patriarchal values in Kerala society. In all the four caste categories, husbands alone enjoyed the privilege of decision making in a considerable number of cases. This dominance is more pronounced among OBCs. A deeper analysis reveals that the dominance of husbands among SCs is noticed only in one project, i.e. in Nedumbassery. In the same manner, in the tribal communities, the husbands had taken decisions independently only in the Karappuzha project. Among the OBCs, male domination in taking decision was obvious in 10 projects. For instance, their dominance was very pronounced in the case of IRE project. Male dominance can be treated as a general tendency in OBCs and forward castes.

According to 60.91 per cent of men, the whole family was involved in the decision making, while a lesser number of women accepted this. Similarly, 62.89 per cent of those who revealed that husbands alone took decision are men, whereas only 37.11 per cent are women. Also, more men (60.14%) had the opinion that husband and wife together took the decision than women.

Nearly 51.51 per cent of total respondents were ignorant of the criteria for fixing compensation. Almost everywhere, there was a feeling that the authorities cheated them on this count. The people had a number of reasons to justify their complaints. Most of these issues were closely related to their economic and social well being. About 64 per cent of the respondents felt that the compensation was inadequate, while 14 per cent thought it as adequate.

About two-thirds of the respondents considered that the land they had lost was fertile and the compensation received is inadequate in comparison with the value of the land they lost. Many people said that their old land was really good for cultivating a variety of crops. It was a great economic support to the family. As majority of the respondents were agriculturists, their whole life was shattered after losing the land. On the other hand, most of these respondents have purchased some land after displacement which is often barren and less in area. This experience is quite widespread, as a sizable number of respondents from eight projects have raised this issue.

The second major reason for the inadequacy of compensation is also related to land. According to about a fourth of the respondents, an equal measure of land costs much more. The DPs find that the compensation they received was not tantamount to the replacement value of the land and assets lost. Another land related complaint was that the land occupied by them was on the roadside and naturally they could get higher prices if it was sold in the open market. Land on the roadside gets much higher price and is in great demand. The enquiry regarding the expectations of respondents about the amount of compensation reveal that 48.07 per cent of the people expected an amount more than four times they actually received. The implication is that the compensation paid to the DPs/PAPs was far below their expectation.

Lodging protest against the project and inadequate compensation seems to be a unique characteristic in the process of land takeover in Kerala. In many cases, the protest (organised movements) started even immediately after the notification. The data sheds light on the same trend. About 45 per cent of the people had lodged protest against the project. Besides the 16 per cent whose case was referred to the court by the project authorities, another five per cent had direct recourse to the court on their own. It is remarkable that two DPs of the Rayons project went even to the Supreme Court to obtain justice. The information regarding how the court settled the case is also not very encouraging. The cases of 15.97 per cent of DPs were pending in the court. These people are leading their lives with uncertainty in their minds. The fact that the court has increased the compensation of 33 (4.75%) DPs may motivate others to follow suit. However, the court has rejected the case of two respondents.

8

Resettlement and Rehabilitation

After having scanned the painful process of the displacement of the victims of development, we come to the final stage of their long pilgrimage, i.e. the struggle the DPs and PAPs had to put up with for a resettlement in life. In order to understand the magnitude of the gap between what the people lost due to land acquisition and what they gained, it is necessary to study the nature of each project and what they had to offer to the affected. Therefore, we will first analyse the rehabilitation and resettlement plans of each project. It will be followed by the actual experience of the sample population.

Resettlement and Rehabilitation

The dictionary meaning of the word to 'rehabilitate', from which rehabilitation is derived, means to restore to rank, privileges, reputation, etc., which one had lost. A second meaning is to put back in good condition (*Webster's New World Dictionary*, 1974). In the fast developing world where the development process physically displaces people through land acquisition, rehabilitation of the displaced deserves greater importance. In this context, the application of the meaning and definition of rehabilitation is to be looked into systematically and analytically. If rehabilitation means restoration of the DPs to their rank, privileges and reputation or putting them back in good condition, it implies that their situation after rehabilitation should be at least equal to their previous state or should, in fact, be better, because of the price they pay for development. In any case, it should not be worse than before.

Acceptance of this principle becomes a sine qua non before one looks into the various aspects and the process of rehabilitation. Resettlement, however, is a one-time relocation with or without other economic, social and cultural support.

Resettlement Schemes by Projects

We have already seen the resettlement schemes of various projects in Chapter 4. A section of the displaced has been assisted by the projects to resettle. The others had no options other than to resettle themselves. 8.1 gives the figures of resettlement either by the project or by individual initiative. About 52 per cent of the displaced in our study had the benefit of project implemented resettlement. The findings show that while all the respondents of KMML and Idukki were resettled by the projects, none of the SIKL, and MVIP displaced and affected households was resettled by the projects. When most of the respondents of Vizhinjam (97.5%), and a vast majority of those of IRE (88.38%) followed by IDA (86.66%), Nedumbassery (85%), and Tiger (76.9%) availed of the resettlement facilities offered by the respective projects, a vast majority of respondents of NTPC (90.19%) and Bakel (76.67%) had the opposite experience. In the case of Bakel, majority were PAPs.

While 36 per cent of the forward castes and STs were resettled by the project, 76 per cent of SCs and 62 per cent of OBCs received the same facilities. That means nearly two thirds of STs and forward castes were deprived of resettlement.

Stages of Rehabilitation of the Displaced

The various stages of rehabilitation of the displaced or for that matter, anyone in need to be rehabilitated, are (1) preparing for resettlement (2) resettlement, and (3) facilitating the establishment of psycho-social, economic and cultural network.

Preparation for Resettlement

The first stage of the rehabilitation process should necessarily start with the decision or intent to acquire land, which is bound to

Table 8.1

Number of People Resettled by Project and Caste

Project	ST N=91			SC N=50		OBC N=287				GEN N=212			Total N=640				Grand Total
	Re-settled	Not Re-settled	NP	Re-settled	Not Re-settled	Re-settled	Not Re-settled	NA	NP	Re-settled	Not Re-settled	NP	Re-settled	Not Re-settled	NA	NP	
IRE	0	0	0	1	0	37	5	0	0	0	0	0	38	5	0	0	43
KML	0	0	0	0	0	17	0	0	0	0	0	0	17	0	0	0	17
IHP	29	0	0	0	0	18	0	0	0	23	0	0	70	0	0	0	70
KIP	4	11	19	0	0	0	3	0	6	0	14	5	4	28	0	30	62
IDA	0	0	0	1	0	20	3	1	0	18	2	0	39	5	1	0	45
SIKL	0	0	0	0	1	0	9	0	0	0	20	0	0	30	0	0	30
NTP	0	0	0	0	1	1	15	0	5	0	48	1	1	64	0	6	71
VSC	0	0	0	0	0	30	30	0	0	0	0	0	30	30	0	0	60
MGR	0	0	0	0	2	0	9	0	0	0	18	12	0	29	0	12	41
VZM	0	0	0	0	0	39	0	1	0	0	0	0	39	0	1	0	40
PTR	0	47	3	0	0	0	0	0	0	0	0	0	0	47	0	3	50
ENA	0	0	0	8	0	6	0	0	0	16	6	3	30	6	0	3	39
BTP	0	0	0	0	0	7	21	0	0	0	2	0	7	23	0	0	30
NIA	0	0	0	28	0	9	0	0	0	20	9	1	57	9	0	1	67
MVP	0	0	0	0	8	0	6	0	0	0	16	0	0	30	0	0	30
Total	33	58	22	38	12	184	101	2	11	77	135	22	332	306	2	55	640
Percentage	36.26	63.74		76.0	24.0	64.11	35.19	0.70		36.32	63.68		51.88	47.81	0.31		100

displace people, or cause loss of their livelihood. In the Land acquisition Act, which is more than 100 years old, in spite of many amendments, the acquisition procedures continue to be unilateral, protecting only the interests of the party for whom land is acquired. The request for land acquisition is placed before the Collector who after studying the proposal notifies the same. This is followed by the identification of possible land losers, measuring their land and assessment of their compensation. Then the compensation is awarded and the notified land is acquired and transferred to the requiring body even in the face of protest by the original land holders. The last straw in the hands of the dispossessed is the recourse to a Court of law for redress, which is beyond the reach of the marginalised. Most dehumanising in the whole process of land acquisition is the denial of the right of the dispossessed to participate in the decision-making process, leading to land acquisition. This turns the existing method of land acquisition into forced eviction. The question which arises then is who prepares whom, how and when for the resettlement? The experiences of our respondents throw light on this aspect of rehabilitation.

The absence of a rehabilitation policy and the poor state of rehabilitation described in Chapter 4 are very conspicuous in the context of the 15 selected projects in this study. All except NTPC of Kayamkulam, show the callous and casual approach of the State Government towards the evicted and their rehabilitation. According to certain bureaucrats interviewed, 'the handsome compensation the state gives is enough to meet all the needs and expenses of the displaced in their post displacement life'. This attitude of the decision-makers is a blatant denial of the right of the displaced and the affected to participate in matters concerning their lives. When we consider the fact that more than 40 per cent of the displaced in India are from among the Tribals who form only 7.5 per cent of the total population (Kothari, 1996: 1477), their resistance to land acquisition can be silenced by giving them false promises. This study shows that a majority of the DPs and PAPs in Kerala are small and marginal farmers and landless unskilled labourers who are powerless and fall for the false promises of the officials. Unless they are empowered by their participation in the process of decision-making regarding land acquisition, there is hardly any scope for their rehabilitation with equity and social justice.

NTPC Kayamkulam was the only project to have conducted an opinion poll among the would be affected on the need for a thermal power plant in Kerala and its location in Kayamkulam (Thomas, 1991:63). Eighty six per cent of the 1510 respondents whose land was acquired gave their opinion in its favour. On the other hand, the ruling party had mobilised public opinion in favour of establishing the Mavoor Gwalior Rayons (GRASIM) presenting it as a panacea for unemployment due to the industrial backwardness of Kerala and as a turning point in the development of Kerala through industrialisation. Therefore, most of the DPs surrendered their land for whatever compensation they received without any resistance. However, recently a senior member of the CPI (M) in Kerala publicly proclaimed that the decision of the then Chief Minister EMS Namboodiripad to invite Gwalior Rayons to establish their factory at Mavoor was a grave mistake (*Manorama*, 13th January 2000). However, these two projects can be considered exceptions.

In the other projects studied, people had no role in the decision related to land acquisition and thereby, in the planning of resettlement. To them, the land acquisition turned out to be forced eviction, which came as a bolt from the blue. So, they could not plan and prepare themselves for resettlement. This can be surmised as the first dehumanising experience the DPs and PAPs faced in the land acquisition process.

Resettlement

The second stage in the process of rehabilitation is resettlement, which facilitates a smooth transition from the original habitation to the resettlement area. Resettlement is defined as the physical implantation in a new colony. It is primarily an economic initiative and is at best a step towards rehabilitation (Fernandes and Asif, 1997: 126).

The first and foremost component in resettlement is the dwelling place the displaced can move into. Among the basic needs to sustain life, shelter comes next to food and clothing. Shelter or housing provide to human beings not only protection from adverse weather conditions, but also the most needed security and a sense of self-esteem. This protection and security are very important for children and women who are more susceptible to health related problems and vulnerable to other social maladies. Phelan et al. (1997: 323) speak of the stigma of homelessness in their study on attitudes towards the poor. It is equally applicable to the displaced in our country.

In a country where there is severe shortage of housing, provision of a house in the resettlement area should become a precondition for land acquisition or eviction. When we look at the resettlement schemes of the selected 15 projects in Kerala which had displaced many families, we understand the gravity of homelessness and its impact. The provisions in the package of some projects was just a house site, whereas some others provided house site and services, some others gave site and house or only jobs or agricultural land; site with basic facilities and money for building a simple house and an unskilled job.

Among the fifteen projects studied, only the Vizhinjam Harbour and VSSC fulfilled this criterion of providing house to the displaced. The Vizhinjam project provided each of the displaced families with a small house of about 250 sq. ft. within four cents of land. Although VSSC had originally made promises to resettle the 400 displaced households in the new settlement colony, only 220 were provided houses and nearly the same number of families were not given the shelter they needed even in 1970, i.e. six years after their eviction. This particular issue was pointed out to the then Chairman of Indian Space Research Organisation (ISRO), Sri Vikram Sarabhai, in a meeting convened by the Pallithura and Veli People's Coordination Committee (PVPCC) on 5 April, 1970. In the said meeting, the ISRO

Chairman regretted the delay in implementing the resettlement scheme of providing land and living accommodation.

The Central Government had already made the payments to the State Government and therefore, rehabilitation was the responsibility of the State Government. He also advised the people to take up the matter with the Collector of Thiruvananthapuram. The PA to the Collector explained that the government had prepared plans and funds would be made available to the Bishop of Thiruvananthapuram, the Rt. Revd Msgr. Pereira for the resettlement and rehabilitation (Minutes of PVPCC, 1970)

On 17-7-1971, the Collector of Thiruvananthapuram stated that 243 families out of the 550 evicted were allotted houses, 70 were allotted house sites and another 237 were yet to be given sites. However, he pointed out that in order to get financial assistance for construction of houses, the beneficiaries required to form a co-operative which would be brought under the existing housing schemes (Minutes of PVPCC, 1971). Although matters looked well on paper and in promises, the ground reality was quite different.

Moving into the new settlement area involves much expenditure of which one is transportation cost. The question here is who pays the transportation or shifting charges? We gathered from the DPs that most of them had to use their own meager resources. Only IRE, KMML and Nedumbassery provided shifting charges.

IRE project in 1975-76 provided each evicted family with 8 cents of land and Rs.300 as shifting charges. But, in 1987-88 and 1993-94, the size of the house plot was reduced to 5 cents and the shifting charges were raised to Rs.10,000. One of the resettlement areas of IRE project is in Kozhikode, an island-like village, surrounded by rivers. The Company made arrangements for boat services to ferry people and goods from and to this resettlement place. Crossing the river is very difficult, especially when people have to depend entirely on the ferry, which has limited service. Drinking water, electricity and toilet facilities were absent in the new village.

In Nedumbassery project, besides payment of compensation fixed by the Tahsildar, the resettlement package of 6 cents of land in a housing colony and a sum of Rs. 10,000/- as relocation cost were provided to each evicted family.

Among the other projects, the resettlement package varied from a small house plot of 6 cents to 10 cents of land as reported in Bakel, IDA, MVIP, IRE and KMML. Among these, only IRE, KMML, NTPC and Nedumbassery were the four projects that promised some basic facilities like drinking water, road and electricity in the resettlement colony. But, in most of these cases, the promises were not kept. This caused serious problems to the displaced.

Besides providing the house site, IRE project in Kollam ensured that the basic facilities such as provision of drinking water, motorable road and electricity to the location were made available.

The Nedumbassery project acquired 36 acres of paddy fields at Akaparambu for the resettlement of 300 evicted households. Infrastructural facilities such as water, electricity and road were not provided although these were part of the deal with the people. Each household was allotted 6 cents of this land. The official report said that all the displaced people were resettled.

The Bakel Tourism Project in Kasargod district disposed of the displaced people with a small house plot of 5 cents. The five displaced families in this project had to mobilise their own resources for resettlement in the newly allotted site. This meant shifting their belongings to the new place, putting up a new house, seeking new job opportunities, getting acquainted with the new place and people, apart from the psychological trauma experienced by all in the family including children.

The Industrial Development Area (IDA) was not any better than the Bakel tourism project in resettling the displaced people. The only difference was that the IDA offered six cents of land instead of the five cents provided by Bakel project as house site. A visit to these locations helped our team members to understand the predicament of the displaced people. The following case studies illustrate the problems of the victims of displacement.

In the case of Ezhimala Naval Academy in Kannur district, the displaced households were provided with a plot of land at

Chorichal and Paruthicaud, varying in size from 10 cents to one acre of land. Here again, the DPs had the same problems as those of Bakel and IDA projects.

Some of the evicted families from Idukki project area were given one acre of land at Amaravathy and ten pieces of coconut palm leaves.

The Karappuzha project is another example of injustice meted out by the displaced people. Almost all of them were Tribals. The R & R officials made an estimate of the value for the house the displaced were living in and made a payment to the family. It was left to the displaced to identify a place, buy the land and build a house of their own.

The state of homelessness attached a stigma to the poor and people reacted negatively. Such reactions and stigma caused social distance of the poor. It also suggests that they face discrimination in social relations, employment and housing which will contribute to the perpetuation of their homeless condition and the public may not support policies that would improve their situation (Phelan et al., 1997: 335). Further, having lost the means of livelihood by their eviction from their original settlement and without any hope for a job, which does not come easily in their new settlement, the project would have done justice had they offered jobs to the displaced people. KMML, VSSC, SIKL, NTPC and Nedumbassery were the few projects that offered some jobs to the displaced people or created job opportunities for them. The Tiger Project was the worst. The Tribals were not given any resettlement package and they had nowhere to go. All these clearly show that a vast majority of the projects do not have a proper resettlement scheme.

Restoration of a Congenial Environment

The third stage in rehabilitation is the restoration of a congenial environment where the host community's support is essential. Rehabilitation, thus, involves replacing the lost economic assets, rebuilding the community systems that have been weakened by displacement, attending to the psychological trauma of forced alienation from livelihood, transition to the new economy which is alien to those living in a predominantly informal society and preparing them to encounter the new society as equals (Fernandes and Asif, 1997: 126). A close scrutiny of all the development projects and their approach in handling the evictees clearly shows that there was no proper rehabilitation of the displaced persons in Kerala between 1951 and 1995. If at all, anything was done, it had not gone beyond the second stage, the resettlement, which was eventually left half way through. Those who represent the government and on whose behalf the land was acquired do not seem to understand the psychological trauma and the social alienation the DPs experience, the innumerable hardships children and women live with and the impact of their refugee status in the host community on their self-esteem and mental health. For instance, the original settlers of Kozhikode (in Kollam district), one of the resettlement colonies of IRE project, despised the new settlers by calling them refugees. Hence, the resettled people have limited interaction with the local people and experience a sort of social isolation.

The MVIP provided four cents of land with the help of the *Gramapanchayat*. SIKL did not have any physical resettlement and all that it could offer was unskilled jobs in the project. The displaced people in Idukki district, a high terrain area, are mostly small and medium farmers. Those families displaced from Mayanna were resettled at Chettikulangara (Chalakudy); Manjapara (Aluva) and the five families from Nadukani were given land at Bhumiaramkulam. The displaced families of Kudavara, Muthukandam, and Vairamani had to go to Ranni, Marumaruti, Madatharuvi, Neeretukavu, Pallikkale and Athikayam, whereas people from Ponnambra, Vairamani were sent to Kaliyar, Vannapuram, Chelachuvadu, Thallakkanam, and Kanjikuzhi. Representatives of those families reported that they were exploited by the authorities by extracting money from them. About 18 officers were suspended on charges of corruption in this regard. A majority of the resettled people sold off their newly allotted land and moved to far off places, because they did not have sufficient money and materials to settle down, develop the land and plant cash crops which would take at least five years before they yield any income. They did not know any occupation other than agriculture, and the meager resettlement package was inadequate for their rehabilitation.

Reasons for Self-resettlement

Out of the 695 persons interviewed, the respondents of 119 (17.12%) households had no option other than to rely on self-resettlement. Among the various factors that forced section of the displaced people is to rely on self re-settlement, the most significant one is that the project had no resettlement programme. Fifty one households (43% of the self-resettled) come under this category, nearly half of them are displaced by Gwalior Rayons of Mavoor in Kozhikode district, a large-scale industry in the private sector.

Another significant factor that motivated people to go in for self-resettlement is the size of the land given. Either no land was given offered to the respondents from the project or the land offered to them was too small. A total of 19 respondents (15.97%) reported this situation. The Nedumbassery Airport of Ernakulam, the Industrial Development Area of Palakkad, and VSSC of Trivandrum are the three main projects involved in creating this situation.

Another important reason that motivated a sizeable number of households (21) to embark upon self-resettlement was that they were not considered by the project for resettlement. More than 50 per cent of these families were evicted by VSSC. According to the respondents, VSSC had double standards in their dealings with the displaced persons. In the first phase of the project, VSSC resettled 220 families, each with a small house plot and an RCC house with a room, verandah, kitchen and toilets. But, the displaced in the subsequent land acquisition were not considered for resettlement. The number of such evictees was small, so was the land involved. Those evicted were unable to organise any protest demonstrations and influence the decision-makers. Therefore, they settled themselves in the vacant plots they could find in the neighbourhood which turned out to be 'puramboke' for some and VSSC land for others.

Similarly, SIKL project of Alappuzha District did not consider some households for resettlement. However, both VSSC and SIKL projects offered one job each to those evicted families, if they had someone technically qualified. Only two respondents from among the displaced families by SIKL project had something positive to speak about self-resettlement. They opted for self-resettlement, because they found better opportunities for employment elsewhere on their own.

Planning of Relocation

It is important to note that only the displaced families needed to be resettled and the relocation planning concerns them. According to 57 per cent of all the DPs, their relocation was planned by R & R officials. They include majority of DPs in IRE, IDA, VSSC, Vizhinjam, Ezhimala, and Nedumbassery. The implication is that the people had little participation in the planning of relocation, except those 22 per cent who had planned the location all by themselves. There is no significant difference when we consider across the caste groups, except that relocation of 76 per cent of SCs whose resettlement was planned by R & R officials.

No village leader was involved in the planning process.

Payment of Relocation Cost

Resettlement of the displaced families involved relocation cost. These expenses of over two-thirds of the displaced families (68%) were paid for by the project officials. For 23 per cent of the displaced, no relocation cost was paid by the project and therefore, these DPs had to meet the expenses all by themselves. The relocation cost was borne by the rehabilitation office for 0.43 per cent of the respondents only. One reason for this state of affairs is the absence of a rehabilitation department in many projects in Kerala. So, these activities are under the purview of the project authorities themselves. Either these offices had no provision for resettlement or they ignored this dimension totally. All of the respondents of KMML and MVIP and a majority of those of IRE, IDA, Vizhinjam, Ezhimala, and Nedumbassery opined that project officials did the payment. In Idukki, 41 per cent of the DPs reported that the government gave them land and all other expenses associated with resettlement were met by the families concerned. For the whole sample, the self paid resettlement constituted 8.33 per cent.

One significant inference from the above is that the project authorities were involved in the payment of the relocation cost of a vast majority (67.72%) of the displaced irrespective of their caste and gender classification. But, the amount, thus, disbursed was nominal without any consideration for the human-days lost and the other troubles involved.

Time Lag Between Displacement and Resettlement

Displacement in itself is a trauma inflicted upon the people in the name of national development by uprooting them from the place and community where they had their social, cultural and psychological roots. Given this psycho-social dimension, any delay in their resettlement is bound to have a serious impact on their post-displacement life. Because of the uncertainties associated with many of the projects, in many cases, the eviction day comes without advance information and people had to vacate the house all on a sudden. The question to be asked is where to go next? The answer to this question is not always easy to find. There are psychological, social and economic problems associated with eviction. None of the projects had planned the resettlement systematically prior to the eviction. Had these been planned with the people involved and implemented, the preliminaries such as housing, infrastructural facilities etc., would have been easy for the people who would be prepared psychologically to face the event creatively with a positive attitude.

But, the uncertainty and the time lag between land acquisition and resettlement made lives miserable for the displaced. A glimpse of the predicament of the people who were displaced was already seen. A major reason for it is the time lag between displacement and resettlement. Eighty two per cent of the DPs got resettled within a year. They include all the DPs of the KMML and Idukki and a majority of those of IRE, IDA, Vizhinjam, Ezhimala and Nedumbassery. But, VSSC and IRE took 2-3 years to resettle a sizeable number of the DPs, particularly those belonging to the OBC.

Place of Stay between Displacement and Resettlement

The place of stay in the transition period between displacement and rehabilitation has significant influence, as this is one of the most difficult stages of the displacement process. The people had to vacate the place where they had been living for many generations. They lost the land, their means of livelihood and all that they had acquired in their life. Many were in a dilemma concerning an alternative place to stay until they found a new place of residence. This study shows that more than three-fourths of the DPs had to stay in a temporary shed built in the new place. It means that the displaced had at first to build a hut in the land provided for resettlement and wait until the house was constructed by the project or by themselves after many months. More than 70 per cent of the displaced of IRE, KMML, Idukki, IDA, VSSC, Ezhimala and Nedumbassery went through this experience. This clearly shows the serious negligence on the part of the project authorities in planning and implementing resettlement properly and in good time.

Seven respondents in NTPC and 11 in Nedumbassery stayed in rented houses. In Bakel project, one respondent stayed in a hut of his friend's place.

First Feeling at Resettlement

With the purpose of understanding the problems of the people after starting a new life, we asked them about their first feeling at resettlement. Nearly 52 per cent of the DPs had the fear of future. Going by the project and the communities affected, a majority of the STs of IHP, KIP, and PTR projects were under the grip of this fear. A substantial number of women too (54%) were among these. This strong emotion definitely shattered their psychological balance in that situation which in turn affected the whole family even in their interpersonal relationships. The same emotion affected all the other communities such as SCs, OBCs, and the forward castes irrespective of the projects.

Another strong feeling that spread among 45 per cent of the DPs was helplessness. That was the dominant feeling of the Vizhinjam and IRE DPs. It is noteworthy that none of them felt the fear of the host population. It may be because the displaced were familiar with the host community, or felt capable of adjustment to such a situation. Another interesting finding is that those who felt happy about resettlement are an insignificant minority (2.14%). Most of them were from the IRE and KMML who had no land of their own and were exposed to the vagaries of nature. They had their huts within the reach of the rough sea. With resettlement, a solution to their perennial problem of finding alternate location during the monsoons was found.

Problems Faced after Resettlement

The life at the place of resettlement is usually accompanied by a host of problems. Financial strain was the main problem reported by 84.05 per cent of the respondents irrespective of their caste and gender. Debt burden is the natural consequence of the financial strain and 17.76 per cent reported it. Rayons and MVIP respondents were the only exceptions. The people who depended on agricultural land and CPRs for their livelihood were forced to live with minimum land after displacement. Some, for example, the Tribals, were in an informal economy and displacement pushed them into a formal economy without adequate preparation. This drastically affected their lives, as they did not know how to spend the amount of compensation in an economically viable manner. And this led to severe financial strain.

About 46 per cent of the DP respondents complained about lack of basic facilities like drinking water, electricity, roads etc., in the new place. Out of this, 18 per cent of these are Tribals and

INDUSTRIAL DEVELOPMENT AREA, PALAKKAD

Pudussery Grama Panchayat of Palakkad district covers an area of 122.24 sq kms with a population of 41,710 (Government of Kerala, Panchayat Directory, 1998: 83). Before 1985, people of the village were happy and self-sufficient in food grains, and had ample opportunity for employment in the primary sector. Nearly 500 acres of land was used for cultivating paddy and veges for their livelihood. Most of the people belong to the OBC. The main occupation of the villagers is agriculture. Toddy tapping was the cottage industry of many villagers. People claimed to have had basic facilities, such as road, water and electricity in the village. There was sufficient land for burial grounds.

Around 750 acres of land was acquired from this Panchayat for Kanjikode industrial estate in the year 1985-86, displacing and affecting around 137 families. Force was used upon the people by the officers in the form of locking their houses, destroying their crops and throwing away the cooking vessels etc., to evict the people. Around 120 evicted families were resettled in the new colony at P. K. Challa by KINFRA project. The criteria for resettlement was that the families which had less than one acre in the acquired area was given five cents of free land at the resettlement colony, besides the compensation for the house and land at market rate. Seventeen families which had more than two acres of land were given only the compensation and without any resettlement facility. The compensation paid was lower than the actual rate of land transaction in the area. Therefore, these families had to rely on self-resettlement elsewhere. They had gone to far away places that no further information about them was available.

The land allotted for resettlement turned out to be on lease for 12 years and the people cannot use the land document for any purpose of transaction including bank loan for housing. This means the government can acquire this land at any time, according to its whims and fancies.

For the resettled, there is no land for cultivation. Being agricultural labourers and farmers, the people are unemployed without land to cultivate and are facing the dire consequence of loss of livelihood.

In the new resettlement colony, people are without drinking water as there are no public taps. The water in the three public wells in the resettlement colony is not fit for drinking. People have no toilets and there is no burial ground. Electricity is still a dream for these villagers.

This project acquired land again in 1997 under notification published in 1994, evicting about 200 families from Pudussery village of Palakkad district. All of them were manual labourers. Those who owned below two acres of land were resettled at Pambukuzhichalla, which lacks basic facilities, such as drinking water, road and electricity. Since they were evicted during the rainy season their households' articles perished. There is no Primary Health Center in the vicinity. The land offered for resettlement was not allotted in time. So, they agitated and got 5 cents of land for each family.

Due to indiscriminate disposal of solid and liquid waste from a sugar factory, water in the community wells became polluted and the people are facing acute shortage of safe drinking water. As the waste from the sugar factory flows into the near by river, the river water also got polluted. Similarly, carbide from a steel factory in the neighbourhood causes serious air pollution.

During rainy season, the colony gets flooded as it is situated in low-lying land, making the whole area filthy and unhygienic. The cowsheds in their small premises also make the surroundings unhygienic during monsoon. In the absence of drainage facilities, the wastewater from one's house flows into house premises of others, causing bickering quarrels among the neighbours. Another major complaint of the DPs was that due to the implementation of this project, they lost their agricultural land and labour opportunity.

The immediate demands of the resettled were safe drinking water, electricity, roads, drainage and transportation facilities. Although Kerala State Electricity Board's substation is very near to their colony, they have not been given electric connection. The Panchayat and other officials do not care for the welfare of the people, rather they despise and abuse the people whenever they approach them for any help. The place is also infested with antisocial elements and political parties make mileage out of the situation. There was no development in this area ever since resettlement of the evicted. KINFRA has not yet operationalised their units in this area. The employment opportunity promised by the project was not given to them so far. Due to the high cost of land, the people are unable to purchase additional land in a better locality for homestead as well as for cultivation. Although the land was acquired by the KINFRA for the industrial purpose, it is lying vacant devoid of any productivity for about 15 years now. Thus, the public purpose for which the land was acquired has not been achieved. The end result is nothing, but causing serious injustice to the people.

women constitute 41 per cent for whom the absence of such facilities affect more. Underemployment was reported by the respondents (41.45%) as another serious problem after resettlement. Of these, 37.7 per cent were women. The Tribal households under the grip of unemployment turned out to be 18.25 per cent of DPs. Going by project, the highest percentage of unemployment was reported by the respondents of Idukki (54.28%) and Nedumbassery (62.68). Lack of toilet facilities was another serious problem in IRE (48.83%) project, and food shortage for the Tribals of Karappuzha project (20.97%). Another unique problem faced by a sizeable number (34.15%) of respondents of Rayons project was social isolation and family disruption.

In the context of resettlement, it is important to remember that the promises made by the officials to provide better facilities to the displaced families were not kept. IRE, and KMML projects authorities had promised better facilities of drinking water, toilets, roads etc., at the time of displacement. A great majority of the respondents of IRE, KMML, Idukki, Nedumbassery and IDA projects had complained that the authorities did not fulfill the promises. This is a serious lapse on the part of the authorities which caused innumerable problems to the households of the DPs making their lives miserable.

Duration of Unemployment

The length of the period of unemployment is another aspect we enquired into. Whereas sixty two per cent of the respondents got job either immediately or within a period of six months, more than one-third of the respondents remained unemployed for a period of 6 to 24 months. They include those who were already unemployed before displacement or did not get any job after displacement. Whether the period of unemployment is either brief or long, it indeed had serious repercussion on the displaced families which had lost their means of livelihood. For the poor people who have a hand to mouth existence, even a single day without employment is a serious threat to their lives. Needless to say that women and children are the worst victims of this predicament.

Looking at the DPs community-wise, one finds that 86.36 per cent did not get employment opportunity immediately after displacement. Among them, women constituted 37 per cent. The depressing story is that majority of the Tribals remained unemployed up to 24 months.

Availability of Amenities Before and After Displacement

In assessing the impact of displacement and rehabilitation, a comparison was made of the availability of amenities before and after displacement. The amenities examined were school, electricity, toilets, drinking water, water for irrigation, employment, medical facilities, market, places of worship, transportation, and recreational facilities.

School

The availability of schools had decreased after displacement. School facilities were available to 92 per cent of the respondents in their vicinity before displacement. It came down to 83.16 per cent after displacement. All the DPs of KMML acknowledged the existence of a school before displacement, but not after. All the DPs of Nedumbassery project had schooling facilities before, but it came down to 68.65 per cent after displacement. In the case of Ezhimala, there was a sharp decline from 97.87 per cent to 23.07 per cent. This difference seems to be because of an increase in the distance of the school from the resettlement area and the difficulty in traversing the hilly terrain.

Nearly two-thirds of the respondents are of the opinion that the quality of school remains the same as in the past. All the respondents of Idukki told us that the quality of the school was better than in the past whereas 76.92 per cent of Ezhimala DPs said that it was worse than the past. Idukki has been one of the few areas in Kerala where facilities like electricity, drinking water and school were not adequately provided. Those who were displaced from the region naturally found better facilities in the resettlement area. In the case of Ezhimala they have been shifted from the vicinity of a school to an interior area.

EZHIMALA NAVAL ACADEMY

An area of 2500 acres was acquired for the Naval Academy at Ezhimala in Taliparamba Taluk of Kannur district in 1983 by evicting nearly 1800 people. The compensation for the acquired land ranged from Rs. 200/- to Rs. 400/- per cent. Resettlement facilities were provided for those who owned an area below 1 acre of land and to the economically poor. The major resettlement colonies are Chorichal colony, Paruthicad 10-cent colony, Paruthicad 1-acre harijan colony and Ettikulam colony.

Sixteen families were resettled in Chorichal colony. This is a hilly area with comparatively less development. Majority of the people were from fishing community, while the remaining were manual labourers. The local Panchayat provided a well in the resettlement colony, but it remains dry most of the time. Therefore people have to spend much of their time to collect water for their daily need. They also complained about the lack of electricity, road and transportation facilities. Thus, the people in this colony are not at all satisfied with their resettlement and the compensation paid for the acquired land.

Paruthicad 10 cent Colony

This is also a hilly region where 30 families were resettled. Their main occupation is manual labour. These people also face lack of basic facilities. They are afraid of another displacement due to qaurry works in the neighbourhood.

Chittadi Colony

Thirteen families were resettled in this colony. The people had no *pattas* for the land they owned before displacement. They protested against the project and were imprisoned for 12 days. Finally, the authorities forcefully evicted them from their houses. These people also lack basic facilities such as drinking water, electricity, road and transportation, etc., in the Chittiadi Colony.

Paruthicad 1 acre Colony

The Scheduled Caste (SC) people were provided 1 acre of land as part of resettlement in this colony. The people were engaged in manual labour.

Ettikulam

Majority of the people in Ettikulam are Muslims. The main occupation of these people is fishing. The process of eviction was very cruel by any standard. It took place during the period of fasting. The people were evicted forcefully with the help of policemen. They had to take refuge in their relatives' houses immediately after the land takeover.

They sold the 10 cents of land allotted to them in Paruthicad 10-cent colony while some others refused to occupy the allotted land. These people were resettled at Ettikulam by the Mosque authorities.

The compensation paid for the land was inadequate. Some of the people approached court for getting increased compensation and they succeeded. There was malpractice in assessing the land and people having some sort of influence, got more compensation. Majority of the land acquired for naval academy was agricultural fields and plantations. Therefore, the people lost their source of livelihood. One family unable to overcome this predicament committed suicide.

There is neither any school nor a primary health centre in their new place which made access to these services difficult. At the time of eviction, the authorities promised to give 25 cents of land as a resettlement package, but actually they provided only 10 cents and an amount of Rs. 9000/- as loan. No preference was given to the evicted local people for jobs related to the project. Now the construction work is in progress with labourers hired from other states like Uttar Pradesh.

The people formed an action committee to get an increased compensation. The committee submitted memorandum to the chief minister and the revenue minister. But, no action was taken in the matter.

Electricity

Electricity is a facility that has improved in many cases. Prior to their displacement about 39 per cent had power supply. In their post-displacement life, nearly 65 per cent had access to electric power in their houses. This is a welcome change.

VSSC, Idukki, Rayons, Vizhinjam, Ezhimala and MVIP respondents largely benefited from the scheme. Power supply for the DPs of Nedumbassery decreased considerably in spite of the commitment made by the project authorities. This appears to be a serious violation of their contract. Such a problem should be seen within the time perspective. Projects like VSSC belong to the

Table 8.2

Availability and Quality of Schools Before and After Displacement

Project	Availability									Quality					
	Yes		No		NA		NP		Total	Better	Worse	Same	NA	NP	Total
	Before	After	Before	After	Before	After	Before	After							
IRE	12	9	31	34	0	0	0	0	43	0	0	13	0	30	43
KML	17	0	0	17	0	0	0	0	17	0	0	17	0	0	17
IHP	70	70	0	0	0	0	0	0	70	70	0	0	0	0	70
KIP	56	56	4	4	2	2	0	0	62	3	1	36	5	17	62
IDA	41	41	3	3	1	1	0	0	45	0	2	42	0	1	45
SIKL	29	29	0	0	1	1	0	0	30	2	6	22	0	0	30
NTP	69	69	1	1	0	0	1	1	71	6	0	62	0	3	71
VSC	59	60	1	0	0	0	0	0	60	26	0	34	0	0	60
MGR	38	39	1	0	0	0	2	2	41	19	0	5	0	17	41
VZM	40	40	0	0	0	0	0	0	40	0	0	40	0	0	40
PTR	45	50	5	0	0	0	0	0	50	13	0	32	0	5	50
ENA	37	9	0	28	0	0	2	2	39	0	30	9	0	0	39
BTP	30	30	0	0	0	0	0	0	30	0	0	20	0	10	30
NIA	67	46	0	20	0	0	0	1	67	1	25	41	0	0	67
MVP	30	30	0	0	0	0	0	0	30	1	0	29	0	0	30
Total	640	578	46	103	4	4	5	6	695	141	64	402	5	83	695
	92.08	83.16	6.61	14.82	0.575	0.575	7.19	8.06		20.25	9.20	57.24	0.7	11.94	100

Table 8.3

Availability and Quality of Electricity Before and After Displacement

Project	Availability									Quality					
	Yes		No		NA		NP		Total	Better	Worse	Same	NA	NP	Total
	Before	After	Before	After	Before	After	Before	After							
IRE	7	15	36	28	0	0	0	0	43	3	6	5	0	29	43
KML	4	4	13	13	0	0	0	0	17	4	12	1	0	0	17
IHP	0	68	69	2	0	0	1	0	70	1	0	0	0	69	70
KIP	9	8	53	53	0	1	0	0	62	7	27	6	16	6	62
IDA	6	1	38	43	0	1	0	0	45	0	13	31	0	1	45
SIKL	29	29	1	1	0	0	0	0	30	1	4	23	0	2	30
NTP	69	69	2	2	0	0	0	0	71	4	1	60	2	4	71
VSC	10	58	50	2	0	0	0	0	60	49	1	10	0	0	60
MGR	0	37	39	2	0	0	2	2	41	0	0	2	0	39	41
VZM	9	30	31	10	0	0	0	0	40	4	0	7	0	29	40
PTR	24	29	26	21	0	0	0	0	50	1	0	24	0	25	50
ENA	13	22	25	16	0	0	1	1	39	13	15	11	0	0	39
BTP	26	26	4	4	0	0	0	0	30	1	0	19	0	10	30
NIA	50	24	17	43	0	0	0	0	67	4	37	25	0	1	67
MVP	15	30	15	0	0	0	0	0	30	16	0	1	0	13	30
Total	271	450	419	216	1	2	4	3	695	108	116	225	18	228	695
Percentage	38.99	64.74	60.28	31.07	0.14	0.28	0.575	0.43		15.54	16.69	32.37	2.58	32.80	100

KOLUMBANS' PREDICAMENT

The house of Karuvellayan Kolumban, the tribal chief of the Urali community who identified the site for the construction of Idukki project, the biggest hydroelectric project in Kerala, is still in darkness without getting an electricity connection. The ingratitude of the Government towards them is a matter of pain for the grandchildren of Kolumban.

It is Kolumban who first showed the site of the Idukki dam to the officials concerned. But even today his relatives do not enjoy any benefit of the electricity generated here. This is the silver Jubilee year of the commissioning of the Idukki project. When Kerala State Electricity Board (KSEB) squanders electricity, Kotha Ponmala, the daughter in law of Kolumban and her family have only kerosene lamps and candles.

Ponmala and her son, namely ND Rajan, live in an Urali settlement known as Kolumban Colony in Kochu Pinavu near Cheruthony. They live in a dilapidated thatched house made of clay walls which cannot even withstand a strong wind. They have only 15 cents of land in the colony. Ponmala's husband Thenan passed away while the children were young.

The family members of the wise tribal chieftain who could foresee the possibility of the generation of power and light from the forest river have only experiences of neglect. The authorities even showed disrespect to the memorial of Kolumban who shared his traditional lore with the nontribals for the progress of society. The monument of Kolumban located near Vellapara forest quarters beside the Thodupuzha-Puliyanmala road is in a state of total neglect. Not a single relative of Kolumban got any job in KSEB project.

Earlier Ponmala was a sweeper in the KSEB office. She ran around the various offices after her retirement to secure a job for her son, Rajan. But, the authorities were not sympathetic towards her plea. According to the KSEB officials they cannot help Rajan as he has studied only up to 4th standard. Earlier, he was given a temporary job for three months which was not renewed.

While struggling with poverty, their only 'reputation' now is that they are descendants of Kolumban. They used to tell these stories to the visitors. The story of Kolumban who had the discreetness that agriculture in Kerala can be supported with a dam across the Periyar river joining the 'Kurvan' and 'Kurathi' hills. Even today visitors come to this hut in the 6th ward in Vazhathopu panchayat to hear the story of Kolumban.

Source: Malayala Manorama, 06-06-2000; p 13.

1960s when electricity was not a commonly available facility and it was provided to them. Nedumbassery belongs to the 1990s when most houses had an electric connection and it had become a basic need. Displacement deprived them of it.

The quality of electricity is assessed by uninterrupted supply and stability in voltage. For 81.67 per cent of VSSC respondents, the quality of this service was better than what they had in the past. Quality of power supply was reported to have deteriorated for 55.22 per cent of the respondents of Nedumbassery and 43.54 per cent of those of Karappuzha project.

Toilets

The proportion of respondents, for whom toilet facility was available, increased from 47 per cent to 76 per cent. This was conspicuous in the case of Idukki, VSSC, Vizhinjam and Ezhimala projects. For the IDA respondents they had toilet facilities neither before nor after displacement.

But, the quality remains the same for most. The quality of toilet facilities was better according to 58.33 per cent of the respondents of VSSC and 50 per cent of those of MVIP, whereas for 76.47 per cent of respondents of KMML, 40.32 per cent of those of Karappuzha, and 38.46 per cent of those of Ezhimala, it was worse than in the past.

Some projects with special allocation for housing, provided toilet facilities, unlike the other projects which had no such provision. For example, Nedumbassery provided special allocation for toilets. Changed circumstances also motivate people to build and improve their infrastructure facilities like housing, toilets add to their self-esteem and the privacy of women. However, those who did not have the toilets had to resort to open defecation (23.45%) which is dehumanising. This had created problems especially for women in crowded and congested areas.

Drinking Water

Availability of Safe Drinking Water

Majority of respondents from all the projects except from KMML and Nedumbassery reported that they had safe drinking water.

Table 8.4

Availability and Quality of Toilets Before and After Displacement

Project	Availability									Quality					
	Yes		No		NA		NP		Total	Better	Worse	Same	NA	NP	Total
	Before	After	Before	After	Before	After	Before	After							
IRE	5	13	38	30	0	0	0	0	43	9	2	2	0	30	43
KML	5	4	12	13	0	0	0	0	17	4	13	0	0	0	17
IHP	2	70	67	0	0	0	1	0	70	2	0	1	0	67	70
KIP	16	14	46	46	0	2	0	0	62	8	25	7	17	5	62
IDA	0	1	44	43	1	1	0	0	45	2	39	3	0	1	45
SIKL	30	30	0	0	0	0	0	0	30	4	5	20	0	1	30
NTP	71	71	0	0	0	0	0	0	71	5	0	62	0	0	71
VSC	25	58	35	2	0	0	0	0	60	35	1	24	0	0	60
MGR	3	37	36	2	0	0	2	2	41	0	0	3	0	38	41
VZM	3	39	37	0	0	0	0	1	40	5	0	3	0	32	40
PTR	46	50	4	0	0	0	0	0	50	3	0	44	0	3	50
ENA	11	24	27	14	0	0	1	1	39	14	15	10	0	0	39
BTP	25	25	5	5	0	0	0	0	30	1	0	19	0	10	30
NIA	57	59	10	8	0	0	0	0	67	9	12	46	0	0	67
MVP	27	30	3	0	0	0	0	0	30	15	0	12	0	3	30
Total	326	525	364	163	1	1	4	4		116	112	256	19	192	695
Percentage	46.90	75.54	52.37	23.45	0.14	0.14	0.58	0.58	695	16.69	16.11	36.83	2.73	27.62	100

Table 8.5

Source of Drinking Water Before and After

Project	Open well		Tube well		River water		Tank		Pipe water		Water hole		Total
	Before	After	Before	After	Before	After	Before	After	Before	After	Before	After	
IRE	22	8	0	0	1	0	0	None	20	35	0	0	43
KML	0	0	0	0	0	0	0		17	17	0	0	17
IHP	2	32	0	0	9	1	0		0	36	59	4	70
KIP	45	54	0	0	1	1	0		2	1	14	5	70
IDA	43	44	0	0	0	0	0		2	0	0	1	45
SIKL	0	0	26	29	0	1	4		0	0	0	0	30
NTP	4	5	0	0	0	0	0		67	66	0	0	71
VSC	60	58	0	0	0	0	0		0	2	0	0	60
MGR	40	39	0	0	1	0	0		0	2	0	0	41
VZM	16	34	0	0	0	0	0		24	7	0	0	40
PTR	26	32	1	0	0	1	0		1	17	22	2	50
ENA	38	34	0	0	0	0	0		1	4	0	0	39
BTP	28	27	1	1	0	0	0		1	1	0	0	30
NIA	67	49	0	1	0	0	0		0	18	0	0	67
MVP	4	0	0	2	10	0	0		15	29	1	0	30
Total	395	416	28	33	22	4	4		150	235	96	11	695
	56.83	59.85	4.2	4.74	3.16	0.57	0.57		21.58	33.81	13.81	1.58	100

But, all the respondents of KMML and 46.2 per cent of Nedumbassery projects did experience shortage of safe drinking water. Water available to the respondents of KMML was contaminated by chemicals and yellow colored oil.

The Nedumbassery project DPs complained that the water in their well was polluted by the proximity of toilets as they were resettled in adjacent plots of 6 cents each. The pipe water supplied as part of the resettlement scheme is contaminated due to improper maintenance of the water tanks.

Environmental problems were reported from Eloor, an industrial area in Ernakulam district. Many cases of Leukemia, respiratory problems and related diseases were reported (*Malayala Manorama*, 15-18 July, 1998) linking them with the pollution of the major industries in this area such as Travancore Cochin Chemicals, Indian Rare Earths Ltd. and FACT. Mavoor Gwalior Rayons of the Birla group which is now known as the Grasim industries in Kozhikode district also caused severe environmental problems in the nearby areas. The water and air pollution caused by this factory has emerged as a controversial issue from 1963, which continues till today as a death knell for a dozen villages. The company is threatening the employees that they will close it down if people protest against the issue. The factory has been forthwith closed as a result of the intense agitation and consequent impact of the ecology.

Source of Drinking Water

After air safe drinking water is the most essential basic need to sustain life. Although open wells were a common source of drinking water among majority of the DPs (56.83%), protection of this source is found to be inadequate. Among the available drinking water sources, pipe water is a protected source, and there has been only a marginal increase from 21.58 per cent to 33.81 per cent after resettlement of DPs. Idukki (51.43%), Nedumbassery (26.87%), and Tiger project (34%) are the three projects which have provided pipe water to the DPs. The Vizhinjam DPs, on the other hand, had a negative story to tell. About 43 per cent who had

Table 8.6

Availability and Quality of Drinking Water Before and After Displacement

Project	Availability									Quality					
	Yes		No		NA		NP		Total	Better	Worse	Same	NA	NP	Total
	Before	After	Before	After	Before	After	Before	After							
IRE	42	43	1	0	0	0	0	0	43	17	23	3	0	0	43
KML	17	17	0	0	0	0	0	0	17	0	17	0	0	0	17
IHP	70	69	0	1	0	0	0	0	70	38	2	30	0	0	70
KIP	53	53	9	9	0	0	0	0	62	9	11	20	17	5	62
IDA	30	28	14	15	1	1	0	1	45	0	36	6	0	3	45
SIKL	30	29	0	1	0	0	0	0	30	2	5	22	0	1	30
NTP	71	69	0	0	0	0	0	2	71	6	1	60	2	2	71
VSC	55	60	5	0	0	0	0	0	60	10	0	50	0	0	60
MGR	38	39	1	0	0	2	2	2	41	1	3	20	0	17	41
VZM	40	30	0	10	0	0	0	0	40	0	17	17	0	6	40
PTR	50	50	0	0	0	0	0	0	50	3	0	47	0	0	50
ENA	17	16	21	22	0	0	1	1	39	4	26	9	0	0	39
BTP	30	30	0	0	0	0	0	0	30	1	0	19	0	10	30
NIA	59	41	8	26	0	0	0	0	67	4	40	21	0	2	67
MVP	30	30	0	0	0	0	0	0	30	23	0	7	0	0	30
Total	632	604	59	84	1	1	3	6	695	118	181	331	19	46	695
Percentage	90.93	86.9	8.48	12.08	0.14	0.14	0.43	0.86		16.97	26.04	47.62	2.73	6.61	100

protected water before were deprived of it after resettlement. This difficulty adds to the misery of the coastal people who have difficulty in getting safe drinking water. It adds to the burden and miseries of women in particular. Now they depend upon open wells, and the quality of the water they use is in question, because of salinity.

A majority of the respondents of IRE project had drinking water from open wells before displacement, but afterwards they had to depend on pipe water the supply of which was irregular. The proportion of people who depended on pipe water had increased after displacement in MVIP. Another important information is that 96.6 per cent of the respondents of SIKL depended on tube well for drinking water before displacement which improved slightly after. In Idukki, those who depended on the natural springs for drinking water before displacement, now had open wells and pipe water.

Availability and Quality of Drinking Water

For 91 per cent of the respondents drinking water was available from various sources (Table 8.4) before displacement. But, after resettlement, accessibility of drinking water came down to 87 per cent. In Nedumbassery, this difference was further widened by 22 per cent (from 88% to 66%).

Eighty per cent of the respondents of IDA, 66.67 per cent of Ezhimala, 53.45 per cent of IRE, 59.70 per cent of Nedumbassery and all those of KMML reported that the quality of drinking water had come down. But, according to 54.28 per cent of the respondents of Idukki project said the quality was better than in the past. Thus, in most cases (75.54%), drinking water was available after resettlement, but quality had deteriorated.

Women in the family have the responsibility of providing drinking water. Availability of drinking water and easy accessibility reduces the burden of women. The overall scenario of drinking water is better than before displacement and therefore, it gave an added advantage to women.

Water for Irrigation

No significant change was noticed in the availability of Water for Irrigation. The change in proportion was from 59.71 per cent to 53 per cent after displacement. In majority of the cases, the response for this question was not relevant because they had no agricultural land.

In the majority of the projects the people had got only less than 10 cents of (mostly 5 or 6 cents) land for resettlement. Hence, there was no possibility for agriculture in such a small area. For instance, all the respondents in KMML and majority in IRE, Karappuzha, IDA, VSSC, Vizhinjam and Nedumbassery, had no possibility for agriculture.

Employment

Availability of employment opportunities came down from 93 per cent to 86.33 per cent after displacement. About 96 per cent of the respondents of Nedumbassery who had employment before displacement came down to 38.80 per cent. The land acquired for this project was mainly coconut groves and paddy fields and people were happy with the work in the fields. There were also many brick making units, which had provided employment opportunities to many villagers. But, after displacement the people had only small plots of land and they lost all chances of employment.

Quality of employment had deteriorated for all of the respondents of KMML and 93 per cent of those of IRE, 84 per cent of those of Ezhimala, 82.08 per cent of Nedumbassery, 82 per cent of IDA, and 74 per cent of Vizhinjam. The quality of employment refers to the nature, type, and remuneration for the job. When people said that the quality of employment was worse than in the past, that meant either the nature of the job was tougher or the remuneration they received was comparatively low.

About 42 per cent of the respondents told that the quality of employment is same as the past, whereas according to 38 per cent the quality had become worse.

Table 8.7

Availability and Quality of Water for Irrigation Before and After Displacement

Project	Availability									Quality					
	Yes		No		NA		NP		Total	Better	Worse	Same	NA	NP	Total
	Before	After	Before	After	Before	After	Before	After							
IRE	2	2	0	0	0	0	41	41	43	0	0	1	0	42	43
KML	0	0	0	0	0	0	17	17	17	0	0	0	0	17	17
IHP	64	42	6	28	0	0	0	0	70	39	4	0	0	27	70
KIP	35	24	27	7	0	0	0	31	62	1	19	10	17	15	62
IDA	27	27	17	17	1	1	0	0	45	0	1	17	0	27	45
SIKL	30	28	0	2	0	0	0	0	30	3	6	19	0	2	30
NTP	71	68	0	1	0	0	0	2	71	1	5	60	3	2	71
VSC	0	0	0	0	0	0	60	60	60	0	0	0	0	60	60
MGR	36	32	2	5	0	0	3	4	41	1	1	18	0	21	41
VZM	1	1	0	0	0	0	39	39	40	0	1	1	0	38	40
PTR	50	50	0	0	0	0	0	0	50	3	0	47	0	0	50
ENA	9	8	29	30	0	0	1	1	39	1	5	33	0	0	39
BTP	30	30	0	0	0	0	0	0	30	0	0	16	0	14	30
NIA	33	29	33	37	0	1	1	22	67	1	17	28	0	21	67
MVP	27	27	0	0	0	0	3	3	30	3	3	23	0	1	30
Total	415	368	114	127	1	2	165	220	695	53	62	272	20	287	695
Percentage	55.71	52.94	16.40	18.27	0.14	0.28	23.74	31.65		7.62	8.92	39.14	2.88	41.29	100

Table 8.8

Availability and Quality of Employment Before and After Displacement

Project	Availability									Quality					
	Yes		No		NA		NP		Total	Better	Worse	Same	NA	NP	Total
	Before	After	Before	After	Before	After	Before	After							
IRE	41	42	1	0	0	0	1	1	43	2	40	1	0	0	43
KML	17	17	0	0	0	0	0	0	17	0	17	0	0	0	17
IHP	70	70	0	0	0	0	0	0	70	36	0	34	0	0	70
KIP	54	54	8	8	0	0	0	0	62	1	32	7	17	5	62
IDA	38	38	6	6	1	1	0	0	45	1	37	6	0	1	45
SIKL	29	26	1	4	0	0	0	0	30	5	4	16	1	4	30
NTP	71	68	0	1	0	0	0	2	71	4	1	60	3	3	71
VSC	49	51	10	9	0	0	1	0	60	8	4	48	0	0	60
MGR	36	35	3	4	0	0	2	2	41	3	6	8	0	24	41
VZM	39	38	0	1	0	0	1	1	40	0	29	9	0	2	40
PTR	49	49	0	0	0	0	1	1	50	4	0	46	0	0	50
ENA	32	27	6	11	0	0	1	1	39	1	27	11	0	0	39
BTP	30	30	0	0	0	0	0	0	30	0	10	10	0	10	30
NIA	64	26	3	41	0	0	0	0	67	0	55	11	0	1	67
MVP	29	29	0	0	1	1	0	0	30	3	0	27	0	0	30
Total	648	600	38	85	2	2	7	8	695	68	262	294	21	50	695
Percentage	93.23	86.33	5.46	12.23	0.28	0.28	1.00	1.15		9.78	37.69	42.30	3.02	7.19	100

Medical Facilities

The availability of medical facilities shows a positive trend with the change of proportion rising from 70 per cent before to 82 per cent after displacement. There is improvement in the availability of this facility in Idukki, IRE, and Rayons. But, it has deteriorated in VSSC, Ezhimala, and Nedumbassery. In some cases relocation brought the people closer to health care centres. That for example, is the case of Idukki project where improvement is not because of project intervention. Rayons operated a medical centre for the employees and the people of the community.

Though the availability of medical facilities had improved, the overall health situation deteriorated, because of the high intensity of environment pollution caused by the Rayons factory. In other cases, the quality of medical facilities remains the same according to 58 per cent of the respondents, while it had deteriorated in the case of Ezhimala (66.67%), Nedumbassery (47.76%) and VSSC (40%). VSSC operated a special medical centre for the resettled. However, according to the people, the quality of services was not up to the mark.

Market

Facilities for marketing are important, especially for those who depend on agriculture for livelihood. All the respondents from Idukki felt that marketing facilities had improved after displacement. But, in Vizhinjam, Ezhimala and Nedumbassery, majority of the respondents was of the opposite opinion.

In Ezhimala, 66.67 per cent of respondents disclosed that the quality of this facility was worse. The overall picture shows that the quality of marketing facilities declined after displacement.

Places of Worship

The availability of places of worship was perceived to be lower compared to the situation before displacement by a majority of the respondents. Before displacement, places of worship were available for 97 per cent of the respondents. It came down to 85.76 per cent

Table 8.9

Availability and Quality of Medical Facilities Before and After Displacement

Project	Availability									Quality					
	Yes		No		NA		NP		Total	Better	Worse	Same	NA	NP	Total
	Before	After	Before	After	Before	After	Before	After							
IRE	11	42	32	1	0	0	0	0	43	1	0	11	0	31	43
KML	17	17	0	0	0	0	0	0	17	0	0	17	0	0	17
IHP	0	70	69	0	0	0	1	0	70	3	0	0	0	67	70
KIP	50	50	12	12	0	0	0	0	62	1	4	35	17	5	62
IDA	28	28	16	16	1	1	0	0	45	0	1	43	0	1	45
SIKL	30	27	0	3	0	0	0	0	30	4	4	20	0	2	30
NTP	71	69	0	0	0	2	0	0	71	4	1	62	2	2	71
VSC	48	38	12	22	0	0	0	0	60	3	24	33	0	0	60
MGR	1	39	38	0	1	2	0	0	41	0	0	1	0	40	41
VZM	39	36	1	4	0	0	0	0	40	0	0	39	0	1	40
PTR	45	50	5	0	0	0	0	0	50	1	0	45	0	4	50
ENA	18	7	20	31	0	0	1	1	39	0	26	13	0	0	39
BTP	30	30	0	0	0	0	0	0	30	0	0	20	0	10	30
NIA	66	36	1	31	0	0	0	0	67	1	32	34	0	0	67
MVP	30	30	0	0	0	0	0	0	30	2	0	28	0	0	30
Total	484	569	206	120	2	5	2	1	695	20	92	401	19	163	695
Percentage	69.64	81.87	29.64	17.26	0.28	0.72	0.28	0.14		2.88	13.23	57.40	2.73	23.45	100

Table 8.10

Availability and Quality of Market Before and After Displacement

Project	Availability									Quality					
	Yes		No		NA		NP		Total	Better	Worse	Same	NA	NP	Total
	Before	After	Before	After	Before	After	Before	After							
IRE	13	14	30	29	0	0	0	0	43	0	0	14	0	29	43
KML	17	17	0	0	0	0	0	0	17	0	0	17	0	0	17
IHP	1	70	68	0	0	0	1	0	70	3	0	0	0	67	70
KIP	52	50	10	10	0	2	0	0	62	1	4	35	17	5	62
IDA	30	29	14	15	1	1	0	0	45	0	1	43	0	1	45
SIKL	30	23	0	7	0	0	0	0	30	1	4	20	0	5	30
NTP	71	69	0	0	0	2	0	0	71	4	1	62	2	2	71
VSC	53	60	7	0	0	0	0	0	60	8	0	52	0	0	60
MGR	25	14	14	25	0	0	2	2	41	0	0	0	0	41	41
VZM	40	3	0	37	0	0	0	0	40	0	5	1	0	34	40
PTR	45	50	5	0	0	0	0	0	50	1	0	45	0	4	50
ENA	23	7	15	31	0	0	1	1	39	0	26	13	0	0	39
BTP	30	30	0	0	0	0	0	0	30	0	0	20	0	10	30
NIA	64	35	3	32	0	0	0	0	67	0	32	35	0	0	67
MVP	30	30	0	0	0	0	0	0	30	2	0	28	0	0	30
Total	524	501	166	186	1	5	4	3	695	20	73	385	19	198	695
Percentage	75.39	72.08	23.88	26.76	0.14	0.72	0.575	0.43		2.88	10.50	55.40	2.73	28.48	100

after. Projects like IDA, Vizhinjam, Ezhimala, and Nedumbassery showed this trend much more obviously. The quality of the places of worship in terms of space, congenial atmosphere and inspiration was perceived to be better by 57 per cent of Idukki respondents, whereas 67 per cent at Ezhimala thought it otherwise.

Transportation

There was a slight improvement in the transport facilities after displacement. It was marked in the case of Idukki, Rayons and VSSC projects, whereas it had deteriorated in Ezhimala, KMML, and Nedumbassery. The quality of transportation refers to its accessibility, frequency of services and proper maintenance of the roads. Only 19 per cent of the respondents said that the quality of transport facilities had become worse, whereas 48 per cent were of the opinion that it remains the same. For instance, in Ezhimala the place of resettlement is in an isolated area, about 20 kms away from a town. The people have to travel such a long distance for most of their daily needs. There is no bus service to the place of resettlement. Consequently for these people the transport facilities were worse than before.

Recreation Facilities

About 83 per cent of respondents reported that recreational facilities such as a playground, cinema, theatre TV centre were available before displacement. This decreased to 72 per cent after displacement. There is deterioration in Ezhimala, because of their relocation far away from centres of entertainment like community centres, theatres, open ground parks, library cum TV centres and especially market places where people socialise. Ninety-six per cent of respondents of IDA, 77 per cent of Ezhimala and 63 per cent of Nedumbassery complained that the quality of recreational facility had become worse after displacement. Idukki was the only exception because recreational facilities were not available before displacement. It was only after their relocation that all these facilities were provided.

Table 8.11

Availability and Quality of Places of Worship Before and After Displacement

Project	Availability									Quality					
	Yes		No		NA		NP		Total	Better	Worse	Same	NA	NP	Total
	Before	After	Before	After	Before	After	Before	After							
IRE	42	42	1	1	0	0	0	0	43	0	0	42	0	1	43
KML	17	17	0	0	0	0	0	0	17	0	0	17	0	0	17
IHP	70	70	0	0	0	0	0	0	70	40	0	29	0	1	70
KIP	57	57	5	3	0	2	0	0	62	0	2	38	17	5	62
IDA	40	29	4	15	1	1	0	0	45	0	16	28	0	1	45
SIKL	30	29	0	1	0	0	0	0	30	1	4	23	0	2	30
NTP	71	69	0	0	0	0	0	2	71	4	1	62	2	2	71
VSC	60	60	0	0	0	0	0	0	60	1	0	59	0	0	60
MGR	38	36	1	3	0	0	2	2	41	4	0	20	0	17	41
VZM	40	31	0	9	0	0	0	0	40	0	0	32	0	8	40
PTR	48	50	2	0	0	0	0	0	50	1	0	45	0	4	50
ENA	33	10	5	28	0	0	1	1	39	1	26	12	0	0	39
BTP	30	29	0	0	0	1	0	0	30	0	0	20	0	10	30
NIA	65	36	2	31	0	0	0	0	67	2	31	34	0	0	67
MVP	30	30	0	0	0	0	0	0	30	1	0	29	0	0	30
Total	671	596	20	91	1	4	3	5	695	55	80	490	19	51	695
Percentage	96.54	85.76	2.87	13.09	0.14	0.58	0.43	0.72		7.91	11.51	70.50	2.73	7.34	100

Table 8.12

Availability and Quality of Transportation Before and After Displacement

Project	Availability									Quality					
	Yes		No		NA		NP		Total	Better	Worse	Same	NA	NP	Total
	Before	After	Before	After	Before	After	Before	After							
IRE	17	32	26	11	0	0	0	0	43	0	9	3	0	31	43
KML	17	1	0	16	0	0	0	0	17	0	16	1	0	0	17
IHP	0	70	70	0	0	0	0	0	70	2	0	0	1	67	70
KIP	18	7	44	33	0	0	0	22?	62	1	29	10	17	5	62
IDA	43	40	1	4	1	1	0	0	45	0	1	43	0	1	45
SIKL	30	27	0	3	0	0	0	0	30	2	4	21	0	3	30
NTP	71	68	0	1	0	0	0	2	71	3	2	62	2	2	71
VSC	31	60	29	0	0	0	0	0	60	27	3	30	0	0	60
MGR	1	39	38	0	0	0	2	2	41	0	0	0	0	41	41
VZM	40	32	0	8	0	0	0	0	40	0	0	31	0	9	40
PTR	45	50	5	0	0	0	0	0	50	1	0	46	0	3	50
ENA	35	11	3	27	0	0	1	1	39	1	27	11	0	0	39
BTP	30	8	0	0	0	0	0	22?	30	0	0	20	0	10	30
NIA	64	27	3	40	0	0	0	0	67	1	39	26	0	1	67
MVP	30	30	0	0	0	0	0	0	30	1	0	29	0	0	30
Total	472	502	219	143	1	1	3	49?	695	39	130	333	19	173	695
Percentage	67.91	72.23	31.51	20.57	0.14	0.14	0.43	7.05		5.61	18.70	47.91	2.73	24.89	100

Table 8.13

Availability and Quality of Recreational Facilities Before and After Displacement

Project	Availability									Quality					
	Yes		No		NA		NP		Total	Better	Worse	Same	NA	NP	Total
	Before	After	Before	After	Before	After	Before	After							
IRE	43	31	0	12	0	0	0	0	43	18	2	13	0	10	43
KML	17	17	0	0	0	0	0	0	17	0	0	17	0	0	17
IHP	0	70	70	0	0	0	0	0	70	0	0	0	0	70	70
KIP	53	36	9	4	0	0	0	22?	62	0	4	36	17	5	62
IDA	41	29	3	15	1	1	0	0	45	0	43	1	0	1	45
SIKL	30	21	0	9	0	0	0	0	30	1	3	19	0	7	30
NTP	71	68	0	1	0	0	0	2	71	4	1	62	2	2	71
VSC	54	57	6	3	0	0	0	0	60	2	0	58	0	0	60
MGR	37	39	2	0	0	0	2	2	41	4	0	20	0	17	41
VZM	40	32	0	8	0	0	0	0	40	1	0	31	0	8	40
PTR	47	50	3	0	0	0	0	0	50	2	0	45	0	3	50
ENA	36	7	2	31	0	0	1	1	39	0	30	9	0	0	39
BTP	30	8	0	0	0	0	0	22?	30	0	0	20	0	10	30
NIA	66	22	1	45	0	0	0	0	67	2	42	22	0	1	67
MVP	15	15	15	15	0	0	0	0	30	2	0	15	0	13	30
Total	580	502	111	143	1	1	3	49?	695	36	125	368	19	147	695
Percentage	83.45	72.23	15.97	20.57	0.14	0.14	0.43	7.05		5.18	17.99	52.95	2.73	21.15	100

More than half of the total respondents said that the quality of recreational facilities remained the same and according to 18 per cent, it had become worse.

Complaints about Resettlement

The process of land takeover and resettlement was not up to the expectation of the people. Among the various complaints of the respondents, inadequacy of compensation was the most prominent. Around 47 per cent raised this issue. Eighty seven per cent of the STs had this tale to tell. They constituted 12 per cent of those who complained about the inadequacy of compensation. Idukki and Karappuzha were the two projects involved in this regard. None of the MVIP DPs had any complaint about their resettlement. Almost all of them got five cents of free land each as a result of the project. They were staying in puramboke (*non-patta*) land before the acquisition and that is what seems to have made them feel happy about the land acquisition and therefore, they registered no complaint. The largest group affected belonged to

TIGER PROJECT – (THEKKADI) IDUKKI

A major portion of the Tiger project area in Thekkadi was used for cardamom cultivation. The fifteen acres of the cardamom estate owned by the tribals were lost when the area of Umikuppa was acquired for the project. These tribals belonging to the Mannan community got the land as gift from Her Highness the Maharani during her reign. With the acquisition of this cardamom estate, these tribals lost their means of livelihood. They were neither paid any compensation nor resettled after their eviction. The rehabilitation package was denied, because they had no documents to prove their ownership of the land. Fourteen families were evicted from Thekkadi for the implementation of this project. The hundreds of labourers who worked in the cardamom estate lost their jobs. But, none of them was paid any compensation. Far worse still is the fact that no rehabilitation package was offered to any of them.

It is estimated that thousands of tribal workers at Umikuppa, Lakshmipara, Naduthottam and Mlappara who depended on minor forest produce, estate jobs and fishing earlier, lost the means of their livelihood because of the project.

forward castes (42.2%) followed by OBCs (39.39%). Prominent among the other complaints were lack of water, electricity, medical care (23.74%) and the inadequacy of land allotted (17.99%). Those who were earlier associated with agriculture earlier complained about the loss of their livelihood.

Another important issue that people raised concerns the lack of infrastructure facilities provided at the site of their resettlement. Lack of drinking water, absence of electricity and medical facilities are some of those issues.

Impact of Displacement on Youth

Unemployment was found to be the most prominent among the impacts of displacement on youth as testified by 68.20 per cent of the respondents. Going by caste, 55.75 per cent of STs, 96 per cent of SCs, 78.19 per cent of OBCs and 55.56 per cent of the general population reported this problem. The gender division shows that 60.55 per cent male and the remaining 39.45 female come under this category. This reflects the acute unemployment situation in Kerala where unemployed men outnumber women. Being a patriarchal society men in Kerala are expected to be the breadwinners of the family. This may be one possibility why men are more anxious about their unemployment. Another reason may be that young men in Kerala have a fancy for white-collar jobs which do not come easily. There is less demand from them for self-employment. This adds to the acute unemployment problem among the young men of Kerala. All the respondents of IRE, KMML and a great majority of the respondents in all projects, except from SIKL and NTPC, were of the same opinion.

Thirty per cent of respondents told us that the displacement had no special impact on the youth. The resettlement programme of SIKL was mainly focussed on giving unskilled jobs. That is why a good majority of them did not complain about unemployment. In NTPC too, there were schemes for self-employment and loans. Thus, the DPs/PAPs of NTPC did not perceive unemployment as a great problem as a result of the project. The youth were not seriously affected by other factors like rise in antisocial elements and communalism.

Impact on Women

Nearly 36 per cent of the respondents complained about lack of availability of jobs for women outside their homes. A majority of the respondents from IRE, V.izhinjam, and all from KMML expressed this opinion. It is significant that all of them are from the fishing community. Prior to the displacement, they had some work or the other related to fishing. Absence of a source of income for women, made them weaker and more dependent on men, even for their minor needs. The difficulty in getting drinking water was reported by 28.48 per cent of respondents, who include majority of the IRE, IDA, Vizhinjam, Nedumbassery and Ezhimala respondents. Providing drinking water to the family is the culturally accepted pattern in Kerala, this burden affected women more than men.

The next major problem was the absence of toilet facilities according to 18.13 per cent of the respondents. Needless to say that women were the worst victims of this problem and relocation made it difficult for open defecation, because of crowded settlements. As many as 28.92 per cent of respondents felt that women were not in anyway affected by the problem of displacement. Among them, 47 came from NTPC project (out of 71). This is in sharp contrast to the situation in other states where a vast majority of women were seriously affected by displacement. The difficulty to get firewood and lack of toilet facilities were problems reported by a considerable number of people.

Studies in Orissa showed that women were the worst affected by displacement among the DPs. Their social, economic and nutritional status deteriorated. Their problems comprised greater economic stress, lower social status, change in workload etc.. Most jobs were given to men. The women could not get jobs easily, because the place of resettlement was usually remote areas. In certain cases, women complained of less work. This is not because of the improved social or economic situation, but because of further deprivation. In many other cases, their workload increased as they were forced to work both at home and outside. But, usually they were low paid unskilled ones. So, there were cases of drunken women in many places. Drunkenness and gambling seem to be modes of escaping the frustration caused by loneliness and unemployment. Drunkenness of men and wife beating make the situation worse (Fernandes and Raj, 1992: 153-56).

Views Regarding Women Getting Low Paid Jobs

We had asked the respondents about their views regarding reasons for unemployment and low paid jobs of women. Lack of job opportunity for women was reported by 17.41 per cent of the respondents. This was endorsed by 54.28 per cent of the respondents of Idukki and 50 per cent of those of MVIP projects. A large number of people (24.02%) opined that it is customary for women to be paid lower wages. This may be attributed to the value system prevalent in our culture according to which women's work is esteemed less. Eighty per cent of the respondents of Vizhinjam, 56.45 per cent of those of Karappuzha, and 57.78 per cent of those of IDA projects held this opinion. 11.85 per cent of respondents were of the opinion that women are capable, but discriminated against solely due to their gender.

Cultural Changes Due to Displacement

Involuntary eviction forces people to leave their fertile land, means of livelihood, house and other assets. One important fallout of displacement is a cultural upheaval. The displaced had to shift to an unknown area where they encounter a different culture manifested in the manner of thinking, expression of feeling, behaviour and ultimately the way of life. Comparatively there is less cultural diversity among the general population in Kerala. The only exception is the isolated pockets of Tribal settlement in forest areas.

Though the DPs in other parts of the country expressed cultural conflicts, it was not so intense in Kerala. About 64 per cent of respondents in Kerala are of the opinion that they had not

Table 8.14

Views Regarding Women Getting Low Paid Jobs

Project	Women not intelligent/ not interested	Women not educated/ trained	Not capable of doing skilled jobs	Capable but discriminated against	Willing to accept any job	Women unable to do all jobs	No suitable job for women	Tradition/ Custom	No Comment
IRE	0	0	0	0	0	3	29	8	3
KML	0	0	0	0	0	9	0	7	1
IHP	0	0	0	0	38	0	0	0	32
KIP	0	5	4	17	0	11	0	35	1
IDA	0	1	1	9	0	2	0	26	7
SIKL	0	0	1	0	24	0	0	0	5
NTP	0	0	0	0	23	0	0	0	47
VSC	0	11	5	12	0	1	0	1	26
MGR	0	0	7	16	0	0	10	8	0
VZM	0	0	0	0	0		7	32	1
PTR	0	0	0	0	21	0	0	19	10
ENA	0	0	0	3	0	0	0	0	36
BTP	0	0	0	2	0	21	0	7	1
NIA	1	1	1	23	0	5	0	24	12
MVP	0	0	0	0	15	0	0	0	15
Total	1	18	19	82	121	26	46	167	197
Percentage	0.14	2.59	2.73	11.8	17.41	3.74	6.62	24.03	28.35

experienced any cultural changes due to displacement. Majority of the respondents from IRE, KMML, Idukki, Karappuzha, Vizhinjam, Ezhimala, Bakel and Nedumbassery and all from MVIP expressed this view. The main reason for this experience is that almost all the people got resettled close to the localities of their original inhabitation. Majority of them remained in their own Panchayats or Taluks even after losing their land. In such cases, there is no question of any cultural change occurring. A significant number of respondents from Karappuzha and VSSC reported drunkenness and gambling as major changes. Drunken behaviour (12.95%) and wife beating are the two cultural changes which dehumanised the women most in the affected households.

The experience in Orissa is somewhat different where drunkenness and gambling were reported to be a major problem in the resettlement areas. The need to survive and the frustration that follows have combined to force some of the DPs into petty crimes like stealing materials from the project. Another area of cultural change is the attitude towards forests, language and culture, especially in projects with a fairly large proportion of tribals (Fernandes and Raj, 1992:156-7).

Impact on Children

Nearly 73.8 per cent of the respondents were of the opinion that displacement did not have any major impact on children. It is generally perceived that displacement would affect health, nutrition and education of children. However, our data show that displacement had no considerable impact on the health of children in Kerala. This is true because Kerala's achievement in the area of human development, especially health and education is outstanding. Around 16 per cent of the total respondents and 53.45 per cent of IRE and 46.15 per cent of Ezhimala and 43.28 per cent of Nedumbassery complained about the lack of school in the new place. This is a negative comment on people who claim 'total literacy' and are greatly concerned about children's education. This complaint may have risen from the longer distance to school in the new place. A shift from private to government school could also be another reason. Caste-wise 44 per cent of SCs, 21.14 per cent of OBCs and 12.39 per cent of forward community expressed this view. None of the STs had this view either. Gender-wise, there was no difference in this regard.

Of the total respondents, five per cent pointed out that children were attracted by antisocial elements. In the case of Rayons, the proportion is 82.9. Generally, children are considered a vulnerable group more susceptible to the diseases and problems in a new environment. Displacement showed no effect on the incidence of illness and malnutrition among children. However, the present study showed that the children remained free from frequent illness and malnutrition. The data also indicate that availability of food was not a problem for the children, as the parents took care of them in spite of all the problem they had to encounter.

The host population generally of a higher SES group consider the resettled in colonies as antisocial and therefore keep a distance. They consider displacement as a punishment. There is no one-to-one relationship on an equal basis, rather they look down on them. This is reflected in the overall situation when the marginalised displaced are resettled.

In Orissa, a significant impact of displacement on children was on education. The decrease in the availability and deterioration of the quality of existing schools had adverse impact on the educational status of children. Since women were busy with work, they had little time to attend to matters relating to the education of children. Another change was that the children did not respect any more the ancestral customs, traditions, religion and language. This, according to the authors, was a part of the alienation and acceptance to the dominant culture required for the adaptation into the new economy (Fernandes and Raj, 1992: 159).

Environmental Impact

Noise Pollution

Kerala, being an industrially backward state the problem of noise pollution is comparatively low. Blasting in Mines and manufacturing process in certain type of industries cause noise pollution. In Kerala, mining activity is comparatively low and the existing mines are minor or medium types without much noise problem.

Ninety four per cent of the respondents did not have any complaint about noise pollution. All the respondents in IRE, Idukki, VSSC, Vizhinjam, Tiger, and Bakel projects reported total absence of noise pollution. But 60.57 per cent of the Rayons respondents said that they experience noise pollution.

Air Pollution

About fifty four per cent of respondents reported that the air was cleaner than in the past whereas 32.67 per cent said that there was no change. However, according to 78.04 per cent of the respondents of Rayons project, there was more smoke and dust particles in the air. Air and water pollution of Mavoor Gwalior Rayons had become an issue that attracted statewide attention. Lives of several villages in the neighboring localities are endangered due to environmental pollution caused by the factory. They are prone to cancer, respiratory and related problems. All the respondents of KMML project also said that there was air pollution due to mining activity.

Most respondents' feedback on the environment is that it is not worse than what it was in the past. This may be due to the industrial backwardness and absence of large scale mining in Kerala. Also, nine out of 15 projects selected for primary data collection are of non-industrial and non-polluting nature.

In Orissa, an increase in TB and asthma was found in certain resettlement sites. Medical specialists claim that the former is linked to malnutrition and the latter is pollution and stress related (Fernandes and Raj, 1992: 152). Studies in Goa too showed the environmental impact of industries and mines (Fernandes and Naik 1999: 81). The industrial activity taking place in the state, particularly industrial estates in the plateau produces effluents of toxic waste that can reach the valley and pollute the springs, sweet water rivers and other water bodies. Studies conducted by Area

Table 8.15
Air Pollution

Project	*Cleaner*	*More Dust/Smoke Particles*	*Same as Before*	*NA*	*Total*
IRE	38	5	0	0	43
KML	0	17	0	0	17
IHP	38	0	32	0	70
KIP	45	6	11	0	62
IDA	9	2	32	2	45
SIKL	13	2	10	5	30
NTP	16	1	52	2	71
VSC	31	0	29	0	60
MGR	9	32	0	0	41
VZM	39	1	0	0	40
PTR	21	0	29	0	50
ENA	38	0	1	0	39
BTP	30	0	0	0	30
NIA	41	3	19	4	67
MVP	5	0	19	6	30
Total	373	69	234	19	695
Percentage	53.67	9.92	33.67	2.73	100

GWALIOR RAYONS MAVOOR (GRASIM)

Gwalior Rayons factory of Birla group is the largest private sector industrial unit in Kerala. Located at Mavoor, 25 kms east of Kozhikode, this factory gives direct employment to about 3000 people and indirect employment to 7000. This industry started manufacturing pulp and staple fibre from bamboo and wood since 1963.

Land was acquired for the industry in 1958 from private individuals paying compensation at the prescribed market rate, which was lower than the actual land value. At that period, displacement was not considered a serious problem as land was easily available elsewhere and Kerala was also going through an experience of inter-district migration.

Further, the starting of the industry was welcomed with many fanfares both by the state government and the local people, because of the employment opportunity it provided.

The issue of PAPs became visible, once the factory located on the banks of the river Chaliyar, began functioning. Since then, i.e. 1963, people began to experience the critical status of the project affected persons (PAPs). Today after 38 years of its existence, the history of Gwalior Rayons of Mavoor remains a great question mark before Kerala's dream of economic development through industrialisation. The industry has not only polluted the river Chaliyar but also caused irreparable damage to the life and ecology of a dozen Village Panchayats and about three lakhs population. Studies conducted by professionals in various fields point to the death knell experienced by the innocent people.

The first sign of Chaliyar pollution surfaced in the form of dead fish floating in large numbers. Thereafter, the unusual rate of acute respiratory infection of the people in the villages began to be noticed. Many other signs and symptoms of diseases began to bother the people. The worst hit was Vazhakad Panchayat, which has an incredible prevalence rate and incidence of cancer, reported to be 21 per cent (*Business Deepika*, March 22-28,1999). Between 1990 and 1994, 199 people succumbed to this deadly disease.

A health survey conducted during November 22-30, 1994 in Vazhakad Panchayat revealed that 213 persons died of cancer during the preceding five years. Further, at the time of the survey ,79 persons were taking treatment for cancer (Chaliyar Agitation, 1999).

In October 1995, the Regional Cancer Centre, Trivandrum, conducted a study based on the death register of Vazhakad and

Areacode Panchayats. Whereas the death rate due to cancer in Kerala is estimated to be 6-8 per cent, the study revealed that the cause of death for 29 per cent of the male and 7 per cent of the female in Vazhaked was cancer. The corresponding figures of Areacode Panchayat were 15 per cent and 14 per cent respectively (Chaliyar Agitation, 1999).

At the instruction of the District Collector, the District Medical Officer (DMO) of Kozhikode prepared a report in July 1995 on the cancer induced deaths in eight Panchayats in the neighbourhood of Gwalior Rayons. His findings are presented in the following table.

Sl. No.	*Name of Panchayat*	*Total Population*	*Death rate per 1000 people*	*Death due to cancer %*	*Death due to respiratory diseases %*
1	Mavoor	26,144	4.2	20	12
2	Peravayal	53,190	3.4	12	19
3	Cheruvannoor	43,785	4.2	12	12
4	Bepur	56,496	4.4	12	12
5	Chemanchery	32,652	4.0	9	3
6	Ramanattukara	26,845	8.0	12	19
7	Faruk	46,825	2.0	3	18
8	Olamana	45,733	4.0	11	31

Source: Chaliyar agitation, 1999.

Worse still is the fate of the employees of Gwalior Rayons as shown in the table below. Whereas the death rate in Kerala is 6.1 per 1000,the death rates in all the seven Panchayats except Ramanattukara has been rather low. But the percentage of death due to cancer and respiratory diseases in these villages has been abnormally high when we compare the rate of cancer deaths in Kerala, which is 6-8 per cent of the total deaths.

If the aforesaid is the fate of the people in the Panchayats in and around Mavoor, the life of the employees of Gwalior Rayons is in a very serious danger.

The data given below are based on the records of the ESI hospital of Mavoor Gwalior Rayons, where the 3000 strong employees and their dependents avail the health care and treatment facilities. On an average a thousand and odd patients from three thousand households report for treatment every month with aliments of the above categories. However in the month of August 1998 the number of patients shot up from one third to nearly one half the number of Grasim employees. This shows that the morbidity among the employees' households is very high.

Grasim Employees' Treatment Records

	Diagnosis													
Month	*Asthma*	*Bronchitis*	*Acute Pharyngitis*	*Other respiratory diseases*	*Influenza*	*Allergy*	*Skin disease*	*Ophthalmic disease*	*Blood pressure*	*Anemia*	*Diseases of the ear*	*Diseases of the urinary balder*	*PUO*	*Total*
April	118	151	28	100	223	71	88	64	85	25	25	50	32	1060
May	92	145	77	63	248	20	87	26	10	10	10	10	25	823
June	100	150	85	74	256	35	96	35	14	15	10	6	14	890
July	110	157	86	54	239	38	100	40	20	16	10	5	17	892
August	147	100	106	65	360	108	135	90	82	27	20	35	72	1347

Source: Chaliyar Agitation 1999.

The mortality rate of the Grasim employees is worth studying. Between 1989 and April 1995, 98 employees of the pulp division died. Out of these cancer accounted for the death of 20 per cent. All these point to just one thing which is that the project affected persons (PAPs) cannot be limited to the land acquisition for setting up a development project, but it has to be extended to further include the victims of environment pollution caused by the project all along its life. Grasim (Gwalior Rayons) is a typical example of the negative impact of industrialisation.

wide Environmental Quality Management (AEQM) and TERI revealed the evidence of land, air and water pollution in many of the mining areas in Goa and its adverse effect on the population (Ibid., 82). In that sense Kerala is somewhat different from other states because of low industrialisation.

Conclusion

A general perception prevalent among authorities concerned and the public is that compensation paid for land acquired is adequate for the DPs/PAPs to began life anew. Therefore all the processes associated with displacement and resettlement are to be seen in this context. Based on this assumption, many projects do not have an R&R scheme worthy of its name. What is provided is limited to the bare minimum, just to make people believe that something is being done for the welfare of the displaced out of the magnanimity of the project authorities. The project authorities view the money invested on R&R as no-productive and therefore, to be written off. As they are unable to bring down the expenses of raw materials, machinery, infrastructure, and recurring expenses, they try to economise on the only area where they have control i.e., compensation and resettlement.

The victims of development bear the brunt of this attitude which is revealed in the site selection, size of the homestead, and infrastructural and other facilities offered to the displaced. The experiences of Nedumbassery, Ezhimala, Thiruvananthapuram airport, IDA, and Vizhinjam give ample evidence to this. The project authorities influenced only by the management principles of cost effectiveness, often lack human consideration. They do not even bother to find a place for the displaced to stay in the interim period between displacement and rehabilitation. The affected have no participation in determining their future place of stay, though it has a decisive influence on their life opportunities.

However, unlike in the other states, no serious impact of displacement was noticed on youth, women and children in Kerala. Since the places of relocation of most of the displaced in Kerala were somewhat close to their original habitation, no serious cultural changes were experienced by them. Very often, finding adequate land for resettling of the displaced persons in the urban areas was found difficult in Kerala. This may be one of the reasons why many of the displaced from urban areas are resettled in comparatively rural areas. For instance, the displaced persons from the site of Thiruvananthapuram airport were offered relocation at Bharathannur near Palode, which is a village in the same district.

9

Towards a Humane Policy of Land Acquisition, Displacement and Rehabilitation

We have attempted to study in this report, the extent and nature of displacement and deprival by development projects in Kerala 1951-95. We reaffirm that this study deals with only planned and often forced displacement in the name of national development. Examining the magnitude of the problem, we drew a brief historical sketch of the pre-independence and post-independence scenario of displacement in India. We, then, tried to understand its extent and nature in Kerala.

The task before us was to make a longitudinal study of a very complex problem covering a period of 45 years from 1951 to 1995. Quantitative as well as qualitative data regarding all aspects of displacement had to be collected, analysed and systematised from primary as well as secondary sources in order to prepare a comprehensive database. Simultaneously, the activists working with the affected people had to be sensitised and mobilised with a view to making them demand their right to just compensation and comprehensive rehabilitation. Ultimately, the study is intended to influence the government and decision makers to formulate a just rehabilitation policy, minimising displacement and providing all the facilities required for the betterment of the lives of those who have made enormous sacrifices for the development of the nation. Corresponding to these three approaches, we used three methodologies, namely conventional research for systematic data collection and analysis, participatory research to conscientize the social activists and through them the affected people, and action research for mobilisation. Combination of these three methodologies is a unique feature of this study.

The study was carried out in three phases. In the first phase, all the gazette notifications on land take-over from 1951 to 1995 were scanned thoroughly and classified. In the second phase, secondary data regarding the projects for which land was acquired, the communities displaced and resettled and the compensation paid were collected from government departments, collectorates and research centres. Out of 34,233 notifications, only 1,105 referred to an area above five hectares. From these, 153 projects were identified as having a significant magnitude of displacement. From among these, 15 projects were specifically selected for the third phase of detailed primary data based study. The choice of the projects and the sample were based on the nature, type, age and location of the project, and the type of people affected by them. This phase was preceded by a series of meetings with social activists from different regions of Kerala in order to ensure their involvement in the study. A team of field investigators was selected jointly and trained to conduct the interviews with appropriate schedules carefully prepared and pre-coded. The analysis of data and report writing were done by the core-team.

In this concluding Chapter, we shall briefly recall the nature and magnitude of the problem and highlight the major findings of this study from which will emerge a third part consisting of general reflections on the core issue of displacement. We shall, then, offer a critique of the existing laws on land acquisition and the draft rehabilitation policies and conclude by proposing some viable alternatives in the form of a more humane policy for land acquisition, displacement and rehabilitation.

Displacement: Problem and Methodology

The first feature, we pointed out is the striking paucity of data on displacement, resettlement and rehabilitation in India. Nevertheless, piecing together the available data of persons displaced or otherwise deprived of livelihood by the major categories of projects like mines, dams, industries, sanctuaries etc., researchers have come to a conservative estimate of not less than 2.13 million DPs/PAPs. Through extrapolation of these figures, we can safely assert that at least 30 million persons have been displaced or affected by these projects from 1951 to 1995. Studies also point out that a large proportion of the victims of development is from the weakest and marginalised sections like the Tribals, Dalits and other backward communities. It is, because, many mines, water resource projects, tourist resorts and sanctuaries are located near the forest or rural areas which are more thickly populated by these sections of people.

We, then, give an overview of Kerala, its land and people with special emphasis on the Kerala model of development, its strengths and weaknesses. Though Kerala is rated high in the human development index, it is riddled with numerous problems of underdevelopment. As in the rest of India, so also in Kerala, the major categories of projects that have resulted in substantial displacement or deprival are water resources, industries, power and mining projects, defence establishments, wildlife sanctuaries, tourism, housing, farms and fisheries, transport and human resource development.

Major Findings of the Study

In this section, we shall highlight the major findings of the study, touching on the extent and type of land acquired, number and type of persons displaced, profile of the respondents, the process of land takeover, amount of compensation paid, the manner of paying it and its utilisation, and finally, the extent and manner of resettlement and rehabilitation of the displaced and project affected persons.

Extent of Land Acquired

The total area of land acquired or used for development projects in Kerala during the period 1951-1995 works out to 1,55,263.52 hectares which is four per cent of the total geographic area of the

State. Of this, private land constitutes 66 per cent (1,01,824.50), forest land 26 per cent and common land about one per cent. The exact status of the remaining 7.4 per cent is not known. Considering the large extent of forest land, Kerala has (27%) with very little common land, the total area acquired is very significant. For a small state with a population density of 749 per sq km, a small plot acquired is likely to affect many people.

The new projects that have taken off and are about to be implemented under various categories will require an additional area of 14,452.86 ha. This is mainly for the new Kannur airport, Kannur power project, Kerala Road Transport Project, expansion of Vizhinjam harbour and Thiruvananthapuram airport and various industries. It is about 9.31 per cent of the area acquired for development projects during 1951-1995. Many more are in the planning stage. If we were to include them, then, several times this area will be acquired during the next decade.

Displacement: Magnitude and Categories

The total number of persons affected by development projects in Kerala during the period under review came to 5,52,233. It is 1.90 per cent of the population of Kerala in 1991. Of these, 40 per cent were displaced (DPs) and the rest were project affected persons (PAPs). The number of people to be displaced and affected by the proposed projects is estimated to be 1,16,000. This constitutes 21 per cent of the total affected by development projects during the 1951-1995 period. If we take the already displaced and affected together with those proposed to be affected, the total would come to 7,11,249 which constitutes 2.44 per cent of the population of Kerala in 1991.

The schemes that have displaced and affected the largest number are industries (2,22,814), water resource projects (1,33,846), transport (1,51,623), educational institutions and environment protection projects like parks and sanctuaries (over 14,000 each). Most of those affected by these categories are Tribals in Wayanadu, Idukki and Thiruvananthapuram districts. Forests are their sustenance. Fishing harbours, the Ezhimala Naval project,

VSSC and Thiruvananthapuram Airport have displaced mostly fisherfolk and OBCs, along with some SCs. Thus, the most affected categories in all the projects were the weaker sections.

Profile of the Respondents

The selection of the respondents for the third phase was based on demographic as well as socio-economic factors. Age-wise, more than three-fourth of the respondents were above 40 with the highest concentration in the 60 and above age group. This choice was deliberate, meant to ensure that those whom we interviewed were knowledgeable about the process of deprival. They offered us valuable information on displacement-related problems. Though, we wanted to ensure equal representation of males and females, the actual proportion turned out to be 56: 44, because of the hesitation of women especially in Tribal communities to come forward for interviews. This is an indication of greater male dominance among the Tribals of Kerala than among the other communities. The same was true about the SCs and OBCs displaced by certain projects. In all the castes, more than 80 per cent of the widowed were females.

Religion-wise, 53 per cent of the respondents were Hindus, 30 per cent Christians, 12 per cent Muslims and the rest belonged to the Tribal religions or some others. Caste/Tribe-wise the highest concentration of STs was in the Idukki, Karappuzha and Tiger Projects. The seven per cent of SCs in our sample were scattered over several projects especially in the agricultural regions. Most of the OBCs were fisher-folk in the coastal belt. Against the average family size of 5.3 in Kerala, that of our sample was 4.89. As against the Kerala sex ratio of 1,036, the sample gave a picture of 954. The ratio varied across the caste group, STs - 858; OBCs - 937; Forward Castes - 998 and SCs - 1,029.

Thus, the STs had the lowest sex ratio in our sample. This and the other features like the difficulty men experienced in interviewing women can be symptoms of gender discrimination among them as well as of lack of proper pre-natal or post-natal care. It may also be attributed to greater poverty, lower nutritional level, lack of access to medical care and poor sanitation etc. They are also signs of greater poverty and malnutrition among the DPs/PAPs than among the rest of the Kerala population and of higher infant mortality among girl children of the DPs/PAPs. Besides, the Tribals whose proportion is very small, seem to have been neglected in Kerala. Their educational status is low and landlessness high among them. This neglect seems to have had an adverse impact on women. This phenomenon is considerably different from other States where the Tribals form a substantial proportion of the population. Their experience shows that the Tribal, and to some extent, Dalit women have a higher social status than their high caste counterparts. So, it is easier for men to interview them. In a similar study, conducted in Orissa, the family size among the displaced Tribals was 5.25, which is also lower than the state average (Fernandes and Raj, 1992). But, the sex ratio of the Tribals in Orissa in 1991 was 1,002 and was higher in districts like Phulbani where the resources are abundant.

About 22 per cent of our sample was illiterate and 43 per cent could hardly read and write. Nearly 61 per cent of these two categories were females. This is an anomalous finding in a State that is supposed to be totally literate! The anomaly regarding land ownership is that more people became legal owners of land after displacement than before it. But, the area owned by them declined in most cases. It is, because, much of the land given was only for the homestead and not agricultural. As a result, those who had agricultural land were reduced to homestead-owners. That also explains why the percentage of the landless declined from 12 to one, while that of persons with less than 50 cents increased from 45 to 70 after displacement or deprival. Also, the proportion of those owning more than one acre decreased showing a leveling of the land ownership pattern.

Among other economic consequences of displacement, is a decline in the proportion of those having an income of less than Rs.5,000 from nine per cent to 2.45 per cent. This is accompanied by a considerable increase from 41 per cent to 67 per cent in the number of persons having an annual income of Rs.5,000-10,000. There is also a consistent lowering of the proportion of respondents belonging to the higher income group of Rs.10,000 to 50,000. Those in the highest class above Rs. 50,000 remained unaffected. Eighty one per cent of the respondents were in the income group below Rs.15,000. Thus, about six per cent of the lowest category was able to climb up, while 18 per cent of those in the higher income groups came down. The ratio of those who lost out in this process to those who gained is 3:1. The net outcome of displacement seems to be a rise in the percentage of families below the poverty line from 50 to 70, if we take an annual income of Rs.10,000 as the cut off point. This general trend is reflected in all the caste categories.

Occupation-wise, a fourth of the respondents were labourers before displacement and 22 per cent were agriculturists. About four per cent were from the salaried class, 11 per cent depended on fishing and one third were jobless. After the project came into the area, the percentage of cultivators decreased from 22 to 15, while that of the jobless increased to 40 per cent. There was hardly any significant change in the proportion of other categories. Unemployment among men was greater (9.47%) than that among women (7.7%), as many could not find a job after losing earlier opportunities in agriculture. Thus, one witnesses a general lowering of the economic status of the DPs/PAPs. The negative impact is felt more by women than by men. The percentage of housewives increased from 48 to 55 after displacement, because of the loss of labour opportunities for women who had worked earlier in agriculture and manual labour. Now, they have no opportunities outside their homes.

The socio-economic status (SES) class of the respondents was calculated on the basis of land ownership, occupation, income, education and ownership of cattle and poultry. Five SES categories were worked out: Lower lower class (LLC), lower class (LC), middle class (MC), upper middle class (UMC) and upper class (UC). About 78 per cent of the respondents belonged to the LLC and 19 per cent to the LC indicating that the vast majority of the affected population belonged to the weaker sections. Only three per cent belonged to the MC and one person each to the two higher classes. This pattern was almost uniform in all the projects. The vast majority of the ST, SC, and OBC belonged to the LLC. About 90 per cent of the LLCs owned less than 50 cents of land. Forty four per cent of the two lowest classes were employed in agriculture, animal husbandry, fishing and casual labour. Nearly 71 per cent of the LLCs and 61 per cent of the LCs had an annual income between Rs.5000 and 10,000. Others had slightly higher incomes. Thus, the data show that the vast majority of the victims of displacement were from the marginalised sections. As a result, the lowest socio-economic groups have been further marginalised by the project.

The Process of Land Takeover

We tried to find out the source from which the affected people got the first information about the project. In 50 per cent of the projects, the main source was officials or the related departments. Some came to know of it from other villagers or from the notification or through the radio and newspapers. Political and local leaders had little role in passing on the information to the people concerned. This is strange in a highly politicised and unionised State like Kerala. Local leaders did very little after the announcement of the project. Only in a few projects like Idukki, Ezhimala and Nedumbassery, they tried to unite the people against the project, while in some others the leaders discussed the matter among themselves. Some called a meeting of the people and discussed the issue. Sixteen per cent of the respondents reported that the leaders openly supported the project. That had negative implications for the affected people.

The response of nearly half of them to the announcement of the project was fear of losing land and house, a feeling of helplessness, anger, despair and fatalism. The people could not approach their leaders, because they were either passive or supported the project. About a third were happy, because they expected to improve their prospects by getting jobs in the project. But many were disappointed later. A majority of them did not face any specific problem immediately after the announcement of the project. Over one-fourth reported that they were prevented from cultivating the land and all development projects were stopped. The problem of rumour-mongering to scare the affected people by anti-social elements was common in many places. Those who were, thus affected were mainly the Tribals and other rural poor.

An important reason why the rest did not raise many problems is that the officials promised to provide better living conditions in the resettlement site. The three most important promises were job (38%), land for land (30%) and house (15%). Though 9 of the 15 projects promised employment for the affected people, only a few fulfilled these promises. As a result, there were many complaints from the affected people about the project officials and about their condition after loss of livelihood. Forty three per cent of the respondents thought that the officials were indifferent and unhelpful, and only 15 per cent found them helpful. Most of the STs and SCs had negative feelings towards the project authorities. However, many of the OBCs were able to develop relatively good rapport with them. The time lag between demarcation and displacement for 70 per cent of the respondents was six months to two years. Only about 15 per cent were displaced in less than six months. Fourteen per cent were not displaced even after two years. This time lag between demarcation and displacement intensified the agony of the affected persons.

Compensation

The amount of compensation paid in Kerala is higher than in most other States. But, it is approximately one-third of the real market value of the land lost. However, other assets got a fairly good compensation based on the returns from them. But, the officer concerned has the discretion to judge the value of the assets. This usually leads to corruption. In many cases, the people had to bribe the officials. Thirty eight per cent did not spend any money to get the compensation, 23 per cent had to spend Rs.500 to 2,500 and a few spent Rs.10,000 to 50,000 for court expenses. Litigation also involved a lot of travel for the poor people with their complaints to the project authorities. About 90 per cent of the DPs/PAPs who received compensation, got it fully through a bank account, while more than a fifth of the respondents had not received any compensation. Twenty per cent received the amount immediately after the Award, while 80 per cent received it immediately after land take-over. Involvement of middlemen was very little in Kerala.

The major share of the compensation amount was spent on land purchase and house construction. Some had to use a part of it to repay loans and for social functions like marriage. Very few spent any part of the money they got for productive purposes like purchasing livestock or starting a business. Building a house was the priority of 90 per cent of the SCs and half the number of STs, OBCs and forward castes or about 62 per cent of all the respondents. It is, because, the project did not resettle them. So, they had to build a house for self-resettlement. Thus, the poorest among them had to invest most of their compensation on a new house, because they had lost their old one to the project which did not have a resettlement package. So, they had little possibility of beginning life anew.

Joint decision-making either by the spouses or the whole family was the prevalent pattern in the spending of the compensation amount. In about 30 per cent of the cases, the husband alone took the decision, whereas wife alone deciding was very rare. This reveals a tendency of male dominance -- an expression of the patriarchal values in Kerala. It was more prevalent among the forward castes and OBCs than the SCs and Tribals. Thus, despite their neglect, lower literacy and lower nutritional status, the Dalit and Tribal women seem to retain their traditional higher status within the family compared to the others.

Nearly half of the respondents were unaware of the criteria for fixing compensation. Almost everywhere, there was a feeling that the authorities cheated them. Sixty four per cent of the respondents felt that the compensation they received was inadequate. Only 14 per cent were satisfied with what they received. Nearly half of the affected people expected an amount four times higher than what they actually received. Land related complaints came mostly from the agriculturists who formed a majority of the DPs/PAPs. They felt that the land they lost was fertile on which they could cultivate a variety of crops, whereas what they got after displacement was mostly barren and non-productive. Secondly, they thought that an equal measure of land cost more than what they received as compensation. Hence they could not replace the assets lost.

Lodging protests against the project and inadequate compensation accompanied the process of land take-over. The aggrieved party does it either individually or through an organised movement under the leadership of a political party or local leaders. Forty five per cent of the DPs/PAPs lodged complaints with project or revenue officials individually against inadequate compensation. Most of them were from the poorer sections. The upper classes went to the court directly to secure justice. Most poor persons could not afford it, as it is a prolonged battle involving high expenses. They found the attitude of the authorities quite negative in responding to their complaints. Red tapism and corruption delayed the disposal of their legitimate demands. Thus, the poor had to cross numerous hurdles to get their grievances redressed. But, it is significant that in 33 cases, the court sanctioned a higher compensation. The Communist Party (Marxist) organised mass movements in Idukki, while the Church leaders took up the issue in VSSC, Thumba. Both succeeded in getting resettlement colonies for the DPs. They are among fewer than a dozen projects in Kerala with a rehabilitation scheme.

Resettlement and Rehabilitation

Though fewer than a dozen projects in Kerala had a resettlement package, we chose a bigger number of resettled persons in our sample in order to study its impact. Half of the DPs in our study had the benefit of project implemented resettlement. While all the KMML and Idukki project respondents were resettled by the project, none of the respondents of SIKL and MVIP projects received this benefit. A majority of the respondents of Vizhinjam,

Nedumbassery, IRE, IDA projects availed of the resettlement facilities offered by the projects. But, hardly anyone in the Bakel project had this advantage. About three-fourths of the SCs and 62 per cent of forward castes took advantage of the resettlement facilities offered by the projects, while only 36 per cent of the STs and forward castes were able to avail of them. Around 17 per cent of the affected people had no option other than to rely on self-resettlement, because the projects like Grasim had no resettlement programme, or the size of the land given was too small or no land was given. Though Nedumbassery Airport, IDA Palakkad and VSSC Thiruvananthapuram projects had rehabilitation packages, they did not provide sufficient land for all the displaced. So, many of them had to resettle themselves.

SIKL and VSSC projects offered one job each to the evicted families which had a technically trained person. That is obviously biased in favour of the better off sections who have more opportunities of technical education than the Tribals and other backwards. In most projects, relocation was planned by the R & R officials. The affected people had little participation in this decision, nor was any village leader involved in the planning process. The relocation cost of nearly half the number of DPs was paid by the project. In other cases, the DPs had to meet the expenses by themselves, mainly because of the absence of a rehabilitation scheme in the project. Nearly 82 per cent of the DPs got resettled within a year after their displacement. In a few projects, it got prolonged even up to 2-3 years. The quality of resettlement was considered poor by most of the affected persons.

For over half the number of the displaced, the fear of the future and helplessness was the predominant feeling at their resettlement. Unlike in some other States like Orissa, none of them expressed any anxiety about the treatment they received from the host population, because they knew them earlier. Only those belonging to the upper class considered the settlers a nuisance and looked down on them. Only a very small proportion of the DPs, mostly from the IRE and KMML projects felt happy about their resettlement, because previously they had no land of their own and lived in small huts, exposed to the vagaries of the rough sea. With resettlement, they could get a small plot and house of their own free from nature's threats. Three-fourths of the DPs had to stay in temporary sheds built in the new place for several months till a permanent house was built for them by the project authorities or by themselves. Some stayed in rented houses or with friends until their new house was ready. They had to undergo these hardships due to the negligence of the project authorities in planning the resettlement programme.

Financial strain and debt burden due to prolonged unemployment lasting for a period from 6 months to two years aggravated the condition of more than one-third of the respondents. About 54 per cent of the Tribals in Idukki were the most affected as many of them lost their livelihood with nothing to replace it. The people who depended on agricultural land and CPRs for their livelihood were forced to live with minimum land in the post-displacement era. They were in an informal economy and displacement pushed them into a formal economy without adequate training or preparation. Besides, they did not know how to spend the compensation amount in a productive manner. Some were cheated in the process, thereby increasing their financial strain.

Nearly 46 per cent of the respondents complained about lack of basic facilities like safe drinking water, toilets, electricity, medical care, marketing, places of religious worship, education, transport and recreation. Women are the most affected by these drawbacks as they had to take care of the household chores, get provisions in time, attend to cooking, cleaning and upbringing of children. It should also be remarked that a sizeable proportion of the respondents from different projects acknowledged that some of these facilities were better provided in the resettlement project. Inadequate compensation and the difficulty of finding a suitable job, especially for women, loomed large among the complaints.

Though many cultural changes are experienced by the DPs in other parts of the country, 64 per cent of the respondents in Kerala were of the opinion that they had not experienced any such change due to displacement. Its main reason is that most of them were resettled fairly close to the earlier location. There was a slight increase in drunkenness and gambling in Karappuzha and VSSC project resettlement areas. According to a sizeable proportion of the respondents, displacement did not have any serious impact on the youth and children. The influence of anti-social elements on children and the youth was minimal. Displacement had no impact on the incidence of illness and malnutrition among children. Kerala being an industrially backward State, air and noise pollution was minimal except in Grasim and in the Kalamassery area where several industries are concentrated. Nine out of 15 projects selected for this study were of a non-polluting nature. On the whole, the impact of displacement had both positive and negative aspects, and affected differentially the settlers in the different projects.

Core Issues Around Displacement

One can, thus, see that the DPs/PAPs are victims of a lopsided process in which those who pay the price of development stand to lose their livelihood and get further impoverished and marginalised. Ironically, the official sources like to call them 'beneficiaries of development projects'. That is indicative of the arbitrariness of the policy followed by the government. The origin of this arbitrary policy to acquire land at the discretion of the State can be traced back to the concept of 'eminent domain' according to which any land which does not have an individual owner is *terra nullius* (nobody's land) and belongs to the State. Its second facet is that the State can take over even individual assets for a 'public purpose'. But, what this public purpose is has not been defined till now. Leaving such wide powers to the government can only lead to abuses whereby the rich and the powerful appropriate for themselves a large proportion of national wealth by depriving the poor and powerless of their paltry livelihood. Besides, in many cases, much more land is taken over than is needed and left unused for years benefiting neither the project nor the deprived. This is a national waste of precious resources. There are also signs of sequential exhaustion, because of which the objectives of land take-over may not be realised.

The mode of acquiring land is another issue that affects the poor negatively. The Land Acquisition Act, 1894 is an enabling and overriding piece of legislation. It does not impose any obligation on the State or the project authorities to search for non-displacing or least displacing alternatives before opting for a people-displacing project. The people have a right to a life with dignity (Art.21), and the right to inhabit any part of the Indian territory (Art.19.1e). But, the Act deprives the people of these rights, often forcefully, without their involvement in the decision concerning the loss of their livelihood. They are displaced without their consent and on terms fixed by the displacing agency without their knowledge. Their exclusion from the decision concerning their very survival reduces them to a state of helplessness and fatalism.

Another very unjust feature of the present mode of land take-over is the paltry compensation the owners are given. Compensation is fixed on what the State calls the market value of the land taken over and not on its replacement value. The market value is calculated as the average of the registered price for three years preceding the notification. But, it is a public secret that the registered value is usually between a third and half of the real price. Consequently, however high the market value offered, it remains far too low for the persons deprived of their livelihood to start life anew. They have to apportion the amount received among various needs like buying a new piece of land -- which may not be of the same quality as the one they lost, build a house and seek other basic amenities like water, electricity etc.. Added to it is the anxiety they feel about finding a new job, educational facilities for children, health services, marketing facilities and so on. Even if land for land is given or a job on the project ensured for one in the family, there are many other resettlement needs the family has to attend to. All these add an enormous burden on the displaced family.

Another aspect that is ignored by the government and the project authorities is that the displaced persons are not compensated for the common property resources like the forest, grazing lands and water resources on which many of them have depended for their livelihood for centuries. In India, around 40 per cent of the DPs/PAPs are Tribals and probably, an equal number belong to the other assetless rural poor groups. They are thrown out of their traditional occupations of services to the communities like barber, scavenger, cobbler, carpenter, smith, tailor, etc., and forced into a new economy that is alien to them. Often they are reduced to the status of cheap labour, mostly daily wage earners and at times, bonded labourers.

Besides, the DPs of fewer than twelve projects in Kerala have received the benefit of resettlement by the project. In most other States, their proportion is about a third. The rest are not even given this minimum. In many cases, resettlement itself is very inadequate and the facilities provided are poor. The powerful classes among the DPs/PAPs are able to get more benefits from the project in the form of compensation and jobs than the powerless. The disadvantaged status is true particularly about those from the backward communities and regions where compensation is calculated at low rates. Idukki is one of many such examples in our study. The main reason for neglecting the DPs/PAPs is that the officials are expected to implement the project in the most economic manner. They do it by cutting down on compensation and rehabilitation, while the machinery and other infrastructure are imported at high costs from foreign governments and companies. As a result, national development has in practice become a process of transferring resources from the rural poor communities, which have sustained themselves on their land and traditional occupations, to the corporate sector, to whom their livelihood is only a source of profit and raw material to produce goods for the middle class consumers (Sharma, 1978: 68).

The implications of this approach have to be studied particularly in the context of its negative impact on the powerless like the Tribals and Dalits. Gender-wise, it affects women more than men. It is they who have to ensure the regular supply of water, fuel, fodder and food for the household. When they are resettled in areas where these facilities are far to fetch or rare to find, they are put to great strain. Most cultures demand more privacy from women. They need better hygienic conditions as they have to bring up the children. These are often not available in the new set-up.

The DPs/PAPs from the powerless classes are at a great disadvantage also in the matter of getting a job after displacement/deprival, as most of them are either illiterate or of low educational standard. Consequently, if they do get jobs, they are mostly unskilled, as skilled jobs require higher qualifications and training. Unless the projects offer them educational and training facilities, they have no prospects of improving their livelihood and social status. Being deprived of the CPRs, the DPs/PAPs become agents of environmental destruction. For example, for sheer survival, they have recourse to cutting down trees indiscriminately for firewood and to other destructive practices.

Even in the process of payment of compensation, the affected people have to undergo an enormous amount of harassment and economic loss. Delay in paying compensation puts them into serious financial difficulties like getting into a debt trap. The poor do not have the sustaining power required for a long court battle. Often, the middlemen and moneylenders cheat them in the manner of utilising the amount received by way of compensation. Very few DPs/PAPs can afford to invest the money in productive assets. Much of the compensation is spent on repaying debts or incurring social expenditures after ensuring a habitat. Consequently, they have very few economic resources to rely upon to begin life anew.

The consequences of displacement are seen not only at the economic level of the affected people, but also in the psychological, social and cultural areas of their life. The tension and mental agony they have to face while rebuilding their life lead many men to mental depression and frustration. This may result in creating a low self-image in them and their taking to alcohol and wife beating, among other coping mechanisms. At times, it results in the break up of family relations. Children may take to the influence of anti-social peer groups and the cinema culture, leading them to delinquency and crime. Once the well established social relations in the previous community are broken up, the new settlers have to seek integration into the new host communities. Though there were very few such cases in Kerala because of its peculiar culture, studies in other States have shown that often the host population is not friendly or are even hostile to them. At the cultural level, many of their cherished values, traditions, norms and practices have to be given up to bring them in tune with the modernising influences. Thus, they have to go through a whole series of psychological, social and cultural adjustments, besides coping with the challenges of economic deprivation. But, the *Land Acquisition Act* and the R&R packages where they exist do not attend to these factors.

A cost-benefit analysis of the major development projects implemented in the country brings us to the stunning discovery that the Planning Commission's criterion of 1:1.5 cost-benefit proportion has rarely been realised in any of them. We ourselves did not do such a study in Kerala. But, the Public Accounts Committee of the Parliament revealed that no major dam has been completed since independence within the amount earmarked for it. Time over-run of five to ten years goes with cost overrun of 500 per cent to 700 per cent. In its 1975-76 report, the PAC pointed out that the real achievement of 12 major irrigation projects in India came to an average of only 64.4 per cent of the originally estimated area for irrigation (Singh, Kothari and Amin, 1992:178). Studies point out that these problems are caused by a combination of factors like lack of proper planning, overestimating benefits in order to get the approval of the Planning Commission, deforestation of the catchment area and the consequent siltation of the reservoirs. As a result of these, the life of most dams has been reduced by half or more. With such gross under-utilisation of national projects, one is led to question the viability of many of them. And a large number of the poor have been displaced for them. These revealing findings urge us to look for alternatives which we shall take up in the final section.

Efforts in Policy Formulation

Basic to the issues discussed above and the enormity of the problem, is the conspicuous absence of a national policy, leave alone a law, on resettlement and rehabilitation. We only have an enabling law on displacement. In the light of its impact on the powerless that we have seen above, we shall now proceed to a critique of the existing laws on land acquisition as well as the draft rehabilitation policies of the government, in order to see whether they attend to these issues.

The Existing Laws

Three States have laws on rehabilitation. Beginning from 1975, Maharashtra passed ad hoc orders providing for land for land and amenities to dam DPs. They were enacted into a law in 1976, amended in 1986 as the *Maharashtra Project Affected Persons Rehabilitation Act 1986.* It received the President's assent in 1989. It applies only to irrigation DPs, but is being amended again to include all types of displacement. The *Madhya Pradesh Pariyojana Ke Karan Visthapit Vyakti (Punhsthspan) Abhiniyan, 1985* is applicable to irrigation projects in which the affected zone exceeds 50 ha. or the benefit zone exceeds 200 ha. or when a whole village is submerged. It does not apply to inter-state schemes like Sardar Sarovar. Its application to non-irrigation projects is left to the State Government's discretion. Till the 1970s, Karnataka used to provide forest land to the DPs. It stopped with the depletion of forests and the *Forest Conservation Act, 1980* (Fernandes, 1990:36). In 1987, its legislature passed the *Karnataka Resettlement of Project Displaced Persons Act* which took seven long years to receive the President's assent in 1994. Orissa had a few GOs in the 1970s and 1980s. It promulgated a policy for irrigation project DPs in 1994 and one for industry DPs in 1998. NTPC promulgated a policy in 1991 and a Revised Version in 1993 (NTPC, 1993). Coal India promulgated its policy in December 1994 (CIL, 1994). But, the country as a whole does not have a rehabilitation law or policy. Thus the existing policies and laws are more exceptions than the rule.

The failure to formulate a policy has to be seen also in the context of several Supreme Court judgements. In the Bombay Pavement Dwellers Case, 1985, for example, the Supreme Court held that the right to work and to a livelihood (that involved the poor occupying the pavements) is an integral part of the right to life with dignity under Article 21 (AIR, 1985, 3 SCC: 343-345). However, in this as well as in a later Calcutta High Court judgement, the judiciary held that though poverty compelled the pavement dwellers to occupy public land, they had no fundamental right to do so (Vaswani, 1992: 158-159). In other words, the right to life with dignity is recognised, but not considered enforceable, particularly if the rights of the poor clash with those of the middle class. So, the State is not bound to enforce the right of the former.

The apathy on rehabilitation and the absence of a policy can be considered an integral part of this contradiction. In 1985, the Ministry of Welfare, Government of India, prepared a rehabilitation policy for the Tribals. The Committee working on it suggested that a national policy be prepared covering all the DPs, not Tribals alone, and that rehabilitation be an integral part of the projects above a certain size, whether executed by the public, private or joint sector. It also stated that the policy should have legal authority and should be binding on the Government as well as the implementing agency (Government of India, 1985a). The Government waited for 8 years before formulating a national policy (MRD, 1993). It was revised in 1994. Also, the Ministry of Water Resources Development drafted a policy in 1993 (WRD, 1993). In 1994-95, more than 1,500 NGOs and thousands of DPs/PAPs went through a process of reflecting on the draft MRD policy and prepared a People's Alternative, which was presented to the Secretary, Ministry of Rural Development, in October 1995. A new draft was got ready three years later, but is yet to be promulgated.

This delay as well as the seven year waiting for the President's assent to the Karnataka Law and the three year waiting for the Maharashtra Amendment of 1986 are indicative of a lack of commitment to rehabilitation. The same can be said about official silence on the draft policy. Moreover, policies are often evolved under pressure from the funders, particularly the World Bank. Only exceptionally do they emerge from awareness among a few policy makers, of the injustice caused to the DPs. For example, the reasons the 1991 draft of the NTPC policy gave for formulating it were delays caused by agitations by the DPs, cost rise, the bad name the Company gets and the refusal of funders to give loans in the absence of a policy. Rehabilitation to deal with the people's sufferings is not mentioned in it, though its subsequent versions do (Fernandes and Chatterjee, 1995). Similar are the reasons given by the Central Government in the letter it wrote to the State Governments in 1980 on the need to formulate a rehabilitation policy. This, as well as internal evidence, leaves one with the impression that the recent flurry of activity around rehabilitation policies is the result of pressure from the World Bank, not of conviction on the part of the Government (Fernandes and Paranjpye, 1997:5).

When such schemes are formulated under pressure, many of those who have to implement them are not committed to them. As a result, many of them have not been implemented properly. For example, the Sardar Sarovar Rehabilitation scheme was prepared as a response to the agitation against the dam and because the World Bank was involved in it. But, many government officials responsible for it present displacement by the dam and the consequent resettlement as Tribal development. Those who oppose the dam are, therefore, presented as persons having a vested interest in the poverty, illiteracy and backwardness of the Tribals (Debnath, Choube and Agarwal, 1992). Little wonder then that according to reports, resettlement has suffered after the World Bank withdrew from the project, because commitment to the DPs on the part of those concerned is low.

In a few cases, there has even been going back on a good policy. For example, till the 1950s, the State of Hyderabad had a fairly good policy on rehabilitation. When the Nizamsagar dam (1923-1931) was constructed, the Nizam decreed that the rehabilitation of its 13,489 DPs should be an integral part of the project, that no cash compensation should be given lest peasants, not adequately exposed to the monetary economy, drift. They were to be resettled in model villages in the command area, given land for land, houses, water and other facilities provided according to approved plans and with due regard to sanitation. Nine thousand DPs accepted the scheme. The rest were given cash compensation. This scheme was followed for the Thungabhadra dam (1945-53) that submerged 65 villages.

Changes began with Nagarjunasagar (1958-1969). Rehabilitation colonies were built, but on dry land away from the command area. The changes got intensified with Sriramsagar (Pochampad) that caused 2,00,000 DPs by official count and 2,40,000 according to others (Guggenheim, 1990). The committee appointed to study resettlement suggested a "modified rehabilitation policy" which gave to the DPs the option of either going to the rehabilitation centres or to any other place of their choice. Even this modified scheme was changed for the more than 1,00,000 DPs of the Srisailam project. Cash compensation became the norm and much of it was spent on bribes or was cornered by middlemen (Reddy and Reddy, 1987: 9-11). Thus, the Nizam's policy has been abandoned in the context of more rapid displacement than in the past, pressure from the medium and big farmers who want to cultivate land in the command area, shortage of other good land, and a growing population. *The Land Acquisition (Amendment) Bill 1998* is in the same direction. It tries to take away the few rights the DPs/PAPs have under the LAQ.

Kerala cannot even boast of a draft. During this study, officials kept telling us that the compensation in the State is higher than that in most others and that it takes the place of rehabilitation. The analysis of the situation given above should suffice to show that this claim is unacceptable. Fewer than a dozen projects in Kerala have had a rehabilitation package, mostly drawn under pressure of agitation by the people, sometimes led by political parties and at other times by others like Church leaders. But, for these few projects, the State that boasts of its high human development record has neglected rehabilitation completely. We have seen that as a result, the social and economic status of most DPs/PAPs particularly the Tribals and Dalits has deteriorated after deprival. Women among them are the worst sufferers of this neglect.

The Draft Rehabilitation Policies

In the context of these developments, we cannot comment on any draft or real policy in Kerala. So, we shall now analyse the policies and laws being formulated by the Ministries at the Centre and see whether they are an improvement on past policies. Do they provide a strong enough basis for acceptance by the DPs/PAPs? Though there are major differences between the drafts prepared by the Ministry of Rural Development, we shall restrict ourselves to the documents of 1994 and 1998 since they are the latest versions. We shall not discuss the Water Resources policy, because it has been abandoned in favour of the Rural Development draft.

Common to all the policies and drafts is the assumption that displacement is inevitable. It can be argued that displacement itself is a consequence of the present pattern of development, and as such it cannot be considered inevitable. Its rationale should, therefore, be questioned. But, no policy does it. However, there are some differences. The 1993 draft formulated within the Ministry does not support "displacement as a deliberate choice" (Sinha, 1996: 1455). While considering it inevitable, it expresses a sense of guilt over the price the DPs/PAPs have paid for the success of planned development, particularly the failure to rehabilitate them. This draft seems to represent the thinking within the Ministry that formulated it. There is some people-orientation in the former, while the latter is totally production-oriented. The 1994 draft formulated after reactions of 15 Ministries and Departments (as such can be called the stand of the Government of India), omits the sections that speak of past failures or betray qualms of conscience about displacement. It begins by stating that with the new economic policy, there will be more investment and more land will have to be acquired especially in the Tribal regions (MRD, 1994: 1.1 and 4.1). Its implication is that more displacement should be taken for granted, particularly of the Tribals.

The drafts do not mention the right of the victims to participate in the decision concerning the project, leave alone being its part owners. More importantly, they are based on the colonial concept of eminent domain, whose two principles are (1) CPRs and other assets without individual *pattas* are State property and (2) the state alone has the right to decide the public purpose and deprive its citizens even of their individual assets (Ramanathan, 1999). Instead of attending to this lacuna, the 1993 and 1994 drafts state that given the acknowledged superiority of the *Land Acquisition Act 1894,* all land should be acquired exclusively under it and that other enabling laws should be amended in consonance with it (No. 8.1).

The National Policy for Resettlement and Rehabilitation of Displaced persons (NPRR) is an improvement on the two previous drafts. It has many positive aspects as well as shortcomings (Fernandes & LAAB, 1998; *EPW*, Oct. 17-24, 1998). It states that displacement should be minimised. So, people-displacing projects should be the last option after studying non-displacing and least displacing alternatives (2.1a and 3.3.3). It recognises that displacement results in "state-induced impoverishment" (2.1a) and that "no developmental project can be justified if a section of society is pauperised by it" (3.1.2). The project should be explained to those to be affected by it, in order to get their co-operation or even consent (2.1d). They may question every aspect including its public purpose and environmental impact (3.1.3 and 3.1.25). The definition of the DPs/PAPs goes beyond landowners to include those who depend for sustenance on land owned by others or on the CPRs (3.1.5). As such, compensation should be given for the CPRs and other livelihood lost. The welfare of the DPs/PAPs is a precondition of the project (3.1.2). Rehabilitation is mandatory and should go on side by side with the project (3.1.4) and should be prior to dislocation (3.1.9). The DPs should be resettled as communities (3.1.14) and should have a better lifestyle after displacement than before it, because they pay the price of development (3.1.12). They should be the first beneficiaries of jobs and other project benefits (3.1.18-23). Often moneylenders and other outsiders usurp land in the area to be acquired after news spreads about the possibility of a project. When the project is notified, they get most benefits meant for the DPs/PAPs. As protection against it, the Policy Statement includes among the DPs/PAPs only those who were residents of the area three years before the notification under section 4.1 of the *Land Acquisition Act, 1894* (LAA) (3.1.8). Land for land is recommended as compensation or rehabilitation to all the DPs/PAPs and is mandatory for Tribals (3.2.2).

NPRR 1998 also has some shortcomings. The 'public purpose' for which land is acquired under LAA has not been defined more than a century after its enactment. In the absence of a definition, courts have generally accepted as 'public purpose' whatever the government declares, including transfer of land to the private sector. Abuses are intrinsic to this stand. In project after project, more land than required is acquired and then sold for profit (ISED, 1996). The social activist DP/PAP combine has been demanding a restrictive definition to include only schemes of genuine welfare of the biggest possible number, such as educational and health institutions and housing for the poor. The Policy Statement says that the project should be according to the public purpose, but does not define it or state that it should be defined in a restrictive manner. Besides, it does not give adequate importance to the cultural aspects except in the rehabilitation of the Tribals. Nomads are mentioned only in passing. The gender issue does not receive the importance it deserves. Though made mandatory, rehabilitation is not mentioned as a right. Thus, it remains a welfare measure. Past DPs/PAPs are alluded to, but their rehabilitation is not mentioned.

Significantly, a policy is not legally binding. It requires a law, but NPRR 1998 makes no provision for it. We are told that Coal India has rejected the policy, because it states that a plan for land reclamation should be prepared two years before a mine is abandoned for possible return to the people or to resettle others. Coal India finds it too expensive. We also hear that the former ministry for welfare had rejected the stipulation that people should not be displaced from wildlife sanctuaries and parks. NGOs have been demanding joint protected area management that will use also the conservation traditions of the forest dwellers and ensure their as well as wildlife right to life. This clause has not been included in the policy.

These lacunae have to be seen in the context of the decision to formulate the *Land Acquisition Amendment Bill 1998* that was expected to come up in the winter 2000 session of the Parliament. To understand this decision, we shall first analyse the *Land Acquisition Act 1894*. This law was enacted for colonial purposes and is based on the principle of eminent domain. It enables the State to deprive people of their sustenance without their consent. There is no provision in it to search for non-displacing or least displacing alternatives before opting for a people-displacing project. The public purpose according to which it is to be done has not been defined till today. It requires the displacing project to compensate only individual *patta* land. There is no obligation to compensate families depending on the CPRs and those who live by rendering services to the village as a community. Compensation is based on the market value, not on replacement value (Ramanathan, 1996). A major abuse is that many projects acquire more land than required and then transfer it for other purposes. For example, less than a third of the 3,764 ha. acquired for the HAL-MIG plant at Sunabeda in the Koraput district of Orissa in 1966 has been used till now. Its 468 predominantly Tribal displaced families have not been resettled nor has the land been afforested. It has been lying unused since then (Pandey, 1998: 35). According to a recent report, some of it is being sold to a private party (ISED, 1996), obviously at a high profit. While not excluding land-based rehabilitation, the LAA places no obligation on the displacing authority to rehabilitate the DPs. Rehabilitation is recognised as a right of the DPs/PAPs. Displacement is taken for granted. No effort is made to minimise it or to reduce its impact on the poor in particular.

Thus, clearly identifiable classes pay the price of development and its benefits reach other equally identifiable classes. As such the claim to its superiority is far fetched. On the other hand, the policy makers have a fairly good understanding of rehabilitation. The drafts do not require the DP/PAP's consent before being deprived of their sustenance. But, they allude to rehabilitation as a necessity without calling it a right. They discuss the possibility of compensating the CPRs, of the need to attend to the DPs' cultural, social, economic and psychological rehabilitation etc. Their major shortcoming is that they leave decisions about the land for land and rehabilitation in the hands of the state government and do not make them mandatory. They also lack a good monitoring body. Besides, they refer to future DPs alone, not to those displaced and not resettled during the last four decades. So, they cannot be acceptable to the DPs though they are an improvement on the past.

Land Acquisition Amendment Bill 1998

One would expect the above deficiencies to be removed in any law that replaces the LAA. On the positive side, the Bill stipulates that the proposal from the project authorities should be complete in all respects before it reaches the Collector. This clause will inhibit proposals to be rushed through for external considerations. It also wants land records to be updated after the Notification under Section 4.1. It raises the solatium from 30 per cent to 100 per cent.

But, its negative points outweigh the positive. No provision is made in the bill against abuses like over-acquisition. Nor does it recognise the DPs' right to rehabilitation. It contradicts most provisions of the Draft Policy 1998 which includes among the DPs/PAPs, all who depend for sustenance on the acquired land, whether they have a *patta* or not. The Bill limits compensation to *patta* owners. It only keeps a door ajar for the other dependants to claim a share of the compensation. The Bill includes among the DPs/PAPs all those owning a site in the area, on the day of the Notification under Section 4.1, not three years before it, as the draft policy suggests. It will encourage the exploiters to spread rumours among the poor, buy small plots before the Notification and corner most benefits meant for them. The LAA gives to the affected persons one month after the notification under Section 4.1

to file objections. By all counts, it is too short a time for the DPs/PAPs, most of whom are poor and illiterate, and hear about the Notification several months later. This is being reduced to 21 days by the 1998 Bill. It is too short a time for the poor. Studies show that even the present three years are inadequate for them to prepare themselves for the change-over to a new life, particularly since no effort is made by the project authorities to train them for it (Mahapatra, 1994: 43-48). The Bill does not remedy this situation, but only tries to shorten the time between the first notification and the final takeover.

The existing law requires the Notice to be published in two newspapers, one of them in the local language. It has to be displayed in the *Panchayat* Office. The Amendment Bill states that the notification under 6.1 should be published in one local newspaper, preferably (not mandatorily) in the local language. So, it becomes extremely difficult for the DPs/PAPs to know about it and becomes easier for the State to acquire land without encumbrances. At present, the administration has to deal with each objection individually. The Bill states that the Collector will hear them at a Public Meeting (5.2), not individually. He/She can then proceed with the Notifications. This is a good way of reducing people's rights by pretending to solicit their participation. It dispenses with individual response to each objection. The affected families are, thus, deprived of the possibility of knowing how their concern has been dealt with. The Award on compensation is to be displayed and the takeover completed within 60 days after it. So, the process from the 1st Notification under 4.1 to hearing objections, under Section 5, the second Notification under 6.1 and the final acquisition will be completed within a year (16.3).

The policy speaks of replacement value for compensation. The Bill limits itself to the 'market value' and we have discussed its meaning in an earlier section. The Bill speaks of the need to rehabilitate the DPs/PAPs. The Bill only brings rehabilitation to the statute book by stating that where a law exists, the DPs may lay a claim to it (6.5). The Collector will then decide its nature (9.2). The amount spent on it will be adjusted against compensation. The displacing agency does not have a duty to resettle and rehabilitate the DPs/PAPs. According to the LAA, the DPs/PAPs may approach a Lower Court against the Collector's award. The Bill allows an appeal against the Award only in the High Court (18.1). Powers of the Lower Court are to be transferred to a Tribunal made up of bureaucrats that may include the Collector. The poor cannot approach the High Court. Instead, the bureaucrats sit in judgement on objections against the decisions of one of their own. So, one of the accused may end up as the judge (Fernandes, 1998b).

Thus, the main purpose of the Amendment Bill seems to be to make acquisition easier for the Corporate Sector. It reduces the already limited rights of the people under the Land Acquisition Amendment Act 1894. More power will be vested in the bureaucracy and the Collector made all powerful. Judicial processes are sought to be short-circuited and time-limits reduced. The Bill does not even mention people's consent before displacement. The need to minimise displacement is ignored. The public purpose is not defined. The Act and its amendments as well as the draft policies revolve around three basic issues. The first is the as yet undefined public purpose. It is an integral part of the Eminent Domain on which Indian land and forest laws are based. Its assumption is that all the natural resources and all land not having an individual *patta* is State property. So, no compensation need to be paid for the CPRs though they are the sustenance of a large number of communities. Secondly, the State alone has the right to decide what is a public purpose and displace even individual owners without their consent. This goes against the spirit of Articles 19.1.e and 21 of the Indian Constitution. Thirdly, the Bill assumes that if the affected individuals are given 'adequate' monetary compensation for the assets acquired, then they need no other benefits. The market value that is its norm is significantly less than the real value as most court cases and negotiations have shown. Based on the Eminent Domain, the Bill confers on the State the power to decide the market value. The Indian Industry resists any move towards replacement value and opposes the very idea of rehabilitation. That seems to be the reason why the Union Cabinet decided on October 31, 1998 to accept the amendments to the Land Acquisition Act and reject the draft policy. We hear from reliable sources that the same decision was repeated in October, 2000 and that the Amendment Bill was introduced in the winter session of the Parliament. But, the rehabilitation policy was not be promulgated.

Search for Alternatives

It is in this context that we need to search for alternatives to these policies and laws. Our contention is that a new law should be worked out based on a policy that does not have the shortcomings mentioned above. There is a consensus among social activists and social analysts that minimising displacement should be the basic principle governing the choice and location of development projects. It should ensure the participation of the DPs not only in planning and implementing rehabilitation, but also in the very decision concerning the project that displaces them. No people-displacing project should be approved till non-displacing and least displacing alternatives are studied and proved to be non-viable. The public purpose should be defined in a restrictive manner (NCPR, 1995). There should be no displacement without the people's prior informed consent after they are convinced that it is the only alternative, according to the restrictive public purpose. The project, thus, approved according to this public purpose should be explained to those to be affected by it in a language and manner they can understand. Information regarding the project and all its implications should be speedily and more effectively disseminated through various channels to avoid the spread of false rumours. For this, the project officials can use fora like the village *panchayat* or *Gram Sabha*. It may be accorded final sanction only after the people accept it as necessary according to such a public purpose.

Thirdly, the DPs/PAPs should be defined in such a way as to include not only landowners, but also its other dependants and those of the CPRs. Persons to be affected by the project should be involved in the identification of the assets to be acquired, of persons to be displaced or otherwise deprived by it, and in fixing the criteria for compensation. Compensation should be according to the replacement value. It includes the market value of the land, replacement of the house (or money to build it according to the prevailing PWD rates), replacement of the CPRs, of the social and cultural systems which the people lose, making every affected person literate and training them technically to take up jobs in the project. It should also quantify the loss of livelihood by the artisans, barbers, landless labourers and others who depend on services to the village as a community, quantify loss in the form of social pollution. It should quantify the psychological trauma of displacement, break up of family links and community institutions as well as the facilities and amenities they enjoyed earlier. It should also include the cost of preparing the DPs to begin life again, of training them to cope with the changes, of replacing the CPRs acquired and of rebuilding the community that breaks up after displacement (Dhagamwar, 1997). Provision should be made to take care of those who do not own *patta* and were living on common property or *puramboke.* The mode of paying compensation should be just and prompt so as to ensure that unnecessary delays are avoided, sparing the beneficiaries additional expenses for repeated travel to the project office, bribing the officials or paying the middlemen. The matter should be settled at the project level, as far as possible, without pushing the poor to engage in court cases which they can ill afford.

In those cases where displacement is inevitable, rehabilitation should ensure that the lifestyle of the DPs/PAPs is better after displacement than before it, because they pay the price of development. At present, rehabilitation is viewed as a welfare measure, provided by the authorities at their mercy. It has to be considered a right of the deprived and as social investment for the nation, even though it may cause some additional expenses for the project. The trauma caused by displacement demands such a compensatory measure. The transition period between displacement and resettlement should be reduced to the minimum, otherwise the displaced would be put to extra hardships like looking for a temporary shelter in huts, rented houses or being at the mercy of relatives. The DPs should be resettled before work on the project begins. The issue concerning Tribals, Dalits and women should be given special attention as they are the most affected with their own unique problems.

Those who pay the price of the project should be the first beneficiaries of its benefits like jobs, supply of provisions etc.. If they are trained to take up most jobs, very few persons will need to come from outside. The local people can then be given loans and grants to improve their houses and give them on rent to these few outsiders. So, no land should be acquired for townships. There should be no forced eviction from the protected areas. In planning rehabilitation, one may encourage even part ownership of the project by those deprived of their livelihood, if their CPRs are acquired for it (Sharma, 1993). The people will, thus, be a part of the management. They may have to be trained to take up this responsibility. They may even decide to appoint professional managers on their behalf. It is to be their decision. Some of these principles such as the need to train the DPs/PAPs apply particularly to women from the marginalised groups, because they have less access to the benefits of the project and other modern outputs than even men from their class do (Fernandes, 1996).

Since the displacing agency cannot do justice to rehabilitation, some suggest an independent body, which may even be a Ministry, to ensure that displacement is minimised, and when it does occur, that the DPs are rehabilitated properly (Dhagamwar, 1989: 173-175). Some also point to the need for ongoing participatory monitoring and evaluation by an agency independent of the project. Its findings should be made available to the project authorities as well as the DPs. It will help the former to take appropriate action when needed and the latter to deal with their trauma better than they have been able to do till now (Mankodi, 1989). A long term regional plan is essential to prevent multiple displacement (Fernandes, 1995a).

All maintain that the cost of rehabilitation should be borne by the project. Proper and successful rehabilitation, thus, includes the whole process beginning from short-term grants as survival assistance during the transition, forming proper credit structures for rebuilding the house, agricultural and other assets, replacing CPRs at an early stage, attending to land reclamation and pastures etc. Community institutions that are weakened by displacement have to be strengthened. If the DPs are resettled in an existing village, they have to be reconciled to the host population particularly in matters concerning the use of the grazing land and other CPRs (Mahapatra, 1994: 61-71).

A separate law may govern land purchase by companies, whether they are in the Public or Private Sector. It can be analogous to labour laws that govern what is a private contract between the employer and the employee, but fix the minimum conditions. Here, conditions such as a price based on replacement value may be fixed. Another possibility is for the Industry to take land on lease and pay the owner a rent equivalent to twice the value of its produce.

If these provisions make a project too expensive, that is reason enough to search for cheaper alternatives. They are available and technically feasible. They only require a political will and some new thinking. The poor cannot be sacrificed for the profit of the entrepreneur.

Conclusion

Ultimately all the problems connected with displacement, resettlement and rehabilitation can be traced back to the present pattern of development which does not sufficiently take into account the enormous sufferings the poor and powerless sections of society have to undergo. As a result, focus has shifted to the economic viability of the project. The country lacks a social policy. The absence of a rehabilitation policy and law is only a reflection of this frame of mind. Liberalisation further intensifies the process of sacrificing the people, the poor in particular, especially women among them, to the profit of the entrepreneur.

There can be no national development till this process is reversed. The narrow concerns of profit have to give way to the ultimate goal of improving the quality of human life. We do not oppose profit. What we strongly advocate is '*development with a human face*'.

Appendix

APPENDIX

Type of Land Acquired (in Hectares) for a Representative Set of Projects

	Name of Project	Private	Common	Forest	Total	Source
1.	Chulliar Dam.	NA	NA	NA	165	Project Report, Revamping and Consolidation Programme, Gayathri Project Stage I& II, 1998.
2.	Idukki Hydro Electric Project.	15.58	00	5463.84	5479.43	Revenue Divisional Office, File No. 766/78, Idukky.
3.	Kallada Irrigation Project.	284.68	00	2144.32	2429	Chief Engineer, KIP, Kottarakara, 1998.
4.	Karppuzha Irrigation Project.	809.7165	NA	NA	1174	Report by Kayal, Nellarachal.
5.	Kutiadi Irrigation Project.	404.86	NA	NA	1052.63	Project Report, Kutiadi Irrigation, 1998.
6.	Kutiadi Augmentation (Banasurusager).	7.69	00	1277.00	1284.69	Project Report, PWD, Irrigation.
7.	Meenkara Irrigation.	NA	NA	NA	250	Office of the Asst. Exe. Engineer
8.	Muvattupuzha Valley Irrigation Project.	713.81	00	1.79	715.40	Office of the Exe. Engr., MVIP, Thodupuzha.
9.	Pothundy Dam.	NA	NA	NA	982.82	Project Report from Irrigation Office, Nemmara, 1967.
10.	Neriamangalam Hydro Electric (HE).	00	64.80	32.06	96.86	Office of the Asst. Exe. Engr, Civil Division, Kallarkuty, Adimali.
11.	Sengulam.	00	00	29.1	29.1	Do
12.	Panniar HE (Ponmudi, Anayirangal Dam).	00	5	764.4	769.40	Do
13.	Idamalayar HE.	00	00	2930	2930	Do
14.	Peringalkuth HE.	00	00	285	285	Do
15.	Sholayar.	00	00	870.5	870.5	Do

Contd...

Contd...

	Name of Project	Private	Common	Forest	Total	Source
16.	Sabarigiri.	00	00	1951	1951	Do
17.	Lower Periyar.	00	00	44.5	44.5	Do
18.	Chaliyar River Valley (Proposed).	545	245	640	1430	Office of the Superintending Engr., Information and Planning, Kozhikode.
19.	Kanjirappuzha Irrigation.	1160	35	00	1195	Office of the Exe. Engr., Siruvani, Palakkad.
	Total	3,941.34	349.8	17,989.51	24,690.33	
Industrial Projects						
1.	Apparel Park at Menamkulam.	31.34	13.73	00	45.07	Office of the KINFRA, Oral Information from Project Consultant, Vellayambalam.
2.	SIKL, Cherthala.	NA	NA	00	48	Office of the Personnel Manager, SIKL, Cherthala.
3.	Chemical Industrial Estate & Development, Aroor.	6.39	00	00	6.39	District Industries Center, Alappuzha.
4.	Cochin Refineries Limited.	141.73	00	00	141.73	LAO, Vytila, Cochin.
5.	Coir Park 1 & 2, Cherthala.	16.78	00	00	16.78	District Industries Center (DIC), Alappuzha.
6.	Conventional Industrial Estate, Thekkil.	00	11.36	00	11.36	DIC, Kasargod.
7.	Development Area, Ananthapuram.	00	42.13	00	42.13	DIC, Kasargod.
8.	Development Area, Urathamchal.	00	43.72	00	43.72	DIC, Kasargod..
9.	Development Area and Development Plot, Anthur.	24.01	00	00	24.01	DIC, Kannur.

Contd...

Contd...

	Name of Project	Private	Common	Forest	Total	Source
10.	English Indian Clays Ltd.	3.66	NA	00	78.15	Office of the Draftsman, Oral Information, English Indian Clays Ltd., Kochuveli.
11.	Automobile Tyre Factory Appollo, Perambra.	13.09	00	00	13.09	Collectorate, File No. 1477/75, Thrissur.
12.	Export Promotion Industrial Park, Kakkanad.	72.87	00	00	72.87	Office of the Asst. Engineer, KINFRA, Kakanad
13.	Hindustan News Print Mill, Velloore.	277.34	00	00	277.34	Personnel Officer, Hindustan Newsprint Mill, Velloore.
14.	Hindustan Petroleum Corporation Ltd., Kanjikode.	NA	NA	NA	9.29	LAO, LA Register and Award File, 1990.
15.	Indian Oil Corporation Ltd., Parippally.	28.13	00	00	28.13	LA General, File No. LA_2 -9295/92, Civil Station, Kollam.
16.	Indian Telephone Industries Ltd., Pudussery.	NA	NA	NA	40.34	LAO, LA and Award File, Kottaikokam, 1990.
17.	Industrial Development Area, Pudussery.	54.31	00	00	54.31	Manager, Oral information, DIC, Palakkad.
18.	Industrial Estate, Pappanamcode.	NA	NA	00	6.89	Deputy General Manager, SIDCO, Thiruvananthapuram.
19.	Industrial Growth Center., Kannur.	105	00	00	105	LAO, Award Register, Thalassery.
20.	Instrumentation Ltd., Pudussery.	00	00	00	242.91	Administrative Office, Pudussery.
21.	Kanjikode Industrial Township.	299.59	00	00	299.59	LAO, Oral information from Clerk, Palakkad
22.	Kerala Ceramics Company Ltd., Madayi,	NA	NA	00	102.82	Oral Information from a villager.
23.	Malabar Cement, Walayar.	00	00	339	339	Civil Engineer, Malabar Cements Ltd.

Contd...

Contd...

	Name of Project	Private	Common	Forest	Total	Source
24.	Mavoor Gwaliyor Rayons.	55.15	00	00	55.15	Collectorate, Award No. 1/60, 1/64, 25/67, Kozhikode
25.	Peruman Special Refractries.	12.15	00	00	12.15	LAO- General, File No. A5-1015/89, Civil Station, Kollam.
26.	Deve. Areas and Deve. Plots, Chengannur.	6.28	00	00	6.28	DIC, Alappuzha.
27.	Deve. Areas and Deve. Plots, Punnpra.	23.19	00	00	23.19	DIC, Alappuzha.
28.	Development Areas and Deve. Plots, Kottakadavu.	19.09	00	00	19.09	DIC, Alappuzha.
29.	SIDCO, Nallavattanam.	3.44	00	00	3.44	Land Manager, SIDCO.
30.	Steel Complex, Chevayur.	17.80	00	00	17.80	Works Manager, Oral Information, Steel Complex.
31.	Sugar Factory, Menompara.	NA	NA	NA	44.53	Manager, Oral Information, Administrative Office.
32.	Technopark, Thiruvananthapuram.	32.26	60.73?	00	92.99	Special Tahsildar, Addl. LA Unit, File No. A_2/379/92. Thiruvananthapuram
33.	Traco Cables Company Ltd., Irumpanam.	NA	NA	00	14.57	Personnel Manager, TRACO, Cochin.
34.	FACT, Udyogamandal Division.	20.2429	00	00	307.6923 **	Estate Manager, FACT, Udyogamandal Division, Cochin.
35.	FACT, Cochin Division.	636.4372	00	00	636.4372	Estate Manager, File No.141-2, FACT, Cochin Division.
36.	HMT Ltd., Kalamassery.	316.1943	00	00	316.1943	Land Manager, HMT Ltd.

Contd...

Contd...

	Name of Project	Private	Common	Forest	Total	Source
37.	Travancore Titanium Products Ltd., Thiruvananthapuram.	NA	NA	00	30.47	Works Manager, Oral information, Travancore Titanium Products Ltd.
38.	Hindustan Latex Ltd., Peroorkada.	NA	NA	NA	4.66	Primary data.
	Total	2216.41	171.67	339	3341.45	
Non-Hydel Power Projects						
1.	120 Mega Watt Diesel Generator Power Plant, Nallalam.	10.85	00	00	10.85	Office of Exe. Engr.-thermal, Vydhuthi Bhavan, Pattom.
2.	66 KV Sub Station of Puthencruz	1.82	00	00	1.82	Office of the Exe. Engr., Vydhuthi Bhavan, Pattom.
3.	220 KV Substation, Andoorkonam.	14	00	00	14	Exe. Engr., File No. 4593/82/LA_3, KSEB, Thiruvananthapuram, 1998.
4.	220-400 KV Switching Plant, Areecode.	20.21	00	00	20.21	Vydhuthi Bhavan, Pattom.
5.	K.S.E.B. Substation, Uduma.	30.77	00	00	30.77	Asst. Engr., Oral Information, KSEB, Kasargod.
6.	National Thermal Power Corporation.	79.35	364.37	00	551.79	R & R Office, Choolatheruvu.
7.	220 KV Substation, Kasargod.	31.94	00	00	31.94	Special Deputy Collector, KSEB, Award Register Vol. I, Kozhikode
8.	Wind Farm, Kanjikode.	NA	NA	NA	21.58	Exe. Engr.- Thermal, Vydhuthi Bhavan, Pattom.
	Total	188.94	364.37	—	682.96	
Defence Units						
1.	Naval Academy, Ezhimala.	NA	NA	NA	850	LAO-II, Correspondence File, Thalikkavu, Kannur.

Contd...

Contd...

	Name of Project	Private	Common	Forest	Total	Source
2.	Kerala Armed Police Camp, Pathanamthitta.	12.64	00	00	12.64	RDO, LA File, Adoor.
Environment Protection						
1.	Elephant Project, Tahriyode.	88.49	00	00	88.49	Collectorate, File No. B6-20048/92 dtd 7-4-1992, Wayanadu
2.	Elephant Project – Marayoor.	NA	NA	NA	30.15	RDO, Devikulam
3.	Periyar Tiger Reserve, Malappara.	NA	NA	NA	54.36	RDO, File No.4926/83, Devikulam
Tourism						
1.	Bakel Resort Development Corporation.	59.51	00	00	59.51	Manager, Bakel Resorts Devt. Corporation, Kasaragode.
2.	Veli Tourism.	NA	NA	00	9.24	Collectorate, Thiruvananthapuram.
Urban/Rural Development						
1.	Medical College, Trissur.	18.96	00	00	18.96	Collectorate, File No. R Dis E_1-34708/84, R Dis 60051/83, Thrissur.
2.	District Town Planning Scheme for Elamkulam extension	47.63	NA	00	47.63	Town Planning Section, Greater Cochin Devt. Authority (GCDA), Cochin.
3.	Medical College, Alappuzha	32.48	00	00	32.48	LAO- General, Alappuzha.
4.	Edappally Housing Accommodation Scheme.	6.51	00	00	6.51	LAO, KSHB, Thiruvananthapuram.
5.	Elamkulam West housing scheme.	39.29	00	00	39.29	Town Planning Section, Greater Cochin Devt. Authority (GCDA), Cochin.
6.	Housing Colony , Nadakavu.	5.29	00	00	5.29	LAO, File No. 1064/82, Collectorate, Kozhikode.

Contd...

Contd...

	Name of Project	Private	Common	Forest	Total	Source
7.	Housing Accommodation, Chelavur.	17.34	00	00	17.34	Chief Engineer, Oral information, Housing Board, Kozhikode.
8.	Municipal Stadium & Park Tiruvalla.	6.08	00	00	6.08	RDO, File No. B_2. 107/87, Thiruvalla.
9.	Thrikkakara Sub-Urban Accommodation.	15.32	00	00	15.32	LAO, Panampally Nagar and Thiruvananthapuram File No. 1243/80, A-1243/80, 1243/87.
	Total	349.54	—	—	1293.29	
Farms and Fisheries						
1.	Attapadi Goat Farm, Agali, Palakkad.	NA	NA	NA	6.92	LAO, LA Register and Award file, 1987, Kottaikakom.
2.	Fish Cultivation Farm, Pallippuram	12.24	00	00	12.24	Collectorate, File No. R Dis 3432/61, Thrissur.
3.	Seed Farm, Edathuruthy.	8.42	00	00	8.42	Collectorate, File No. R Dis 2746/61, Thrissur.
4.	Seed Farm, Pazhayannur.	9.84	00	00	9.84	Collectorate, Thrissur.
5.	Fish farm, Eranholi.	NA	NA	NA	11.96	Office of the Fish farm, Thalassery.
6.	Seed farm, Anakayam.	NA	NA	NA	10.98	Office of the Seed farm, Anakayam.
7.	State Seed Farm, Eravattur.	11.96	00	00	11.96	Office of the Seed farm, Oral information from Clerk.
8.	CTCRI, Sreekariyam.	NA	NA	00	44.53	Oral information from a Villager
Transport						
1.	Aroor–Cherthala Bye - Pass - NH 47.	NA	NA	00	5.63	LAO-Highways, Alappuzha.

Contd...

Contd...

	Name of Project	Private	Common	Forest	Total	Source
2.	Ernakulam - Kayamkulam Broad Gauge Railway.	NA	NA	00	487.22	LAO-Railway, Alappuzha and Deputy Exe. Egnr., Railways, Ernakulam.
3.	Ettumanoor- Eratupetta Road.	4.45	00	00	4.45	Collectorate, LAO, Award Register No. G_5-50830/94, Vol.V to VIII and G_5. 30105/94, Vol. IV to VI, Kottayam.
4.	Kalpata Bye-Pass.	10.57	00	00	10.57	RDO, Oral Information, Wayanad.
5.	Karipur Airport.	45.96	00	00	45.96	LAO, Award Register No. 5/95 to19/95, Malappuram.
6.	Nedumbassery International Airport, Cochin.	489.29	00	00	489.29	LAO-I, II, and III, Ankamaly.
7.	Needakara Fishing Harbor.	2.02	00	00	2.02	Exe. Egnr.- Fisheries, Kollam.
8.	Thalassery-Mahe Bye-Pass NH-47.	35.06	00	00	35.06	LA- II, Kannur.
9.	Tharkassery Harbor.	NA	NA	00	1.21	Exe. Egnr.- Fisheries, Oral Information, Kollam.
10.	Thiruvananthapuram International Airport.	10.53	00	00	10.53	Land Manager (Oral Information), Airport, Thiruvananthapuram.
11.	Vizhinjam Harbour.	NA	NA	00	40.16	Collectorate, File No. A_{11}. 334/85. Thiruvananthapuram.
12.	Calicut Bye-Pass-17 (Mapuzha- Arapuzha).	NA	NA	NA	22.33	LAO-I, Award Register, B 128/83, Kozhikode.
Educational Institutions						
1.	Centre for Water Resource Development and Management, Kozhikode.	NA	NA	NA	63.62	Registrar, CDWRDM.

Contd...

Contd...

	Name of Project	Private	Common	Forest	Total	Source
2.	Cochin University of Science and Technology.	4.05	44.99	00	49.04	Engineering Section, File No.44/ E_4 - 4/65-66, Cochin University.
3.	Coconut Research Station, Pilicode.	16.19	00	00	16.19	RDO, File No. R. Dis. 2765/69 dt. 21-8-70, Kasargod.
4.	Government Polytechnic, Purakady.	8.24	00	00	8.24	Collectorate, File No.B_6/ 19159/97, Wayanad
5.	Expansion of Govt. Polytechnic Kodumba.	NA	NA	NA	8.29	LAO, LA Register and Award, Kottikakom, 1986.
6.	Kerala Agricultural University, Vellanikara.	379.56	00	00	379.56	Collectorate, File No- E3 18498/70, Thrissur.
7.	Mahatma Gandhi University, Kottayam.	NA	NA	00	42.51	LAO-General, Collectorate, Kottayam.
8.	NSS Engineering College, Akathethara, Palakkad.	00	00	00	50.61	Civil section, NSS Engineering College, Akathethara.
9.	Regional Agricultural Research Station (RARS), Kumarakom.	NA	NA	00	44.76	Dept. of Economics, RARS, Kumarakom.
10.	Sri.Sankaracharaya Sanskrit University.	25.10	00	00	25.10	Dept. of Development, Sanskrit University, Kalady.
Social Welfare						
1.	Punalur Rehabilitation Centre.	4.01	00	00	4.01	LAO-General, File No.138/95 B, Civil station, Kollam.
Others						
1.	Treatment Plant for Calicut Drainage.	15.74	00	00	15.74	Collectorate, File No. 4869/76, Kozhikode, 1976.

Bibliography

AIR. (1985). "Olga Tellis and Others vs Bombay Municipal Corporation and Others". All India Reporter: Supreme Court SCC, pp. 545-590.

Areeparampil, Mathew. (1996). "Industries, Mines, and Dispossession of Indigenous Peoples: The Case of Chottanagpur," in Walter Fernandes and Enakshi Ganguly Thukral (eds.). *Development, Displacement and Rehabilitation: Issues of a National Debate.* New Delhi: Indian Social Institute, pp.102-07.

Asif, Muhammed. (1999). "Land Acquisition Act, Need for an Alternative Paradigm", *Economic and Political Weekly,* Vol.34, No.25, pp. 1564-6.

Babbar, Vinod. (1991). "Land Acquisition and Transfer: National and Sectoral Resettlement Policies Participatory Approaches", Paper Presented at the World Bank and Electrobars Sponsored Conference on Resettlement in Power Projects, Samta Catarina, 4-14 May.

Baboo, Balgovind. (1991). "Big Dams and Tribals: The Case Study of the Hirakud Dam Oustees in Orissa", *Social Action*, Vol. 41, No. 3, pp. 288-303.

Baboo, Balgovind, Ashok Kumar and S.K. Pattanaik. (1987). "Development displacement: A Case Study of Koraput District", working paper presented at the seminar on Development and Displacement. Bula: Institute for Study of Society and Culture, Dec.20-21

Bhuskute, R.V. (1997). "The Maharashtra Rehabilitation Act 1989", in Walter Fernandes and Vijay Paranjpye (eds.). *Rehabilitation Policy and Law in India: A Right to Livelihood.* New Delhi: Indian Social Institute, pp. 169-191.

Brennan, Frank. (1995). "Parliamentary Responses to the Mabo Decision", in M.A.Stephen (ed.), Mabo; *The Native Legislation: A*

Legislative Response to the High Court Decision. St Lucia: Queensland University Press, pp.1-25.

Bureau of Industrial Promotion. ---. *Report on Industrial Potential Survey in Palakkad District*. Thiruvananthapuram: Government of Kerala.

Cernea, Michael M. (1996). "Public Policy Response to Development Induced Population Displacement", *Economic and Political Weekly*, Vol.31, No. 24, June 15, pp. 1515-23.

Cheria, Anitha. (1996). *Ecodevelopment in Nagarhole, India; A Critique*. Unpublished Paper circulated by the Documentation Centre, Indian Social Institute, New Delhi.

Chief Engineer, (1998). Kallada Irrigation Project, Kottarakara.

Chief Engineer, Oral information, Housing Board, Kozhikode.

CIL. (1994). Resettlement and Rehabilitation Policy of CIL. Calcutta: Coal India Ltd.

Civil Engineer, Malabar Cements Ltd., Walayar, Palakkad.

Colchester, Marcus. (1986). "An End to Laughter? The Bhopalapatnam and the Godavari Projects," in Edwards Goldsmith and Environmental Impact of Large Dams. Vol. II: Case Studies. Comelford: Wardbridge Ecological Centre, No. 99, pp. 245-54.

CMIE. (1986). *Basic Statistics Relating to the Economy*, Vol. I & II. Bombay: Centre for Monitoring Indian Economy.

Collectorate, (1994). Land Acquisition Office, Award Register No. G5-50830/94, Vol. V to VIII and G5. 30105/94, Vol. IV to VI, Kottayam.

Collectorate, (1997). File No.B6/19159/97, Wayanad.

Collectorate, (1961). File No. R Dis 2746/61, Thrissur.

Collectorate, (1961). File No. R Dis 2746/61, Thrissur.

Collectorate, (1961). File No. R Dis 3432/61, Thrissur.

Collectorate, (1970). File No-E3 18498/70,Thrissur.

Collectorate, (1975). File No. 1477/75, Thrissur.

Collectorate, (1976). File No. 4869/76, Kozhikode.

Collectorate, (1983). File No. R Dis E1-34708/84, R Dis 60051/83, Thrissur.

Collectorate, (1984). Land Acquisition Office, File No. G2 -46339/84, G2 -3213/86, G2 -22449/87, Kottayam.

Collectorate, (1985). File No. A11. 334/85. Thiruvananthapuram.

Collectorate, (1991). Land Acquisition Office, Award No. 1/91 dt. 4-2-91, Palakkad.

Collectorate, (1992). File No. B6-20048/92, dtd 7-4-1992, Wayanad.

Collectorate, Award No. 1/60, 1/64, 25/67, Kozhikode.

Collectorate, Thiruvananthapuram.

Collectorate, Thrissur.

Dani, Sujata G. (1991). "Tribal Land Alienation in Giridih District", Mussoorie: Lal Bahadur Shastri National Academy of Administration (mimeo).

Das, S. P. and S. S. Singh. (1985). "Koel-Karo Hydro Electric Project, Bihar", Paper Presented at the Seminar on Big Dams in India. Ranchi : Xavier Institute of Social Service, February 18-20.

Datta, Chandan and Rashmi De Roy. (1986). *Big Dam in Narmada*. Vol. II. New Delhi: Environmental Services Group World Wildlife Fund-India.

Debnath, D.C., M. B. Choube and Shyam S. Agarwal. (1992). "Recent Innovations in Resettlement," Paper Presented at the World Bank and Electrobars Sponsored conference on Resettlement in Power Projects. Santa Catarina, May 4-14.

Debnath, Biswanath. (2001). "Environment and Social Impact Management of Transport Project". Paper presented in the seminar conducted by Public Works Department, Government of Kerala, 24 August.

Department of Forests. (1990). *Management Plan: Chimoni Wildlife.*

Department of Forests. (1990). *Management Plan: Chinnar Wildlife.*

Department of Forests. (1990). *Management Plan: Neyyar Wildlife.*

Department of Forests. (1990). *Management Plan: Peppara Wildlife.*

Department of Forests. (1990). *Management Plan: Wayanad Wildlife.*

Dept. of Development, Sanskrit University, Kalady.

Dept. of Economics, Regional Agriculture Research Station, Kumarakom.

Deputy General Manager, SIDCO, Thiruvananthapuram.

Desai, AR. (1981). "Tribes in Transition" in Buddhadeb Chadhuri (ed.). *Tribal Development in India*. New Delhi. Inter India Publications, pp. 510-18.

Dhagamwar, Vasudha. (1989). "Rehabilitation: Policy and Institutional Changes Required", in Walter Fernades and Enakshi Ganguly Thukral (eds.), (op. cit.), pp. 171-184.

District Industries Centre (DIC), Kannur.

District Industries Centre (DIC), Kasargod.

District Industries Centre (DIC), Alappuzha.

Elangovan et al. (1997). "Transport Scenario: New Initiatives", *Kerala Calling*. Vol. 17, No. 10, August. Department of Public Relations. Government of Kerala, pp.49-52.

Engineering Section, (1966). File No-44/E4 -4/65-66, Cochin University.

Executive Engineer, (1982). File No. 4593/82/LA3, Kerala State Electricity Board.

Fernandes Walter and Naik. (1999). *Development Induced Displacement in Goa 1965-95: A Study on its Extent and Nature.* New Delhi: Indian Social Institute and Goa: Indian National Social Action Forum.

Fernandes, Walter. (1999). *The Land Acquisition (Amendment) Bill 1998. For Liberalisation or for the Poor*. New Delhi. Indian Social Institute.

----(1999). *The Land Acquisition (Amendment) Bill, 1998, For Liberalisation or for the Poor.* New Delhi: Indian Social Institute.

----(1998). "Land Acquisition (Amendment) Bill, 1998-Rights of Project Affected Persons Ignored", *Economic and Political Weekly*, Vol.33, No.42&43, pp. 2703-06.

----(1998a). "Development-Induced Displacement in Eastern India", in S.C. Dube (ed). *Antiquity and Modernity in Tribal India: Vol. I: Continuity and Change Among the Tribals.* New Delhi: Inter-India Publishers, pp. 217-301.

----(1996). "Development-Induced Displacement and Benefit-Sharing by the Victims", Second International Conference on Displacement and Refugees, Oxford University, September 17-20.

----(1995). "An Activist Process Around the Draft National Rehabilitation Policy", *Social Action*, Vol. 45, No. 3, July-Sept., pp. 277-298.

----(1995). "Development-Induced Displacement in Orissa". Quantitative Report. Unpublished.

----(1986). Construction Workers, Powerlessness and Bondage: The Case of the Asian Games", *Social Action*, Vol. 36, No.3, July-Sept., pp.264-291

Fernandes, Walter and Vijay Paranjpye. (1997). "Hundred Years of Displacement in India: Is the Rehabilitation Policy an Adequate response?" in Walter Fernandes and Vijay Paranjpye (eds.) op. cit. pp. 1-34.

Fernandes, Walter and Vijay Paranjpye (Eds.). (1997). *Rehabilitation Policy and Law in India: A Right to Livelihood.* Pune: Econet and New Delhi: Indian Social Institute.

Fernandes, Walter and Mohammed Asif. (1997). *Development-Induced Displacement in Orissa 1951 to 1995: A Database on its Extent and Nature*. New Delhi: Indian Social Institute.

Fernandes, Walter and S. Anthony Raj. (1992). *Development, Displacement and Rehabilitation in the Tribal Areas of Orissa.* New Delhi: Indian Social Institute. (mimeo).

Fernandes, Walter, Philip Viegas, Geeta Menon and K.T. Chandy. (1985). *Forests, Environment and Forests Dweller Economy in Chattisgarh*. New Delhi.

Forest Department. *Periyar Tiger Reserve*, a Brochure by the Wildlife Wing of the Kerala Forest Department.

Gadgil, Madhav. (1983). "Forestry with a Social Purpose" in Walter Fernandes and Sharad Kulkarni (eds.). *Towards a New Policy: Peoples Rights and Environmental Needs.* New Delhi: Indian Social Institute, pp.111-33.

Ganguly Thukral, Enakshi. (1996). "Development, Displacement and Rehabilitation Locating Gender", *Economic and Political Weekly*, Vol.31, No. 24, June 15, pp.1500.

Ganguly Thukral, Enakshi. (1989). "Dams: For Whose Development?" in Walter Fernandes and Enakshi Ganguly Thukral (eds.), (op.cit.), pp.39-61.

George, K.K. (1994). *Whither Kerala Model*? in International Congress on Kerala Studies. Abstracts. Vol. 5. Thiruvananthapuram. AKG Centre for Research and Studies, pp.8-10.

Good, Byron J. (1996). "Mental Health Consequences of Displacement and Resettlement", *Economic and Political Weekly*, Vol.31, No. 24, June 15, pp. 1504-08.

Gopinathan Nair, P.R.G. (1978). *Education and Economic Changes in Kerala*. Centre for Development Studies, Thiruvananthapuram.

Government of Kerala. (1998). *A Survey on Tribals in the Catchment Area of Chaliyar Irrigation Project*. Chief Engineer Investigation, Irrigation Department, Thiruvananthapuram.

Government of India. (1968). Report of the 23rd Estimates Committee of the Parliament. New Delhi: Government of India.

Goyal, Sangeetha. (1996). "Economic Perspectives on Resettlement and Rehabilitation", *Economic and Political Weekly*, Vol.31, No. 24, June 15, pp.1461-67.

Greater Cochin Development. Authority (GCDA), Town Planning Section, Cochin.

Guggenheim, Scott. (1990). "Development and Dynamics of Displacement", in Aloysius P. Fernandes (eds.), op. cit. pp.9-26.

Gulati, Leela, Ramalingam and I.S. Gulati. (1994). *Gender Profile: Kerala.* New Delhi: Royal Netherlands Embassy.

Heuze-Brigant, Gerard. (1991). "Singuli Super Thermal Project: Heavy Investment and Social Havoc", *Social Action*, Vol. 43, No.3, July-Sept, pp.304-22.

Halliburton, Murphy. (1998). "Suicide: A Paradox of Development in Kerala", *Economic and Political Weekly*, Vol.33, No. 36 & 37, pp. 2341-45.

Indian Bureau of Mines. (1999). *Statistical Profiles of Minerals, 1998-99.* Ministry of Steel and Mines. Nagpur.

Indian Mineral Year Book. (1997). *Mineral Review and Foreign Trade.* Vol. 2. Nagpur: Indian Bureau of Mines.

ISED (1996). *Development, Displacement and Rehabilitation in Orissa, 1950-1990.* Bhubaneswar: Institute of Socio-Economic Development.

Issac, Thomas. (1997). "People's Campaign for 9th Plan", *Kerala Calling,* Vol. 17, No. 7, May. Department of Public Relations: Government of Kerala.

Iyer, L.A., Krishna. (1968). *Social History of Kerala.* Vol. 2. Dravidian Book Centre.

Joy, M.S. (1997). *Kerlathile Vanyajeevi Sangethangal (Mal)* Thiruvananthapuram. State Institute of Languages.

Kar, N.C. (1991). *Social, Economic and Cultural Impact of NALCO on Local Tribal in Damanjodi Project Area.* Bhuvaneshwar: Nabakrushna Choudhury Centre for Development Studies.

Karunakaran, C.K. (1992). *Keralathile Vanangal Noottandukaliloode (Mal).* Thiruvananthapuram: State Institute of Languages.

Karunakaran, C.K. (1995). *Keralathile Vanangal-2 (Mal).* Thiruvananthapuram: State Institute of Languages.

Kerala Forest Department. (1992). *SC/STs in The Forests of Kerala: Settlement-wise* (Tables 1 to 10), pp. 16-19.

Kerala Forest Department. (1994). *SC/STs in the Forests of Kerala: Facts and Figures.* Forest Information Bureau.

Kerala State Electricity Board. (1997). *Power Systems Statistics.* Thiruvananthapuram: Government of Kerala, pp. 11-12 and 21.

Kerala State Land Use Board. (1976). *Project Report on Kuriarkutty Karappara Project (Irrigation Part).*

Kerala State Land Use Board. (1981a). *Land and Water Use Efficiency in Peechi Irrigation Project Command.*

Kerala State Land Use Board. (1981b). *A Note on Increasing Land and Water Use Efficiency in Chalakudy Irrigation Project Command.*

Kerala State Land Use Board. (1981c). *Land Use Efficiency in the Command Area of Periyar Valley Irrigation Project.*

Kerala State Land Use Board. (1995). *Land Resources of Kerala State.* Thiruvananthapuram: Government of Kerala.

KINFRA. (1999). *KINFRA: Strategic Locations.* Brochure by Kerala Industrial Infrastructure Development Corporation.

Kocherry, Thomas. (1997). "Fish Workers' Struggle and Victory", *Integral Liberation*, Vol.1. No.1, pp.32-6.

Kothari, Ashish and Shekar Singh.(1988).The Narmada Valley Project: A Critique. New Delhi: Kalpavriksh.

Kothari, Ashish, Prathibha. Pande, Shekhar Singh and Dilnavaz Variava. (1989). *Management of National Parks and Sanctuaries in India: A Status Report*, New Delhi: Environmental Studies Division, Indian Institute of Public Administration.

Kothari, Smithu. (1996). "Whose Nation? The Displaced as Victims of Development", *Economic and Political Weekly*, Vol.31, No. 24, June 15, pp. 1476-85.

Krishna N. R. and R. K. Sachdeva. (1990). "Coal Mining Project: Rehabilitation and Resettlement of Displaced Population," in Aloysius P. Fernadez (op. cit), pp.105-113.

KSEB. (1996). *Idukki Hydroelectric Project*: A Brochure by KSEB, November 1996.

Kunhaman, M. (1990). *Economic Development and Social Change.* Thiruvananthapuram: Research Review Publications Committee, University of Kerala.

NSS Engineering College, Civil Section, Akathethara, Palakkad.

Land Acquisition Office-General,(1992). File No. LA_2-9295/92, Civil Station, Kollam.

Land Acquisition Office-II, Kannur.

Land Acquisition Office-General, (1989). File No. A5-1015/89, Civil Station, Kollam.

Land Acquisition Office-II, Correspondence File, Thalikkavu, Kannur.

Land Acquisition Office, (1986). LA Register and Award, Kottaikakom.

Land Acquisition Office, (1990), LA and Award File, Kottaikakom.

Land Acquisition Office, (1990). LA Register and Award File.

Land Acquisition Office, Angamaly.

Land Acquisition Office, Award Register No. 5/95 to 19/95, Malappuram.

Land Acquisition Office, Award Register, Thalassery.

Land Acquisition Office, Collectorate, Thiruvananthapuram.

Land Acquisition Office, File No. 1064/82, Collectorate, Kozhikode.

Land Acquisition Office, Harippad, Alappuzha.

Land Acquisition Office, Kerala State Housing Board, Thiruvananthapuram.

Land Acquisition Office, LA Register and Award File, 1987, Kottaikakom.

Land Acquisition Office, Oral information from Clerk, Palakkad.

Land Acquisition Office, Panampally Nagar and Thiruvananthapuram File No. 1243/80, A-1243/80, 1243/87.

Land Acquisition Office, Vytila, Cochin.

Land Acquisition Office, Alappuzha.

Land Acquisition Office-General, Alappuzha.

Land Acquisition Office-General, Collectorate, Thrissur.

Land Acquisition Office-General, File No.138/95 B, Civil Station, Kollam.

Land Acquisition Office-Highways, Alappuzha.

Land Acquisition Office-I, (1983). Award Register, B 128/83, Kozhikode.

Land Acquisition Office-I, II, and III, Angamaly.

Land Acquisition Office-Railway, Alappuzha and Deputy Executive Engineer, Railways, Ernakulam.

Land Manager (Oral Information), Airport, Thiruvananthapuram.

Mahapatra, L.K. (1990). "Rehabilitation of Tribes Affected by Major Dams and Other Projects in Orissa," in Aloysious P. Fernandes (ed), *A Report on the workshop on Rehabilitation of Persons Displaced by Development Projects*. Bangalore: Institute for Social and Economic Change and Myrada.pp.85-99.

Mahapatra, L.K. (1994). *Tribal Development in India: Myth and Reality*. New Delhi: Vikas Publications.

Manager, Bakel Resorts Development Corporation, Kasaragode.

Manager, Oral Information, District Industries Centre, Palakkad.

Mankodi, Kashyap. (1989). "Displacement and Relocation: Problems and Prospects," in Walter Fernandes and Enakshi Ganguly Thukarāl (eds.), (op.cit.), pp 135-163.

Mathew, A. (1987). *A History of Educational Development in Kerala*. New Delhi: NIEPA.

Mathur, Hari Mohan and David Marson (Eds). (1998). *Development Projects and Impoverishment Risks-Resettling Project Affected People in India*. New Delhi: Oxford University Press.

Mathur, P.R.G. (1975). "Transfer and Alienation of Tribal Land and Indebtedness in Kerala". *Journal of Kerala Studies*. Vol II, Part.II.

Ministry of Steel and Mines. (1986). Annual Report 1985-86, New Delhi: Ministry of Steel and Mines.

Morse, Bradford and Thomas Berger. (1992). *Sardar Sarovar: Report of the Independent Review*. Ottawa: Resources Futures International Inc.

MRD. (1993). The Draft National Policy for Rehabilitation of Person Displaced as a Consequence of Acquisition of Land. New Delhi: Ministry of Rural Development, Government of India.

MRD. (1994). The Draft National Policy for Rehabilitation of Persons Displaced as a Consequence of Acquisition of Land-Cabinet Note. New Delhi: Ministry of Rural Development, Government of India.

Murphy Halliburton. (1998). "Suicide: A Paradox of Development in Kerala", *Economic and Political Weekly*, Vol.33, Nos. 36 & 37, pp. 2341-5.

Nampoothiriad, K.D. (1994). *Water Resources of Kerala State*. International Congress on Kerala Studies, Abstract, Vol. 4, Thiruvananthapuram: AKG Centre.

Naoroji, Dadabhai. (1988). *Poverty and Un-British Rule in India*. New Delhi: Commonwealth Publications.

Nayak, D.N. (1996). *Study on Mining Impact*. University of Goa.

NCA (1984). Sardar Sarovar Project Resettlement and Rehabilitation Programme: A Supplementary Report. Bhopal : Narmada Control Authority.

NCPR. (1995). National Policy for Development-Induced Displacement and Rehabilitation of Persons Displaced as a Consequence of Acquisition of Land. Pune: The National Campaign for Peoples Resources.

NCPRR. (1998). National Policy for Rehabilitation of Persons Displaced as a Consequence of Acquisition of Land. New Delhi: Ministry of Rural Development, Government of India.

NTPC. (1993). Rehabilitation Policy. New Delhi: National Thermal Power Corporation.

NTPC. (1996). *The Power to Care.* A Brochure by National Thermal Power Corporation Ltd., December 1996.

Office of the Assistant Engineer, Oral Information, Kerala State Electricity Board, Kasargod.

Office of the Assistant Executive Engineer Civil Division, Kallarkuty, Adimali.

Office of the Assistant Engineer, Oral Information, Thiruvananthapuram.

Office of the Assistant Engineer, KINFRA, Kakanad.

Office of the Bakel Development Corporation, Kasargod.

Office of the Draftsman, Oral Information, English Indian Clays Ltd., Kochuveli, Thiruvananthapuram.

Office of the Executive Engineer – Fisheries, Kollam.

Office of the Executive Engineer – Fisheries, Oral Information, Kollam.

Office of the Executive Engineer – Thermal, Vydhuthi Bhavan, Pattom.

Office of the Executive Engineer, Siruvani, Palakkad.

Office of the Executive Engineer, Vydhuthi Bhavan, Pattom.

Office of the Executive Engineer, Muvatupuzha Valley Irrigation Project, Thodupuzha.

Office of the Fish Farm, Thalassery.

Office of the KINFRA, (1999). Oral Information from Project Consultant, Vellayambalam.

Office of the Land Manager, (Oral Information) Thiruvananthapuram Airport.

Office of the Personnel Manager, Steel Industries Kerala Ltd., Cherthala.

Office of the Seed Farm, Oral Information from Clerk.

Office of the Seed Farm, Anakayam.

Office of the State Seed Farm, Perambra.

Office of the Superintending Engineer, Information and Planning, Kozhikode.

Oomman, M.A. (1971). *Land Reforms and Socioeconomic Change in Kerala*. Madras: CLS.

ORG (1992). Chilka Lake: Nature's Gift, A Warning to TATAs and Other Polluters. Bhubaneswar: Orissa Khushak Mahasanga Press.

Pandey, Balaji. (1998). *Depriving the Underprivileged for Development.* Bhubaneshwar: Institute for Socio-Economic Development.

Patkar, Medha. (1998). "The People's Policy on Development, Displacement and Resettlement: Need to Link Displacement and

Development", *Economic and Political Weekly*, Vol. 33, No. 38, pp. 2432-3.

Personnel Manager, TRACO Cables Ltd., Cochin, Ernakulam

Personnel Officer, Hindustan Newsprint Mill, Velloore.

Phelan et al. (1997). 'The Stigma of Homelessness: The Impact of Label Homeless on Attitudes Towards Poor Persons", *Social Psychology*, Vol 60, No. 4, pp 323-37.

Pinto, Ambrose. (1998). 'Fillip to Land Transfers-Land Acquisition Bill, 1998", *Economic and Political Weekly*, Vol. 33.

Planning Commission. (1987). High Priority Irrigation Projects in the Seventh Plan. New Delhi: Planning Board, pp. 101-11.

Prabhakaran. (1996). "Tribals' Cup of Woes is Full". *The Hindu*, October 28.

Prakash, P.A. (1998). "Gulf Migration and its Economic Impact: The Kerala Experience," *Economic and Political Weekly*, Vol. 33, No. 50, pp. 3209-13.

Project Report from Irrigation Office (1967). Nemmara.

Project Report, (1998). Kutiadi Irrigation Project.

Project Report, (1998). Revamping and Consolidation Programme, Gayathri Project Stage I& II.

Project Report, Kutiady Augmentation Project, PWD, Irrigation.

Resettlement & Rehabilitation Office, Kayamkulam Combined Cycle Power Project, Choolatheruvu.

Rajan, Irudaya, et al. 1999. *India's Elderly: Burden or Challenge*. New Delhi. Sage Publishers.

Ramachandran, K.K., N.J.K. Nair, S. Mohan (---). *Study on Human Elements of Environmental and Ecological Impacts of Idukki Project (Interim report for the period April 1983 to April 1984).* Thiruvananthapuram: Centre for Earth Science Studies.

Ramanathan, Usha. (1996). "Displacement and the Law", *Economic and Political Weekly*, Vol.31. No. 24. June. 15. pp. 1486-91.

Ramesan, R. (1990). *Management Plan: Thattekad Bird Sanctuary.*

Ramanathan, Usha. (1999). "Public Purpose: Points for Discussion", in Walter Fernandes (ed.). *The Land Acquisition (Amendment) Bill 1998*, New Delhi: Indian Social Institute, pp. 19-24.

Reddy, I.U.B. (1989). Towards Rehabilitation of People Affected by Large Development Projects in Backward Tribal Areas: A Study in NALCO Upper Kolab Project Areas of Koraput District, Orissa, Ph D

Thesis Submitted to the department of Architecture and Regional Planning, Kharagpur: Indian Institute of Technology (unpublished).

Reddy, Narasingh and K. Muthyam Reddy. (1987). "Dams and Displacement.: The Andhra Experience", Paper presented at the seminar on Problems of Displacement due to Development. Burla: Institute for the Study and Culture, Dec.21-23.

Registrar, Centre for Water Resource Development and Management (CWRDM), Kozhikode.

Report by Kayal, Nellarachal.

Revenue Divisional Office, (1970). File No. R. Dis. 2765/69 dt. 21-8-70, Kasargod.

Revenue Divisional Office, (1978). File No. 766/78, Idukki.

Revenue Divisional Office, (1983). File No.4926/83, Devikulam, Idukki.

Revenue Divisional Office, Devikulam, Idukki.

Revenue Divisional Office, File No. B2. 107/87, Thiruvalla.

Revenue Divisional Office, Land Acquisition File, Adoor.

Revenue Divisional Office, Oral Information, Wayanad.

Revenue Divisional Office, Oral Information, Wayanad.

Rural Development Bureau. (1996). *Vikasana Guide*. Rural Development Department, Government of Kerala.

Samuel, N M. (1991). Census of India, Series.12, Final Population Totals.

Saradamoni, K. (1994). "Women, Kerala and Some Development Issues", *Economic and Political Weekly*, pp. 501-09.

Savyasaachi, (1998). *Tribal Forest-Dwellers and Self Rule, The Constitute Assembly Debate on the Fifth and Sixth Schedules.* New Delhi: Indian Social Institute.

Sen, Amartya and J. Dreze (Eds.). (1998). *Indian Development: Selected Perspectives.* New Delhi: Oxford University Press.

Sen, Sunil. (1979). *Agrarian Relations in India* 1793-1947, New Delhi: People's Publishing House.

Shariff, Abusakh. (1999). *Indian Human Development Report*. Oxford University Press, p.7.

Sharma, B. D. (1978). *Tribal Development: The Concept and the Frame.* New Delhi: Prachi Prakashan.

Sharma, B.D. (1993). "Community Control over Natural Resources and Industry: The Significance of the Mavalibhata Declaration," in Walter Fernandes. (ed). *The Indigenous Question: Search for an Identity.* New Delhi: Indian Social Institute, pp. 107-122.

Singh, Mridula and Ranjan Kumar Samantaray. (1992). "Whatever Happened to Muddavat Chenna? The Tale of Nagarjuna Sagar," in Enakhi Ganguly Thukral (ed). *Big Dams Displaced People: Rivers of Sorrow, Rivers of Change*. New Delhi: Sage Publications, pp. 54-76.

Sinha, B. K. (1996). " Draft National Policy for Rehabilitation: Objectives and Principles", *Economic and Political Weekly*, Vol. 31, No. 24, June 15, pp.1453-60.

Soman, C.R. (1998). *Arogyarangathe Mikacha Nettang*al *(Mal)* in *Swathanthryathinte Anpathu Varsh*am. Thiruvananthapuram. Public Relations Department. Govt. of Kerala, pp.206-21.

Somasekharan Nair, (1998). *Towards a Land Use Policy for Kerala, The Indian Express* dated 8-12-1998, p.11

Sooryamoorthy, R. (1997). *Consumption to Consumerism: In the Context of Kerala*. New Delhi: Classical Publishing Co.

Special Deputy Collector, KSEB, Award Register Vol. I, Kozhikode.

Special Tahsildar, (1992). Additional Land Acquisition Unit, File No. A2/379/92. Thiruvananthapuram.

Sreedhara Menon, A. (1979). *Social and Cultural History of India: Kerala*. New Delhi: Sterling Publishing Pvt. Ltd.

Sreedharan, E M. (1998). 'Information Technologiyum Keralavum (Mal)", in *Swathanthryathinte Anpathu Varshangal*

State Planning Board. (1992). *Economic Review*. Thiruvananthapuram: Government of Kerala.

State Planning Board. (1994). *Annual Plan Proposals 1995-6*. Thiruvananthapuram: Government of Kerala.

State Planning Board. (1997). *Economic Review*. Thiruvananthapuram: Government of Kerala.

State Planning Board. (1998). *Economic Review*. Thiruvananthapuram: Government of Kerala.

State Planning Board. ----. *The Peoples' Campaign for Ninth Plan in Kerala: An Introduction*. Thiruvananthapuram: Government of Kerala.

Sunny George. (1994). *Kerala Model of Development: Lessons and Non-Lessons in International Congress on Kerala Studies*. Abstracts, Vol. 5. Thiruvananthapuram. AKG Centre for Research and Studies, pp.6-8.

Superintendent of Presses. (1998). *Administrative Report*. Irrigation Department, Ernakulam.: Government of Kerala, pp.25-9.

Superintendent of Presses. (1998). *Administrative Report*. Public Works Department. Thiruvananthapuram: Government of Kerala, p.3.

Tharakan, Michael. (1984). "Socio-economic Factors in Educational Development: Case of 19th century Travancore", *Economic and Political Weekly*, Vol. 19, No. 45, November 10, pp.1913-28 and No.46. November 17, pp 1959-69.

The Malayala Manorama Daily, dt. 1-3-2000, p11 (Vamanapuram).

Thomas, E J. (1997). *Keralathinte Samoohakhadanayum Roopantharavum (Mal).* Kottayam. DC Books.

Upadhyay, Sanjay and Bhavani Raman. (1998). Land Acquisition and Purpose. New Delhi: The Other Media.

Vallil, Gopinathan. (1990). *Management Plan: Aralam Wildlife.*

Varma, S.C. (1985). Human Resettlement in the Narmada Basin. Bhopal: Narmada Valley Development Authority.

Vaswani, Kalpana. (1992). "Rehabilitation Laws and Policies: A Critical Look," in Enakshi Ganguly Thukral (ed.). *Big Dams, Displaced people: Rivers of Sorrow, Rivers of Change.* New Delhi: Sage Publication, pp 155-169.

Viegas, Philip. (1992). "The Hirakud Dam Oustees: Thirty Years After," in Enakshi Ganguly Thukral (ed.). (Op. Cit.), pp. 29-53.

Viswanath, Leela. (1993). *Social Mobility Among Scheduled Caste Women in India.* New Delhi: Uppal Publishing House.

Vydhuthi Bhavan, Pattom, Thiruvananthapuram.

Works Manager, Oral Information, Steel Complex, Chevayur, Kozhikode.

Works Manager, Oral Information, Travancore Titanium Products Ltd., Thiruvananthapuram.

World Bank. (1994). Resettlement and Development: The Bankwide Review of Projects Involving Involuntary Resettlement, 1986-93. Washington D.C.: Environment Department, the World Bank.

WRD. (1994). Modified Draft National Policy for Resettlement and Rehabilitation of Persons Affected by Reservoir Projects. New Delhi: Central Water Commission.

Zacharia, K.C. and Irudayarajan, S. (1997). *Kerala's Economic Transition: Determinants and Consequences.* New Delhi: Sage Publishers.

Zakariah et al. (1994). *Demographic Transition in Kerala in the 1980's.* Thiruvananthapuram: Centre for Development Studies.

Index